MW00425119

CALMLY TO POISE THE SCALES OF JUSTICE

*A History of the Courts of the
District of Columbia Circuit*

Written by

Jeffrey Brandon Morris

with the assistance of
Chris Rohmann

for
**The Historical Society of the
District of Columbia Circuit**

CAROLINA ACADEMIC PRESS
Durham, North Carolina

ISBN 0-89089-645-3
LCCN 2001086402

Carolina Academic Press
700 Kent Street
Durham, North Carolina 27701

Telephone (919) 489-7486
Fax (919) 493-5668
www.cap-press.com

Printed in the United States of America

To Dona
With Love

Contents

List of Illustrations

Foreword

Prior to my 1993 appointment to the Supreme Court of the United States, I spent thirteen absorbing years on the bench of the Court of Appeals for the District of Columbia Circuit. It is a court like no other in the nation. In the view of many court watchers, it is second in importance only to the Supreme Court. Its history, and the history of the prominent federal District Court allied with it, should be better known. Established by Congress at the very time Washington, D.C., became the nation's capital, the courts of the District of Columbia Circuit gained judicial authority both federal and local in character. From the start and continuing to this day, a substantial number of major cases finally resolved by the Supreme Court originate in the District of Columbia Circuit.

The special character of this circuit, fully revealed in the twentieth century, springs from its dominant role in adjudicating government cases. Close to 70 percent of the suits lodged in the Court of Appeals involve the United States or a federal agency or officer on one side or another. The D.C. Circuit also differs from the regional circuits in that its appellate judges are drawn not from a particular set of states, but from a nationwide pool.

I consider it my great good fortune to have served on the D.C. Circuit. For thirteen years I thrived in the challenges that daily trooped before the Court of Appeals, a bench uncommonly vibrant on two complementary counts: the quality of its members is matched by the complexity and significance of the cases on its docket. As the years unfolded, I became ever more certain that the history of the District's federal courts should be told in a manner accessible to interested lay readers as well as lawyers. My colleagues were of the same mind. Under the stewardship of the Historical Society of the District of Columbia Circuit, the decade-long endeavor was launched and sustained. Legal historian Jeffrey Morris, our unanimous choice as author, agreed to devote his fine mind and hand to the formidable undertaking. I am pleased that in 2001, the bicentennial year of the federal courts of the District of Columbia, Professor Morris's comprehensive account of the courts' evolution is in print. *Calmly to Poise the Scales of Justice* illuminates the pathmarking contributions this circuit has made to law and justice in the United States. May the volume lead to further scholarly exploration.

Ruth Bader Ginsburg
Associate Justice
Supreme Court of the United States

Preface

My immersion in the District of Columbia Circuit began just over thirty-five years ago, with a paper written during my last year of law school on the judges and criminal decisions of the U.S. Court of Appeals for that circuit. My interest was initially spurred because the fathers of two of my friends sat on the Court. At that time, the only literature on the Court of Appeals consisted of articles about particular cases and on matters of the Court's administration. There was just one book, an anthology of opinions of one of the Court of Appeals' most distinguished judges, Henry W. Edgerton.

That paper provided the groundwork and stimulus for my doctoral dissertation at Columbia University, a much expanded study of the work of the Court of Appeals. After completing the dissertation, I moved on to cultivate other scholarly vineyards, although five years in Washington at the end of the 1970s as a member of the staff of Chief Justice Warren E. Burger gave me the opportunity to talk with the Chief Justice about his experiences on the Court of Appeals, to renew old acquaintances on that court, and to become newly acquainted with others of its judges.

Nevertheless, the D.C. Circuit was but a memory when Chief Judge Patricia M. Wald telephoned to ask if I would consider writing the history of the Court of Appeals and its predecessors. The only significant contribution to the literature on the Court since I had written my dissertation was a short history commissioned by the Court on the occasion of the nation's bicentennial. Although my initial reaction was to leave well enough alone, in the end I yielded because of the opportunity it offered to return to the subject of my earliest scholarship with the insights gathered over twenty-five years.

Writing the history of a single court is, in itself, a major undertaking. My task became far more complicated when the Historical Society of the District of Columbia Circuit yielded to the blandishments of Judge Gerhard

A. Gesell and his colleagues and commissioned a book that would not only trace the history of the Court of Appeals, but would embrace the U.S. District Court for the District of Columbia as well. The result was an enormous undertaking, yielding a long, sprawling manuscript, which required far more than the usual amount of shaping, cutting, and rewriting.

In that endeavor, I have been assisted by Chris Rohmann, a perspicacious editor and a talented writer, whose contribution to the finished work has been so substantial that it is properly recognized on the title page. In the revision of the book, I have also been invaluably assisted by the president of the Historical Society, Daniel M. Gribbon of Covington & Burling. Mr. Gribbon was no figurehead overseer of this project, but a hands-on participant without whom this book might not have seen the light of day.

Notwithstanding the substantive contributions of these two collaborators and of the many other contributors acknowledged below, all the judgments made in this book, as well as any errors, are those of its author.

A project of this magnitude is never completed without an accumulation of debts. I owe special appreciation to the Chief Judges of the Court of Appeals and of the District Court during the span of this project — Patricia M. Wald, Abner J. Mikva, and Harry T. Edwards; Aubrey E. Robinson Jr., John Garrett Penn, and Norma Holloway Johnson — with particular thanks to judges Wald, Mikva, and Robinson for the many courtesies they extended to me in the book's initial stages. Linda Ferren, the talented former Circuit Executive of the District of Columbia Circuit, was enormously helpful on a wide range of matters, as were members of her staff, including Jill Sayenga, Nancy Stanley, and Jackie Morson. Among the many others who worked at the U.S. Courthouse, particular mention should be made of James M. Davey, former Clerk of the U.S. District Court, and Linda C. O'Donnell of the staff of then-Judge (now Justice) Ruth Bader Ginsburg.

I am indebted to a number of libraries, including that of Touro Law School and its entire staff, headed by Daniel Jordan. The Harry S. Truman Presidential Library in Independence, Missouri, helped make a stay of few days very productive. Most of all, I am indebted to the library of the U.S. Court of Appeals for the District of Columbia Circuit. Its head librarian, Nancy Lazar, not only made her staff and other resources readily available, but offered many insights into the work of the Court of Appeals. I profited from the assistance of Theresa Sentella and Warren Juggins. Linda Baltrusch was not only enormously helpful in tracking down hard-to-find sources, but also proved a superb companion with whom to talk through research problems.

Over the years, a number of students have written papers on the work of the courts of the District of Columbia Circuit under my direction. Many of these were of assistance in writing this book. I ought particularly to single out the work of Vincent Geoghan of The City College of the City University of New York, Weslie Resnick of Barnard College, and Christopher Smith of the University of Pennsylvania. I have also benefitted from the able services of a number of research assistants, including Seth Muraskin, Richard Jacobson, Donna McElhinney, and Christine Lindwall of Touro Law School, and Shelly Hein of the University of Montana Law School. M. Raye Miller, of the Touro Law School, must be given special mention for her exceptional insights into the work of the courts of the District of Columbia in the nineteenth century.

I am indebted to Jeffrey Liss, of the D.C. Bar, and his colleagues, and to an able team of paralegals at Covington & Burling, for checking the numerous case citations throughout the book. Mary Jane Mullen of Smith College, and the staff of that college's Nielson Library, gave valuable bibliographic assistance in preparing the lists of sources. William Causey and Stuart Newberger of the D.C. Bar aided in the selection of illustrations. The index is the work of the meticulous Barbara Wilcie Kern.

Many scholars — law professors, political scientists, and historians — have offered useful advice over the years. One in particular must be singled out. The late Harry M. Jones of Columbia Law School, who was there at the outset of my research on the D.C. Circuit, not only shared his knowledge of the Court of Appeals and drew upon his friendships to facilitate access to the judges of that court, but critiqued my early work and, in all ways, was a role model for how professors should interact with students.

Over thirty-five years, judges of the U.S. Court of Appeals and of the U.S. District Court have been extraordinarily generous with their time, willing to sit down and talk with me, often at great length, about their work and the work of their courts. In writing this book, I have relied upon my notes from extensive interviews and conversations in the 1960s and 1970s with David L. Bazelon, Warren E. Burger, Harold Leventhal, Henry W. Edgerton, Charles Fahy, and Carl McGowan. During the course of this project I interviewed Spottswood W. Robinson III, George E. MacKinnon, Malcolm Richard Wilkey, Patricia M. Wald, Abner J. Mikva, and Ruth Bader Ginsburg of the Court Appeals. The District Court judges with whom I spoke were William B. Bryant, Oliver Gasch, John H. Pratt, Aubrey E. Robinson Jr., John J. Sirica, June L. Green, Harold H. Greene, Thomas A. Flannery, Gerhard A. Gesell, George H. Revercomb, and Louis F. Oberdorfer.

At the beginning of this project, two extraordinary judges oversaw the work: Ruth Bader Ginsburg, who was Chair of the Historical Society, and Gerhard Gesell. Judge Gesell's enthusiasm for the project was unbounded and he gave generously of his time for it. He took it so seriously and professionally that, prior to three full days of interviews, he prepared a series of memoranda as a basis for his discussions with me. Even without time to prepare, Judge Gesell was an enormous intellectual force, but with this preparation he was a wonder to behold. It is my great regret that he did not live to see the publication of this book. Fortunately, Justice Ginsburg has, and honors it with its foreword. Few persons this author has met during his lifetime have come near to combining her formidable intellect, judiciousness, and thoughtfulness.

Following the death of Judge Gesell and the elevation of Justice Ginsburg to the Supreme Court, the role of judicial shepherd was performed ably and graciously by Judge Louis F. Oberdorfer, who succeeded Justice Ginsburg as Chair of the Historical Society. The Society's Historian, Maeva Marcus, an old and good friend, has provided valuable insight and perspective.

The writing of a book consumes a great deal of time, too much of which is taken away from one's family. I can only say a deep "thanks" to David Brandon Morris and Deborah Helaine Morris for the sacrifices they made, as well as to my talented wife and companion, Dona Baron Morris, who was forced yet again to share a large chunk of her life with a book.

Jeffrey Brandon Morris
December 29, 2000

Introduction

This book is a history of two of the most important courts in the United States, the U.S. Court of Appeals and the District Court for the District of Columbia, and their antecedents. It attempts to trace the development of these courts over two centuries, to portray some of their most influential judges, and to consider the most important decisions and case lines. Some of the most memorable cases in American history have taken place in the D.C. Circuit, and more justices of the United States Supreme Court have been drawn from the Court of Appeals than from any other court. The Court of Appeals is now the undisputed chief tribunal for administrative law in the United States, and the District Court has become a principal venue for cases involving the separation of powers.

From the outset, the major court for the District of Columbia was an unusual hybrid. The Circuit Court of the District of Columbia, which existed from 1801 to 1863, had most of the trial and appellate authority of other federal courts of that era, but also heard civil and criminal matters that elsewhere would have come before state courts. This meant a diet of litigation over real property, commercial transactions, and family matters, as well as prosecutions for local crimes. The richness of that jurisdiction was qualified somewhat, however, by the confined geographical area of the District, its small population, and its rather specialized economy.

Far more important to the docket of the Circuit Court and its successors have been the cases derived from the courts' location in the nation's capital. These have ranged from prosecutions for contempt of Congress and political corruption to state trials of presidential assassins, from trials and appeals arising from political demonstrations and alleged breaches of national security to cases testing the powers of Congress, the President, and the independent regulatory agencies. Moreover, for well over a century, the power to issue the writ of mandamus to order a federal official to perform a nondiscretionary action was held uniquely by the Circuit Court and its successor, the Supreme Court of the District of Columbia—an authority that provided a vital forum for oversight of the executive branch.

The courts of the District have been closely involved in the development of the city of Washington ever since its beginnings as a provincial village with muddy streets and grand designs. The racial mix of the population, the dominance of the federal government in Washington's economy, the involvement of Congress in the District's affairs, and the absence of representative institutions for most of the city's history have contributed to shaping the courts' unique role in the life of the District. The impact of the legal system on African-Americans—and vice versa—has been a constant factor, and the courts of the District have repeatedly played an important role in the struggle for racial civil rights.

This history proceeds more or less chronologically from the founding of the D.C. Circuit in 1801, shortly after the federal capital was established at Washington, through the 1980s. Each of the ten chapters is devoted to an important stage in the courts' history. They are demarcated by the lifespans of the present courts' predecessors or by significant eras—particularly those defined by presidencies in which the work of the courts was greatly affected by appointments to the Circuit bench and, in some cases, by bitter clashes between the executive and the judiciary.

The Circuit Court of the District of Columbia existed from 1801 until its abolition, in part for political reasons, in 1863. It had both trial and appellate jurisdiction, and a docket of both federal and local cases. In its first few years, the Court heard two notable prosecutions born of the contentious political climate of the young republic, including the trial of several participants in the Aaron Burr conspiracy. It also decided a range of cases spawned by the developing city, from local misdemeanors to litigation over land speculation. In this period, the landmark *Kendall* case established the Circuit's unique role in overseeing the actions of high officials of the federal government.

The Supreme Court of the District of Columbia succeeded to the jurisdiction of the Circuit Court in 1863. The Court decided *Kilbourn v. Thompson*, the most important nineteenth-century case limiting Congress's power to investigate, heard the prosecution for political corruption of the Star Route conspirators, and played a central role in the growth of the federal city. In the case of Charles Guiteau, the assassin of President James A. Garfield, it gave the most important opinion on the test for criminal insanity issued by any American court during the century.

The Court of Appeals of the District of Columbia was created in 1893, assuming the appellate authority of the D.C. Supreme Court. During the first three decades of the twentieth century, both courts heard, most notably, a number of controversial labor cases, including challenges to the use of secondary boycotts and contempt citations in labor disputes and a test of the District's minimum wage law. In this period, two prosecutions attracting nationwide attention were conducted in the District Court: the trials of those involved in the Teapot Dome scandal and a trial of prominent local bank officers at which two former presidents of the United States testified. During this era, the judges of the Circuit, especially of the Court of Appeals, were increasingly chosen from all over the country, setting a pattern that still holds true.

The courts of the District of Columbia Circuit, especially the Court of Appeals, were the beneficiaries of the enormously enhanced role and power of the federal government brought about by the New Deal. During the presidency of Franklin Delano Roosevelt, seven appointments to the Court of Appeals changed its character and philosophy considerably. Two of its judges, Fred Vinson and Wiley Rutledge, later became Supreme Court justices. Administrative law began to become an important area of law in the United States, and the Court of Appeals became a major participant in its growth. Both the Court of Appeals and what now was titled the District Court of the United States for the District of Columbia began to wrestle with civil rights cases of increasing importance.

President Harry Truman appointed several of the strongest appeals court judges of the century, in particular David L. Bazelon, Charles Fahy, and E. Barrett Prettyman. Some of the most pressing domestic issues Truman encountered as President—civil rights, loyalty-security, and labor relations—made their way into both courts during his administration, resulting in some of the courts' most significant jurisprudence. The courts proved critical in the battles against segregation in housing, public accommodations, and schools in the District of Columbia. In the uneasy political atmosphere of the early years of the Cold War, the courts handled several high-profile loyalty cases cautiously, tending to defer to the political branches. The era was bracketed by two incendiary cases arising from labor-management conflicts of considerable political significance: the contempt prosecution of United Mine Workers leader John L. Lewis and the litigation over Truman's seizure of the steel mills.

In the years of Dwight D. Eisenhower's presidency during the 1950s, the courts wrestled repeatedly with volatile questions, especially in the areas of loyalty-security issues and criminal law. These struggles opened a fissure between the District Court and several of the judges of the Court of Appeals, as well as causing clashes among the judges of the Court of Appeals, especially between David L. Bazelon and the newly appointed Warren E. Burger. By the end of the 1950s, the Court of Appeals had become one of the nation's most closely watched courts, with a reputation for boldness and innovation, as well as for attracting controversy.

During the 1960s, the U.S. Court of Appeals for the District of Columbia Circuit was emerging as the nation's second most important court, its prominence deriving from the ability of its judges, the quality of its jurisprudence, and a docket more varied than virtually any other court in the country. This period, too, saw the appointment to the Court of a number of outstanding jurists, including J. Skelly Wright, Carl McGowan, and Harold Leventhal. In such areas as landlord-tenant relations and mental health, the Court of Appeals reshaped legal doctrines in a manner favorable to the poor of the disenfranchised District, and it greatly expanded the rights of criminal defendants. Concurrently, the Court continued to employ its rich administrative-law docket to press the regulators to represent the interests of the public rather than those of the regulated industries.

Rarely in the history of the United States has the government been challenged so often and so momentously as in the District Court for the District of Columbia during the presidency of Richard M. Nixon. It was through these confrontations that the District Court came of age as a national court, becoming the focal point for great tests of American constitutionalism in a cascade of separation-of-powers issues, including the struggle for control of the Nixon tapes, and the battle over publication of the Pentagon Papers.

While the two major courts of the District of Columbia Circuit lost their "state court" jurisdictions in the early 1970s, in that decade they achieved milestones in poverty and mental-health law, civil rights, and administrative law, particularly concerning the environment. In a period of explosive growth and rapid changes in government regulation, arising in a time of a weakened presidency, a more assertive Congress, and an active public-interest bar, the judges of the Court of Appeals engaged in a crucial dialogue about how courts should review administrative agencies and interpret statutes. By the end of the decade, the Court of Appeals for the District of Columbia Circuit was the nation's premier administrative tribunal.

In the 1980s, the era of Ronald Reagan's presidency, the dockets of both courts of the District of Columbia Circuit reflected the perennial concerns

that have confronted and defined the Circuit from the beginning: cases involving the city of Washington, civil rights, and the rights of the insane;
prosecutions for political corruption and malfeasance and for attempted
assassination of the President; constitutional tests of the separation of powers and First Amendment freedoms. The accelerating drive toward deregulation shaped much of the Court of Appeals' administrative-law docket, and
one case in the Circuit affected just about every American—the antitrust
prosecution that led to the dismantling of the Bell Telephone system. During this period, appointments to the Court of Appeals gave it a conservative majority for the first time since the 1950s. It remained, however, as it
has been throughout its history, a court of extremely able judges holding
strong, sometimes clashing, views.

CALMLY TO POISE THE SCALES OF JUSTICE

Chapter 1

"Compact in Situation, United in Interest, and Happily Placed"

*The Courts' Creation and Early Years,
1801–60*

On the third of June 1800, the first President of the United States to live and work in the District of Columbia arrived by coach for a visit. Well aware of the opposition to the location chosen for the federal city, the crusty, incorruptible New Englander expressed to those who would soon become his neighbors the hope that "all the reluctance which remained... will soon be removed."

For John Adams this would be more a ceremonial than a working visit. However, on his first full day in the District the President rode across Rock Creek Bridge, at K Street, to inspect the building that would be his residence and place of work, visited the Treasury building, and was given a tour of the unfinished Capitol. Reflecting later on what he had seen of the capital during his visit, Adams, usually no enthusiast, would write, "I am well pleased with the whole."

One source of pleasure was the arrival, just before he left, of his nephew by marriage, thirty-year-old William Cranch. For Cranch, a close friend of the President's son, John Quincy Adams, the chief executive's visit was something of a personal triumph; for years the ambitious young lawyer had been after the elder Adams to visit the city. Within a year, Cranch would become one of Adams' "midnight judges," appointed in the last hours of the President's term.

In the District of Columbia, as he did with federal courts throughout the nation, Adams tried to use his power of appointment to secure Federalist influence on the judiciary by selecting as judges, marshals, and U.S. District Attorneys able and energetic men who were also strong Federalists. The most lasting of all these appointments was William Cranch, who would serve on the Circuit Court of the District of Columbia for fifty-four years.

The courts established for the District of Columbia in February 1801 inherited a jurisdiction which had already been shaped by dreams and disappointments, rivalries and disputation. The City of Washington and the District of Columbia were the product of a dream of a magnificent capital for a great republican experiment. The District of Columbia was formed by the cession to the United States of land in Maryland and Virginia bordering the Potomac (the Virginia side was ceded back to the state in 1846). The District embraced two thriving towns—Alexandria, by 1795 the seventh largest port in the United States, on the Virginia side, and Georgetown on the Maryland side.

When Congress first convened there, in November 1800, the District was still isolated and undeveloped. The congressmen discovered a rudimentary, uncomfortable town lacking not only in commerce but also in the social and cultural amenities they had enjoyed in Philadelphia. The city's primary characteristic was incompleteness. Spacious avenues began amid nothing in particular and led nowhere. Small clumps of buildings were separated from each other by virtual wilderness. Still unrealized were the broad boulevards, classical structures, monuments, and parks envisioned in Pierre L'Enfant's design for the city.

The expectations of the Potomac boosters that the capital would attract commerce and culture were in the short run sorely disappointed. The hopes that the building of the city could largely be funded by the sale of lots to the public, as well as the dreams of great fortunes derived from the sale of land in the District, were also unfulfilled, and resulted in an extraordinary amount of litigation over land titles. Over three-quarters of the lots made available to private buyers were purchased by a syndicate composed of James Nicholson, James Greenleaf, and America's richest man, Senator Robert Morris of Pennsylvania. By the time the government moved to Washington in 1800, relatively little development had occurred, much of the land was encumbered, the area had developed a reputation as a bad investment, and Congress had already been called upon to appropriate money for the city.

Although the land for the District of Columbia had been ceded in the early 1790s, Congress had made little use of its power, granted in Article I, Section 8 of the Constitution, to legislate for the District. Congress did delegate power to build the city to the three District Commissioners appointed by the President. Until full jurisdiction was vested in the United States in December 1800,[1]

---

1. See *United States v. Hammond,* 1 D.C. (1 Cranch) 15 (1801).

the laws and institutions of Maryland governed on the eastern side of the Potomac and those of Virginia on the western side, and Georgetown and Alexandria retained the powers of municipal corporations. From 1790 until 1801, the inhabitants of the area ceded by Maryland and Virginia voted in the local and federal elections of the respective states; in 1801, however, the United States assumed exclusive jurisdiction over the ceded areas and inhabitants of those areas no longer voted.

Creation of Local Government and the D.C. Court System

The organization of the courts of the District of Columbia occurred during a momentous few weeks between late January and March 4, 1801, when Thomas Jefferson took the oath of office. Those final days of Adams' term were marked by events that had profound implications for the constitutional future of the United States. Not the least of these was Adams' appointment of his Secretary of State, John Marshall, to be Chief Justice.

While the lame-duck, Federalist-controlled House of Representatives was balloting to decide the deadlocked presidential election between Jefferson and Aaron Burr, the bill reorganizing the federal judiciary reached the President's desk for signature. Although this law did not affect the District of Columbia, it needs mention. In the Judiciary Act of February 13, 1801, Congress reformed the far from perfect federal judicial structure created in 1789.[2] The Act established six new circuit courts with both trial and appellate jurisdiction, ended circuit riding by the justices of the Supreme Court, and created thirteen new circuit judgeships. It also greatly increased the original jurisdiction of the circuit courts and made it easier to remove litigation from state to federal courts.

In the charged political atmosphere of early 1801, the new law appeared to the opposition Republican Party not just as a job-creating vehicle for Federalist politicians; it also looked like a mechanism whereby the Federalist Party, which had lost control of both Congress and the Presidency in the 1800 elections, could maintain power through the appointment of life-tenured federal judges. Suspicions were not allayed by Adams' swift appointment of a number of Federalists to the new judgeships. The new act and Adams' appointments established the background against which legis-

---

2. 2 Stat. 89.

lation for governance of the District of Columbia and judicial appointments were viewed.

After finally resolving the presidential election (it took thirty-four ballots, from February 11–17, before the House elected Jefferson), Congress had just two weeks to pass legislation specifically affecting the District. That was addressed in the Act of February 27, 1801, the main achievement of which was the creation of a judicial system for the District of Columbia.[3] The District was divided into two counties: Alexandria County, on the west side of the Potomac, and Washington County, on the east. Within those counties lay three incorporated cities: Alexandria, Georgetown, and the newly created City of Washington. The rather large unincorporated areas of the two counties were governed by levy courts, which were constituted of justices of the peace; these had the power to assess taxes, pay for the maintenance of bridges and roads, provide for a poor house, grant liquor licenses, and police the areas.[4] Until Congress acted further, the laws of the respective states were to remain in force in each county. At the time, Congress did not carefully consider the degree of home rule the District would be allowed, nor its possible representation in Congress.

The new court system for the District of Columbia was headed by a Circuit Court composed of three judges; an Orphan's Court for each county, which dealt with trusts and probate matters; and a United States District Court, staffed by the Chief Judge of the Circuit Court. The Circuit Court had appellate jurisdiction over the justices of the peace and, by error or appeal, over the District Court. The Circuit Court and the District Court each had its own Clerk and Marshal and each county had a Register of Wills.

The Circuit Court's original jurisdiction was broad, encompassing not only most of the authority of a federal circuit court, including its appellate jurisdiction, but also that of a state trial court. Under the new law the Circuit Court's procedures were to conform to whichever state it was sitting in. A litigant who lost in the Circuit Court was entitled to appeal to the U.S. Supreme Court by writ of error or appeal if the matter in dispute exceeded $100 (the amount was raised in 1816 to $1,000).

---

3. On the Act of February 27, 1801, 2 Stat. 103, see 1 D.C. (1 Cranch) v–viii.

4. It was not until May 1802 that Congress chartered a municipal corporation for the City of Washington, providing for a Mayor appointed by the President and a City Council elected by the 325 men eligible to vote. In 1812 Congress provided the city of Washington with a new charter which authorized an elected Mayor and a twenty-person council. There would not be salaried police in the towns themselves until 1842; until then, law enforcement was the work of constables, overseen by the Court.

The Circuit Court, especially during its early years, exercised many powers which were executive and legislative in nature. The Court appointed the Coroner of the County of Washington; appointed, discharged, and accepted the resignations of constables; acted on petitions for licenses to open new ferries and established the selling prices of liquors for taverns. The District's courts had no building of their own until the mid-1820s. For a generation, when the Circuit Court sat in Washington, the judges held forth in taverns, hotels, and private homes, and, when they could, in the Capitol itself. During much of this time, the Clerk and Marshal used their homes as offices, rented quarters, or used a room in the Capitol.

The District Court would not prove to be an important institution at first. The early federal district courts were basically maritime courts and, during this period, the significance of Georgetown and Alexandria as ports declined.

The Midnight Judges

Working at breakneck speed between February 27, 1801, when the legislation creating the District of Columbia judicial system was passed, and midnight March 3, when his term expired, President Adams made his appointments to the D.C. courts. To the Circuit Court he appointed Thomas Johnson (as Chief Judge), James Marshall, and William Cranch, all of whom were confirmed without controversy.

The nomination of Thomas Johnson (1732–1819) suggests the caliber of man Adams wanted to head the judiciary of this undeveloped but promising jurisdiction. Johnson was perhaps the most prominent Marylander in American public life, having served as a delegate to the first and second Continental Congresses, as Governor of Maryland, as Chief Judge of the General Court of Maryland, and, briefly, as a justice of the Supreme Court of the United States. However, Johnson declined the appointment to the Circuit Court. As a result, the first man to actually serve as Chief Judge, William Kilty (1757–1821), was appointed by President Jefferson. The English-born Kilty had come to the United States in 1774, fought in the Revolution, and practiced as a surgeon before turning to the law. He compiled the laws of Maryland at the request of its legislature. Kilty left the D.C. court in 1806 to serve as Chancellor of Maryland, a position he held until his death.

James Marshall (1764–1848), brother of the Chief Justice, was Adams' second appointee to the Circuit Court. Although he was described by John

Marshall's great biographer, Senator Albert J. Beveridge, as possessing "ability almost equal to John Marshall and wider and more varied accomplishments," comparatively little is known of him, partly because his tenure on the Court was so brief. After only two years on the Circuit Court, James Marshall resigned and moved to Winchester, Virginia, where he practiced law and managed the family's land interests. He was the moving party in the great Fairfax land case, *Martin v. Hunter's Lessee*, and outlived his great brother by almost thirteen years.[5]

Adams' third, and lasting, appointment was his nephew by marriage, William Cranch (1769–1855). Cranch was connected to the Adams clan by way of his mother, Mary Smith Cranch, Abigail Adams' sister. He attended Harvard with his first cousin, John Quincy Adams, and in 1795 he married Anne Greenleaf, the sister of James Greenleaf. Even before his marriage Cranch had agreed to move to Washington to manage the affairs of the Morris-Greenleaf-Nicholson land speculation syndicate.

Cranch's early years in Washington were tumultuous, as he found himself at the center of an enormous speculative bubble, followed by the bankruptcy and collapse of the partnership and the ensuing litigation. There is no suggestion that Cranch himself engaged in shady practices, and he seems to have retained the respect of each of the warring partners. He would, however, be often called as a witness in his own court in the Maryland cases to which Greenleaf was a party.

When the syndicate failed, Cranch returned to the practice of law, after turning down a proposal to publish a newspaper with his sister-in-law's husband, Noah Webster. However, as late as November 1800, Cranch's economic state was so precarious that he was considering taking in boarders. There remained the Adams connection. Although no speculator himself, John Adams had not lost his respect for his "sensible and worthy nephew," whom he saw as "very much like one of my own sons." When a vacancy

---

5. *Martin v. Hunter's Lessee*, 14 U.S. (1 Wheat) 304 (1816). The degree to which the relationship between the two Marshall brothers affected the decisions of the two courts cannot be known. In *Scott v. Mandeville*, 1 D.C. (1 Cranch) 115 (1803), a suit over a bond where the question of the commission for taking depositions was to be governed either by the law of Virginia or the law of Congress, Cranch's Circuit Court Reports include the following: "Marshall, J., said that he had been informed by the Chief Justice of the Supreme Court of the United States that it was the opinion of that court that the laws of Virginia were to be considered in this district, with regard to the general laws of the United States, as the common law is considered with regard to the statute law, viz., that it is not altered without negative words or an absolute inconsistency, so that both cannot stand together."

arose among the D.C. Commissioners in January 1800, Adams appointed Cranch to the position. Less than two months later, he appointed him to the Circuit Court. Cranch was not yet thirty-two.

Marbury v. Madison

Adams' nominations for the Circuit Court and the Orphan's Court, as well as those of the men he chose as Marshal of the District of Columbia, U.S. Attorney, and Registers of Wills for each county, were confirmed without incident. However, his nominations of justices of the peace triggered a controversy that led to one of the most important cases in American constitutional law.

In the Act of February 13, 1801, Congress had provided for justices of the peace for the District. They would serve five-year terms and have the same powers as their counterparts in Maryland or Virginia. In Virginia, at least, the position had some value as a starting place for a political career. Congress had left it to the President to appoint as many justices of the peace as he thought appropriate. Adams appointed twenty-three for Washington County and nineteen for Alexandria County. It is far from certain that the District of Columbia, with a population of 15,000 in 1801, needed forty-two minor judicial functionaries. Once again, Adams sought to fill the positions with pillars of the Federalist community.

Although all forty-two nominees had been confirmed by the Senate on March 2, some of their commissions were not delivered before Adams left office. Secretary of State John Marshall had been responsible for affixing the great seal of the United States to the JPs' commissions, while his brother, James, was charged with delivering some of them. After Jefferson assumed the presidency, he determined that thirty JPs—fifteen for each county—were enough. He refused to allow the commissions of seventeen of Adams' appointees, then made five additional nominations himself. Among the seventeen were William Marbury of Washington County and Townshend Hooe, William Harper, and Dennis Ramsey of Alexandria County—all prominent businessmen and landowners. These men chose to sue Secretary of State James Madison for their positions, probably more to embarrass the Jefferson administration than for the positions themselves.

Marbury v. Madison was not decided until more than two years of their five-year terms had expired. James Marshall testified in the proceedings in the U.S. Supreme Court; his brother, the Chief Justice, whose failure to affix the seal of the United States to the commissions in a timely manner had triggered the litigation, wrote the opinion for the Court. The opinion held that the men were indeed entitled to their commissions, but that the remedy they had asked for—issuance of the writ of mandamus by the

Supreme Court—could not be granted, because Congress had violated the Constitution when it had increased the original jurisdiction of the Supreme Court by authorizing it to grant such writs. The decision thus established the power of the Court to review and hold acts of Congress unconstitutional.[6]

It should be noted that, had the putative justices of the peace sought the writ of mandamus from James Marshall's court, they might have won the case. This, however, could have precipitated a confrontation between the administration and the Circuit Court.

Administration of the Local Court System

The Circuit Court for the District of Columbia met for the first time in Washington County on March 23, 1801, probably using the room in the Capitol assigned to the Supreme Court. At this first session, eleven attorneys were admitted to the bar. Charging the grand jury that was formed, Chief Judge William Kilty spoke of the creation of a "community compact in situation, united in interest and happily placed in that center from which must emanate the collected wisdom of united America."

Similar proceedings occurred in Alexandria in April 1801, at the old Hustings Court in Market Square. Congress had required the Circuit Court to hold four sessions each year in each of the District of Columbia's two counties; by the Act of May 3, 1802, this was reduced to two terms annually in each county. However, as early as March 1803, the Court itself ordered a special session in Alexandria County for criminal trials.

The Act of February 27, 1801, authorized the Circuit Court to appoint a Clerk in each county and the President to appoint a Marshal for the District of Columbia. The duties of the Clerk, as described by Deputy Clerk John A. Smith in hearings before the House of Representatives in 1837, were not unlike those of the Clerk's office today: "He is almost constantly employed waiting upon the Court, lawyers, suitors, witnesses, or some other of the vast number of persons with whom, and for what, he is obliged to transact business." Uriah Forrest, the first Clerk appointed for Washington County, died in 1805 and was succeeded by William Brent, a member of a prominent Republican family, who held the position for forty-three years.[7]

---

6. *Marbury v. Madison*, 5 U.S. (1 Cranch) 137 (1803).

7. The third Washington clerk (1848–63) was John Smith, who had been Brent's deputy.

Although some of the duties performed by federal marshals were similar to those undertaken by marshals or their deputies in some jurisdictions today—serving subpoenas, summonses, writs, and warrants—the Marshal of the District of Columbia had additional duties and his prestige was far higher. The Marshal was responsible for the jail; he served as Marshal of the Supreme Court of the United States, where he was expected to keep order; and from the outset, the office entailed participation at great ceremonial occasions. These ceremonial duties would evolve into responsibilities for maintaining order at public functions in and around the presidential mansion; by James Monroe's second term the Marshal had become a social aide to the President.

As in most American court systems in the early nineteenth century, the minor judicial officials and court officers in the District of Columbia relied heavily upon fees for their incomes. Only the Circuit Court judges were paid a salary; most of the court officers received modest per diems. This system invited abuse, and at least the appearance of impropriety was ever present. No less an observer than William Cranch believed that many prosecutions were prompted by witness fees. Justices of the peace and constables were usually paid more for convictions, and there were many complaints of JPs abusing their authority and taking advantage of the poor.

This was also true of the running of the jail. Each debtor, runaway slave, and criminal was expected to reimburse the Marshal's expenses. If a free African-American, falsely accused of being a slave, was able to prove he was a free man but could not pay the jail fees, the Marshal could sell him into slavery for reimbursement. Moreover, the Marshal was permitted to retain any profit. Not until the Civil War, when it was found that the Marshal of the District of Columbia was earning twice what U.S. marshals elsewhere earned—even making a profit on the feeding of prisoners—did Congress finally give the Marshal an annual allowance.

Unique Factors Affecting the Work of the Courts

From the first, the D.C. Circuit possessed several characteristics that set it apart from most American courts. For one thing, it had dual jurisdiction, that of a federal court and that of a state court of general jurisdiction. The latter, until the creation of a separate Criminal Court in 1838, included the hearing of local criminal cases. Further, the location of the court at the seat of government meant that from time to time some of the ordinary civil suits, criminal prosecutions, and probate matters it heard under its "state" jurisdiction involved national figures and thus attracted national attention. Trials of presidential assassins and of corrupt members of the executive and legislative branches would become a feature of its work, as would cases involving charges of contempt of Congress. The Circuit Court would also come to be recognized for its status as the one court in the United States with power to grant a writ of mandamus compelling a Cabinet member to perform a nondiscretionary duty.

Consequently, from the very beginning the courts of the District of Columbia were far more influential than might have been anticipated from their geographically tiny and underpopulated jurisdiction. For nearly two centuries, that jurisdiction has yielded a jurisprudence rich in cases involving oversight of the federal government and separation of powers.

Beyond the singular fact of their jurisdiction—partly federal, partly state, and partly national—the federal courts of the District of Columbia Circuit have, throughout their history, been affected by a number of special factors. These include, among others, the comparative insignificance of the District's private commerce, the population size and racial mix of the District, and the selection of judicial personnel from a wide geographic area. Congressional supremacy over the District and, much of the time, the absence of representative institutions have also played a part. From 1800 to 1860, the Circuit Court's contrast with other federal courts could be seen most clearly in the paucity of cases arising from commercial activity, the status of Washington's African-American population, and the antiquated substantive laws governing the District.

Economic development was slow in the District of Columbia, the mercantile class relatively small, and the diversity of economic opportunities limited. Thus, we do not see in the District of Columbia Circuit Court many important maritime or customs cases, or many cases involving the powers of private (as distinguished from municipal) corporations, or any important cases involving the interpretation of contracts and other disputes over the sale of merchandise. While government was, of course, the "business" of the District of Columbia, the federal presence in the city was quite small (there were only 137 federal employees in 1800) and its activities limited; in the period prior to the Civil War, public law litigation was unusual in the District. In addition, by 1860 the seat of the government had still not succeeded in attracting the commerce, wealth, and population likely to produce important private law litigation and sustained case lines.

The impact of the legal system on African-Americans, and of African-Americans on the law, has been a constant factor throughout the history of the courts of the District of Columbia Circuit. In the early nineteenth century, laws governing African-Americans in the city of Washington were far less severe than in most slave states, although they became harsher with time as whites grew increasingly concerned that if freedmen were permitted "privileges" in the District denied elsewhere in the South, the area would be overrun by freed blacks. Nevertheless, African-Americans participated in a wider range of activities than in possibly any other American city save New Orleans.

When Congress hurriedly cobbled together a legal system for the District in February 1801, it provided that, unless and until it changed them, the laws of Maryland and Virginia as they were in 1801 would continue in force. As the Circuit Court was also required to follow the procedures of the state in which it was meeting, its judges had to be familiar with the procedural and substantive law of two states, as well as with whatever changes Congress made. The duality of law in the District caused substantial litigation; for example, until Congress acted in 1812, certain promissory notes that were negotiable in Washington County were non-negotiable in Alexandria County.

Beyond disrupting commercial arrangements, many of the laws the judges had to apply, especially in criminal cases, were already antiquated in 1801 and mandated barbaric punishments, including branding (with a great key heated by a jailer), whipping, and the pillory. On the Alexandria side of the Potomac thirty crimes were punishable by death, and fourteen on the Maryland side, including the theft of as little as five shillings. Such cases came before the courts from the outset. The judges themselves lobbied for the erection of a penitentiary, "instead of hangings, whippings and burnings on the hand," as Judge Buckner Thruston put it in a charge to a grand jury. In order to avoid imposing these medieval penalties, judges declined to punish many common offenses; in other cases prosecutors charged or juries convicted under weaker alternatives. When circumstances allowed little leeway to prosecutors, juries, and judges, the Court itself often requested executive clemency. Indeed, the implementation of a capital sentence was rare; only three executions were carried out between 1801 and 1850.

Early Political Cases

From the very beginning, important cases of a political nature came before the District's courts. During the decade, the courts dealt with two particularly explosive political cases, one a criminal libel prosecution of the journalistic voice of the Jefferson administration, the other dealing with part of the alleged treasonous conspiracy involving Aaron Burr.

The National Intelligencer Case

Shortly after assuming the presidency, Thomas Jefferson persuaded Samuel Harrison Smith, a good friend and moderate Republican, to move to Washington to establish a newspaper which would speak for the administration. The *National Intelligencer*, a four-page tri-weekly, ultimately became the leading newspaper in the District and flourished for a half century.

On June 12, 1801, just three months after Jefferson took office, Smith published a letter defending the President's removal of Federalist marshals and U.S. Attorneys. The letter charged that the courts had "been prompt to seize every occasion of aggrandizing Executive power, of destroying all freedom of opinion, of executing unconstitutional laws, and of inculcating by the wanton and unsolicited diffusion of heterodox polities, the doctrines of passive obedience and non-resistance."

For the era, this was not particularly strong stuff, but it offended Judges James Marshall and William Cranch sufficiently that they ordered the U.S. District Attorney—over the dissent of the one Jefferson appointee, Chief Judge Kilty—to institute a seditious libel prosecution against Smith. Neither Marshall nor Cranch had been on the bench long enough to be legitimately considered the focus of the criticisms.

The prosecution of Smith was another symptom of the partisan bitterness of the early years of the Republic. During Adams' administration, Federalist justices, judges, jurors, and marshals in the Northeast had joined in seditious libel prosecutions against Republican politicians, newspaper editors, and printers. Basing his defense upon the Constitution, Smith argued that the public officials were being criticized only in an official capacity, and therefore the criticism was protected by the First Amendment.

The U.S. District Attorney, a Jefferson appointee, refused to have anything to do with the case, beyond handing the paper to the grand jury and expressing the sentiments of different members of the Court. The grand jury returned a presentment, but refused to indict. Eventually, the case was dropped, but not before it had become a *cause celebre*, had exacerbated tensions between the Republicans and the judiciary, and had nudged Jefferson closer to countenancing the attempt by congressional Republicans to abolish the federal circuit courts—though not that of the District of Columbia.[8]

---

8. A number of private libel and slander cases were brought in the Circuit during this period. One of the most piquant involved two of the master architects of the capital, Benjamin Latrobe and William Thornton, who met in court over Thornton's poem mocking Latrobe's design for the main gate of the Naval Yard.

Bollmann and Swartwout

Following his duel with Alexander Hamilton in 1804, former Vice President Aaron Burr, now a political pariah in New York and Washington, looked to the West for his future. What precisely he had in mind remains a mystery to this day. He engaged in a series of suggestive conversations with foreign diplomats and Washington acquaintances, tailoring descriptions of his plans to the dreams and biases of different listeners. It may be plausibly argued that he intended to settle a contested land claim, to seek a new political base, to organize a military expedition to wrest control of Spain's North American colonies for the U.S., or to separate the western states and territories from the United States.

Caught in the web spun by Burr were Dr. Justus Erich Bollmann (or Bollman), a German-born physician, and Samuel Swartwout, the brother of John Swartwout, an important cog in Burr's Tammany machine. For their participation in Burr's scheme, both men would be charged with treason in the most important criminal prosecution brought in the District of Columbia during its first sixty years.

General James Wilkinson, commander of the American army and governor of the Territory of Louisiana, was a critical figure in Burr's plans. Wilkinson was a scoundrel in the pay of the Spanish government, although it is not clear whether either Burr or Thomas Jefferson, who had appointed him, knew this. In 1806, Bollmann and Swartwout carried to Wilkinson a coded letter from Burr. Wilkinson would later claim that the letter proposed a conspiracy to "revolutionize" Louisiana and then move to conquer Mexico.

Wilkinson had Bollmann and Swartwout arrested by military order, without a warrant, and held incommunicado. He confiscated their papers, denied them access to counsel and the courts, ignored writs of habeas corpus issued by the territorial courts, and had them transported to Washington, where they were held in a military prison. On January 22, 1807, in reply to a request from Congress for information, Jefferson named Burr, "whose guilt is placed beyond question," as the prime mover in a conspiracy to sever the Union and attack Mexico. The following day, Walter Jones, the U.S. Attorney, acting on instructions from the President, asked Chief Judge Cranch to issue a bench warrant charging Bollmann and Swartwout with treason and holding them for trial.

The audience for the argument before the Circuit Court was vast—indeed, the House of Representatives adjourned to allow its members to attend. On January 24, a petition for habeas corpus was filed with the Court. On the 27th, the divided Circuit Court held that the bench warrant to arrest

Bollman and Swartwout for treason should issue. Cranch dissented. On the 30th, the Court, Cranch again dissenting, ruled that Bollmann and Swartwout should be held for trial and not admitted to bail. Judge Allen B. Duckett relied heavily upon the depositions of Wilkinson and General William Eaton to find probable cause, arguing, as well, that the President's message provided substantial corroboration. Judge Nicholas Fitzhugh concurred.[9]

Cranch's dissent is one of the most eloquent civil liberties opinions in early American law. Had it been written a century later, one would have found in it the same principles reflected in Holmes' classic opinion in the *Abrams* case and Brandeis's in *Whitney v. California*.[10] Cranch wrote:

> In times like these, when the public mind is agitated, when wars, and rumors of wars, plots, conspiracies and treasons excite alarm, it is the duty of a court to be peculiarly watchful lest the public feeling should reach the seat of justice, and thereby precedents be established which may become the ready tools of faction in times more disastrous. The worst of precedents may be established from the best of motives. We ought to be on our guard lest our zeal for the public interest lead us to overstep the bounds of the law and the Constitution; for although we may thereby bring one criminal to punishment, we may furnish the means by which an hundred innocent persons may suffer.
>
> The Constitution was made for times of commotion. In the calm of peace and prosperity there is seldom great injustice. Dangerous precedents occur in dangerous times. It then becomes the duty of the judiciary calmly to poise the scales of justice, unmoved by the arm of power, undisturbed by the clamor of the multitude.

In the Supreme Court, that great, if often tipsy, advocate Luther Martin argued for the defendants. The High Court heard three days of argument before concluding that there was insufficient evidence of levying war to justify the commitment of Bollmann and Swartwout. Writing for the Court, Chief Justice Marshall held that levying war "must be brought into operation by the assemblage of men for a purpose treasonable in itself, or the fact of levying of war cannot have been committed."[11]

---

9. *United States v. Bollmann and Swartwout*, 1 D.C. (1 Cranch) 373 (1807).

10. *Abrams v. United States*, 250 U.S. 616, 624–31 (1919); *Whitney v. California*, 274 U.S. 357, 372–80 (1927).

11. *Ex Parte Bollmann and Ex Parte Swartwout*, 8 U.S. (4 Cranch) 73 (1807). Neither Bollmann nor Swartwout stood trial with Burr in Richmond, although Bollmann was called as a witness. In rendering his famous opinion on constructive treason in the Burr trial, Marshall moved away from those parts of his *Bollmann and Swartwout* opin-

Cranch emerged from the tempest with honor. Writing on the day the Supreme Court decided *Bollmann and Swartwout*, he stated:

> It happened, from a singular and unforeseen coincidence of strange circumstances, that I should be the first to resist the hand of arbitrary power, and to stem the torrent, which has at length yielded and is now turning the other way. Although I have not for a moment doubted the correctness of my opinion, yet it is a source of great satisfaction to find it confirmed by the highest judicial tribunal in the nation. I congratulate my country upon this triumph of reason and law over popular passion and injustice—upon the final triumph of civil over the military authority, and of the practical principles of substantial personal liberty over the theoretical doctrine of philosophic civil liberty.

The Cranch Court

At one time or another in its early days, the District of Columbia Circuit Court was the object of all the eternal complaints made about courts: congested calendars, cumbersome procedures, interminable delays, needless expenses. Beyond these, however, the Circuit Court seems to have had real problems with decorum. Besides the noise and confusion in the courtroom, there was a lack of civility all around: members of the bar and members of the bench vilified each other and feuded among themselves. One attorney, describing the unruly courtroom, exclaimed, "What a beargarden!" To understand the reasons for the problem, we must look more closely at the judges of the Cranch Court.

From 1815 to 1845, the same three judges constituted the Circuit Court of the District of Columbia—William Cranch, Buckner Thruston, and James S. Morsell—an extraordinarily long period of stability for a court. Cranch served for fifty-four years (forty-nine as Chief Judge), Morsell for forty-eight, and Thruston for thirty-six. Thruston's service equals the longest tenure of any justice of the Supreme Court of the United States. If only because of the longevity of their service—three times that of the other seven judges who sat on the Court during its sixty-two years—their work demands attention.

---

ion which had appeared to embrace the English view of constructive treason, i.e., that anyone who had played any part, however remote from the scene of the action, was guilty of treason. Marshall's charge to the jury in *United States v. Burr* is found in Appendix B, 8 U.S. (4 Cranch) 469.

William Cranch

The name Cranch is familiar to virtually everyone who has studied American constitutional law, for 5 U.S. (1 Cranch) 137 (1803) is the official citation for *Marbury v. Madison*. But apart from his role as the reporter of that landmark case and other Supreme Court decisions, William Cranch has been little remarked in legal histories. He was an able jurist, and his judicial tenure was about as lengthy as any in American history. From the evidence, Cranch was a careful, diligent judge. If he was not completely nonpartisan during the bitter struggles between Federalists and Republicans in the early years, he was sufficiently fair and well regarded for Thomas Jefferson to elevate him, in 1806, to the Chief Judgeship, where he presided for almost half a century.

A man of extraordinary energy and diligence, he discharged not only the duties of a Circuit Judge but those for which the Chief Judge was solely responsible — presiding over the District Court and hearing appeals from the decisions of the Commissioner of Patents.[12] He also undertook an enormous number of law-related projects and other civic duties, as well as engaging in a few commercial activities.[13] But it is for his work as reporter of the decisions of the Supreme Court from 1801 to 1816 that Cranch has gained a measure of immortality. Cranch's nine volumes of Supreme Court reports begin with John Marshall's assumption of the Chief Justiceship and the Court's new practice of rendering written opinions. Cranch regularized the practice of reporting lawyers' arguments and introduced summaries of the principal points decided by the opinion, although his summaries are difficult to read.

---

12. The Chief Judge was also supposed to hold the Criminal Court, created in 1838, when the Criminal Court judge was disabled. It is not clear whether it ever was necessary for Cranch to perform this duty. As Chief Judge of the District of Columbia, Cranch administered the constitutional oath to Millard Fillmore on July 10, 1850, upon the death of Zachary Taylor.

13. Cranch and President Jefferson were among the thirteen trustees of the first public schools organized in the District. Cranch and John Marshall were officers of the Washington Monument Society and the Washington chapter of the American Colonization Society. Cranch was president of the Capitol Hill Seminary for Young Ladies, president of the Society for the Promotion of Temperance, and an organizer of the Washington Library Company. In 1826 Cranch was inaugurated as one of the first two professors of law in the District (William Thomas Carroll was the other), at the Columbian College. Cranch's childhood friend, John Quincy Adams, now President, attended his inaugural lecture. Cranch also edited *Cranch's Patent Decisions: Laws of the United States Relating to Patents and the Patent Office, Together with Decisions* (1848).

By the War of 1812, the pressure of his own judicial business, the increased workload of the Marshall Court, and his tendency to procrastinate conspired to delay the publication of the Supreme Court opinions for a considerable period after they had been delivered. A group led by Justice Joseph Story and Attorney General Richard Rush sought Cranch's removal. He stepped down just at the time Congress passed a law creating an official reporter for the Court with an annual salary.

Cranch continued, however, to report the decisions of his own court. As a result, much of what we know about the work of the Circuit Court, and about Cranch himself, comes from his five volumes of decisions (plus a one volume index-digest) containing 2,100 cases spanning the years 1801–40. To the modern eye, the reports are not entirely satisfactory. Statements of facts are cryptic, the judges' rationales tightly compressed, and opinions in the contemporary sense included for only a relative handful of cases. Still, if the cases suggest more than they tell, they offer considerable insight into the range of work which came before the Court.

Less is known than one would like about Cranch the man. He was the father of ten — five sons and five daughters. In the sketchy record there are glimpses of a patient, modest man, nowhere near as prickly as his Adams relations, but just as diligent and upright. He seems to have found great joy, not in power, but in sunsets and flowers, poetry, music, and chess. A religious Unitarian opposed to slavery, alcohol, and dueling, Cranch seems to have possessed no trace of sanctimoniousness. "Patient, painstaking and learned," as Walter S. Cox, a judge of the Supreme Court of the District of Columbia in the latter part of the century, described him, he may have been simply too *nice* to deal effectively with his irascible colleague Thruston and some of the fractious advocates who appeared before him.

Thruston and Morsell

Buckner Thruston was the first of James Madison's two appointees to the Circuit Court. Born in Virginia in 1764, he practiced law in Kentucky and served in the Virginia Assembly and as first clerk of the Kentucky Senate. Thruston declined appointment as judge of the Supreme Court of the Orleans Territory and in 1805 was elected United States Senator from Kentucky. On his appointment to the Circuit Court in 1809, Thruston was succeeded in the Senate by Henry Clay. A Latin scholar and mathematician, Thruston was a highly intelligent man with a quick mind. But he was also opinionated, impatient of legal learning and lawyers, and extraordinarily hard to get along with: a textbook curmudgeon.

After James Madison's appointment of James S. Morsell in 1815, the Circuit Court's membership would remain stable for thirty years. Little is known of Morsell. He was born on Maryland's Western Shore in 1775 and was among the first group of lawyers admitted to the bar of the Circuit Court. He practiced law in Georgetown, where he also lived, until his appointment to the Court. Judge Cox described Morsell as "a plodding, patient and industrious judge." Morsell served on the Circuit Court for forty-eight years. After the Court was abolished in 1863, he retired to his farm in Maryland and died there the day after his ninety-fifth birthday.

The Thruston Problem

One of the major factors—perhaps the prime factor—affecting the work of the Circuit Court for over a third of a century was the cantankerous Judge Thruston. Even if Article III federal judges boast a greater than average share of strong personalities, Thruston was in a special class, so much so that an ad hoc congressional committee was established in 1837 to investigate the charges brought against him by two members of the bar of the Court, William L. Brent and Richard S. Coxe. Thruston was accused of gross and avowed ignorance of the law; insolent, quarrelsome, and rude behavior towards the bar; habitual inattentiveness; and negligence in the discharge of his official duties. The congressional hearings neither exonerated nor condemned Thruston, but the record yields remarkable insights into the atmosphere in which the Court functioned.

Thruston may have been intelligent and, in some areas, learned, but there is little doubt that he was temperamentally unfit for the bench. Cranch's reports frequently record cases decided in Thruston's absence; he was often two or three hours late for the court sessions. Tardiness and ignorance of what had gone before did not, however, prevent him from rapidly developing an opinion of the case, which he then pursued without disguising his partisanship, not even from the jury.

These traits were exacerbated by Thruston's open contempt for legal learning. In one prosecution described in Cranch's notes, Thruston disagreed with his colleagues that two of the charges should be thrown out. "He said it might be good law, but that the law books would ruin the country by driving common sense out of court." Thruston's dislike of the formal law and its practitioners was not unique among Republicans of the day. Indeed, his impatience with the technicalities of common-law proceedings put him ahead of, rather than behind, his time; but it could not but alienate able practitioners.

A trial judge with a short fuse, interacting bluntly with advocates of "combustible and explosive tempers," in a courtroom not known as a model of dignity and decorum, was bound to explode. There was a pattern: Thruston would become impatient with the lawyers and interrupt them, provoking a sharp reply; at this, the judge would get more exercised, making remarks like, "If I had the power I would expel you from the bar and I would commit you to prison."

Thruston's behavior towards his judicial colleagues was little better. He differed with them openly on matters of judicial administration. He believed that grand juries were kept in session long after they should have been discharged and opposed multiple indictments. He believed (not unreasonably) that Cranch indulged too much argument. He made no effort to keep these differences private, but denounced the evils he perceived in open court. Thruston's breaches of courtroom decorum might have been fewer or less indecorous had Cranch been firm rather than patient, not only with his irascible colleague but with the overzealous advocates as well. Cranch was ever anxious not to give more offense to Thruston and thereby excite more outbursts, for "when the paroxysms passed off, the judge appeared to be himself again, and to be polite and friendly. Thus we rubbed along for twenty-five years."

It was widely believed that Thruston suffered from a form of mental illness. Thruston himself described it as a "partial intellectual derangement and particularly hypochondriasis" causing "peevishness and irritability." John Quincy Adams, blunt as his father, wrote that Thruston "is partially insane but knows it and avows it."

Jurisprudence of the Early Courts

Observers have differed in their assessments of the importance of the D.C. Circuit Court in this period. In the volume of the Oliver Wendell Holmes Devise *History of the Supreme Court of the United States* dealing with the early Marshall Court, Herbert Johnson argues that "[w]ithin the galaxy of federal circuit courts the Circuit Court of the District of Columbia was a star of first magnitude." But in a later volume, G. Edward White observes that "comparatively little law was generated," adding that "the District's minor role as a legal center was the result of its small population."

Certainly, one does not see in Cranch's reports the creation of an Americanized and modernized common law, as it is possible to see in Gibson's Pennsylvania, Shaw's Massachusetts, or Story's First Circuit. As was the case with many American courts before the Civil War, the Circuit Court for the District of Columbia was a *useful* court: useful in untangling those legal knots that made it difficult to alienate land or to buy and sell merchandise. During this period, the "federal" jurisdiction of the D.C. Circuit Court — the jurisdiction it shared with U.S. circuit courts throughout the country — was a relatively unimportant part of its docket. If the Court's location in Washington brought before it, in both civil and criminal matters, important figures in American public life, little law of lasting importance resulted in these years. Only with the *Kendall* case in 1837 did the Circuit Court begin to carve out what would develop into the most uniquely important characteristic of the federal courts of the D.C. Circuit: their use as the forum for suits against high federal officials.

The federal courts during this period, with the exception of those in the territories, were specialized courts hearing limited classes of cases — admiralty and maritime cases, seizures and forfeitures under U.S. revenue and navigation laws, the prosecution of a few federal crimes, suits under federal laws such as patent and copyright, and diversity cases between citizens of different states. Relatively few cases in these "federal" specialties came before the D.C. Circuit Court, save patent and some criminal cases.

Most of the docket of the Circuit Court of the District of Columbia was made up of cases that, in other jurisdictions, would be heard by state courts, where the bulk of litigation involving ordinary people transpired. These were cases involving property, contracts, wills, and the family — fairly simple disputes, although certainly meaningful for the litigants. A large number of cases involved the speculative land operations in the District in the 1790s. It took a half century of litigation relating to the collapse of Greenleaf, Morris, and Nicholson to fully untangle the complications. The record of the most important of these cases, *Pratt v. Law and Campbell*, is contained in 900 folios.[14] If the stakes were higher in this case than in most — it put at issue the ownership of 2.4 million square feet of land in Washington — in its complexity it was quite typical of many land disputes emerging out of the early development of the District. And many of them, including *Pratt*, were ultimately decided by the U.S. Supreme Court.

Criminal Prosecutions

Until the establishment of a separate Criminal Court in the District in 1838, the Circuit Court for the District of Columbia was unique among the federal circuit courts because it had not only the powers and jurisdiction of the other circuit courts but also jurisdiction over all crimes and offenses committed

---

14. 13 U.S. (9 Cranch) 456 (1815).

within the District, whether or not they were violations of federal law. A number of the early criminal cases are period pieces, in form if not in substance. Among the cases recorded by Cranch were indictments for keeping a "bawdy" or "disorderly" house, for keeping a billiard table for public use without a license, for cheating at cards, and for cruelty to a horse in a public street.[15]

There were a number of indictments relating to the fighting of duels, some with prominent defendants. Cranch indicated his opposition to dueling in a charge to the grand jury in 1820, after Stephen Decatur had been killed by a disgraced naval officer. A law banning duels in Washington was passed in 1829, but dueling pistols continued to be part of the attire of members of Congress from the South and West. Many duels were fought just outside the city limits in Bladensburg.

One case involving dueling, decided by the Criminal Court in 1842, raised an important separation of powers issue—one which would recur in later years with prosecutions of corrupt members of Congress. A member of Congress, about to fight a duel with another Congressman, was arrested on a warrant issued by Judge Thruston upon probable cause. The defendant argued that under Article I, Section 6 of the Constitution, he was privileged from arrest unless there had been an actual breach of the peace. The U.S. Attorney took the position that the privileges of members of Congress ought to be kept within narrow limits, if they were to be tolerated at all. Judge James Dunlop held the privilege unavailable and required the defendant to give security to keep the peace and prohibited him from leaving the District for the purpose of fighting a duel for the period of one year, under penalty of forfeiting $3,000.[16]

Separation of powers questions were raised in another prosecution of a prominent politician, former Tennessee (and future Texas) governor Sam Houston. Houston was charged with battery for the caning of Representative William Stanberry of Ohio after Stanberry had accused him of fraud on the floor of the House. After Congress convicted Houston for contempt of Congress, the Circuit Court held that the contempt conviction was not a bar to criminal prosecution for the same assault and battery. The Court fined Houston $500 after considering "the situation of the parties, their high

15. See, for example, *United States v. Burch*, 1 D.C. (1 Cranch) 36 (1801); *United States v. Mary Rawlinson*, 1 D.C. (1 Cranch) 83 (1802); *United States v. Polly Rollinson*, 2 D.C. (2 Cranch) 13 (1811); *United States v. Duvall*, 2 D.C. (2 Cranch) 42 (1812); *United States v. Bascadore*, 2 D.C. (2 Cranch) 3 (1811); *United States v. Logan*, 2 D.C. (2 Cranch) 259 (1821).

16. *United States v. Wise*, 1 Hay. & Haz. 82 (1842).

standing in society, the original provocation, the deliberate revenge, the great outrage upon the public peace, the severity of the battery, and the mitigating circumstances."[17]

Perhaps the most notorious defendant to appear in the District's courts was Representative Daniel Sickles, who was tried in April 1859 for the murder of his wife's lover, Philip Barton Key, the playboy U.S. Attorney for the District of Columbia. Although there was not the slightest doubt that Sickles had committed the crime, the jury deliberated for seventy minutes and acquitted.[18]

Although concepts about the rights of criminal defendants have ancient roots, just a small handful of cases in the early years of the D.C. courts foreshadow modern notions. In one such case, in 1802, the Circuit Court, citing Blackstone, instructed a jury that "no confession, extorted from the prisoner, by threats of punishment, or obtained by the promise of reward or favor, was evidence against him." Four years later, the Circuit Court held that a jury should disregard a confession made under threats or promises of favor; however, in a ruling more akin to recent Supreme Court decisions, the Court also declared that facts discovered in consequence of the confession were good evidence.[19]

A perennial debate in jurisprudence surfaced in the Circuit Court early in its existence. In an 1802 case a defense attorney attempted to inform the jury that they were judges of the law as well as of the fact in criminal cases. He began to argue the substantive point to them when Judges Kilty and Marshall interrupted and stopped him. Cranch's dissent, echoed by David Bazelon over 160 years later, stated that "he held it to be an important point in favor of the liberties of the people that the jury, in criminal cases, had a right to decide the law as well as the facts."[20]

In 1831, acting at the request of President Andrew Jackson, Congress substantially modernized the criminal code. Among the reforms were the abolition of capital crimes except for treason, murder, piracy, and rape committed by slaves.

---

17. *United States v. Houston,* 4 D.C. (4 Cranch) 261 (1832).

18. *United States v. Sickles,* 27 F. Cas. 1074 (1859).

19. *United States v. Pumphreys,* 1 D.C. (1 Cranch) 74 (1802); *United States v. Hunter,* 1 D.C. (1 Cranch) 317 (1806).

20. *Commonwealth of Virginia v. Zimmerman,* 1 D.C. (1 Cranch) 47, 48 (1802). Compare Chief Judge Bazelon's opinion (concurring in part and dissenting in part) in *United States v. Dougherty,* 473 F.2d 1113, 1138–44 (1972).

The Kendall Case

The unique role the courts of the District of Columbia have in oversight of high officials of the federal government dates from an 1837 ruling of the Circuit Court affirmed by the U.S. Supreme Court. This landmark case, *United States ex rel. Stokes v. Kendall*, established that the Circuit Court for the District of Columbia had the power to grant a writ of mandamus to compel a member of the Cabinet to perform a nondiscretionary duty.[21]

Amos Kendall, Postmaster General under Andrew Jackson and Martin Van Buren, was an exemplary, if partisan, public servant, and the most influential member of Jackson's "kitchen cabinet." Jackson made Kendall Postmaster General in 1835 to clean up a mess in the Post Office Department. A man of probity and a superb administrator, Kendall eliminated gross over-expenditures and tried to terminate the near-incestuous relations between department officials and private contractors.

The case arose after Kendall refused to pay a claim made by Stockton and Stokes, a firm of intercity coach operators. The claim was allegedly due under a decision of his predecessor, but Kendall was unable to find a legitimate basis for it—both he and President Jackson believed it fraudulent. Congress directed the Solicitor General of the Treasury to make a determination of right according to principles of equity. The Solicitor General allowed the original claim plus $40,000; Kendall credited the original claim but refused to authorize the additional amount.

Stokes sued for the balance by way of a writ of mandamus from the Circuit Court. The Postmaster General responded with a letter to the Chief Judge, respectfully denying that a court of the District of Columbia, established for local purposes, could possess jurisdiction to inquire into the official conduct of the President and heads of the departments. They were, after all, subject to impeachment for neglect of duty. Kendall further argued that, as he was subject solely to the direction and control of the President, the courts lacked the power to compel even a mandatory duty.

Cranch ruled for Stokes, holding that the Circuit Court did have the power to issue mandamus to an executive branch official. He wrote:

> This Court has all the jurisdiction which any other circuit court of the
> United States can have in its circuit, and much more.... This Court

---

21. *United States ex rel. Stokes v. Kendall*, 5 D.C. (5 Cranch) 163 (1837). Prior to this decision, it appeared that no Circuit Court in the United States possessed the authority to issue a writ of mandamus to a government official. See *M'Intire v. Wood*, 11 U.S. (7 Cranch) 504 (1813).

has power to call before it every person found in the district, from the highest to the lowest; and it is upon this power that they all depend for that protection which the law extends over them.

The case was appealed to the Supreme Court, which held that while the President was beyond the reach of process, mandamus could be used to enforce an executive officer's duties for which the President was not responsible. Further, the High Court ruled that the Circuit Court for the District of Columbia had jurisdiction because in 1801 it had succeeded to the powers of the Maryland courts, which had the power to issue mandamus to an executive officer, commanding him to perform a ministerial act required of him by law. Three justices dissented.[22] President Martin Van Buren then urged Congress to withdraw jurisdiction from the Circuit Court; the bill passed the Senate but not the House of Representatives.

So much litigation arose in the wake of the *Kendall* cases that in 1840 Justice John Catron, in an unrelated opinion, wrote, rather hyperbolically, "Between the Circuit Court of this district and the executive administration of the United States there is an open contest for power." In that case, *Decatur v. Paulding*, the Supreme Court confirmed the basic position of the Circuit Court, that if a duty was not merely administrative, but required the exercise of official judgment, the Court could not properly interfere.[23]

On the whole, under *Kendall* the Circuit Court for the District of Columbia was recognized to have remarkable power; but in the years before the Civil War that power was narrowly exercised.[24] Not until the passage of

---

22. *Kendall v. United States ex rel. Stokes*, 37 U.S. (12 Pet.) 524 (1838), on remand, *United States ex rel. Stockton v. Kendall*, 5 D.C. (5 Cranch) 385 (1838).

23. *Decatur v. Paulding*, 39 U.S. (14 Pet.) 497 (1840), in which the widow of Stephen Decatur had invoked the jurisdiction of the Circuit Court to direct the Secretary of the Navy to pay her a second pension.

24. Examples of the Circuit Court's refusal to broaden its power include *Ex Parte Schaumberg*, 1 Hay. & Haz. 249 (1846), in which the Court denied mandamus to order the reinstatement of the commission of a first lieutenant that was to be held "during pleasure" of the President; *United States ex rel. Goodrich v. Guthrie*, 2 Hay. & Haz. 151 (1854), aff'd, 58 U.S. (17 How.) 284 (1855), in which it rejected mandamus to the Secretary of the Treasury to pay the salary of the Chief Justice of the Territory of Minnesota, in a dispute as to whether he could properly be removed by the President before the end of his four-year term; and *United States v. Seaman*, 2 Hay. & Haz. 151 (1854), aff'd, 58 U.S. (17 How.) 225 (1855), where the court denied mandamus in a quarrel between the printers for the Senate and the House of Representatives over who was to be paid for printing the agricultural portion of the annual report of the Commissioner of Patents.

the Mandamus and Venue Act in 1962 would the federal district courts have general power to grant mandamus relief in original actions. Until then, there was conflicting authority as to whether the federal district courts outside of the District of Columbia could issue injunctions or declaratory decrees against federal officers to accomplish the same result as might have been accomplished by mandamus.

African-Americans and the Law

In 1800 the black population of the District of Columbia was 4,027, of whom 783 were free men. Hired slaves formed the core of the labor force that built the Capitol and then restored it after it was burned by the British in the War of 1812. The slave trade in the District of Columbia continued until 1850, while slavery itself continued in the District until April 16, 1862. However, Washington would become one of a very few cities in slave jurisdictions where free blacks outnumbered slaves — a relative oasis of freedom surrounded by two slave states. In 1860, the District (which by that time occupied only the Maryland side of the Potomac) had a population of 14,316 African-Americans, of whom 11,131 were free.

The first District of Columbia law aimed at freed African-Americans was enacted in 1808; it imposed a five-dollar fine on any African-American out after 10 p.m. Two years later the Mayor and the City Council enacted a "black code" requiring free blacks to register with the municipal authority and always to carry with them a certificate of freedom. Further restrictions were imposed during the 1820s, and more followed the Nat Turner rebellion of 1831 and a major racial riot in 1836 — one precipitated by whites.

When emancipation of slaves in the District of Columbia became a national political issue during the 1840s, tensions grew. There was general relief in Washington when Congress abolished the slave trade in the District as part of the Compromise of 1850. However, during the decade before the Civil War considerable efforts were made in the District to slow the increase of the freed black population, and there were episodes of rigid surveillance and police brutality. By the Civil War, the District had a substantial community of free African-Americans with a rich network of supportive institutions, but only forty-two percent of that population was literate, and just three percent were professionals or business persons.

The Circuit Court's record in cases involving African-Americans during this period is mixed; the unsurprising conclusion is that, in court as well as out, it was more advantageous to be white than black. A slave could not be a witness in a lawsuit where a free white man was a party (although Cranch thought otherwise), nor could a contract between master and slave be enforced at law or in equity.[25]

In 1821, William Costin, a trusted messenger of the Bank of Washington and the most respected black man in the city, brought a test case in the Circuit Court challenging the newly strengthened black code. He argued that the Corporation of Washington did not have the authority to prescribe "the terms and conditions upon which free Negroes and mulattoes may reside" because Congress could not delegate powers to the city that were unconstitutional, and "the Constitution knows no distinction of color." Cranch upheld the ordinance on the ground that a state or municipality could, in the interest of protecting society, restrict any group that, irrespective of proved misconduct by individual members of the group, appeared likely to disturb the peace. However, he then held that the ordinance could not be applied to Costin and others with long residence in Washington.[26]

Blacks fared far worse in the criminal justice system than whites; their arrest rate was much higher and their testimony against whites was not considered good evidence. Before the 1831 reform of the criminal laws, offenses by slaves were often subject to barbaric punishment. Yet, as it did with other antiquated laws, the Court sometimes bent the law to avoid inflicting those penalties.[27]

In Washington, unlike Virginia, procedures existed whereby wrongfully enslaved persons could petition for their freedom; and the petitioner often won. There were a number of indictments for aiding the escape of slaves, including one, in 1821, for aiding a slave owned by Justice Bushrod Washington. The Circuit Court records also chronicle numerous actions for the return of fugitive slaves.[28]

---

25. *Thomas v. Jamesson*, 1 D.C. (1 Cranch) 91 (1802); *O'Neale v. Willis*, 2 D.C. (2 Cranch) 108 (1814); *Negro Richard v. Van Meter*, 3 D.C. (3 Cranch) 214 (1827), citing *Negro Joseph Brown v. Wingrad*, 2 D.C. (2 Cranch) 300 (1822).

26. *Costin v. Corporation of Washington*, 2 D.C. (2 Cranch) 254 (1821).

27. For example, in 1813 Jacob Bruce was accused of conspiring to burn down a house; if he were a slave it would have been a capital offense, but the Court accepted an informal paper as proof of manumission and he was not harshly punished. *United States v. Negro Jacob Bruce*, 2 D.C. (2 Cranch) 95 (1813).

28. *United States v. Negro Pompey*, 2 D.C. (2 Cranch) 246 (1821). Actions for the return of fugitives included petitions by the putative owners, affidavits supporting the arrest of fugitive slaves, warrants of arrest, depositions, court orders to deliver fugitive slaves, and remands of fugitive slaves to their owners.

Changes in Judicial Administration

As early as 1815 the need for a building to house the Circuit Court, municipal offices, and a penitentiary was recognized as a high priority by the Washington city government. When the cornerstone for the City Hall, which would also house the courts, was laid at Fifth and D Streets, N.W., on August 22, 1820, there was a great municipal celebration. At 240 feet long, 176 feet wide, and sixty feet high, the three-story building was one of the largest in the city. It was used by the Circuit Court, the Orphan's Court, and the Register of Wills.

Changes in the court system occurred slowly. As with many American courts, business increased far beyond expectations because of population growth and the unanticipated litigiousness of citizens, and the problems were dealt with by patchwork legislation. By the 1820 term, the Circuit Court was able to complete only half of its business. The following year, 1,200 lawsuits were awaiting trial. Congress dealt with this by increasing the upper monetary limit, in cases in debt and damages that the justices of the peace could handle, from $20 to $50.[29] As a result, in just two years the business of the Circuit Court fell drastically, from 1,300 civil actions to 150.

However, the criminal business of the Court increased greatly in the 1830s, and in 1838 a separate Criminal Court was established. Although the Criminal Court shared the courtroom and clerk of the Circuit Court, it was presided over by a separate judge. Each year two terms were held in each county. In the event of the disability of the Criminal Court judge, the Chief Judge of the Circuit Court was authorized to hold Criminal Court.[30] By the 1840s the Circuit Court was back to holding four terms annually, each about a month to six weeks long. Jury cases were heard first, then equity business. The Criminal Court sat between Circuit Court terms.

Toward the end of Cranch's tenure, pressures to change the Court system increased. One of the most influential proponents of change was Henry May, an attorney who had been disbarred by the Court and went on to be elected to Congress from a Baltimore district. Chief Judge Cranch, who was May's neighbor and an old friend of his father, had issued the disbarment after a distressing courtroom incident. May had won a jury verdict in a usury case, but the judges set the verdict aside. Still smarting from that rebuke, May, in another case, stated in open court that the proceedings filled him with disgust. Cranch consulted with his colleagues, then dismissed May

---

29. Act of March 1, 1823, 3 Stat. 743.
30. Act of July 7, 1838, 5 Stat. 306; Act of February 20, 1839, 5 Stat. 321.

from the bar. May exclaimed, "Dismissed! say rather loosed from the things I loathe!" and stalked out of the courtroom.

But in his attack on the Court, May was not just carrying out a vendetta. The weaknesses that concerned him were real. The court system was antiquated, its procedures were cumbersome, and it was expensive. By 1850, when May launched his reform effort in Congress, Thruston was gone (replaced by James Dunlop in 1845), but Morsell was in his thirty-sixth year on the bench and Cranch, in his fiftieth, was so disabled by age and deafness that he was unable to perform his duties. (It was undoubtedly because of Cranch's condition that Congress, on May 27, 1852, empowered any judge of the Circuit Court to hold the District Court.)

Although Jacksonian democracy had swept the country in the previous decades, Cranch and Morsell, shaped in the heyday of Federalism and moderate Republicanism, hung onto the old ways. It must have been particularly galling for lawyers to find judges virtually nullifying the right to jury trial by directing verdicts. While this was commonplace in the District, it attracted considerable attention in the litigation over the estate of the very wealthy John P. Van Ness, which was contested by a Mrs. Connor, who plausibly claimed to be Van Ness's widow and sued for her share of the estate. The jury split 7–5 for the claimant, but the Court directed a verdict for the other side. The Supreme Court refused to hear an appeal, holding that the judgment below was not final, but Mrs. Connor's claim ended there. Counsel, outraged at what they termed usurpation of the jury system, inserted an indignant advertisement into the *National Intelligencer*.

In 1850 Congress considered a proposal which would have retained the Criminal Court but abolished the Circuit Court, replacing it with three courts: common pleas, chancery and probate, and appeal. Instead of taking that course, however, Congress established a commission to revise, simplify, digest, and codify the laws of the District. The commission's proposed revision of the laws was submitted to a popular vote in 1857 and defeated, 3,872–1,646. Reform of the court system would not take place until the middle of the Civil War, and even then, matters of judicial administration would not be the primary motive.

~

The city of Washington, which had 3,000 residents in 1800, was home to 61,000 in 1860. The population of the entire District, including Georgetown and the unincorporated rural areas, had grown more than five-fold to 75,000, even though its Virginia shore had been shed. Federal employment had grown from 137 to over 2,000. Yet the capital remained incomplete and provincial. The Washington Monument was frozen at 154 feet. The Capitol dome was not yet complete. Slops were still dumped in alleys, and the main thoroughfares were clogged with mud and dust. Anthony Trollope, visiting at the beginning of the Civil War, wrote in his travelogue *North America* that parts of the city were "wild, trackless, unbridged, uninhabited, and desolate."

But the city had begun to fill up with churches, schools, and charitable institutions. A great aqueduct brought water into the city, its avenues were lighted by gas, cultivated gardens flourished. New roads, bridges, and canals had ended the District's isolation. But a great tempest was about to sweep the nation. It would transform the nation's capital, and the courts of the District of Columbia would be swept into its vortex.

Chapter 2

War and Transformation
The Republican Court, 1861–92

The election of Abraham Lincoln in 1860 marked the beginning of the preeminence of the Republican Party in national politics and in the life of the District of Columbia—a period that would transform the capital and its courts. It was a Republican Congress that abolished the Circuit Court in 1863, an episode perhaps unique in American history: the abolition of a court by Congress for partisan political reasons. The old court was replaced by the Supreme Court of the District of Columbia. Its first judges (called justices) were Lincoln appointees, Republicans from the North and the border states, men he could count on. Of the remaining ten men who served as judges until the structure of the District's judicial system was again reformed in 1893, seven were appointed by Republican presidents.

It was also a Republican Congress that abolished slavery in the District and a Republican Congress that united the District under a territorial government in 1871. Although the territorial system was short-lived, it endured long enough to fundamentally transform the face of the city. By the end of the quarter-century following the Civil War, a beautiful city had arisen, attracting not only office-seekers but men and women of science, culture, and wealth; a city which could no longer be fairly called provincial.

Washington was at the center of America's bitterest war. The city was a symbol of immense value to both sides—its capture a major object of the Confederacy, its defense a major concern of the federal government. As the hub of the Union's war effort—the place decisions were made, contracts granted, money appropriated—wartime Washington was a magnet for profiteers and spies, favor seekers and influence peddlers. Troops arrived daily at wharves and railroad stations; for a time, even the East Ballroom of the White House quartered soldiers. The wounded were everywhere—in hotels and warehouses, schools and seminaries, churches and private houses. Even the City Hall, where the courts met, served as a hospital.

The city was utterly transformed by the Civil War. Prior to 1860, Washington had been growing by about 500 persons a year, but in four years of war the population nearly doubled; at its height it reached about 140,000. The war also brought massive inflation (131 percent between 1861 and 1866), along with horrifying slums and a huge increase in crime. Nevertheless, much good did come to the District from the war. Slavery was abolished. Municipal services were modernized and expanded: by the end of the war, Washington possessed a salaried fire chief and firefighters, a 150-person police force, a completed aqueduct and new water supply system, and the city's first municipal garbage carts. Perhaps most important, it was during the Civil War that Washington, for the first time, engaged the hearts of the American people as a symbol of the Union.

Throughout its thirty-year life (1863–93), the Supreme Court of the District of Columbia, vested like its predecessor with the jurisdiction of both a state and a federal court, performed a central role in the development of the city. In addition, in its unique national jurisdiction owing to its location at the seat of government, the D.C. Supreme Court was often asked to deal with cases with important separation-of-powers ramifications, to issue writs of mandamus to officials of the executive branch, and to try prosecutions for political corruption involving both local and national figures. It also continued to hear significant race-relations cases and began to develop an important jurisprudence dealing with the insanity defense.

Creation of the D.C. Supreme Court

The attempt in 1850 to reform the court system of the District of Columbia had failed, partially because reform in judicial administration usually occurs very slowly and long after the need, but mainly because the problem was more with the elderly judges than with the court system itself. The changes in the Circuit Court bench upon the death of William Cranch in 1855 certainly helped. James Dunlop, comparatively young at sixty-three, was elevated to the Chief Judgeship and thirty-seven-year-old William Merrick was appointed to fill Dunlop's chair. However, by the beginning of the war Dunlop was slowing down and the third judge, James Morsell, who had been on the Court forty-six years, was eighty-six. The Criminal Court judge, Thomas H. Crawford, was seventy-five. After March 1862,

Crawford's health did not permit him to sit much and he died on January 27, 1863.

There were also, however, systemic deficiencies in the administration of justice in the District of Columbia. Procedures were antiquated, the jail was old and horribly overcrowded, and a reform school was needed. But nothing in the Court's structure required drastic overhaul, nor was the bar calling for such change. The passions of war were responsible. The Circuit Court and the Criminal Court were abolished primarily to get rid of a single judicial "pest"—William Matthew Merrick.

Merrick was the pivotal figure in the Court's handling of petitions for habeas corpus seeking the discharge of soldiers who had enlisted while minors without parental consent. Merrick's decisions often went against the interests of the army and the Lincoln administration, incurring their ire and that of Republicans in the Congress. His actions on the bench raised clear, if unfair, doubts about his loyalty to the Union, suspicions which may have been fueled by his background. He was a Marylander and a Democrat, appointed to the Circuit Court by Franklin Pierce.

The most controversial of Merrick's decisions involved Jeremiah Lyons, a young Pennsylvania soldier whose discharge by way of habeas corpus was sought by his father after he had been unable to persuade the Secretary of War. Merrick ordered the discharge. Although military counsel, the U.S. District Attorney, and Brigadier General Lawrence P. Graham argued that under military orders, a soldier could not be discharged on the ground of minority, Merrick read the order to mean that the army would not *on its own* discharge a soldier for that reason, but that it would leave the matter to the civil power. "At all times, and particularly in times of war," Merrick added, "the civil order should be preserved and made superior to the military."

Merrick issued the writ again in a similar case, a little more than two weeks later, on October 19, 1861, this time to General Andrew Porter, the army's Provost Marshal for the cities of Washington and Georgetown. On the following day, the first day of the new term of the Circuit Court, Secretary of State William Seward—next to Lincoln the most powerful man in the administration—ordered Porter to establish a strict military guard over Merrick's residence, but not to confine him, stating that "it may be sufficient to make him understand that at a juncture like this when the public enemy is as it were at the gates of the capital the public safety is deemed to require that his correspondence and proceedings should be observed." On instructions from the President, Seward also directed the First Comptroller of the Treasury to withhold Merrick's salary until further notice.

Outraged at finding an armed sentinel at his door, Merrick refused to attend court. The remaining judges, Dunlop and Morsell, ordered Porter to show cause why he should not be held in contempt for obstructing the habeas corpus process. Porter did not appear in court; rather, the U.S. District Attorney submitted an affidavit explaining that the President had ordered him not to serve the order and had suspended the writ of habeas corpus with regard to soldiers in the District of Columbia.

Four days later, on October 30, 1861, Chief Judge Dunlop, calling this a case "without a parallel in the judicial history of the United States," announced the Court's decision.[1] The opinion emphasized both the practical and the constitutional limits on the Court's powers. The President, having prevented the deputy from executing the process of the Court, had assumed responsibility for the general's acts. But as the Court had no physical power to enforce its process against the President, the case was closed. In a separate opinion, Morsell protested against "the right claimed to interrupt the proceedings in this case." Echoing Merrick's earlier sentiment, he said that the supremacy of the civil authority over the military cannot be denied" and that the Court "ought to be respected by everyone as the guardian of the personal liberty of the citizen." The sentinel was withdrawn from Merrick's house two and a half weeks later; Merrick rejoined his brethren and received his salary on time.

But the incident was not forgotten. Just over six months later, a bill was introduced in the Senate to abolish the courts of the District of Columbia and create a new system. Drafted by Senator Ira Harris, a former New York state judge, the bill proposed a court system modeled on that of New York State.[2] There is little doubt that the bill's supporters were concerned not about the efficiency of the courts of the District of Columbia but about the loyalty of its judges. In the floor debate, Harris argued that Congress had the power under the Constitution to abolish any federal court except the U.S. Supreme Court, but did not directly come to grips with the question of whether Congress had the power under the Constitution to terminate the life tenure of judges by abolishing courts. The bill squeaked through the Senate by a vote of 19–16, and was easily approved by the House of Representatives. Lincoln immediately signed it into law.

---

1. *United States ex rel. Murphy v. Porter*, 2 Hay & Haz. 394, (1861).
2. The U.S. Supreme Court later held that because the Act of March 3, 1863, was substantially the same as the New York statute, it was to receive the same construction. *Metropolitan R.R. Co. v. More*, 121 U.S. 558 (1887).

By the Act of March 3, 1863, a single court replaced the circuit, district, and criminal courts of the District of Columbia.[3] The new court, the Supreme Court of the District of Columbia, possessed the same powers and exercised the same jurisdiction as the Circuit Court, both local and federal. The three judges of the old Circuit Court were replaced with four justices. The new Supreme Court had general jurisdiction in law and equity. Each judge could hold a district court in the same manner and with the same powers and jurisdiction as district courts possessed everywhere in the United States. Each of the judges could hold criminal court, with the same jurisdiction as the old Criminal Court. Whereas a quorum of two judges of the Circuit Court had previously been required, each of the justices of the new court was empowered to try cases by himself at "special term." The decisions of each of the judges individually in "special term" were reviewable by the full court in "general term."

Congress sought to assure the loyalty not only of the judges but also of the bar and of the District's constables. Under the Act, every judicial officer of the United States government was required to take the so-called iron-clad loyalty oath. When 117 out of 142 constables refused to take the oath, their commissions were revoked by the Court. Two prominent lawyers, James Mandeville Carlisle and William J. Stone, chose not to practice before the Court rather than take the oath. Even after the U.S. Supreme Court held the oath unconstitutional, the District Supreme Court continued to administer it.

It was certain that Lincoln would not appoint Merrick to the new court. It was also considered probable that Morsell, because of his age, would not be appointed. But it had been expected that the able Dunlop, who had been among the first judges in the country to sustain the naval blockade of the South imposed by Lincoln, might receive an appointment. He did not. For the new four-judge tribunal, Lincoln instead chose two sitting Republican members of Congress and one former Republican congressman, along with a local attorney who, it was said, was the only man in Alexandria to have voted for Lincoln in 1860. Ward Lamon, Lincoln's former law partner and close confidant, remained Marshal of the District of Columbia, while another close friend of the President, Return J. Meigs, was named Clerk. (Meigs was also commissioned to revise and codify the laws of the District, another effort at codification that failed.)

Morsell retired to a farm in Maryland, where he lived to be ninety-five. Dunlop remained vigorous until he died suddenly in his eightieth year.

---

3. 12 Stat. 762.

Merrick returned to Maryland to practice law and engaged in politics. As a Democratic member of the U.S. House of Representatives (1871–73), he voted to preserve the right of appeal from the D.C. Supreme Court to the U.S. Supreme Court in all cases where it then prevailed, stating that the people of the District "have suffered enough by injurious legislation. Let them at least have the guardianship of that great tribunal which administers the Constitution and laws of these United States for the protection of all the people of the country."[4] After the Democrats finally returned to the White House, with the election of Grover Cleveland in 1884, Merrick received a remarkable vindication. In 1885 he was appointed to the Supreme Court of the District Columbia, where he served a little more than three years, until his death in early 1889.

The most serious problem with the 1863 statute was the generous jurisdiction given the United States Supreme Court to review the D.C. Supreme Court. Review was available by writ of error or appeal where the jurisdictional amount was only $1,000, and minor cases from the District of Columbia added to the burdens of the High Court during Reconstruction. Finally, in 1879, the jurisdictional amount for taking appeals to the U.S. Supreme Court was raised to $2,500, which considerably reduced the flow of cases to its doors.[5]

Nonjudicial duties continued to be vested by Congress in the major courts of the District. In 1865, for example, in order to deny the Democratic mayor and Board of Aldermen the power over voting lists, Congress authorized the D.C. Supreme Court to appoint a commission to prepare a list of voters. The resulting commission was made up entirely of Republicans.

In the fifteen years following the 1863 legislation, some minor revisions were made in the court structure of the District of Columbia. In 1867 the D.C. Supreme Court was given concurrent jurisdiction with the justices of the peace of petty civil suits (most claims between $50 and $100) and authority to review decisions of the justices of the peace in smaller claims. The Orphan's Court, which had survived the 1863 changes, was abolished in 1870 and probate jurisdiction given to the D.C. Supreme Court. Also in 1870, a Police Court was created to relieve the D.C. Supreme Court of such minor criminal offenses as simple assault and batteries.[6]

---

4. Congress was considering raising the jurisdictional amount from $2,000 to $5,000. Merrick argued that the lower threshold should be maintained.

5. Act of February 25, 1879, 20 Stat. 320.

6. Act of June 17, 1870, 16 Stat. 153.

Wartime Cases

Sitting in the nation's capital, the courts of the District of Columbia were called upon to decide cases on a variety of matters arising from the Civil War. There was plenty of criminal business, as the war brought an efflorescence of brothels, boisterous soldiers, pickpockets, and bullies. More important were the habeas corpus cases already discussed and the cases involving captured navy vessels, confiscations of enemy property and fugitive slaves.

Soon after the beginning of hostilities, President Lincoln, on his own authority, imposed a naval blockade against the Confederacy. Almost immediately the constitutionality of the order was challenged. On May 21, 1861, the British schooner *Tropic Wind*, sailing from Richmond, was seized in or near the mouth of the James River by the U.S. ship *Monticello*. A libel was for condemnation of the ship and its cargo, valued at $22,000. James Carlisle, attorney for the master of the *Tropic Wind*, went to court, where he disputed the President's power to proclaim the blockade and attacked the administration's position that the United States could blockade the South without recognizing the Confederacy as a belligerent. So long as the South was considered part of the Union, the lawyer argued, United States treaty commitments forbade it to inhibit the commerce of neutral powers in southern ports.

The case was heard by Chief Judge Dunlop, sitting in admiralty as a district judge. He upheld the blockade as a valid exercise of the President's power as Commander-in-Chief.[7] War declared by Congress was not, Dunlop held, the "only war within the contemplation of the Constitution." Furthermore, Dunlop found, the status of the insurrection was a *political* question to be determined by the executive branch: "Whether insurrection has...become so formidable in power as to have culminated into a civil war, it seems to me must also belong, as to its decision, to the same political branch of government." Although the U.S. District Attorney ultimately dismissed the case and returned the vessel to its owner, Dunlop's approach was upheld two years later by a closely divided Supreme Court. That Court was unanimous on the point that the blockade was constitutional once it had been ratified by Congress.[8]

---

7. *United States v. The British Schooner Tropic Wind,* 2 Hay & Haz. 374 (1861).

8. Prize Cases, 67 U.S. (2 Black) 635 (1863). While the D.C. prize court lacked the importance of those in New York and Philadelphia, the Potomac flotilla continued to make captures which were adjudicated as prizes. Prize law was the wartime face of an age in which governmental functions were subcontracted out to enfranchised small-scale entrepreneurs. When a vessel of a belligerent power was forcibly captured at sea, it was brought to a prize court to be condemned under the laws of war. Prize adjudica-

During the war Congress provided by statute for the confiscation of property of individuals adhering to the enemy—both those who went south and did not return and those in the North who gave aid and comfort to the enemy.[9] Confiscation might be for life or absolute. Proceedings were to be instituted in federal courts by a libel or information filed by the U.S. District Attorney. If the owner appeared in court, there would ordinarily be a hearing.

On the whole, the confiscations were not successful, as local district attorneys hesitated to begin them and judicial procedures were slow. From May 1863 to September 1865, there were fifty-two cases docketed in the D.C. Supreme Court and twenty-seven forfeitures of real and personal property worth a total of $33,265. However, from those proceeds came the fees of the U.S. District Attorney, the Marshal, and the Clerk, which could amount to over twenty percent. Chided by the House of Representatives for the slow pace of confiscation in the District, Attorney General Edward Bates replied, "The law is highly penal, and therefore, in the judicial proceedings, the courts will take care that the forms prescribed are minutely observed, and that the acts which constitute the guilt and consequent forfeiture are properly alleged and strictly proven."

No business presented to the courts of the District of Columbia during the Civil War was more delicate than that involving the treatment of fugitive slaves. Policy decisions were made by the Lincoln administration, at least for the first two years of the war, but the application of that policy was the responsibility of the D.C. courts and of the Marshal—Lincoln's friend Ward Lamon—and it was potentially explosive.

The Lincoln administration's "border-state strategy" required continued enforcement of the Fugitive Slave Law of 1850 in Washington, where a large number of fugitive slaves (mostly from Maryland) had fled—even after slavery in the District was abolished in April 1862. Indeed, in an opinion by Chief Judge Dunlop on May 30, 1862, the Circuit Court held in no uncertain terms that fugitive slaves in the District were to be treated like any other fugitives from justice.[10]

---

tion was central to the waging of the Civil War because it was essential in carrying out the naval blockade of the Confederacy, for the Union did not have enough of its own ships. The prize court was responsible for adjudicating ships as prizes. Under its authority, the ship and its cargo were auctioned and part of the proceeds remitted to the owner, captain, and crew of the vessel that was the captor.

9. Act of August 6, 1861, 12 Stat. 319; Act of July 17, 1862, 12 Stat. 989.

10. *United States ex rel. Copeland,* 2 Hay. & Haz. 402 (1862).

One year later, the newly created D.C. Supreme Court considered the application of the Fugitive Slave Law in the District in the case of an escaped slave named Andrew Hall. He had been arrested by the Marshal on a warrant issued by Justice Andrew Wylie at the instance of a Maryland slaveholder, George W. Duval. The Court, made up of four Lincoln appointees, divided 2–2. Each justice delivered an opinion discussing the Court's jurisdiction as a "federal court" under the Fugitive Slave Law. Chief Justice David Cartter held that the new court was "essentially...a Circuit Court of the United States, subject to all the legislation affecting such courts," with the power to execute that law. Justice George P. Fisher agreed, holding that the constitutionality of the Fugitive Slave Law had been settled by the U.S. Supreme Court, that it was applicable to the District of Columbia, and the D.C. Supreme Court had power to execute it.

In a tortuous opinion, Justice Wylie took the position that the courts of the District had been omitted from the coverage of the Fugitive Slave Law. Justice Abram Olin, agreeing with Wylie, held that since the abolition of the Circuit Court, no court in the District had the power to execute the law.[11] At that announcement, Hall's owner grabbed his slave and tried to make off with him. A donnybrook ensued in the courtroom and police had to separate the brawling parties. Hall was taken to the station house, where he was "rescued" by the military; he subsequently won his freedom by enlisting in the Union army.

After this fiasco, the District Supreme Court, exercising a power granted it by the Fugitive Slave Law, appointed a Circuit Court commissioner, Walter S. Cox (who would later become one of the most distinguished judges of the Court), to administer the Fugitive Slave Law. But the public mood began to change and enforcement in the District became increasingly difficult. For the next few years, an escaped slave or a kidnapped freeman might more realistically hope for the intervention of Union soldiers or mobs rather than expect to be set free by the Court or the Marshal. In July 1864, Congress finally repealed the Fugitive Slave Law.

Postwar Race Relations in Washington

The fate of African-Americans in the District of Columbia for almost a century was determined by events which took place in the first thirteen years after the Civil War. The racial atmosphere for African-Americans in Wash-

---

11. *In re Hall*, 6 D.C. (1 Mackey) 10 (1863).

ington had improved during the war. The District's slaves were emancipated, the repressive "black codes" passed in the early years of the century were repealed, and Congress required the local governments in the District of Columbia to open schools for black children.[12] In 1865, the year the war ended, African-Americans marched in Lincoln's second inaugural parade and a black minister preached in the chamber of the House of Representatives.

But equality had not been achieved. Prejudice and fears among whites remained and grew. A committee of the Washington City Council opposed giving the vote to blacks, stating, "The white man, being the superior race, must...rule the black." When the issue was put to referendum in 1865, Washington's all-white electorate rejected black suffrage by a vote of 6,591 to 32 and Georgetown's by 465 to 0.

Nevertheless, in the first years after the war, as a result of efforts in Congress and the newly created local government, more progress was made than in the previous sixty years and possibly more than would be made in the next eighty. In December 1866, over President Andrew Johnson's veto, Congress guaranteed the vote to blacks, without a literacy qualification. In 1869, a law making black men eligible for jury duty was passed. In the same year, Washington's City Council, which had seven black members, banned discrimination in places of public entertainment and the following year extended the ban to restaurants, buses, and hotels.

However, the wave crested in 1870, and soon ebbed. The new city civil-rights ordinance was challenged in a test case;[13] after being upheld at trial and again on appeal, it was simply ignored. In 1872, another ordinance aimed at ending discrimination in public places was passed by the territorial legislature and was therefore applicable to the entire District. A supplementary law was passed in 1873. Several cases brought to enforce them were won at trial but reversed on technical grounds. Although they would prove a dead letter for almost eighty years, these ordinances would again be employed in the 1950s in litigation which ended segregation in public accommodations.

---

12. The Act of May 21, 1862, 12 Stat. 407, provided for black schooling. Under the Act of April 16, 1862, 12 Stat. 376, freeing the District's slaves, slaveowners were compensated for their material loss. Of one thousand claims for compensation for 3,128 freed slaves, all but forty-four were granted. The average compensation was $300. The commission that awarded compensation met in the courtroom in the City Hall and employed a slave dealer from Baltimore for his expertise.

13. *Mayor etc. v. Honey & Holden*, Supreme Court of District of Columbia, Criminal Court, May 31, 1871 (Box 30, Nos. 8946–9140, National Archives).

Violations of civil rights laws in the District occurred with mounting frequency, and usually with impunity. However, in 1883, in a case which attracted national attention, an African-American visitor from Connecticut brought suit under the criminal provision of the federal civil rights law of 1875 after a restaurant had refused to seat him in a dining room with whites but offered to serve him in the pantry. The offending restaurant was fined $500; but it was a pyrrhic victory, as the case merely served to strengthen white animosities in the District. Two months later, the U.S. Supreme Court held the same law unconstitutional when enforced in the states, although it remained enforceable in the District of Columbia and its rural environs.[14]

During the next two decades, blacks filed over a dozen civil rights suits in the District of Columbia. A few were won—some with pointed one-penny damage awards—others simply dismissed. The local civil-rights ordinances enacted during Reconstruction were never repealed nor declared unconstitutional. But they disappeared so completely from view that, when a new code of laws for the District was drawn up in 1929, there was no mention of them whatever. Long before that, a high, unscalable wall of caste had risen to block the path of the District's blacks to political influence, economic progress, and social equality.

The Growth of the City

Between 1865 and 1878, the District of Columbia underwent several dramatic changes in the structure of its governance and experienced extraordinary physical growth. At the end of the war, the District encompassed two cities, Georgetown and Washington, each of which had elected mayors and city councils with circumscribed powers to tax and spend. The part of the District not coming within the two cities, the County of Washington, was still governed by a levy court.

In January 1871, Congress significantly altered the governance of the District. The two cities and the county were placed under a single territorial government. The Territory of the District of Columbia had a governor appointed by the President and a two-house legislature. The District was also allowed an elected, non-voting delegate to the Congress. The federal government was responsible for the salaries of the appointed officials, but was not required to pay for city improvements.

---

14. *Robinson v. Memphis & Charleston R.R. Co.*, 109 U.S. 3 (1883).

The territorial government lasted only three years. In 1874 Congress, without debate, replaced it with a commission, and in 1878 eliminated all vestiges of home rule and made the commission form of government permanent. The commission consisted of two civilians appointed by the President, one to be a Republican and the other a Democrat, and an officer of the Army Corps of Engineers, who was responsible for public works. The 1878 law pledged the U.S. government to meet half of the city's annual budget, but every entry in the detailed budget required congressional approval.

Nonetheless, in its short, controversial lifespan, the territorial government was responsible for enormous changes in the District. In 1871, it was not even certain that Washington would remain the nation's capital. A campaign was afoot to move the seat of government to St. Louis. Washington, as Horace Greeley wrote in 1867, was "not a nice place to live in. The rents are high, the food is bad, the dust is disgusting, the mud is deep and the morals are deplorable." By 1874, the city no longer was an object of derision.

The man most responsible for this metamorphosis was Alexander Shepherd. Indeed, no one, including even L'Enfant, did more to ensure Washington's ultimate emergence as an attractive, appealing city. Shepherd was at home in an era of strong and not completely scrupulous entrepreneurs in both business and politics. As head of the Board of Public Works under the territorial government (1871–73) and then as Governor of the Territory (1873–74), Shepherd conceived and implemented a grandiose plan to revitalize and expand the city's infrastructure. He found the money, dictated the program, and refused to be deflected from the tasks he undertook. What stood in the way, he overrode. In three years, the city was transformed. For the first time, Washington had clean, well-paved, well-lit streets and unrivaled urban sanitary facilities.

But the price was high. The program cost three times what had been planned and ran up an illegal debt of nineteen million dollars. By 1873 the city was bankrupt. In these conditions, the new government—effective and popular but vulnerable to attack for arrogance, secrecy, corruption, and rigged elections—could not last. A coalition of liberal Republicans, D.C. property owners outraged at the enormous rise in their assessments, and Democrats hoping to restore the District's prewar political structure, brought it down.

The memory of Shepherd's profligacy must have contributed to the refusal of Congress for ninety years to permit even partial home rule, even at the cost of perpetuating government by a commission easily penetrated by local businessmen and conservative members of Congress. An anti-Shepherd backlash can be seen in decisions of the D.C. Supreme Court, such as the 1879 case *Roach v. Van Riswick*.[15] There, the Court, aware of the "instinctive reluctance on the part of bench and bar, to recognize the legislation of the late government of the District as valid, so far as it transcended the limits of strictly municipal action," and of the "lurking doubt which existed from the beginning and has never been dispelled, as to the constitutional power to create such an anomalous entity as the late District government," sharply confined the power of the U.S. Congress to delegate powers of legislation to any local legislature of the District of Columbia.

The New Court

Created as a four-judge tribunal in 1863, the Supreme Court of the District of Columbia was enlarged to six by statutes creating additional judgeships in 1870 and 1878.[16] Of the fourteen justices who served during the period 1863–92, eleven were Republicans appointed by Republican presidents, the other three were Democrats appointed by Grover Cleveland, the one Democratic president during this period. (See fig. 2.1.) The members of the Supreme Court of the District of Columbia were recruited from a national base. Only two of the justices were born in the District and only four were residents at the time of their appointment. The rest came to the Court from Maryland (3), Ohio (2), Delaware, New York, Alabama, Michigan and Wisconsin. None of these judges was a star of the first magnitude, but the first Chief Justice of the D.C. Supreme Court, David Cartter, is worthy of consideration here.

Chief Justice Cartter
David K. Cartter (1812–1887) was a massive man with unruly black hair and large eyes set in a pockmarked face. A perceptible stutter apparently did not limit his effectiveness as a stump speaker. A strong-minded radical from Ohio, he had been a leader of the Salmon P. Chase forces at the 1860 Republican Convention; at the critical moment, he rose to announce the shift of Ohio's votes to Lincoln, starting the tide that produced Lincoln's nomination.

---

15. 11 D.C. (MacArth. & M.) 171 (1879).
16. Act of June 21, 1870, 16 Stat. 160; Act of February 25, 1879, 20 Stat. 320.

Lincoln rewarded Cartter by making him Minister to Bolivia in 1861, then named him to the new court in 1863. Cartter became close to Secretary of State William Seward and Secretary of War Edwin Stanton (and, later, to Ulysses Grant), but he was not universally liked by members of the cabinet; Attorney General Edward Bates described him as a "fierce partisan, an inbred vulgarian and a truculent ignoramus."

David Cartter was a visible Chief Justice who was not wont to confine himself strictly to judicial business. He routinely presided over mass meetings of the citizens of Washington and was not deterred by his office from speaking out. After the fall of Richmond, for example, at the Grand Illumination of the buildings of Washington, Cartter gave a speech calling for the execution of Jefferson Davis and Robert E. Lee. During the terrible night of Lincoln's assassination, Cartter conducted a court of inquiry, interviewing witnesses with the aid of a soldier-stenographer, an island of efficiency in a sea of chaos.[17]

Few judges of the D.C. Circuit could have been as well prepared as Cartter was for patent cases, an important part of the Court's docket in these years. He himself held several patents, including one for a ventilating device for windows, which was used for over a generation in the courthouse. Cartter seems to have been extremely sensitive about the spelling of his name, making the point, often with profanity, that he was not "a common Carter." If his name was misspelled in a pleading—the two t's had to be crossed separately—it is said that he would throw it on the floor.

The Work of the Court

As the population of the District continued to grow, the courts heard more cases and were expected to perform a greater variety of functions. From 1879 to 1893, three justices of the D.C. Supreme Court were generally available for trial term and three sat in General Term. Opinions were still rendered orally. After a thirty-three-year hiatus, bound publication of the reports of the D.C. courts resumed with the 1873 term, through the efforts of Chief Justice Cartter, members of the bar and Justice Arthur MacArthur, who was the editor.

The quarters of the Court were also modified. It is said that when the courts were reorganized in 1863, the new clerk, Return J. Meigs, found not

---

17. Hearing of the attack on Lincoln, Cartter had ordered a hackman to drive him to the Peterson House, where Lincoln had been taken. The terrified man insisted that he was too frightened to drive, whereupon Cartter pushed him into the hack and drove the horse at a gallop to the President's bedside.

a single lock on the doors of the City Hall and that one of his first functions was to obtain a large stone and lay it up against the outside door. At one time, the City Hall housed not only the courts, the municipal government, and prisoners, but also private law offices and boarders. However, the United States purchased the District's share of the building and in 1881 it was remodeled with an appropriation secured by Chief Justice Cartter.

The Court's Federal Jurisdiction

The Supreme Court of the District of Columbia bore only a marginal resemblance to other federal trial and intermediate appellate courts. Though it heard a considerable number of patent cases, its admiralty, copyright, bankruptcy, customs, and immigration cases were fewer and less significant than those in the more important federal jurisdictions. The Court primarily was the high court of a city lacking in commercial viability. Its local jurisdiction was nevertheless varied, encompassing such areas as divorce and personal injury actions and criminal prosecutions.

During this period, the Court's federal jurisdiction brought before it many of the types of cases that would, over the years, illustrate its unique position in the federal court system by virtue of its location at the seat of government. These included prosecutions of presidential assassins, cases involving government corruption, a major test of the limits of Congress's investigatory power, and cases arising from its role in oversight of the executive branch.

Assassination and Insanity

One of the "specialties" of the federal courts of the District of Columbia has been prosecutions for the assassination or attempted assassination of the President of the United States. Several of those have involved the plea of not guilty by reason of insanity. From its beginning, Washington, as the nation's seat of government, has attracted more than its share of the mentally ill—people imagining conspiracies against them, imploring help, or bent on revenge.

The first provision by the City of Washington for the care and maintenance of "lunatics" was made by contract in 1806. Dorothea Lynde Dix drafted the law establishing the Government House for the Insane, which opened in 1855. Its object was to provide "the most humane care and enlightened curative treatment [for those] whose minds are more or less erratic." President Fillmore himself helped select the site, on a plateau overlooking the Anacostia River. The grounds were as beautiful as the panorama, with graded walks, green lawns, and flowering gardens. Because commitment to an institution is often a legal matter, the staff of what became known as St. Elizabeths Hospital became expert at forensic psychiatry. For well over a century, the physicians of St. Elizabeths agitated for reform in the treatment of the mentally ill by the courts.[18]

Some of the country's mentally ill have always been attracted to Washington because the President resides there. The vast majority have been harmless, but of the eleven known attempts on the lives of sitting presidents during the nineteenth and twentieth centuries, seven took place in Washington — the assassinations of Lincoln and Garfield and the attempts on Jackson, Truman, Reagan, and Clinton (two).[19] Most of those who tried — successfully or not — to assassinate a president have been prosecuted in the federal courts of the District of Columbia. Such high-profile state trials gave the courts their first national prominence and established an ongoing aspect of their jurisdiction — although one created by an accident of geography.

The first known attempt to assassinate a president in Washington was Richard Lawrence's attempt on the life of Andrew Jackson on January 30, 1835. An English-born immigrant and unemployed drifter, Lawrence seems to have believed that he was the rightful heir to the thrones of England *and* the United States. He saw Jackson as standing in his way. As the President was leaving the Capitol after attending a funeral, Lawrence fired two pistols. Both misfired. Lawrence was immediately arrested and taken at once to Chief Judge Cranch in chambers.

At Lawrence's trial before Cranch, it took the jury just five minutes to decide that the prisoner was not guilty, "he being under the influence of insanity at the time he committed the act." Since there was then no asylum in Washington and as the Court was of the opinion that it would be dangerous "to permit him to be at large while under this mental delusion," Lawrence was remanded to prison until some other safe and humane provision could be made for him.[20]

---

18. During its first century, nearly one in ten (145 out of 1,480) of the publications of the staff of St. Elizabeths were in the field of forensic psychiatry. However, after the U.S. Court of Appeals for the District of Columbia finally began to address the subject comprehensively, in 1954, St. Elizabeths' physicians were not always happy with the results of the seeds they had sown, as patients were released into society, often with little medical or social-service support.

19. There were also attempts on the life of Theodore Roosevelt after he left the Presidency and on Franklin Roosevelt before he assumed the office, neither of which happened in Washington.

20. *United States v. Lawrence*, 4 D.C. (4 Cranch) 518 (1835).

The D.C. Supreme Court's connection with the trial of those involved in the conspiracy to assassinate Lincoln and other high officials was more peripheral, as they were tried by a military commission. Four of the eight accused conspirators were sentenced to death after a trial wholly lacking in the spirit and substance of due process. The condemned included Mary Surratt, who owned the boarding house where several of the conspirators, including her son, John, had met. In the middle of the night before the scheduled execution, her counsel roused Justice Andrew Wylie and secured a writ of habeas corpus.

The next morning, General Winfield Scott Hancock, military governor of the District of Columbia, appeared in court with Attorney General James Speed and informed the judge that President Johnson had suspended the writ of habeas corpus in the District — "especially this particular writ" — and had directed the immediate execution of the sentences. Like Dunlop and Morsell in 1861, Wylie had no alternative but to yield, but, like his predecessors, he protested vigorously the military's "determination to treat the authority of this court with contempt."

John Surratt was apprehended almost a year and a half after the assassination, after the popular mood had calmed, and was tried by a civilian court. Although D.C. Supreme Court Justice George P. Fisher's charge to the jurors all but directed them to reach a guilty verdict, there was a hung jury. Surratt was not tried again.

The Trial of Charles Guiteau

President James A. Garfield was shot by Charles Guiteau on July 2, 1881, at the B & O Railway Terminal at Sixth and B streets on his way to a much-needed vacation. He clung to life until September 19. The trial of his assassin — the most celebrated insanity case of the nineteenth century — began on November 14.

The trial judge, Walter S. Cox, was an able jurist, prudent and honorable, neither petty tyrant nor bitter partisan. Washington-born, Cox had made his career in the District. Before his appointment to the D.C. Supreme Court in 1879, Cox had served the D.C. Supreme Court as commissioner in fugitive slave cases and as Auditor. By coincidence, Cox had been counsel to two of the conspirators in the Lincoln assassination trial, Michael O'Laughlin and Samuel Arnold, both of whom were sentenced to life imprisonment.

Of all the trials involving those who have made attempts on the life of the President, that of Guiteau came the closest to being a circus, both in the courtroom and in the journalistic sensationalism that surrounded it. Guiteau was a pathetic figure — slight and sallow, shabby, friendless, rejected by most of his family even before the assassination. A man with peculiar religious convictions, Guiteau claimed that his act was divinely inspired. At one point, the prosecution asked Guiteau on the witness stand, "Did it occur to you that there was a commandment, 'Thou shalt not kill?'" Guiteau responded, "If it did, the divine authority overcame the written law."

Cox gave Guiteau a scrupulously fair trial—perhaps too fair. The defendant insisted on serving as his own co-counsel, thereby undermining his own defense and the dignity of the Court. He constantly interrupted the proceedings with bizarre outbursts, often insolent or arrogant. Cox chose to tolerate the interruptions rather than have Guiteau gagged or removed from the courtroom, in part to permit the jury to observe his mental condition. Although feeble defenses were attempted as to jurisdiction and causation, the only real issue in the ten-week trial was his sanity, on which subject Cox chose to allow a wide range of testimony.

All the problems that still plague the insanity defense surfaced at the Guiteau trial: conflicting expert witnesses (the prosecution put on twenty-three, the defense, thirteen); the gap between medical and legal standards; the conflict between those who believe in unfettered free will and those who believe human behavior is conditioned by heredity, environment, and life experience. As with John Hinckley exactly a century later, the defendant had a history of delusions and there was patent evidence of severe maladjustment, but there was also convincing evidence that the details of the crime had been thought through and carried out rationally.

If the trial was undignified because of Guiteau's antics, it was nevertheless fair, and Cox took care not to commit reversible error. His instruction to the jury rested on the *M'Naghten* rules, the test governing the defense of not guilty by reason of insanity then employed in Great Britain and in almost every American jurisdiction. The rules required the jury to determine whether "the party accused was labouring under such a defect of reason, from disease of the mind, as not to know the nature and quality of the act he was doing; or as not to know that what he was doing was wrong."[21] *M'Naghten*, then as now, was vulnerable to the fact that many crimes committed by the mentally ill are the work of persons who can distinguish right from wrong but are unable to restrain themselves.

The jury took less than half an hour to bring in a verdict of guilty. Cox sentenced Guiteau to death, stating, "One cannot doubt... that you understood the nature and consequences of your crime or that you had the moral

---

21. *M'Naghten's Case,* 10 Cl. & F. 200 (1843).

capacity to recognize its iniquity." The D.C. Supreme Court affirmed in an opinion by Justice Charles P. James.[22] Justice Joseph P. Bradley of the U.S. Supreme Court denied a petition for habeas corpus. President Chester A. Arthur, Garfield's successor, refused to stay the execution to appoint a commission of experts to inquire into Guiteau's mental state. On June 30, 1882, five months after the trial ended and less than a year after he had shot Garfield, Guiteau mounted the scaffold. Before his execution he sang a hymn he had written; it began, "I am going to the Lordy, I am so glad."

The Guiteau trial was in many ways a pathetic and shabby affair. Yet it was also an important state trial which contributed to the restoration of stability after the assassination, and a landmark in the history of the insanity defense in the United States, confirming the primacy of the *M'Naghten* right-wrong test not only in the District of Columbia but in virtually every American jurisdiction. Over seventy years would pass before there would be as lively a debate over the appropriate standard for criminal responsibility. That, too, would be prompted by the courts of the District of Columbia, with the 1954 decision in *Durham v. United States* (see chapter six).

The Star Route Scandal

As the courts of the national capital, the D.C. Circuit courts have often been the forum for prosecution of important cases of political corruption. Among the most important prosecutions for governmental corruption in the nineteenth century were those involving the Star Route frauds. At issue were contracts for private delivery of the mails to sparsely populated regions of the United States—army posts, homesteads, mining camps. The pledge to carry the mail with "certainty, celerity, and security" was symbolized on the department registers by three stars; hence the routes came to be known as "star routes."

In the years following the Civil War, the nation was expanding so rapidly that Congress gave the Post Office Department—the largest government office, containing one-half of the federal bureaucracy—discretion to add more trips on these routes and adjust compensation. Predictably, this led to abuse.

---

22. *United States v. Guiteau*, 10 F. 161 (1882), aff'd, 12 D.C. (1 Mackey) 498 (*Jam-Hag*(c)-MacA) (1882).

Note: When reported, the judges' votes in a decision are given parenthetically at the end of the case citation, as above, if they are not specified in the text. The majority and minority are separated by a slash (solidus) and the (abbreviated) names of those issuing written opinions are italicized. See Appendix B for a key to abbreviations.

Favored contractors offered impossibly low bids, then, after the contracts were awarded, "improved" their service, raised their fees, and received fat profits. Oversight of the 75 million miles ridden annually would not have been easy even for honest, capable public officials; but the Post Office was slow to act even after it became apparent that the expenditures for the routes far exceeded congressional appropriations. The network of corruption involved Department officials, contractors, and politicians, including members of Congress.

Irregularities in the Star Route service were first disclosed in the Washington *Patriot* in 1872. There were congressional investigations in 1874 and 1876, but not until 1878 were any prominent people implicated. Although the frauds were costing the government an estimated six million dollars annually, they were not a major issue in the 1880 campaign because officials of both parties were tainted. President Garfield appointed a reformer as Postmaster General and directed him and the Attorney General "not only to probe this ulcer to the bottom, but to cut it out." When he became President, Chester A. Arthur chose Benjamin H. Brewster, who was already acting as special counsel for the government in the Star Route case, as Attorney General.

On March 4, 1882, Stephen Dorsey, who had been secretary of the Republican National Committee, former Assistant Postmaster General Thomas Brady, and six others were indicted for conspiracy to defraud the government. Two lengthy trials before Justice Andrew Wylie proved frustrating for the government and ultimately futile. Although Brewster personally handled parts of the first trial, the government was out-lawyered and hurt by defense delays, by a barrage of hostile newspaper publicity, and possibly by jury tampering. In a trial lasting a little over three months, there were 115 witnesses and 3,600 exhibits. Two defendants were acquitted and two were convicted; the jury hung as to the rest. Wylie, who appeared sympathetic to the prosecution, set aside the verdicts because of the irregular conduct of certain members of the jury and what he termed its "general unreasonableness."

The second trial, which began in September 1882 and lasted nine months, was anticlimactic. Public interest had waned and Brewster did not appear. Despite Wylie's severe charge to the jury, all the defendants were acquitted. Civil suits brought in the District of Columbia to recoup some of the illegal payments were also unsuccessful, as were prosecutions for jury tampering arising from the first trial. By then, cynics were murmuring (as they would a century later during the Iran-Contra affair) that the cases were simply providing a substantial income for the special counsel.

The trials illustrated the risks of overwhelming a jury with unimportant evidence and the damage that could be done to a strong case by lawyer delays and a hostile press. In its issue of June 21, 1883, *The Nation* editorialized, "No American jury is equal to a case tried under such conditions: overloaded, overwhelmed, distracted and lost in the mere mass of so-called evidence." Yet, despite their failure in the courtroom, the Star Route cases led to much-needed housecleaning in the postal service and a reform of the mail-delivery system, and also contributed to the movement for civil service reform. For the courts of the D.C. Circuit, the cases also constituted an early instance of what would become an important part of their jurisdiction: supervisory control over executive departments.

Separation of Powers: Kilbourn v. Thompson

Prior to 1857, contempt of Congress was punished directly, by the houses of Congress themselves, although, as demonstrated in the 1832 Sam Houston case, such punishment was not a bar to prosecution for a related criminal offense. In 1857, however, Congress provided by law that if witnesses failed to appear when summoned to testify, refused to answer pertinent questions, or declined to turn over requested information, they could be prosecuted in the federal courts for criminal contempt. *Kilbourn v. Thompson*, the most important separation of powers case of the era, tested the limits of congressional power in a prosecution brought under the statute. It proved seminal in defining Congress's investigatory powers.

Kilbourn arose in the politically charged atmosphere of the 1876 election year and was related to the failed experiment in territorial government of the District of Columbia and the ethics of some of Alexander Shepherd's friends and business associates. Hallett Kilbourn was one of those friends who had made fortunes from Shepherd's urban development program. In the course of an investigation into the failure of a bank controlled by former Territorial Governor Henry Cooke, the Congress sought information from participants in a Washington real estate pool which included Cooke, Kilbourn, and others. When Kilbourn refused to produce certain papers and to answer questions put to him by the House committee — instead accusing it of employing "naked arbitrary power... to investigate private business, in which nobody but me and my customers have concern" — the House cited him for contempt and committed him to the District jail.

At the request of the Speaker of the House, a District grand jury indicted Kilbourn under the 1857 statute. However, when the Marshal sought to take custody of Kilbourn, the House refused to turn him over. Kilbourn petitioned for habeas corpus. Chief Justice Cartter ordered Kilbourn's release, holding that in passing the 1857 law, Congress had deprived itself of its power to punish contempt. Prosecution under the statute was the exclusive means by which an uncooperative witness could be brought to testify.

Kilbourn then sued members of the committee, the Speaker of the House, and the Sergeant-at-Arms, John G. Thompson — who had originally arrested Kilbourn on the Speaker's warrant — for false imprisonment. At trial, the defendants claimed that they were immune from suit under the Speech and Debate Clause of the U.S. Constitution. The Supreme Court of the District of Columbia agreed with all the defendants. The Supreme Court of the United States agreed that the members of Congress were immune from suit, but reversed as to Thompson.

The High Court held that the investigatory and contempt powers of Congress were limited by the Constitution and could be reached by judicial review. Congress did not possess, Justice Samuel F. Miller wrote, "the general power of making inquiry into the private affairs of the citizen." Congress was limited to inquiries relating to matters over which it had jurisdiction. As it had not been contemplating legislation when it investigated the real estate pool, what it had done was outside its power.[23] *Kilbourn v. Thompson* would prove to be the leading case interpreting the power of Congress to investigate until the Teapot Dome cases of the 1920s, when it was sharply qualified.

Although the U.S. Supreme Court took a narrow view of congressional power, it took a broad view of the immunity of members of Congress from suit. That immunity, as the Court would reiterate a century later in *Hutchinson v. Proxmire*, was not narrowly confined to speeches and activities, but protected other legislative business as well.[24] However, if the members of the House and the Speaker were immune from suit, the *Kilbourn* decision found that the underlying conduct of the House was nevertheless properly reviewed by a suit against a House employee. This principle is still good law and was pivotal to the 1969 U.S. Supreme Court decision in *Powell v. McCormack,* which also arose in the D.C. Circuit (see chapter eight). *Kilbourn* and *Watkins v. United States,* a 1957 Supreme Court decision in a case also coming from the D.C. Circuit (see chapter six), remain the most

---

23. *Kilbourn v. Thompson,* 103 U.S. 377 (1880). Thompson was left personally liable for Kilbourn's false imprisonment. Three times juries rendered generous verdicts against Thompson; two of these were set aside by Justice Walter S. Cox. After a jury verdict of $37,500 in the third trial, Cox ordered a remittur of $17,500 and Congress appropriated $20,000 to pay the judgment. *Kilbourn v. Thompson,* 11 D.C. (MacArth. & M.) 401 (1883).

24. *Hutchinson v. Proxmire,* 443 U.S. 111 (1979).

important precedents (although not dispositive) restraining Congress from fishing expeditions into private lives.

Oversight of the Executive Branch

In the years after the Civil War, the federal government took on more functions and its small bureaucracy grew. The first independent regulatory commission, the Civil Service Commission, was established by the Pendleton Act in 1883 to prepare and administer rules for a limited classified civil service. The Interstate Commerce Commission was created in 1887 to regulate the railroads, but within a few years it was chiefly engaged in collecting and publishing statistics.

In 1880, the Supreme Court of the United States confirmed that the Supreme Court for the District of Columbia had inherited from the D.C. Circuit Court exclusive review, by way of mandamus, of an executive official's performance or nonperformance of a duty imposed by law.[25] A few of these cases arose in each term of the D.C. Supreme Court. Although none of the cases occurring during the period 1863–92 were momentous, this power continued to serve as some restraint on the executive and as a central example of the D.C. Circuit's uniqueness. In several cases, the D.C. Supreme Court granted the writ of mandamus and the U.S. Supreme Court reversed.[26]

Review of the executive branch by way of mandamus occurred most often with the most important agencies in that "Department of the Great Miscellany," the Interior Department—the Pension Office, the General Land Office, and the Office of Indian Affairs. By 1891, the Pension Office had some 6,000 employees and 500,000 cases pending—many spurred by the efforts of claim agents and attorneys. The D.C. Supreme Court held in *United States ex rel. Miller v. Raum* that it would not interfere by mandamus in the Pension Commissioner's interpretation of the law as to the amount due as a pension for a given disability. The Supreme Court affirmed.[27]

---

25. *United States v. Schurz,* 102 U.S. 378 (1880).

26. See, for example, *United States ex rel. Key v. Frelinghuysen,* in which the Court ordered the Secretary of State to pay certain Mexican claims and was reversed in relevant part by the Supreme Court. 13 D.C. (2 Mackey) 299, 306 (1883), 110 U.S. 63, 76 (1884).

27. 18 D.C. 556 (1890), aff'd, 135 U.S. 200 (1890).

~

The core of the court structure Congress created in 1863 was left in place for thirty years. By then, the population of the District (230,392 in the 1890 census) had tripled since the outset of the Civil War. The number of government employees was 23,000, twice what it had been at the height of the war. The Capitol dome and the Washington Monument had been completed. The Potomac marshes were being drained and Rock Creek Park developed.

Washington had become a magnet, attracting some of America's most interesting people. In 1877 Henry Adams, that most intellectually snobbish of all the Adams clan, abandoned Cambridge for Washington, stating that "this is the only place in America where society amuses me or where life offers variety." New financial capital flowed into the District—assets in District banks tripled between 1880 and 1890—but the new wealth was primarily in real estate, which became the city's third principal industry, after government and tourism. Washington's public buildings still gleamed white, in contrast to the sooty patina that covered the nation's industrial cities.

In 1891, Congress finally turned its attention to the problems of the federal judiciary, and created the U.S. courts of appeals. Two years later, it would again overhaul the structure of the courts of the District of Columbia. The primacy of the D.C. Supreme Court would not endure. Joining it would be a court which would eventually emerge as one of America's most important.

Chapter 3

Beginnings of a National Reputation
Changes in the D.C. Circuit, 1893–1932

The four decades from 1893, when Congress created a solely appellate court for the District of Columbia, to 1932, when Franklin D. Roosevelt was elected President, were eventful years for the country. Although generally marked by prosperity, this period began and ended in economic depression. Indeed, the years spanned by this chapter can be demarcated by two great marches on Washington in which the poor and unemployed came to petition the federal government for relief—that of Coxey's Army in 1894 and that of the Bonus Marchers in 1932.

The procession of each "army" through the nation to Washington demonstrated the increasing expectations Americans had of their national government and the growing symbolism of the capital. Both revealed a growing belief that new conditions—urbanization, industrialization, labor-management strife—demanded action by the national government; and both reflected a widespread understanding that what was happening in Washington was essential to the growth and well-being of the nation.

The march of Coxey's Army was born of the severe depression which swept the United States in 1893. Led by Jacob Coxey, a self-made business-man from Ohio, a ragtag band of 500 unemployed men arrived in Washington on the first of May 1894. Coxey's demands were vague, even eccentric, but the central message was unmistakable—that the federal government should use its credit to create jobs. After Coxey and two others walked across the Capitol grounds and were refused entrance to the Capitol, they were arrested. The police then dispersed the other marchers, wielding clubs and charging on horseback; fifty-two people were beaten or trampled.

Coxey's was the first great march on Washington to lobby the government. Soon, others would grasp the image of Washington as a national soapbox and the Mall would regularly be thronged with demonstrators for causes noble and ignoble. As the importance of the work of the federal government grew, many groups with social and political agendas established national headquarters in Washington. This was the new environment in which the courts of the District of Columbia operated.

During the years 1893–1932 the work of the federal courts throughout the nation increased measurably in both quantity and importance. Not all the areas of growth in other districts were important to the courts of the District of Columbia, however. For example, because of the city's lack of industry, few of the first sustained encounters with the federal laws regulating the marketplace occurred in Washington. On the other hand, Prohibition brought about not only an enormous increase in federal criminal cases in the District but also for the first time prompted consideration in depth of the Fourth and Fifth Amendments. One can detect as well, especially toward the end of this period, the seeds of two major sources of the unique power and prestige of the courts of the D.C. Circuit: their position as the venue of important state trials and their role in oversight of the federal administrative agencies.

The city of Washington doubled in size between 1893 and 1932, from 230,000 in the 1890 census to nearly half a million. Federal employment likewise grew steadily, from 24,000 in 1891 to 70,000 in 1930, with a bulge to 120,000 during the First World War. The city continued without home rule, under the governance of three commissioners. Government by commission proved to be relatively inexpensive and there was relatively little corruption, although the commissioners were often greatly influenced by the Board of Trade, which, in turn, often represented the interests of banks and the real estate lobby. Even minor matters could necessitate an act of Congress, and governance became increasingly complex and unwieldy as Congress surrounded the commissioners with independent or quasi-independent agencies, which numbered twenty-five by 1928.

The entire city benefitted enormously from planned development. In 1902 a commission headed by Senator James McMillan of Michigan proposed a comprehensive program for regional development. The plan was faithful to Pierre L'Enfant's vision, reaffirming the commitment to a stately and monumental city which would itself be a work of art. The McMillan Commission made provision for monumental buildings on the Mall, great parks, and scenic roadways along the Potomac from Great Falls to Mount Vernon. By 1932 most of the Commission's plan had been realized.

Where black Washingtonians were concerned, the story was far less happy. The Wilson administration segregated government cafeterias and screened off the desks of black employees. The federal and local civil-rights acts of Reconstruction were a dead letter, and by the First World War segregation was virtually total. Employment in both the federal and District governments was all but foreclosed to blacks for any but the most menial positions. By 1916 the only African-American holding office by presidential appointment in Washington was Robert Terrell, a judge of the Municipal Court.

The Court of Appeals of the District of Columbia

Between 1893 and 1909 the judicial system of the District of Columbia achieved the shape it would retain through much of the twentieth century. There would be two "superior" federal courts, closely resembling what would in 1911 become the model for the federal court system: one trial court and an appellate court available to every litigant who lost at the trial level—a forum for correcting errors at trial and a mechanism for ensuring uniformity in the work of the trial judges. There would also be inferior courts for petty crimes, minor civil suits and small claims, whose decisions would be appealable to the new Court of Appeals.

For almost a century the federal court system for the nation had been so structured that judges might hear on appeal decisions they had made at trial. That system ended with the creation of the circuit courts of appeals in 1891. The new, solely appellate tier of courts was crafted primarily to relieve the justices of the U.S. Supreme Court of the large number of trivial federal appeals, but it also resulted from developing sensibilities that appeals should not go "from Philip drunk to Philip sober." Similar concerns moved the Congress in 1893 to reshape the court system of the District of Columbia by removing the appellate jurisdiction of the Supreme Court of the District of Columbia and vesting it in a newly created Court of Appeals of the District of Columbia.

The reform was spurred by members of the District's bar, who appear to have been concerned about delays in the D.C. Supreme Court (by 1893, delays in the disposition of cases were averaging fifteen to eighteen months), as well as about the appropriateness of judges reviewing in general term their own and their colleagues' work in special term. A committee of members of the bar, chaired by Martin F. Morris, a noted attorney and professor at Georgetown Law School (and who would be appointed to the new Court of Appeals in 1893), prepared the draft legislation. A number of influential attorneys, including Walter Davidge, Enoch Totten, and Henry Wise Garnett, opposed the legislation, as did some of the justices of the D.C. Supreme Court, although not Chief Justice Edward Bingham. Some unsuccessful efforts were made (presumably by Populist members of

Congress) to limit the terms of the judges of the new court, to cut the amount of their salaries, and to require that no more than two of the three judges of the new court be of the same political party.

By the Act of February 9, 1893, Congress created the Court of Appeals of the District of Columbia, initially composed of three justices.[1] The Act was signed into law by the outgoing President, Benjamin Harrison, but it was Grover Cleveland who named the Court's first three members. The Court was organized and convened on May 1.

Its jurisdiction encompassed appeals from final orders, judgments and decrees of the District Supreme Court, and appeals from certain inter-locutory orders (such as the granting of injunctions and appointment of receivers, a matter of concern to members of Congress), as well as occa-sions when "it will be in the interest of justice to allow the appeal." The new court also succeeded to the D.C. Supreme Court's power to hear ap-peals from decisions of the Commissioner of Patents in interference cases.[2] The statute provided for the appointment of justices of the D.C. Supreme Court to fill out panels if for some reason an Appeals Court justice was unable to sit. By law, every opinion of the Court of Appeals had to be re-duced to writing and filed with the clerk before any judgment or order could be entered.

During these years, the inferior court system of the District was reshaped into something less countrified and more professional. In 1901 Congress provided for appeals from the Police Court to the Court of Appeals, and in 1906 a separate Juvenile Court for the District was established, manned by a single justice with a five-year term. Also in 1901, the justices of the peace were officially constituted as an inferior court of the District. This court was reconstituted in 1909 as the Municipal Court of the District of Co-lumbia. In 1921 the Municipal Court was given exclusive jurisdiction over all damage claims up to $1,000 and made a court of record, and the Court of Appeals was given jurisdiction to review its judgments upon petition for writ of error.[3]

---

1. 27 Stat. 434. The Court's name would be changed in 1934 to United States Court of Appeals for the District of Columbia (Act of June 7, 1934, 48 Stat. 926) and then, in 1948, to United States Court of Appeals for the District of Columbia Circuit (Act of June 25, 1948, 62 Stat. 869). Since 1948, the Court's members have been denominated "judge."

2. In 1929 many of the Court's patent cases were channeled to the newly reconsti-tuted U.S. Court of Customs and Patent Appeals. Act of March 2, 1929, 45 Stat. 1475.

3. Act of February 17, 1909, 35 Stat. 623; Act of March 31, 1921, 41 Stat. 1310.

When the Court of Appeals of the District of Columbia was created, Congress inadvertently failed to restrict appeals to the U.S. Supreme Court in a manner similar to what had been provided in the Act creating the circuit courts of appeals two years before. As a result, until 1925 a much wider avenue of appeal was available from the Court of Appeals of the District of Columbia than from other federal appellate courts.[4]

Over the years the caseload of the Court of Appeals increased gradually. As early as 1910—the year in which a courthouse for the Court of Appeals was erected adjacent to the courthouse of the D.C. Supreme Court—the annual report of the Attorney General recommended the addition of two judges for the Court, which was then handling more cases than any of the nine federal circuits save the Second and the Eighth, both of which had four judges. However, the pace of change in judicial administration is such that another twenty years elapsed before the Court received the two additional judgeships. By then, the three routes by which cases reached the Court of Appeals—by appeal from the D.C. Supreme Court, by appeal from the District's inferior courts, and from federal administrative agencies—were all heavily traveled.

The membership and work of the Court of Appeals from 1893 to 1932 may be divided into four periods: that of the original three justices who served as a unit from 1893 through 1904; the years in which the Court was made up exclusively of the appointees of Theodore Roosevelt (1905–17); the Chief Justiceship of Constantine Smyth, a Wilson appointee serving uneasily with Roosevelt appointees (1917–24); and a period of transformation of the docket and enlargement of the Court, during which the holdover Theodore Roosevelt appointees were joined by a Chief Justice appointed by Calvin Coolidge and two justices appointed by Herbert Hoover (1924–33).

The Supreme Court of the District of Columbia

Twenty-seven different men were justices of the Supreme Court of the District of Columbia during this period—too many for anything but a brief group portrait. Six were sitting at the time of the creation of the Court of Appeals; of the others all but five were appointed by Republican presidents: McKinley named three; Roosevelt, four; Wilson, five; Harding, one; Coolidge, one; and Hoover, seven, including three newly created judgeships.

---

4. The Act of February 13, 1925, 43 Stat. 936, provided for review in the Supreme Court by writ of certiorari for all decisions of courts of appeals, including the D.C. Circuit.

Only four of these justices were Washington-born; however, ten were educated at law schools in the District. Almost half were practicing in Washington at the time of their appointment, either in private practice or with the government. Four had been U.S. Attorney for the District of Columbia and six had been either Special Assistant to the Attorney General or Assistant Attorney General. Four had served as president of the District of Columbia Bar Association. One of the justices, Jeter C. Pritchard of North Carolina, had been a United States Senator and four had been members of the U.S. House of Representatives. Two had been state judges and one, Frederick L. Siddons, had been a D.C. Commissioner. Two, James M. Proctor and William Hitz, would be elevated to the Court of Appeals of the District of Columbia, and one (Pritchard) to the Circuit Court for the Fourth Circuit. One member of the Court, Daniel Thew Wright, resigned to avoid impeachment. Two, Thomas Jennings and F. Dickinson Letts, had judicial careers of remarkable length—1918–50 and 1931–61, respectively.

Two particularly high-profile cases drew attention to the D.C. Supreme Court during this period. In *United States v. Morris*, which became known as the Potomac Flats case, a special act of Congress conferred jurisdiction upon the Supreme Court of the District of Columbia to decide perhaps the most important case affecting the development of the city of Washington to ever come before the courts of the District of Columbia.

After the great flood of February 1881, during which the waters of the Potomac reached to the foot of Capitol Hill, Congress had acted to change the river's channel to improve navigation and to use the earth dredged out of the river to elevate the 300 acres of sediment known as the Potomac Flats, high enough above the normal water level to create both a buffer against floods and an area for recreation. By acts of Congress in 1882 and 1886, the D.C. Supreme Court was given "full power and jurisdiction" over all claims by putative property holders within the area of the proposed improvements.[5] The intention was to quiet title in the United States as to any unfounded claims to title and, if the Court held that anyone other than the United States had a right to any of the land or water, to ascertain its value with a view to condemnation.

United States v. Morris was first brought in 1887, ultimately decided in 1895, and affirmed by the U.S. Supreme Court in 1899.[6] It involved many claims by corporations and individuals, including those of Martin F. Morris, who had purchased the major portion of Kidwell's Meadows, fifty-seven

5. Act of August 2, 1882, 22 Stat. 198; Act of August 15, 1886, 24 Stat. 335.
6. 17 D.C. (6 Mackey) 90 (1887) (*Bin*-Jam-Mer), 18 D.C. (7 Mackey) 8 (1888), 23 Wash. Law Rep. 745 (1895), aff'd, 174 U.S. 196 (1899).

acres of land lying within the Potomac River. The most extensive claims were those of the heirs of Chief Justice John Marshall and his brother, James, to the whole bed of the river.

In a thirty-three page opinion, Justice Alexander B. Hagner held that Maryland had ceded the land to the United States, which held it in trust for the benefit of the City of Washington, for whose use it had been dedicated. The land, the Court held, was not vendible to private persons. It did find that certain lots might be so injuriously affected by the improvements that their owners would have a right to compensation from the government to the extent of their injury.

Two decades later, the D.C. Supreme Court was the setting for another case that attracted wide national attention, this one notable for the appearance of two ex-presidents as witnesses. It involved an apparent vendetta by the Wilson administration, which carried on a comprehensive, political and public investigation of the Riggs National Bank, one of Washington's oldest. The bank filed a bill in equity seeking an injunction to restrain the government from continuing its harassment and charging the Secretary of the Treasury and other high officials with conspiracy to wreck the bank. The government responded by hiring Louis D. Brandeis, among others, as special counsel.

The equity proceeding was interrupted when the government brought charges of making false official statements against the bank's president, vice president — two of the city's leading citizens — and a former cashier. The defendants were represented by Frank Hogan and Daniel O'Donoghue, who later became a justice of the D.C. Supreme Court. Defense counsel called former presidents William Howard Taft and Theodore Roosevelt as character witnesses. After Roosevelt testified, he passed in front of the jury box and shook his finger at the jury, saying "I expect you to do the right thing." After deliberating for nine minutes, the jury acquitted. With the failure of the prosecution, the war against the bank ended.[7]

The Alvey Court

In his appointments to the Court of Appeals of the District of Columbia, Grover Cleveland chose to view the Court as a national rather than a local

---

7. *Riggs Nat'l Bank v. Comptroller of the Currency, et al.,* 44 Wash. Law Rep. 434 (1916).

court. Reflecting this, two of his three nominees, Richard H. Alvey and Seth Shepard, came from outside the District.

Alvey, the Court's first Chief Justice, was born in 1826 on Maryland's Western Shore. During the Civil War he had spent six months in prison for his secessionist views. In 1867 he was elected Chief Justice of the Fourth Maryland Circuit, which made him not only a trial judge but also an associate judge of the Maryland Court of Appeals, the state's highest court. Alvey's reputation was such that when a vacancy arose in 1883, the governor of Maryland was virtually forced to appoint him Chief Justice. Thus, at the time he was appointed Chief Justice of the D.C. Court of Appeals, Alvey had been a judge for twenty-six years, ten of them as Chief Justice of Maryland.

Alvey appears to have been a workaholic and in some respects a remarkably unsociable man. At the formal memorial service in Washington after Alvey's death, one of the speakers noted that he "never visited his friends, never took part in social affairs, and it is said he accepted but one invitation to dinner in Hagerstown" in the many years he lived there. Nevertheless, Seth Shepard called him "an ideal associate and an incomparable chief." Alvey's opinions were the most scholarly of the first three justices of the Court of Appeals. Alvey retired at the end of 1904 at the age of seventy-eight and died in 1907.

Seth Shepard served twenty-four years on the Court of Appeals, half of them as Alvey's successor as Chief Justice. Shepard was born in Washington County, Texas, in 1847. During the last years of the Civil War he served in the Fifth Texas Mounted Volunteers of the Confederate Army. After the war he practiced law in Texas until his appointment to the Court of Appeals. The respect in which he was held by Democratic representative David Browning Culberson of Texas, the prime congressional mover of the law creating the Court of Appeals, undoubtedly facilitated Shepard's appointment to the Court. It was, however, a Republican, Theodore Roosevelt, who in 1905 elevated Shepard to the Chief Justiceship. Shepard's opinions are crisp and clear, and continue to read well. He retired in 1917 at the age of seventy and died a few months later.

Martin F. Morris was born in Washington in 1834. He was a Roman Catholic, attended Georgetown University and studied for the priesthood before turning to the law. Morris was a prolific writer, a professor of law at Georgetown beginning in 1876. As one of the owners of Kidwell's Meadows, he became a major party in the great litigation over ownership of the Potomac Flats, which would be decided against him. Morris chaired the committee of the bar whose work led to the 1893 judicial reorganization. An able judge, Morris served until retiring in 1905. He died in 1909.

Jurisprudence

The new Court of Appeals showed little compunction about reversing the Supreme Court of the District of Columbia, doing so more than one-third of the time in the very first volume of its reported decisions. Opinions tended to be short, although Chief Justice Alvey would from time to time explore the byways of the law. Sixty-one cases are reported in 1 App. D.C.'s 537 pages and as much as forty percent of the space is given over to statements of the case and lawyers' arguments. There was also very little of "the dissenting business" on the Alvey Court. There is but one dissent reported in the first volume—it is the very first case reported and the dissenter was the Chief Justice.[8]

During the eleven years the first three justices of the Court of Appeals sat together, the tribunal was essentially a state supreme court. If there were those who saw the Court, as Justice Morris put it in his retirement address, as a "great federal tribunal intended to deal with questions as broad as the federal union," they envisioned the Court's future more than its present. In the first one hundred cases decided by the Court of Appeals there are almost none of the staples of federal courts elsewhere in the country—admiralty, customs, copyright, diversity.[9] Nor, during the Alvey Chief Justiceship, was the Court's new role as a "national court" much in evidence, although the justices did hear appeals from decisions of the Commissioner of Patents rejecting patent applications and in patent infringement cases.

Rather than illustrating the work of the federal government or offering glimpses into the political life of the nation, as they would later, the early decisions of the Court of Appeals primarily reflect the growth of Washington. They show a city being paved and remodeled. New brick buildings—schools, homes, hotels—are under construction. Sewers, electricity, elevators are being installed. Land deals are being cut and real estate prices are escalating. Cases involving property development occur in suits for partition, foreclosures, attachments, suits for an accounting, and those to remove clouds on title.

The new court's very first case, *Bush v. District of Columbia*, revealed differences within the Court in approaching the interpretation of statutes which continue to this very day. The case involved a recently passed law controlling saloons. Two weeks after the statute became law, a saloon keeper

---

8. *Bush v. District of Columbia*, 1 App. D.C. 1 (1893) (*She-Mor/Alv*).

9. The first hundred cases are reported in 1 App. D.C. and one-third of volume 2.

was convicted in Police Court for operating without the license required by the new law, even though his license under the old ordinance did not expire for several months. On appeal, Bush prevailed by a vote of 2–1. Justices Shepard and Morris thought the Police Court's interpretation of the new law was "unconscionable and unjust" and could not believe that Congress would have closed all the saloons in the city until new licenses were obtained. Chief Justice Alvey dissented, arguing that "terms more comprehensive and unequivocal could not have been employed." It was not the Court's place, he said, "to restrict the plain meaning of the statute...to relieve what would appear to be a hardship or injustice to individuals."[10]

Although little of the early work of the D.C. Court of Appeals was "national" in character, in its first years the Alvey Court confronted one of the most important contempt of Congress cases of the nineteenth century. *Chapman v. United States* was the first criminal prosecution under the 1857 statute which made contempt of Congress an indictable offense in the federal courts.

When Elverton R. Chapman, a broker in sugar stocks, was called before a Senate committee investigating the possible corrupt influence of the American Sugar Refining Company on the Senate, he refused to testify and was indicted for contempt. On appeal, Chapman argued that the contempt statute was unconstitutional, that the Senate lacked the power to make the inquiry, and that the questions put to him were not pertinent. Writing for the Court, Chief Justice Alvey upheld the contempt statute, ruled that the Senate had jurisdiction to investigate accusations against its own members, and held that the questions put to Chapman were pertinent. Chapman was then tried in the D.C. Supreme Court, found guilty by a jury and sentenced to a month in jail and a $100 fine. The Court of Appeals affirmed, distinguishing the case from *Kilbourn v. Thompson* because "there was no unconstitutional search into private affairs of the witnesses." The U.S. Supreme Court reviewed the case by way of habeas corpus. Citing Chief Justice Alvey by name, the High Court left the result undisturbed.[11]

In the first years of the twentieth century, the Court of Appeals dealt with several petitions for the writ of mandamus aimed at officials of the Department of the Interior, concerning Native Americans. One of these, *Lone Wolf v. Hitchcock,* culminated in a U.S. Supreme Court decision so signifi-

---

10. *Bush v. District of Columbia,* 1 App. D.C. 1 (1893).
11. *Chapman v. United States,* 8 App. D.C. 302 (1896), 164 U.S. 436 (1896), dismissing writ of error, 8 App. D.C. 320 (1896), cert. denied, 166 U.S. 721 (1897).

cant that it has been called "the Indians' Dred Scott decision."[12] The case involved an 1892 agreement between the federal government and the Kiowa, Comanche, and Plains Apache Indians for some 2.5 million acres of land to be sold to the United States. Although an 1867 treaty stipulated that three-quarters of the adult males in the tribes had to consent to such a transfer, the agreement was submitted to the Senate with many fewer than the required number of Indian signatures and with many signatures obtained by "deceit, fraud and bribery." After eight years of delaying tactics on the part of the Native Americans, the agreement was ratified by the Senate.

Lone Wolf, leader of the Kiowa, first sought to block implementation of the agreement in the courts of the Oklahoma Territory. Unsuccessful there, he and others from the three tribes filed suit in the Supreme Court of the District of Columbia. On June 20, 1901, Justice A. C. Bradley upheld the United States, stressing Indian dependence on the United States and the political nature of the congressional enactments. The Court of Appeals rejected the Indians' arguments, including the contention that the final agreement offered them only a fraction of the land's value and that the remainder of the land could not support them. The U.S. Supreme Court, too, upheld the agreement, holding that Congress had made a good faith effort to give the Indians full value for the land. As to the charges of fraud, bribery and chicanery, the High Court took refuge in the political-question doctrine, holding that "as Congress possessed full power in the matter, the judiciary cannot question or inquire into the motives which prompted the enactment of the legislation."[13]

The *Lone Wolf* case came to dominate federal policy in Indian affairs. It implied that congressional power was plenary and established in law the wardship status of the Indians. It effectively held that Congress could unilaterally diminish Indian reservations and could force allotment upon reluctant Indian wards, and it presumed that Indians were not competent to negotiate for themselves. As one observer put it, "*Lone Wolf v. Hitchcock* firmly secured the Indian's place as second-class citizens in America."

The Roosevelt Court, 1905–17

Between 1905 and 1907, Theodore Roosevelt reconstituted the Court of Appeals in such a way as to leave his stamp upon it for three decades. With

---

12. The characterization is from Judge Phillip Nichols Jr.'s concurring opinion in *Sioux Nation v. United States*, 601 F.2d 1157, 1173 (Ct. Cl. 1979).

13. *Lone Wolf v. Hitchcock*, 19 App. D.C. 315 (1902), aff'd, 187 U.S. 553, 568 (1903).

the retirements of Alvey and Morris in 1905, Roosevelt promoted Shepard to the center chair and appointed Charles Holland Duell and Louis Emory McComas to the other seats. Duell resigned the next year and McComas died in 1907; they were replaced by Charles H. Robb and Josiah A. Van Orsdel, respectively. The court would remain intact for a decade, until halfway through Woodrow Wilson's first term; Robb and Van Orsdel served together for just one month shy of thirty years.

Charles Robb was born in 1867 in Vermont. He practiced law in Bellow's Falls and served as State's Attorney for Windham County before going to Washington in 1892 to become Solicitor of the Bureau of Internal Revenue. He was then Special Assistant to the Attorney General for the prosecution of frauds in the Post Office Department. At the time of his appointment to the Court of Appeals in 1906, Robb, by then Assistant Attorney General, was only thirty-eight years old. His tenure on the Court was marked by a keen interest in patent matters and a ready wit. Robb remained on the Court of Appeals until 1937 and died in 1939.[14]

Josiah A. Van Orsdel, born in Pennsylvania in 1860 and admitted to the bar there, settled in Wyoming in 1891. There he served in the state House of Representatives, as Attorney General, and as associate justice of the Wyoming Supreme Court. Van Orsdel came east in 1906 to serve as an Assistant U.S. Attorney General; he argued the Philippine Tariff case before the U.S. Supreme Court. As a judge, he was an early pioneer in the area of administrative law. Although a certain self-righteousness marks his style in constitutional cases, Van Orsdel wrote briefly and to the point. He died in 1937, while still on the bench.

The Theodore Roosevelt Court, like the Alvey Court, bore little resemblance to a "national court" save in its patent and trademark jurisdiction. But that jurisdiction accounted for a great deal of its docket: thirty-six of the eighty-two cases reported in 36 App. D.C. (covering less than a year in 1907–08) were patent and trademark.[15] There were various routes to raising patent issues in the federal courts, but the Court of Appeals of the Dis-

---

14. Charles Robb was the father of Roger Robb, whom Richard Nixon would place on the Court of Appeals of the District of Columbia Circuit in 1969.

15. There were, for instance, cases involving the trademarks "tabasco," "shredded whole wheat," and "health food," and patent cases involving a dust shield for a typewriter, a cigar bunch shaping machine, a process for covering tennis balls, and commercial explosives. See decisions reported in 30 App. D.C. at 191, 299, 329, 334, 337, 348, 411. Thomas Edison also appears in 30 App. D.C. (at 321), as the loser in a patent case.

trict of Columbia was the only court in the country with direct jurisdiction to review the decisions of the U.S. Commissioner of Patents. Further, the Court made an important contribution to setting up guideposts governing Patent Office procedures.

The majority of reported cases of the Court of Appeals from 1905 to 1916, however, were local—personal injury, homicide, contract, estate—reflecting, sometimes unhappily, the lives of those who lived in Washington. There were several appeals in prosecutions arising out of mishandled abortions. The constitutionality of Sunday blue laws was considered and upheld. The court also upheld the finding of a trial judge (Daniel Thew Wright) that a child who had "one-eighth or one-sixteenth Negro blood" but who had "no physical characteristic which affords ocular evidence suggestive of ought but the Caucasian" had properly been excluded from a white public school.[16]

Jurisprudence

The decade of the "Teddy Roosevelt Court" essentially corresponds to the second half of the Progressive era in the federal government. Notwithstanding, few cases coming before the D.C. courts in this period involved Progressive legislation. Of those that did, the most important was *McNamara v. Washington Terminal Company.*

Edward McNamara was a locomotive fireman who received fatal injuries in a collision in which his employer had been negligent. The case revolved around the constitutionality of Section 3 of the Employers Liability Act of 1906, one section of which provided that no contract of employment could be used by an employer as a defense to an employee's suit for negligence. The railroad argued that this section was unconstitutional because it infringed upon the right to contract, which had been elevated to constitutional status by the 1905 Supreme Court decision in *Lochner v. New York.*[17] A unanimous Court of Appeals upheld the law in a strong opinion by Justice Robb which waved away arguments of right to contract: "After all, the right to contract is hedged about with many restrictions, and must always yield to the common good."[18]

---

16. *Wall v. Oyster*, 36 App. D.C. 50 (1910) (*She*-CRobb-Van). Abortion cases, see e.g. *Maxey v. United States*, 30 App. D.C. 63 (1907) (*She*-CRobb-Van); *Thompson v. United States*, 30 App. D.C. 352 (1908) (*She*-CRobb-Van). The blue-laws case was *District of Columbia v. Robinson*, 30 App. D.C. 283 (1908) (*Van-She*-CRobb).

17. 198 U.S. 45 (1905).

18. *McNamara v. Washington Terminal Company*, 35 App. D.C. 230 (1910) (*CRobb-She*-Van).

Of the handful of "national" cases that came before the Court of Appeals during this period, the most significant one involved the use of the secondary boycott in labor disputes and the use of the contempt power against labor and labor leaders; it reached the U.S. Supreme Court twice. It involved an attempt to enjoin a successful boycott led by the American Federation of Labor against the Buck's Stove and Range Company in many areas of the West and Midwest. Because of the personalities involved, the dispute transcended the labor-management controversy that had inspired the boycott. James W. Van Cleve, the president of Buck's, was also president of the National Association of Manufacturers; the AFL, led by Samuel Gompers, the most powerful labor leader of his time, was represented in court by Alton B. Parker, who had been the Democratic candidate for President in 1904.

The action was brought in 1907 in the District of Columbia, where the AFL had its headquarters. The D.C. judges' attitudes proved to be no friendlier to unions than those of federal judges elsewhere. Chief Justice Harry M. Clabaugh of the D.C. Supreme Court issued a temporary injunction in December 1907 and a permanent one several months later, restraining the AFL, its officers, and others from promoting what he held to be an unlawful boycott. The injunction was largely upheld by an atypically split Court of Appeals, Chief Justice Shepard dissenting in part.[19]

While Clabaugh's decision was on appeal, Gompers delivered a speech in New York in which he claimed to be honoring the order but declared that union members were nonetheless not "compelled to buy" any Buck's products. Gompers and two other union officials were held in contempt by the D.C. Supreme Court. On appeal, Justice Van Orsdel, writing for the Court, upheld the contempt citations, stating that "contempt may be committed by both innuendo and insinuation." Dissenting, Chief Justice Shepard argued that part of the injunction was void because it violated the First Amendment.[20]

By the time the cases reached the United States Supreme Court, in 1911, the appeals of the original injunction were moot because the parties had reached a settlement.[21] In the appeals of the contempt judgments, the High Court agreed with the majority of the Court of Appeals in part, but threw the case back into the lap of the D.C. Supreme Court to decide if they wished to bring criminal proceedings against Gompers and his colleagues

---

19. *American Federation of Labor v. Buck's Stove & Range Company*, 33 App. D.C. 83 (1909) (*CRobb-Van*(c)/*She*).

20. *Gompers v. Buck's Stove & Range Co.*, 33 App. D.C. 516 (1909) (*Van-CRobb*(c)/*She*).

21. *Buck's Stove & Range Co. v. American Federation of Labor*, 219 U.S. 581 (1911).

for violation of their decree.[22] On trial before the D.C. Supreme Court, the defendants were found guilty and sentenced to prison terms. But the terms were never served: six and a half years after the injunction had first been ordered, the U.S. Supreme Court ended the saga on the ground that "the power to punish for contempt must have some limit in time."[23]

The Smyth Court, 1917–24

The differences among the Court of Appeals judges in *Buck's Stove* were atypical of the Court during Shepard's Chief Justiceship. However, with Shepard's resignation in 1917 and the appointment of Constantine J. Smyth as Chief Justice, the Court of Appeals entered upon a period of far less harmony, in which there were more than hints of bitterness among the judges.

Smyth, the only appointee to the Court of Appeals of a Democratic President between 1893 and 1935, was born in Ireland in 1859 and brought to America when he was eleven. He practiced law in Nebraska and became a major figure in Democratic state politics, serving two terms as state attorney general. He served as Special Assistant to the U.S. Attorney General from 1913 to 1917, having charge of many important antitrust cases. In 1917, Woodrow Wilson appointed him Chief Justice of the Court of Appeals, where he served until his death in 1924.

The opinions issued by the Court of Appeals during the Smyth years are marked by brevity as well as discord. In Volume 48 App. D.C., for example, which covers a twelve-month period in 1918–19, 120 cases are reported. About half are local District of Columbia cases and all but eight of the others are patent and trademark appeals, a continuing staple of the Court.[24] There are dissents in almost ten percent of the cases, not an astounding number these days but remarkable in contrast to the harmonious work of the Court of Appeals just a few years before. Furthermore, dissents appear not only in major cases, such as *United States ex rel. Ashley v. Roper*, which involved construction of the newly passed Harrison Narcotic Act of 1914, but in trivial causes, such

---

22. *Gompers v. Buck's Stove & Range Co.*, 221 U.S. 418 (1911).

23. *Gompers v. United States*, 233 U.S. 604 (1914).

24. There were, for instance, patent cases involving paper drinking cups, drill bits for use in digging oil wells, an improvement relating to engine starters, and a device for launching torpedoes. See 48 App. D.C. at 218, 223, 258, 376. Litigation over trademarks included Aunt Jemima and BVDs; see *Aunt Jemima Mills Company v. Kirkland Distributing Co.*, 48 App. D.C. 248 (1918); *Atlas Underwear Co. v. BVD Company*, 48 App. D.C. 425 (1919).

as actions for debt, where the legal questions themselves were not significant. Several times Chief Justice Smyth dissented without opinion. The norms supporting the outward show of consensus were breaking down.[25]

During these years, the business of the D.C. Supreme Court and of the Court of Appeals grew appreciably because of the First World War, Prohibition, the growing population of the District, and the increased size of the federal government. The volume of business was such that judges of the Court of Customs Appeals were regularly assigned to panels of the Court of Appeals to ease the workload.[26] Local cases still constituted about half of the docket; these were made up, essentially in the same proportions as before, of cases involving real property (although more of these now concerned landlord-tenant questions), estates, contracts, divorce, and personal injury, as well as criminal cases. But several of the decisions in these "local" cases—involving minimum wage law, scientific evidence, and restrictive housing covenants—had far-reaching "national" implications.

It was Prohibition cases that gave the dockets of the D.C. Supreme Court and Court of Appeals the most resemblance to those of other federal courts. The local Prohibition Act took effect in the District on November 1, 1917, nearly two years before the Volsted Act. The district courts of Washington were flooded with liquor cases, many of which reached the Court of Appeals. That court responded sometimes with sympathy, often with impatience, to the "Great Experiment."[27]

Washington continued to play host to demonstrations in support of political causes. None were more consequential than the succession of marches

---

25. See *United States ex rel. Ashley v. Roper*, 48 App. D.C. 69 (1918) (*Smy-Van/CRobb*); *Eisinger v. E. J. Murphy Co.*, 48 App. D.C. 476 (1919) (*Van-CRobb/Smy*); *Hutchins v. Hutchins*, 48 App. D.C. 495 (1919) (*Van-CRobb/Smy*).

26. The U.S. Court of Customs Appeals, established in 1910 and reconstituted in 1929 as the Court of Customs and Patent Appeals, was a separate national court, not a part of the District of Columbia court system. From time to time, some of its judges were designated to sit with the Court of Appeals (as judges of other courts of appeals are now).

27. In *Rudolph v. United States ex rel. Rock*, for example, a divided court held that a first conviction for unlawful possession and transportation of intoxicating liquors was a crime involving moral turpitude, which would permit the D.C. Commissioners to discontinue the pension of a retired police officer. 6 F.2d 487 (1925) (*Van-Mar/CRobb*). But in *United States v. Mattingly*, the Court held that where liquor was seized illegally it had to be returned, notwithstanding the possibility it was contraband. 285 F. 922 (1922) (*Smy-CRobb-Van*). And in *United States v. Franzione*, the Court rejected a libel sought by the United States for materials in the possession of the defendant, clearly designed for the manufacture of liquor, because the statutory scheme provided for a search warrant, which had not been obtained. 286 F. 769 (1923) (*Mar-CRobb-Smy*).

and pickets on behalf of women's suffrage, which reached a peak during the Wilson administration. During a prolonged round of demonstrations in 1917, socially prominent women submitted to arrest again and again: for disorderly conduct, for obstructing traffic, for assembling in a public park without a permit. At first they were jailed for a few days, but as the demonstrations escalated so did sentences, up to sixty days in the District workhouse in Occoquan, Virginia.

The demonstrators' claims that their First Amendment rights had been violated were pursued unsuccessfully in the lower courts in the District of Columbia. The Court of Appeals confronted the problem in a suit for damages for unlawful transfer brought against the D.C. Commissioners and the Superintendent of the District jail. On March 4, 1919, the Court held that the arrests, convictions and imprisonments had been illegal, since no information had been filed justifying their arrest and sentence. The cases were dismissed. By then, Wilson had endorsed the Nineteenth Amendment, granting women the right to vote, which was ratified in 1920.

During the Smyth Chief Justiceship, the Court of Appeals heard about five cases a year involving attempts to mandamus federal officials. One of these, however, proved to be the Court's most important foray into issues arising from the U.S. entry into World War I. Postmaster General Albert Sidney Burleson had denied second-class mailing privileges to the *Milwaukee Leader*, a newspaper owned by Victor L. Berger, after a finding that previous issues had contained seditious matter. Berger sought to force the Postmaster General to restore those privileges. The Court of Appeals was unsympathetic, writing of the newspaper articles, "No one can read them without being convinced that they were printed in a spirit of hostility to our own government and in a spirit of sympathy to the Central powers." Over the dissents of Justices Holmes and Brandeis, the Supreme Court affirmed in a far-reaching opinion by Justice Clarke that sustained the power of the Postmaster General over the press.[28]

Minimum Wage Law

The litigation over the constitutionality of the Act of September 19, 1918,[29] which provided for the fixing of minimum wages for women in the District of Columbia, led to one of the most significant Supreme Court opinions of the century. Although it was overshadowed by the controversy over

28. *United States ex rel. Milwaukee Democrat Pub. Co. v. Burleson*, 258 F. 282 (1917) (*CRobb*-Smy-Van), aff'd, 255 U.S. 407 (1921).
29. 40 Stat. 960. In 1916 the Supreme Court had divided evenly as to a similar statute, in a case which had been argued by Louis D. Brandeis.

the Supreme Court decision in the case, the Court of Appeals' handling of *Children's Hospital v. Adkins* constituted a self-inflicted wound that vividly exposed the tensions within the Court.

In *Adkins*, the D.C. Children's Hospital sought to nullify a Minimum Wage Board order that essentially provided a wage of 34½ cents an hour, or $16.50 a week, for women working in hotels and hospitals. The Supreme Court of the District of Columbia denied the application. When the case was heard by the Court of Appeals in February 1921, Justice Robb was ill. Following the prescribed procedure, Chief Justice Smyth and Justice Van Orsdel designated Wendell P. Stafford, probably the most liberal judge of the D.C. Supreme Court at the time, to sit with them to hear and decide not only *Adkins* but other cases ready for argument. On June 6 the divided Court of Appeals (Van Orsdel dissenting) affirmed the D.C. Supreme Court decision. Over the next two weeks, with Van Orsdel absent, motions for rehearing were denied by Smyth and Stafford (no statutory procedure existed at the time for requesting rehearing *en banc*).

On June 25, Robb wrote to Smyth, informing him that counsel had sent him their application for a rehearing "and insisted, and still insist, that I vote thereon." Smyth took the position that he and Stafford had properly taken part in the motion for rehearing and that the motion was properly disposed of in Van Orsdel's absence. Robb, however, forced the issue; at the direction of Robb and Van Orsdel, and over Smyth's dissent, the clerk entered an order granting a rehearing. In mid-July the Court, dividing 2–1, set aside the order made by Smyth and Van Orsdel.

On November 6, 1922, the Court of Appeals, again 2–1, struck the statute down. The majority relied upon the freedom of contract as protected by the Fifth Amendment. Writing for the Court, Van Orsdel stood foursquare against "the modern trend toward indiscriminate legislative and judicial jugglery with great fundamental principles of free government." Dissenting, Chief Justice Smyth emphasized the presumption of constitutionality, the breadth of Congress's police power over the District of Columbia, and the thorough investigation Congress had made before drafting the law. He concluded that the law was "but a measure to prevent the confiscation of a working woman's labor by those who have the power to do so.... The choicest function of government is to protect the weak against the unrighteous acts of those who are strong economically or physically."[30]

---

30. *Children's Hospital of the District of Columbia v. Adkins*, 284 F. 613 (1922) (Van-CRobb/Smy).

The losing attorney, Felix Frankfurter, commented with some disgust, "It is beyond belief what courts don't know. I don't mean their views but their ignorance of facts and events, even in the field of law." Frankfurter then drafted a thousand-page brief to inform the Supreme Court, but that court, too, was unreceptive, affirming the Court of Appeals by a vote of 5–3. Dissenting from the decision, Chief Justice Taft, hardly a liberal, stated that "it is not the function of this Court to hold congressional acts invalid simply because they are passed to carry out economic views which the Court believes to be unwise or unsound." Justice Holmes also dissented, stating, in a memorable opinion, "Pretty much all law consists in forbidding men to do some things that they want to do, and contract is no more exempt from law than other acts."[31]

The *Adkins* decision was one of the high-water marks of laissez-faire capitalism. Every minimum-wage law in the country, save that of Massachusetts, was effectively nullified. Though sharply criticized in the law reviews and by lay observers, *Adkins* would remain good law until the great Supreme Court "switch" of 1937.

Scientific Evidence

The most influential opinion of the Court of Appeals during the years of Smyth's Chief Justiceship—indeed, one of the most influential in the Court's history—occurred in a local homicide case. At trial in the D.C. Supreme Court, the defense wished to have an expert witness testify about a comparatively new physiological test, which had been used on the defendant, James Alphonso Frye. Chief Justice Walter T. McCoy refused to allow the expert to testify as to the results of the test, nor would he permit the test to be conducted in front of the jury. On appeal, the Court of Appeals affirmed the conviction. In an opinion so succinct that it covers barely a page and one-half, Justice Van Orsdel wrote:

> Just when a scientific principle or discovery crosses the line between the experimental and demonstrable stages is difficult to define. Somewhere in this twilight zone the evidential force of the principle must be recognized, and while courts will go a long way in admitting expert testimony deduced from a well-recognized scientific principle or discovery, the thing from which the deduction is made must be sufficiently established to have gained general acceptance in the particular field in which it belongs.[32]

---

31. *Adkins v. Children's Hospital*, 261 U.S. 525 (1923).
32. *Frye v. United States*, 293 F. 1013 (1923) (*Van-Smy-Mar*). The controversial test

The *Frye* opinion established the national standard for the admissibility of polygraph testimony in particular and expert scientific evidence in general.[33] Years later, another party confessed to the murder for which James Frye was convicted. *Frye* remained good law until 1993, when the Supreme Court decreed a somewhat more generous approach to scientific evidence.[34]

Restrictive Covenants

The most significant case in the District of Columbia involving racial relations during the years 1893 to 1932 was decided in 1924, less than two months after Smyth's death and without the participation of his successor. The decision in *Corrigan v. Buckley* upheld the validity of voluntary racially restrictive housing covenants and thereby raised high barriers throughout the United States to black home ownership or tenancy in white neighborhoods. At issue was a covenant, signed by John J. Buckley, Irene Corrigan, and twenty-eight other white people, that their properties would never be sold to "any persons of Negro blood." When Mrs. Corrigan agreed to sell her lot to a black woman, Buckley sued to nullify the sale.

The D.C. Supreme Court rejected the defendants' claim that the covenants were unconstitutional under the Fifth Amendment and the Due Process, Equal Protection, and Privileges and Immunities clauses of the Fourteenth Amendment and enjoined the sale of the house. The Court of Appeals (Van Orsdel writing, joined by Robb and Judge Orion Metcalf Barber of the Court of Customs Appeals) affirmed.[35] The sole issue in the case, as Justice Van Orsdel saw it, was the power of landowners to make and record such a restrictive covenant. There was no discrimination under the Constitution, because black property owners could impose similar restrictions. Furthermore, the Fourteenth Amendment inhibited the power of the

---

was the systolic blood-pressure deception test, which had not yet gained the standing and scientific recognition among the physiological and psychological authorities it later acquired.

33. The standard was developed further in a series of opinions of Chief Judge David L. Bazelon. See *United States v. Brown*, 461 F.2d 135, 145 n.1 (1972); *United States v. Alexander*, 471 F.2d 923, 955 n.85 (1973). Compare *United States v. Addison*, 498 F.2d 741, 743–44 (1974).

34. *Daubert v. Merrill Dow Pharmaceutical*, 509 U.S. 579 (1993), in which the Supreme Court held that under the Federal Rules of Evidence the *Frye* test no longer applied in the federal courts. Scientific evidence is now admissible, if the trial court determines that the expert's testimony rests on a reliable scientific foundation, even if the theory or technique in question lacks general acceptance.

35. *Corrigan v. Buckley*, 299 F. 899 (1924).

states, not the federal government. Segregation, in and of itself, "cannot be held to be against public policy," Van Orsdel wrote. "Nor can the social equality of the races be attained, either by legislation or by the favorable assertion of assumed rights."

The U.S. Supreme Court, in a puzzling decision which would prove mischievous, dismissed the appeal for want of jurisdiction. Concerned more with establishing its jurisdiction under the 1925 Judiciary Act than with matters of substance, the High Court held that the plaintiff had not raised a substantial constitutional question. Technically, the Supreme Court held only that a racially restrictive covenant was not in and of itself void and that property owners were entirely free to enter into them and abide by them. However, by belittling the issue as to whether the enforcement by lower courts of racially restrictive covenants constituted unconstitutional government action, the Court effectively sent a message to the state courts.[36] After *Corrigan*, the highest courts in nineteen states disposed of that issue on the grounds that the U.S. Supreme Court had already settled it.

In Washington itself, the practical effects were mixed. Only a year later, the block in question in *Corrigan* was occupied by blacks in uncontested tenancy. But the network of interests supporting restrictive agreements, already extensive, was strengthened. Newspapers would not print advertisements offering restricted property for sale to African-Americans. The Washington real estate board's code of ethics advised that property in a white part of the city should not be offered to blacks. The Court of Appeals of the District of Columbia heard four racially restrictive covenant cases in the years between its *Corrigan* decision and the election of Franklin D. Roosevelt, and enforced them each time.[37]

Baseball

One of the notable idiosyncracies of the law has been the national pastime's success, over many years, in avoiding the reach of the Sherman Antitrust Act. Much has been written and speculated about the brief, rather cryptic opinion of Justice Holmes, in which the Supreme Court held that the baseball was merely an exhibition, not trade or commerce, and therefore not subject to the Sherman Act. Little noted has been the 1921 decision of the

36. 271 U.S. 323 (1926).

37. *Torrey v. Wolfes*, 6 F.2d 702 (1925) (Van-Mar-CRobb); *Cornish v. O'Donoghue*, 30 F.2d 983 (1929) (Van-CRobb-Mar); *Russell v. Wallace*, 30 F.2d 981 (1929) (Van-CRobb-Mar); *Edwards v. Westwoodbridge Theatre Co.*, 55 F.2d 524 (1931) (Van-Mar-CRobb-Hitz-Gro).

Court of Appeals of the District of Columbia which the Supreme Court affirmed. Two leaders of the local bar, Hugh Obear and Benjamin Minor, and two giants of the national bar, William Marbury and George Wharton Pepper, appeared as counsel in this case in both the Court of Appeals and the Supreme Court.

In a case brought by a third baseball league, alleging that the American and National leagues had used their monopoly power to drive the new league out of existence, a jury had rendered a verdict for damages against the two major leagues, pursuant to an instruction by the trial court that they were engaged in interstate commerce. The Court of Appeals reversed, in an opinion by Chief Justice Smyth for a unanimous Court. Smyth, as previously noted, had spent four years in the Department of Justice supervising important antitrust cases. His opinion elucidated the rationale by which baseball avoided the antitrust laws for several decades: that baseball was merely an exhibition and was not any part of trade or commerce. In affirming, Justice Holmes stated that "the decision of the Court of Appeals went to the root of the case and if correct makes it unnecessary to consider other serious difficulties in the way of plaintiff's recovery.... [W]e are of the opinion that the Court of Appeals was right."[38]

The "Republican Court," 1924–33

From Chief Justice Smyth's death in 1924 until Franklin Roosevelt became President, the Court of Appeals bench was made up entirely of appointees of Republican presidents. Calvin Coolidge appointed George Ewing Martin as Smyth's successor in 1924. When the Court was enlarged by two in 1930, Herbert Hoover elevated William Hitz from the D.C. Supreme Court and appointed Duncan Lawrence Groner. Hitz's term was short (1931–35) and Groner's eighteen-year tenure will be discussed in the next chapter.

George Ewing Martin was born in Lancaster, Ohio, in 1857 and practiced law there for twenty years. He was serving as a judge of Common Pleas when William Howard Taft appointed him judge of the Court of Customs Appeals in 1911. As a member of that court, he sat by designation on

---

38. *National League v. Federal Baseball Club of Baltimore*, 269 F. 681 (1921), aff'd, 259 U.S. 200 (1922).

the Court of Appeals of the District of Columbia a number of times. Martin served as Chief Justice of the Court of Appeals for thirteen years, retiring in 1937, just before his eightieth birthday. He died in 1948.

By 1924, when Martin became Chief Justice, the caseload of the Court of Appeals had become extremely heavy. Furthermore, the Court was in considerable danger of becoming a specialized patent court. But relief was in sight. In 1929 Congress transferred most of the Court of Appeals' patent and trademark jurisdiction to the Court of Customs and Patent Appeals, and the following year two new judgeships were authorized.[39] However, other changes in jurisdiction attracted new cases to the Court of Appeals. For example, it began hearing appeals from the Board of Tax Appeals, which had been created in 1924 for hearing and reviewing the findings of the Commissioner of Internal Revenue. In 1926, direct appellate review of the Board by the Court of Appeals was provided by statute.[40]

The years 1893–1932 saw the D.C. courts developing two important strands of jurisprudence that would greatly occupy them for the rest of the century and help define their unique position in the federal court system. One of these two lines of business arose from the Courts' involvement in important state trials, of which the most significant in this era were the prosecutions arising from the Teapot Dome scandals of the late 1920s. The other involved their role in oversight of the "administrative state," which was seeded by Populists in the 1890s and took root in the Progressive administrations of Theodore Roosevelt and Woodrow Wilson. This role, which could be detected as early as the *Bush* decision of 1893, blossomed with the Court of Appeals' complex involvement with the federal administrative agencies, which began with the creation of the Federal Radio Commission in 1927.

The Federal Radio Commission

When the Court of Appeals for the District of Columbia was created in 1893, Congress had just begun to take steps toward national regulation of the marketplace with the creation of the Interstate Commerce Commission (1887) and passage of the Sherman Antitrust Act (1890). In the first years of the new century, Congress shifted the federal-state balance to curb the abuses of uncontrolled economic power. It reinforced the Interstate Commerce Commission with the Elkins Act (1903) and the Hepburn Act (1905); strengthened the Sherman Act with the Clayton Act

---

39. Act of March 2, 1929, 45 Stat. 1475; Act of June 19, 1930, 46 Stat. 785.
40. 44 Stat. 2018 (1926), an amendment to the Revenue Act of 1924.

(1914); and created the Federal Trade Commission (1914), which was charged with preventing unfair competition. After the First World War, the size and authority of the federal government continued to grow. It began to take responsibility for electric power in 1920; in 1926 it began to regulate air transport in 1926, and the following year set out to regulate radio.

Congress's creation of the Federal Radio Commission in 1927, which provided for the first comprehensive regulation of the booming radio industry, was also the most important development in the jurisdiction of the Court of Appeals in the first three decades of the twentieth century. A 1912 statute had provided for very limited regulation of the broadcast industry, merely empowering the Secretary of Commerce to license stations.[41] The weakness of that statute and the need for greater regulation became clear after the World War, when there was rapid expansion of commercial broadcasting.

Secretary of Commerce Herbert Hoover attempted to step into the field in 1922 by allocating frequencies. However, in 1923 the Court of Appeals of the District of Columbia, in a mandamus case, held that Hoover lacked the power to do anything more than issue licenses. He lacked the power to allocate frequencies, the Court declared, even when the result of issuing a license would be interference with existing stations.[42] After another adverse court decision[43] and a discouraging opinion from the Attorney General, Hoover left the field and a mad scramble for the broadcast spectrum developed. The need for comprehensive federal regulation of the airways was evident.

Congress addressed the situation with the Federal Radio Act of 1927, which created, on a temporary (year-by-year) basis, a five-person Federal Radio Commission to determine radio stations' wave lengths, power output, and times of operation.[44] From the outset the Court of Appeals of the District of Columbia had an unusual relationship to broadcasting. The 1927 statute provided that any unsuccessful applicant for a construction permit, a station license, or a license renewal would have the right to appeal to the D.C. Court of Appeals and *only* that court. (A license revocation could be appealed either to the Court of Appeals of the District of Columbia or to the U.S. District Court where the station was located.)

The statute further authorized the Court of Appeals, when reviewing an action of the Commission, "to alter or revise the decision appealed from

41. Radio Act of August 13, 1912, 37 Stat. 302.
42. *United States v. Zenith Radio*, 12 F.2d 614 (N.D. Ill. 1926).
43. *Hoover v. Intercity Radio Co.*, 286 F. 1003 (1923) (*Van*-Smy-Mar).
44. Act of February 23, 1927, 44 Stat. 1169.

and enter such judgment as may seem just." Although that power was revoked by a 1930 act of Congress which restricted the Court in FRC cases to purely judicial review, the change was apparently not scrupulously heeded; in a case that arose in the same year, the U.S. Supreme Court was obliged to remind the Court of Appeals that its authority no longer extended so far.[45] (Indeed, how many Court of Appeals judges since then have not considered it their right and duty to "alter and revise" decisions of the regulatory commissions "as may seem just"?) However, since one of every ten Radio Commission decisions was litigated in the courts, the Court of Appeals continued to wield enormous influence in broadcast regulation.

The creation of the Federal Radio Commission occasioned the D.C. Court of Appeals' first deep immersion in the field of administrative law. In just a few years, it rendered a number of significant decisions. In *KFKB Broadcasting Association v. FRC*, the Court affirmed the Radio Commission's refusal to renew the station license of a physician of dubious repute who diagnosed and treated over the air, and in a later case affirmed the Commission's decision not to renew a license where the owner was using the station for anti-Semitic and anti-Catholic attacks and to accuse judges of sundry immoral acts.[46]

The Teapot Dome Scandals

The cases which commanded the most public attention in all the years covered by this chapter were those that grew out of the Teapot Dome scandals. The scandals erupted in an administration headed by a man of "unaffected good nature," but unable "to distinguish between honesty and rascality." In two years and five months, the administration of Warren G. Harding was, as Frederick Lewis Allen put it in his history of the 1920s, responsible "for more concentrated robbery and rascality than any other in the whole history of the Federal Government."

"Teapot Dome," like "Watergate," is an umbrella term for a congeries of scandals, but the primary tempest involved the leasing of U.S. petroleum reserves in California and Wyoming by Secretary of the Interior Albert B. Fall to Edward L. Doheny, head of Pan American Petroleum, and Harry Sinclair, head of the Mammoth Oil Company. Fall accepted $100,000 from Doheny and $260,000 from Sinclair.

---

45. *FRC v. Nelson Bros. Bond & Mortgage Co.*, 289 U.S. 266 (1933), reversing 62 F.2d 854 (1932). See Act of July 1, 1930, 41 Stat. 844.

46. *KFKB Broadcasting Association v. FRC*, 47 F.2d 670 (1931) (*CRobb*-Mar-Van); *Trinity Methodist Church, South v. FRC*, 62 F.2d 850 (1932) (*Gro*-Mar-CRobb-Hitz-Van(c)).

After Harding's death, a congressional investigation led to the appointment of special prosecutors Owen J. Roberts and Atlee Pomerene. Their
work resulted in a total of eight trials in the D.C. Supreme Court between
1926 and 1930, including prosecutions for conspiracy to defraud the U.S.
government, contempt of the Senate, contempt of court, perjury, accepting
a bribe, and giving a bribe. The trials were presided over by Justices Thomas
J. Bailey, William Hitz, Adolph A. Hoehling, and Frederick L. Siddons. Sinclair was acquitted of the charges related to the bribery, but convicted of
contempt of the Senate and contempt of court (for having his jury shad-
owed). In two trials, Doheny was also acquitted. Fall, brought daily into the
courtroom in a wheelchair and shrouded in blankets because he suppos-
edly was dying, was convicted before Justice Hitz of accepting the bribe that
Doheny was acquitted of giving. The Court of Appeals affirmed on April 6,
1931, in an opinion by Justice Van Orsdel. Fall, the first cabinet officer ever
convicted of a felony and imprisoned, was sentenced by Hitz to one year in
prison and a fine of $100,000.[47]

⁓

The Court of Appeals' first four decades ended as they had begun, in a time
of great economic depression. Now, however, the nation was looking to
Washington for assistance far more than it had in 1893. In the spring of
1932 some 60,000 men and women, most of them unemployed and desti-
tute, descended on Washington. They came to demonstrate on behalf of a
bill before Congress calling for immediate payment of a bonus that World
War I veterans were due to receive in 1945. The marchers camped on mud
flats across the Anacostia and squatted in buildings scheduled for demoli-
tion along Pennsylvania Avenue.

Tension mounted after Congress killed the bonus bill and the government was pressed by contractors who wanted the squatters evacuated from
the condemned buildings. Finally, after a fight ended in bloodshed on July
28, President Hoover gave the order to the United States Army to end the
demonstration. The commanding general, Douglas MacArthur, resplendent
in jodhpurs with all his medals, rode down Pennsylvania Avenue on a white
horse, accompanied by his aide, Dwight D. Eisenhower. They were followed
by cavalry (commanded by George S. Patton) with sabers drawn, infantry
with bayonets fixed, and six whippet tanks. Ignoring President Hoover's

---

47. *Fall v. United States*, 49 F.2d 506 (1931) (*Van-CRobb-Gro*). See also *United States
v. Fall*, 10 F.2d 648 (1925) (*Mar-CRobb-Van*); *United States v. Doheny*, 10 F.2d 651 (1925)
(*Mar-CRobb-Van*).

order "to use all humanity," the troops gassed the marchers and burned the Anacostia camp. Hoover sat in Lincoln's office as the red glare spread in the sky to the east.

A few months later, Hoover would be unseated by an electorate that was both angry and afraid. The era of dominant laissez-faire capitalism would soon be over, and a new administration with a new agenda would sweep into office. It would appoint judges with a quite different philosophy from their predecessors.

Chapter 4

The New Deal and Wartime

F.D.R.'s Court, 1933–45

Washington's weather was clouded and cheerless on March 4, 1933, for the inauguration of the new President of the United States. Speaking into the mist and wind, Franklin Roosevelt declared, "This nation asks for action, and action now." If Congress failed to enact a program to fight the Depression, he announced, he would ask for "broad executive power to wage a war against the emergency, as great as the power that would be given to me if we were in fact invaded by a foreign foe."

Thus began a presidency which would transform the United States and many of its institutions. Among these would be the federal courts of the District of Columbia, especially the Court of Appeals. That court would be a beneficiary of the enormously enhanced role and power of the federal government produced by the New Deal. Further, by the seven appointments he made in less than eight years to the Court of Appeals, Roosevelt believed he had secured a court worthy of its enhanced jurisdiction. With the possible exceptions of Lincoln and Cleveland, both of whom constituted new courts with judges whose tenure was long, no President has ever made as great an impact on the courts of the District of Columbia.

Roosevelt took office at the worst moment of the greatest economic catastrophe in American history. Fifteen million people were unemployed. Stock prices were one-quarter of what they had been in 1929 and industrial output had been almost halved. 5,504 banks had closed since 1930. The New Deal was not by any means completely successful at putting people back to work and revitalizing the economy, but it restored hope and staved off political extremism. The banking system was reformed, and federal agencies fostered industrial self-regulation and regulated the sale of securities. The government created millions of jobs, most of them in public works. The government also took the side of organized labor, instituting a national minimum wage and maximum work week and establishing the right to union membership and collective bargaining.

As the power of the federal government grew, so did its size. New independent regulatory commissions were established, along with many new agencies in the executive branch. Increasingly centralized governance meant more and more attorneys working in Washington, both within the federal government and for clients dealing with the government. A large and distinguished administrative law bar developed.

Although hard hit during the early years of the Depression, Washington was not as severely affected as other cities, thanks to the growth of the federal government. While the District's population grew by about one-third during the 1930s—from 487,000 to 663,000—the number of federal employees more than doubled, from about 70,000 when Roosevelt became President to 166,000 by the spring of 1940. Once the war began, that rate accelerated dramatically; by 1942 there were 276,000 civilian federal employees in Washington. In addition, during the New Deal every major industry sent representatives to help frame the codes regulating them, the largest labor unions set up national headquarters in the District, and the number of newspaper correspondents grew appreciably. Under the pressure of its new population, the Washington metropolitan area began spreading beyond the limits of the District.

Like the rest of the country, Washington benefitted from the public-works programs of the New Deal. Trees were planted on the Mall, public buildings were air-conditioned, the National Zoo was improved. During the 1930s Pennsylvania Avenue was cleared of its gas stations, rooming houses, and tattoo parlors. They were replaced by government buildings: large, buff-colored limestone structures with tile roofs. By 1940, the Mall was clear—there was an uninterrupted view from the Capitol to the Lincoln Memorial.

Change was less apparent in two areas: local governance and race relations. F.D.R. was not sympathetic to home rule and appointed unusually inept commissioners. The bright young New Dealers generally "looked upon the city as theirs to use but not to bother about." Nor did Roosevelt openly embrace the cause of racial equality, even though many close to him—not the least of whom was his wife, Eleanor—were forthright in their desire for progress in race relations. Dependent at first upon southern Democrats for passage of his social legislation, and later reluctant to disrupt wartime unity, the President himself rarely spoke out on racial issues.

One-third of Washington's new residents between 1930 and 1940 were black, but few joined the exodus to the suburbs. Most of the District's

African-Americans remained in poverty. Washington's schools were segregated, as were most of the restaurants, theaters, public recreational facilities, and even government cafeterias. Of 9,717 African-Americans regularly employed by the federal government in Washington in 1938, only forty-seven held professional positions; ninety percent had custodial jobs.

Judicial Administration

During the years of the New Deal, the major courts of the District of Columbia were gradually recognized as an integral part of the federal court system. Changes in nomenclature made by Congress confirmed what had already occurred in practice. In 1927 the Supreme Court had recognized the Court of Appeals of the District of Columbia as an Article III court, similar in all respects to the other U.S. circuit courts of appeals. In 1933 the High Court recognized the complete parallel between the two D.C. courts and the circuit courts of appeals and U.S. district courts.[1]

In 1934 Congress changed the name Court of Appeals of the District of Columbia to United States Court of Appeals for the District of Columbia. Two years later the Supreme Court of the District of Columbia became the District Court of the United States for the District of Columbia. In 1937 Congress gave the District of Columbia courts representation on the Judicial Conference of the United States. In 1942 the District of Columbia was finally declared to be a judicial district and the Court of Appeals redesignated as the United States Court of Appeals for the District of Columbia Circuit. The final step was taken in 1948 with the enactment of the Judicial Code (volume 28 of the U.S. Code), when the District Court became known as the United States District Court for the District of Columbia. At the same time, the members of the bench on both courts, who had hitherto been called "justices," were denominated "judges."[2]

---

1. *FTC v. Klesner*, 274 U.S. 145 (1927); *O'Donoghue v. United States*, 289 U.S. 516 (1933). The latter decision resulted from a suit brought by Justices Daniel W. O'Donoghue of the D.C. Supreme Court and William Hitz of the Court of Appeals, challenging the reduction of their salaries and those of other federal officials as part of the government's cost-cutting measures. The Supreme Court held that the D.C. Supreme Court and the Court of Appeals were "constitutional courts" protected by Article III of the Constitution, which contains a prohibition against reducing the salaries of federal judges.

2. Act of June 7, 1934, 48 Stat. 926; Act of June 25, 1936, 49 Stat. 1921; Act of July 5, 1937, 50 Stat. 473; Act of December 29, 1942, 56 Stat. 1094; Act of June 25, 1948, 62 Stat. 869.

But the jurisdiction of the two major courts of the District of Columbia was still unlike that of other Article III courts. The U.S. District Court had civil and criminal jurisdiction over matters that normally would be the preserve of a state court. The Court of Appeals effectively was the final appellate court for the "inferior" courts of the District. In 1938, to relieve the burden on the Court of Appeals, Congress created a sixth judgeship for the Court, and in 1942 it created the Municipal Court of Appeals for the District of Columbia, vested with appellate jurisdiction over the Municipal Court.[3] That court's jurisdiction, in turn, was broadened by consolidation with the Police Court and by the raising of its jurisdictional limit in civil cases to $3,000. Review of the Municipal Court of Appeals by the U.S. Court of Appeals was largely discretionary.

More important, however, than the changes in nomenclature and the modifications in the local court system was the growth of the "national" caseload of the Court of Appeals. During this period the Court repeatedly passed upon questions of national importance and its work became both richer and more influential. Several factors contributed to this growth: the burgeoning administrative law bar in Washington, the District Court's enhanced mandamus and equity jurisdiction, the increased reach of the federal government, and statutes granting the Court of Appeals unique jurisdiction, especially over certain orders of the Federal Communications Commission.

Review of the work of the independent regulatory commissions became an important staple of the work of the Court of Appeals for the District of Columbia during this period. Five new commissions were created, the jurisdiction of three others were substantially enlarged, and the work of the executive departments was enhanced. The District Court for the District of Columbia was the forum for important war-related prosecutions. Among the most important "local" cases during the F.D.R. era were racial civil rights cases dealing with jobs and housing. On the whole, the lower courts of the District of Columbia were not friendly to those civil rights claims; however, in this area the mighty dissents of Henry W. Edgerton in the Court of Appeals not only inspired attorneys seeking to end judicial enforcement

---

In 1943, beginning with volume 75, citation to the reports of the cases of the Court of Appeals was changed from App. D.C. to U.S. App. D.C. Publication of the opinions of the Court of Appeals in the Federal Reporter had begun in 1920, commencing with 258 F. (49 App. D.C.).

3. Act of May 31, 1938, 52 Stat. 584; Act of April 1, 1942, 56 Stat. 190.

of racially restrictive covenants but greatly influenced courts elsewhere in the country.

The Court of Appeals

On March 4, 1933, the Court of Appeals was composed of five justices. Two, Charles H. Robb and Josiah A. Van Orsdel, appointed by Theodore Roosevelt, had been sitting for twenty-five years and their tenure was coming to a close. That was true as well of the seventy-five-year-old Chief Justice, George Ewing Martin, although he had been on the Court of Appeals less than a decade. William Hitz and Duncan Lawrence Groner, both appointed by Herbert Hoover in 1930, were younger men of about sixty. By 1938, all but Groner were gone. In just two and a half years, beginning with Hitz's departure in 1935, Roosevelt completely reconstituted the Court of Appeals for the District of Columbia, making five new appointments (which included the filling of the newly created sixth judgeship) and elevating Groner to the Chief Justiceship.

Confronted by a judiciary largely hostile to his programs, Roosevelt aimed to make his appointments count. The seven judges he appointed between 1935 and 1943 were perhaps the most talented group of men appointed by any President to the Court of Appeals for the District of Columbia. All were staunch New Dealers, although in jurisprudence only three — Wiley Rutledge, Thurman Arnold, and Edgerton — were "modern" judicial thinkers of the kind F.D.R. preferred: unbound by formulae and willing to modify the law to suit the conditions and meet the challenges of the time. However, Roosevelt's impact on this court was limited by the short tenures of a majority of his appointees. Three would last five years or less, another only eight. Only one — Henry W. Edgerton — would exercise considerable influence over the long-run course of the Court.

Groner

Duncan Lawrence Groner was a Virginian, born in Norfolk in 1873 to a family of judges. His maternal grandfather, John Archibald Campbell, and his cousin Lucius Quintus Cincinnatus Lamar, had been justices of the U.S. Supreme Court. Groner practiced law in Norfolk from 1894 to 1921, serving as U.S. Attorney from 1910 to 1913. In 1921 he was appointed to the Eastern District of Virginia, where he occasionally sat with the U.S. Court of Appeals for the Fourth Circuit. Appointed Chief Justice of the Court of Appeals for the District of Columbia on December 7, 1937, Groner served until his retirement in 1948. He died in 1957.

Groner contributed some fine work to the administrative law jurisprudence of the D.C. Circuit. He was an "obedient judge"—if not quite as obedient as Learned Hand—deferential to Congress and to the Supreme Court, and supportive of, though not always captivated by, the work of the administrative agencies. That supportiveness can be seen in cases such as *Miles Laboratories v. FTC*, in which the Court refused to grant a declaratory judgment as to the limits of the Federal Trade Commission's power (in dictating the labeling and advertising of medications) prior to the Commission issuing a complaint. "Even in a case in which it is made to appear that a public hearing will result in irreparable injury," Groner wrote, for a federal court "to assume the right to suspend the Commission's investigation while it determines controversial questions of law or fact, would be a clear assumption of power it does not possess."[4]

Stephens

Roosevelt's first appointee to the Court of Appeals was a conservative New Dealer who had represented the United States in the U.S. Supreme Court in several of the early constitutional tests of New Deal legislation (without notable success). Harold Montelle Stephens was born in Crete, Nebraska, in 1886, and began his law practice in Salt Lake City, where, at the age of thirty-one, he became a judge of the Utah District Court for the Third Judicial District. After four years on the bench, he returned to private practice until, in 1933, he was appointed Assistant Attorney General of the United States. In 1935 he became Administrative Assistant to the Attorney General. Later the same year, on July 27, Stephens was appointed to the Court of Appeals—only the second Catholic to sit on the Court. He served until his death in 1955, the last seven years as Chief Judge.

Stephens was one of the more conservative Court of Appeals judges appointed by Roosevelt. Judge Louis Pollak has characterized him as "a judge of adamantine and literalist principle." Certainly, his approach to the law was considerably more formalistic and less dynamic than that of most of Roosevelt's other appointees to the Court of Appeals. At his best, Stephens was capable of quite fine work. His opinion in *Saginaw Broadcasting v. FCC* was a primer for the Federal Communications Commission on the findings of fact which had to accompany the Commission's decisions on construction permits.[5]

---

4. 140 F.2d 683 (1944) (*Gro*-Edg-Arn).

5. 96 F.2d 554 (1938) (*Ste*-Gro-JMil) See also Stephens' dissent in *Laughlin v. Eicher*, 145 F.2d 700 (1944) (*Edg*-JMil-Arn/*Ste*-Gro).

Stephens also made a major contribution to federal judicial administration, not least in his self-appointed role as a "lobbyist" for the judiciary on Capitol Hill. Stephens worked continuously with the members of the Judiciary Committee—even rewriting the reports of congressional committees—on such matters as omnibus judgeship bills and judicial salaries. He also taught other judges how to lobby Congress, insisting that senators and representatives could not be expected to take an interest in judicial legislation if the judges did not.[6]

Miller

Robert Justin Miller replaced Josiah Van Orsdel on the Court of Appeals in 1937. Miller's career bespeaks a desire not to stay in any one position or place for very long. Born in Crescent City, California, in 1888 and educated in that state, Miller was admitted to the bars of Montana, California, and Minnesota. Between 1921 and 1935 he was successively professor of law at the universities of Oregon, Minnesota, and California and at Columbia, then dean of U.S.C. and Duke law schools. From 1934, while still at Duke, to 1937, Miller was first Special Assistant to the Attorney General and then a member of the Board of Tax Appeals. During this period he was also president of the Federal Bar (1935–36).

Justin Miller was appointed to the Court of Appeals on August 23, 1937, and remained until September 1945. Probably as the result of the shortness of his tenure, he did not leave a substantial imprint on the jurisprudence of the D.C. Circuit. After resigning from the Court, he was president of the National Association of Broadcasters and chairman of the board and general counsel of the National Association of Radio and TV Broadcasters, in addition to being active in numerous other organizations. Miller died in 1982.

Vinson

On December 15, 1937, President Roosevelt made two significant appointments to the Court of Appeals: Frederick M. Vinson, to replace the retiring Charles Robb, and Henry W. Edgerton, to fill the seat left vacant by Groner's elevation. Vinson would serve only five years before leaving for a grander stage. Edgerton, however, would remain on the Court for thirty-three years

---

6. At another point, however, Stephens remarked, rather disingenuously, "The courts have no lobby. They cannot exert pressure on Congress." Stephens also served, from 1943–46, as American chairman of the Joint Committee on Interchange of Patent Rights and Information with Great Britain, for which he was given the Presidential Medal for Merit.

and deserves recognition as one of the great judges in the history of the
D.C. Circuit.

Frederick Moore Vinson was born in Louisa, Kentucky, in 1890. He
served in the House of Representatives from 1923 to 1938, with a one-term
interruption after losing reelection in 1928. Vinson was a calm, friendly, so-
ciable man with the ability to conciliate conflicting views and clashing personalities. His flexibility, pragmatism, and ability to comprehend a multi-
faceted argument and tinker a compromise must have been welcome traits
on an appellate bench.

Despite his brief tenure on the Court of Appeals, Vinson participated in
450 decisions and wrote 128 majority and only six dissenting opinions. For
the most part, these opinions are bland. Lacking the gift of an Arnold or a
Bazelon of finding great issues within seemingly mundane cases, without the
prescience and soul of Edgerton, the compassion and legal dynamism of Rutledge, the flinty integrity and wit of Groner, Vinson was not a major judge.
Yet if Vinson's judicial career, whether on the Court of Appeals or the Supreme
Court, was not of the highest order, his record of public service at very high
levels in all three branches of government was remarkable, as was the trust
this unassuming man could inspire in some of the greatest men of his time.

Edgerton

By contrast, Henry W. Edgerton, judge of the U.S. Court of Appeals from
1938 to 1972, was one of the most influential lower federal court judges of
this century. In a series of dissents in the 1940s and after, Edgerton helped
pave the way for landmark Supreme Court decisions fostering racial equality and protecting civil liberties. Within the Court of Appeals, Edgerton's
intellectual impact on David Bazelon was significant and the influence of
his moral and practical support of Bazelon was profound.

Edgerton, born in Rush Center, Kansas, in 1888, was descended on both
sides from Governor William Bradford of the Plymouth Colony. His father
was an economist with the U.S. Industrial Commission and the Federal
Trade Commission. Edgerton practiced law and served on the staff of the
newly created Legislative Reference Division of the Library of Congress,
then taught law at George Washington, the University of Chicago, and Cornell. A distinguished scholar, Edgerton made important contributions to
the fields of torts and constitutional law. He spent 1934–35 as special assistant to the Attorney General in the Antitrust Division. He was commissioned on December 15, 1937, but completed the academic semester at Cornell and did not take the judicial oath until February 1, 1938. He served on
the Court of Appeals until his death in 1970.

In an article honoring Judge Cuthbert W. Pound, published three years before he was appointed to the bench, Edgerton described the characteristics that would apply to his own judicial career: tolerance of change and its advocates, respect for legislative acts, willingness to modify the rules to suit the conditions of the times, and, when weighing conflicting social interests, to give a little more weight than the orthodox judge to the "unprivileged minority"—married women, working men, foreigners, radicals, criminals, and the unconventional.

Very early in his career, Edgerton began to discover and grapple with issues that would pervade the work of the Court of Appeals one and two generations later. He also revealed an innate sympathy for the underdog—a sensibility that from his time on would be an important, if highly controversial, characteristic of the Court of Appeals. The 1940 case *Johnson v. United States* offers an example. William F. Johnson, a black foreman, had been convicted and sentenced to death for shooting the foreman who had discharged him from his job. Though he pleaded self-defense, Johnson was unable to call a corroborative witness. There was such a witness, though, who had testified at the inquest and whom the government had later tried unsuccessfully to locate. The witness was subsequently found, and the defendant moved for a new trial, but the government opposed the motion, arguing that with due diligence the witness could have been located by the defense for the trial. The motion was denied.

Edgerton, writing for the Court of Appeals, overruled the denial of a new trial. The defendant's court-appointed counsel had neither examined the transcript of the inquest nor filed a timely appeal in the Court of Appeals. Only for the appeal had the trial judge appointed experienced defense counsel. Edgerton wrote, "It would be a strange system of law which first assigned inexperienced or negligent counsel in a capital case and then made counsel's neglect a ground for refusing the new trial."[7]

Rutledge

Similar sensibilities are evident in the work of Roosevelt's next appointee, Wiley Blount Rutledge, who would be the first justice from the District of Columbia Circuit to be elevated to the Supreme Court of the United States. Though his tenure on both courts was short, Rutledge left a substantial jurisprudential legacy (especially on the Supreme Court) and unusually warm personal memories among those he worked with.

---

7. 110 F.2d 562 (1940) (*Edg*-Gro-Rut).

Rutledge was born in Cloverport, Kentucky, in 1894, the son of a Baptist minister. Like Edgerton, Rutledge's career prior to judicial appointment was primarily that of an academic. He taught at the University of Colorado, at Washington University, where he became dean, and at the University of Iowa Law School, where he also was dean. He was one of the only law-school deans willing to testify on behalf of Roosevelt's court-packing plan—a position that greatly contributed to his appointment to the newly created sixth judgeship on the D.C. Court of Appeals.

His work on the Court was painstaking and demonstrated careful use of, but not reverence for, precedent. Like Edgerton and Arnold—as well as Jerome Frank and Charles Clark on the Second Circuit—Rutledge was a legal realist who distrusted labels and who looked past form to function. A good example is his opinion in *McKenna v. Austin*, which weighed "the character as well as the effect" of a legal agreement. A similar impatience with "verbalism" can be seen in *Cotonificio Bustese, S.A. v. Morgenthau*, where a dispute over whether an exaction on raw silk was a "duty" or a "penalty" was resolved in favor of common sense rather than details of nomenclature.[8] In questions of administrative law, Rutledge was generally friendly to the government.

Rutledge was known as a civil libertarian as well as a craftsman. John Paul Stevens called him a man with "an amazing conscience." The most celebrated civil liberties case Rutledge participated in on the D.C. Circuit involved Jehovah's Witnesses who were arrested for selling their newspaper, the *Watchtower*, on the street without a license. Their aim was clearly proselytizing, not profit: they were selling it for a nickel. An Appeals Court majority affirmed the conviction, but Rutledge disagreed. The state cannot, he said, charge for the use of the streets for the interchange of thought. "Taxed speech," he said, "is not free speech. It is silence for persons unable to pay the tax.... This is no time," he said—and Rutledge was writing in 1942—"to wear away further the freedom of conscience and mind by nicely technical or doubtful construction. Everywhere they are fighting for their life."[9]

Arnold

For just twenty-eight months, the Court of Appeals enjoyed the imaginative intelligence and rapier wit of Thurman Arnold. His sixty-five opinions give every indication that had his tenure been longer, he would have made

---

8. *McKenna v. Austin*, 134 F.2d 659, 662 (1943) (*Rut-Vin/Ste*); *Cotonificio Bustese, S.A. v. Morgenthau*, 121 F.2d 884 (1941) (*Rut-Vin-Gro*).

9. *Busey v. District of Columbia*, 129 F.2d 24 (1942) (*Edg-Gro/Rut*).

a judicial career comparable in brilliance to Jerome Frank's on the Second Circuit. But he was not happy on the bench. He seems to have disliked the absolutism and objectivism involved in pronouncing judgment; he felt constricted by precedents and stifled from speaking out on political issues.

Born in Laramie, Wyoming, in 1891, Arnold was educated in the East and practiced law briefly in Chicago before serving in France during the First World War. Arnold had at least five distinguished careers: as a lawyer and politician in the intermountain West; as a legal scholar (he taught at Yale Law School and was dean of West Virginia Law School); as an Assistant Attorney General in charge of the Antitrust Division; as a judge; and again at the bar as the progenitor of one of Washington's great law firms.

While he was on the Yale faculty, Arnold was spending his summers in Washington, where he worked for Jerome Frank on the lawsuit involving the constitutionality of the Agricultural Adjustment Administration, then as a trial examiner with the Securities and Exchange Commission. A principal advocate of Roosevelt's court-packing plan, Arnold, the most outspoken critic of antitrust enforcement in the country, was appointed Assistant Attorney General in charge of the Antitrust Division. During his five-year tenure, the antitrust laws were enforced with vigor.

Taking his seat on the Court of Appeals on March 16, 1943, Arnold served until his resignation in 1945. Not one of his sixty-five opinions is longer than ten pages. At a ceremony in 1991 honoring the centennial of his birth, Patricia Wald praised the quality of his work, which included "ten intricate, exquisitely reasoned patent opinions, most harking back to the theme that large corporate enterprises must not be allowed through proliferating patents to monopolize development in burgeoning scientific fields." His work in cases involving divorce and child custody, abortion, and the death penalty was "compassionate, precise [and] disdainful of legal abstractions that ignored human realities." He also produced a series of opinions on the problems of proving and disproving insanity (discussed in chapter six), which "were a primer and a preview" for the concerns of the Court of Appeals under David Bazelon.

Administrative Law

During the period 1933–45, when the federal government moved from a limited role in domestic matters to manager of the economy and redistributor of wealth, review of the work of the independent regulatory commissions became one of the most important staples of the U.S. Court of

Appeals—perhaps the most important. Because of this work and the way in which it was done, the reputation of the Court began to grow. During the New Deal, five of the eight major regulatory commissions were created—the Securities and Exchange Commission, the Federal Communications Commission, the National Labor Relations Board, the Federal Maritime Commission, and the Civil Aeronautics Board—four of them in the brief period 1934–36.[10] In addition, the jurisdiction of the three existing regulatory agencies—the Federal Power Commission, the Federal Trade Commission, and the Interstate Commerce Commission—was substantially enlarged.

With these developments, administrative law began to be an important area of American law. The Court of Appeals for the District of Columbia would be one of the major contributors to its growth and, in time, would become the chief administrative law court in the country. From the time of F.D.R. to Ronald Reagan, the most significant regulatory commission cases handled by the Court of Appeals came from the FCC, of which the Court was the major overseer, the FPC, and the CAB. The court's long-term impact on the other regulatory commissions, while not insubstantial, was not much greater than that of some of the other circuits.

The shaping of administrative law in the 1930s occurred during a time of economic crisis, wholesale governmental experimentation, and confrontation between the judiciary and the White House. As they had earlier with the ICC and FTC, the regulated industries repeatedly sought to block regulation by resort to the judiciary. The new agencies (including the many executive branch agencies) were bitterly attacked for lawless discretion, unconstitutional combination of prosecutorial and adjudicatory functions, one-sided fact-finding, and lax rules of evidence. The organized bar was generally hostile to the agencies.

In the early years of the New Deal, federal courts invalidated many of the enabling statutes, narrowly construed the powers of the agencies, and closely scrutinized the procedures employed in particular cases. When the dust settled, the effect of judicial review had been to render agency decision making more regularized, generalized, visible, and subject to judicial

---

10. The SEC was created by the Securities and Exchange Act of 1934, 48 Stat. 881; the FCC by the Communications Act of June 19, 1934, 48 Stat, 106; the NLRB by the Wagner-Connery Labor Relations Act of 1935, 49 Stat. 449; the Maritime Commission by the Merchant Marine Act of 1936, 49 Stat. 1985; and the CAB in 1940 as the result of a presidential reorganization plan aimed at achieving the regulatory and promotional objectives of the Civil Aeronautics Act of 1938.

scrutiny and control; but it also made it more cumbersome. Concerted efforts to deal on a government-wide basis with the problems that plagued the agencies, beginning in 1938, culminated in the Administrative Procedure Act of 1946 (see chapter five), which would achieve some uniformity of procedure and some assurance of the application of fairer standards.

During the Roosevelt administration, the influence of the Court of Appeals for the District of Columbia in shaping administrative law was not as great as it would become later. The Supreme Court acted to resolve some of the more urgent problems, the contribution of the Fifth Circuit to the development of administrative law was as significant as that of the D.C. Circuit, and that of the Second Circuit was more significant. Nevertheless, the Court made a lasting imprint on the development of the law regarding such issues as standing before the agency and in the federal courts; the meaning of the requirement of findings of fact; when and whether there could be judicial review of commission orders while an investigation was proceeding; and the amount of discretion to be given by the courts to an agency's choice of procedures. Although arising from disputes concerning particular agencies, these decisions often had bearing on the rules, policies, and procedures of all the administrative agencies. Unlike the courts of some other circuits, the D.C. Court of Appeals was rarely hostile to the agencies, and sometimes friendly; however, it generally kept a tight hand on the reins.

The Federal Communications Commission

Of the eight major regulatory Commissions, the Federal Communications Commission was by far the one most influenced by the D.C. Court of Appeals, because of the Court's virtually exclusive jurisdiction over it. The Communications Act of 1934[11] abolished the Federal Radio Commission and established a permanent Federal Communications Commission to regulate all interstate and foreign communications by wire and radio, including telephone, telegraph, and broadcasting. Under the statute, the U.S. Court of Appeals for the District of Columbia was given jurisdiction over most of the appeals. Over the years, the Court's involvement with the FCC has been so great that it has been called "the upper house of the FCC."

Several cases coming to the Court from the FCC dealt with the right of someone harmed, or likely to be harmed, by commission action, to be heard

---

11. 48 Stat. 106.

by the Commission or to appeal to the federal courts. One of the most important was *Sanders Bros. Radio Station v. FCC.* Though ultimately decided by the Supreme Court on different grounds from those applied by the Court of Appeals, the case illustrates that court's interest in preserving competition on the airwaves. In *Sanders*, the plaintiff was not an applicant for broadcast license, but a competing radio station that claimed potential financial injury from the licensing of a new station. The Court of Appeals granted standing to the plaintiff, holding that Sanders Brothers had sufficient interest to contest the grant of a license and, on the merits, ruled that when the FCC passed on the application, it ought to have made findings of fact as to the potential injury to possible competitors. The Supreme Court agreed, but on a different theory. While the FCC was not required to take into account the possible resulting economic injury to a rival station in such a case, the High Court held, the statute provided an explicit right to judicial review to any person aggrieved or adversely affected by such an order. Thus, even if Sanders could not, on the merits, argue that the grant of the license impermissibly caused it economic harm, it could use that fact as a basis for standing. On the merits, it could then argue that the FCC action was unlawful on some other basis.[12]

The Court of Appeals decision in *Saginaw Broadcasting Co. v. FCC* continues to be influential on the subject of the obligation of the agencies to issue findings of fact to accompany their decisions. Such findings must, the Court held, be more than mere conclusions framed in statutory language (the "ultimate facts"), but must also include the basic or underlying facts from which the ultimate facts were inferred. In his opinion, Justice Stephens wrote that "a reviewing court cannot properly exercise its function upon findings of ultimate facts alone, but must require also findings of the basic facts which represent the determination of the administrative body as to the meaning of the evidence, and from which the ultimate facts flow."[13]

Other Administrative Law

Several of the Court's most important decisions involved the reviewability of commission action. In *American Sumatra Tobacco Corp. v. SEC,* for example, several large corporations, including General Mills and Bulova Watch, sought judicial review of the Securities and Exchange Commission's refusal of their request to keep secret certain information supplied with their applications for registration of their securities. Although the SEC contended

---

12. 106 F.2d 321 (1939) (*JMil*-Gro-Vin), rev'd on other grounds, 309 U.S. 470 (1940).

13. 96 F.2d 554 (1938) (*Ste*-Gro-JMil).

that only commission orders made after notice, hearing, and fact finding were reviewable, the Court of Appeals held that the orders were reviewable.[14]

Another case turning on the issue of reviewability involved the National Labor Relations Board. While lacking widespread implications for other regulatory agencies, *American Federation of Labor v. NLRB* had national political significance. The case derived from a bitter dispute between the AFL and the CIO as to which union would represent all of the longshoremen working for the members of employers' associations at West Coast ports. When the NLRB certified the union as affiliated with the CIO, the AFL appealed to the D.C. Court of Appeals to set the certification aside. The court unenthusiastically threw out the appeal, basing its decision on Supreme Court precedent (Chief Justice Groner, writing for the Court, criticized the High Court for its formalism). While orders restraining unfair labor practices were appealable, the Court held, the National Labor Relations Act did not provide review of a certification decision. Unsurprisingly, the Supreme Court affirmed.[15]

During these years, the Court of Appeals rendered several important decisions dealing with the administrative authority of executive branch officials. In *Glass v. Ickes* the issue was the immunity of a cabinet secretary from suit (the Secretary of the Interior had used a press release to personally criticize a former employee). The Court of Appeals held that the Secretary was absolutely privileged from liability for alleged defamatory statements made in connection with general matters committed by law to his control or supervision.[16] In *Cotonificio Bustese, S.A. v. Morgenthau*, the Court found that where an administrator erroneously held that he was without power to consider a claim, mandamus could generally be used as a remedy.[17]

During this period, the most stinging rebuke the Supreme Court gave the Court of Appeals in the administrative law area occurred in *Perkins v. Lukens Steel Co.* The case involved the Public Contracts Act (Davis-Bacon Act), which assures those employed by government contractors that they will receive at the least the minimum wage prevailing in their "locality" — an area to be defined by the Secretary of Labor. In *Perkins*, the Secretary had defined the locality as stretching from Maine to Kentucky. The Court of Appeals (Justices Miller and Vinson, with Justice Edgerton dissenting) held that this was "an attempt arbitrarily to disregard the statutory man-

14. 93 F.2d 236 (1937) (*Gro-Mar-CRobb-Ste*).

15. *American Federation of Labor v. NLRB*, 103 F.2d 933 (1939) (*Gro-JMil-Vin*), aff'd, 401 U.S. 300 (1940).

16. 117 F.2d 273 (1940) (*Vin-Gro*(c)-Edg).

17. 121 F.2d 884 (1941) (*Rut-Gro-Vin*).

date." The Court issued a very broad injunction which had the effect of suspending the Act for more than a year. In the Supreme Court, an irate Justice Hugo Black criticized the Court of Appeals for the sweep of the injunction, which went, he said,

> beyond any controversy that might have existed between the complaining companies and the government officials.... The case before us makes it fitting to remember that "the interference of the courts with the performance of the ordinary duties of the executive departments of the government would be productive of nothing but mischief."[18]

Civil Rights

In the arena of race relations, the courts of the District generally supported the status quo during this period, with the conspicuous exception of Justice Edgerton. Nowhere was this more evident than in the contentious matter of racially restricted housing covenants. Despite the defeat in *Corrigan v. Buckley* in the 1920s (see chapter three), the battle against restrictive covenants continued in the District and elsewhere. As the white exodus to the suburbs swelled, Washington property owners, real-estate dealers, builders, and banks stood fast against selling or renting to blacks in most sections of the city. In most cases, the federal courts in Washington continued to enforce restrictive covenants. In the 1937 decision in *Grady v. Garland*, the Appeals Court held that, even when other neighboring properties were occupied by blacks, such covenants "constitute valid and solemn contracts and should not be lightly set aside." Justice Stephens dissented, but his concern seemed to be the heavy burden on the landowner.[19]

Nevertheless, by the end of the 1930s there were signs of judicial dissatisfaction, and in 1945 a decision upholding racially restrictive covenants produced a strong and influential dissent from Edgerton. During World War II, virtually all the new housing in the District was restricted to whites. Clara Mays, an African-American government employee, had purchased a home at 2213 Cook Street, N.W. Four of her white neighbors sued to enjoin her from using the property and received an injunction, which she ignored.

---

18. *Lukens Steel Co. v. Perkins*, 107 F.2d 627 (1939) (*JMil*-Vin/*Edg*), rev'd, 310 U.S. 113 (1940). Black was quoting from Chief Justice Taney's opinion in *Decatur v. Paulding*, 14 Pet. (39 U.S.) 497 at 513, 515 (1840).
19. 89 F.2d 817 (1937) (*Van*-CRobb-Gro-Ste-Mar).

Chief Justice Groner, for the majority of the Court of Appeals, held that it was settled law in the jurisdiction that a covenant against black ownership or occupation was valid and enforceable by injunction and that "rights created by covenants such as these have been so consistently enforced by us as to become a rule of property within the accepted policy of the District of Columbia." In his dissent, Edgerton pointed out that in *Corrigan v. Buckley* the Supreme Court had *not* decided whether a racially restrictive covenant was void as against public policy. It would, he wrote, "seem to be unsound policy for a court, in the exercise of its equitable discretion, to enforce a privately adopted segregation plan which would be unconstitutional if it were adopted by a legislature."

In a one-paragraph concurring opinion, Justice Miller indicated some sympathy with Edgerton's position, but believed that at this stage it was either for Congress to change the law or for the Supreme Court to reconsider the constitutional issue. The Supreme Court refused to accept Miller's invitation, denying certiorari, although Justice Frank Murphy and the newly elevated Justice Rutledge dissented from that denial.[20]

Justice Edgerton's dissent in *Mays* gave heart to the lawyers fighting racially restrictive covenants throughout the country and stimulated interest in the problem in the capital and in law journals. His dissenting opinion two years later in *Hurd v. Hodge* would be a more complete formulation of his views, and appears to have greatly influenced both the lawyers who argued and the Supreme Court justices who, in 1948, unanimously declared judicial enforcement of racially restrictive covenants unconstitutional, in an opinion written by Chief Justice Fred Vinson.

The racially restrictive covenant cases of the mid-forties were part of a nationwide attack on the practice by civil rights lawyers. But from the standpoint of James Hurd, the defendant in the principal District of Columbia case, the litigation represented an attempt to protect the roof over his head. In 1944, knowing the property was covered by a restrictive covenant, the Hurds had bought a house on Bryant Street in the Upper Georgia Avenue neighborhood — an all-white block in a neighborhood that had become one-third black. In October 1944 suit was brought in the

---

20. *Mays v. Burgess*, 147 F.2d 869 (1945) (*Gro-JMil(c)/Edg*). Later that year *Mays* came back to the Court of Appeals. Mrs. Mays would not leave the house, because, she said, she could not find another home for her family (which now numbered nine) and because "four colored families had purchased property in the adjoining block." The Court of Appeals affirmed an order of contempt 2–1, Edgerton again dissenting. *Mays v. Burgess*, 152 F.2d 123 (1945) (*Gro-Cla/Edg*).

names of Frederick and Lena Hodge (among others), who had owned their home on Bryant Street since 1909. Mrs. Hodge would declare at trial that she would rather live next door to a white convict, "because he is white and I am white," than to a Negro family "no matter how educated or cultivated." Later, suit was also brought against the three other black families who purchased houses on the same block in 1945, and a separate action was brought against Raphael Urciolo, a white lawyer-realtor who made his living selling property in white neighborhoods to blacks.

The black families were defended by Charles H. Houston, vice-dean of Howard Law School, who also had represented Clara Mays. Houston unsuccessfully sought to have Justice F. Dickinson Letts disqualify himself because he lived in premises covered by a restrictive covenant.[21] At the trial, Houston was able to expose the racial attitudes of the plaintiffs, lay out the broad problem of housing for blacks, and probe the network of interests keeping Washington segregated. Still, he did not win. Basing his decision upon the history of Court of Appeals rulings upholding the validity of such covenants (and finding insufficient black penetration in the area to permit application of the exception the Court of Appeals had carved out), Letts enforced the covenants.

By the time *Hurd v. Hodge* came before the Court of Appeals, in November 1946, that Court had heard a total of seven cases involving racially restrictive covenants. Ten of the justices who had heard these cases had upheld the covenants; only Justices Rutledge and Edgerton had voted the other way. On May 26, 1947, the Court affirmed, Justices Clark and Wilbur Miller in the majority, Edgerton dissenting. Justice Clark wrote that the Court of Appeals was not willing "to reverse and annul" what it had previously said on the subject and thereby destroy contracts and land titles based on those earlier decisions.

Edgerton argued that the covenants were invalid under five different theories. They were void as unreasonable restraints on alienation, because their enforcement by injunction was inequitable, and because their enforcement violated the 1866 Civil Rights Act, infringed the Due Process Clause of the Constitution, and was contrary to public policy. "It is strangely inconsistent," he wrote, "to hold as this court does that although no legislature can authorize a court, even for a moment, to prevent Negroes from acquiring and using particular property, a mere owner of property at a given moment can authorize a court to do so for all time."[22]

---

21. *Hurd v. Letts*, 152 F.2d 121 (1945) (*per curiam* Gro-Edg).
22. *Hurd v. Hodge, Urciolo v. Same*, 162 F.2d 233 (1947) (*Cla-WMil/Edg*).

In June 1947 the Supreme Court granted certiorari in restrictive covenant cases coming out of Missouri and Michigan, and in October granted certiorari in the D.C. cases. Charles Houston, Phineas Indritz, and Spottswood Robinson worked on the briefs in the Washington cases, Loren Miller and Thurgood Marshall in the state cases. The 149-page brief in the Washington case admitted its debt to Edgerton's dissent. Eighteen *amicus* briefs were filed in support of the civil rights claimants, including one by the Truman administration.

The Supreme Court's decisions came down on May 3, 1948. Writing for a unanimous Court, Chief Justice Fred M. Vinson held, in the state cases, that judicial enforcement of racially restrictive covenants was state action which violated the Equal Protection clause. In *Hurd v. Hodge*, Vinson held that by enforcing the covenants the District Court had violated the 1866 Civil Rights Act, which prohibited government denial of the right to own and occupy property on account of race, and that such enforcement was at odds with the Fourteenth Amendment.[23] After this decision, the District Court for the District of Columbia would hold that the courts could not enforce any aspects of restrictive covenants.

In other areas of civil rights, as well, the D.C. courts lagged behind the Supreme Court. Perhaps the outstanding notable example of this was a 1937 case involving the New Negro Alliance, one of the nation's first and most successful grassroots protest movements for civil rights. Its campaigns against job discrimination in stores in the District employed picketing, boycotts, and other assertive tactics. When a grocery chain brought suit against the Alliance, the District Court entered a restraining order prohibiting the use of picketing, boycott, inducement, intimidation, or physical force to keep people out of the stores.

On appeal the Alliance was represented by Belford V. Lawson (whose wife, Marjorie, would be appointed Juvenile Court judge by President Kennedy) and Thurman L. Dodson. William H. Hastie, Thurgood Marshall, and James M. Nabrit assisted the legal effort. The Alliance contended that what was at issue was a labor dispute and that Congress, in the Norris-La-Guardia Act, had prohibited the federal courts from restraining peaceful picketing in labor disputes. The unanimous Court of Appeals, all five justices sitting (the only F.D.R. appointee then on the Court was Stephens), held that the controversy was not a labor dispute within the statute, but a

---

23. *Shelley v. Kramer*, 334 U.S. 1 (1948), *Hurd v. Hodge*, 334 U.S. 24 (1948). Only six justices heard the cases, as Justices Reed, Jackson, and Rutledge recused themselves.

racial dispute and an interference with the company's right to choose its employees and conduct its business as it chose.[24]

The Supreme Court reversed, holding that the matter *was* a labor dispute within the Norris-LaGuardia Act.[25] The decision not only gave African-Americans an effective method for fighting discriminatory hiring practices, it also aided the cause of white labor. By the time Franklin Roosevelt outlawed discriminatory policies by companies receiving defense contracts and established a Committee on Fair Employment Practices on June 25, 1941,[26] the New Negro Alliance's victories had led to the employment of some 5,000 African-Americans in Washington businesses.

Wartime Prosecutions

During and after World War II, the U.S. District Court for the District of Columbia was the seat of some of the most important prosecutions for wartime sedition and other possibly treasonous activities by enemy sympathizers. It was also a forum in which foreign nationals convicted of war crimes by international tribunals sought review by the federal courts.

Perhaps the most virulent Nazi propagandist in the United States, George Sylvester Viereck, was tried and convicted in the District Court for violation of the Foreign Agents' Registration Act. As the law required, Viereck had registered with the Secretary of State as an agent and supplemented that registration by filing every six months. He had admitted to being an agent and correspondent for several German publications, but he chose not to divulge what he viewed as his personal activities. These included financing and controlling a publishing house which produced German propaganda, as well as writing or soliciting propaganda articles which had been inserted into the Congressional Record by friendly members of Congress and mailed out by the tens of thousands under congressional frank.

Viereck was tried and convicted in 1942. The trial record is 1,700 pages long, and there were several thousand pages of exhibits. His appeal argued, as one ground for reversal, the prejudicial misconduct of the prosecution, citing as an example the conclusion of its summation: "The American

24. *New Negro Alliance v. Sanitary Grocery Co.*, 92 F.2d 510 (1937) (*Van-CRobb-Mar-Gro-Ste*(c/d)).
25. 303 U.S. 552 (1938).
26. Executive Order 8801, June 25, 1941.

people are relying upon you ladies and gentlemen, for their protection against this sort of crime, just as much as they are relying upon the protection of the men who man the guns in Bataan Peninsula.... As a representative of your government I am calling upon every one of you to do your duty."[27]

The Court of Appeals, Vinson writing, upheld the conviction. On the central legal issue, the scope of the duty to report under the Foreign Agents' Registration Act, the Court said that the government had the right "to know from all that is going on around the country that which may be subsidized by principals outside the country. The foreign purse can have a lot to do with the conviction expressed under the smoke-screen of free speech." The Supreme Court reversed. The opinion contained sharp criticism of the prosecution, but the basis for reversal was that the law should not have been interpreted to require agents to disclose activities that were not on behalf of foreign principals. Justices Black and Douglas dissented.[28] Viereck was retried and again convicted. On appeal, the convictions were affirmed.[29]

Viereck was also one of the defendants in the most politicized trial of the war, the mass trial of Nazi sympathizers known as the "great sedition trial," which had been spurred by the President and which took place in the District Court in 1944. In July 1941 the government began to present evidence concerning the activities of right-wing groups to a D.C. grand jury. That grand jury, the first of three, heard 221 witnesses (including members of Congress) in fifteen months. Three indictments were issued. The third, returned on January 3, 1944, charged the defendants under the Smith Act with conspiracy involving officials of the German government to destroy democracy in the United States and establish a fascist government by causing insubordination and disloyalty in the armed forces. Thirty defendants were charged in *United States v. McWilliams*, a veritable Who's Who of crypto-Nazis: leaders of nativist organizations like William Dudley Pelley, chief of the Silver Shirts, and former Communist Joseph E. McWilliams, whose Christian Mobilizers were given to beating up people on the streets of New York; writers and small publishers like Frederick Elmhurst and Elizabeth Dilling; propagandists like Viereck; and members of the German-American Bund. Six of the thirty defendants, including Viereck and Pelley, were already serving sentences for sedition. All but three were overt anti-Semites.

---

27. *Viereck v. United States*, 318 U.S. 236, 247–48 n.3 (1943).

28. *Viereck v. United States*, 130 F.2d 945 (1942) (*Vin*-Gro-JMil), rev'd, 318 U.S. 236 (1943).

29. *Viereck v. United States*, 139 F.2d 847 (1944) (*Dobie*(4th Cir.)-JMil-Arn).

However disloyal each of the defendants may have been, the government did not have a very strong case for its indictment—a dragnet conspiracy charge against unpopular defendants who were being punished for their unpleasant associations. The government lacked evidence of a "worldwide Nazi movement" that specifically sought to subvert the armed forces. It had no evidence that any but a handful of the defendants had direct contacts with the Third Reich or had received money from Germany. There were also problems with the alleged conspiracy: some of those indicted had never even met; there was no satisfactory proof that the defendants had been in contact with members of the armed forces; most of the accused had never expressed their opinions in the District of Columbia. However, it was possible to overcome many of these drawbacks because, if a conspiracy was found, each conspirator became responsible for the acts and deeds of the others.

The case was tried in the District Court by Chief Justice Edward Clayton Eicher. The Iowa-born, sixty-six-year-old Eicher had been appointed to the bench by Franklin D. Roosevelt after a career in practice, in Congress (1933–39), and on the Securities and Exchange Commission (1939–42). Eicher's pretrial rulings were supportive of the government. He held the charges specific enough, allowed the removal of all the defendants to Washington, and ruled that those activities of the defendants which antedated the Smith Act were relevant to demonstrate intent and the origins of the conspiracy.[30]

It was an awful case for the judge to try. For more than seven months, Eicher tried to be fair while being goaded, badgered, and bullied. An audience of friends and followers of the defendants hooted and applauded. The defense played to the jury with skeptical questions and sarcastic asides. Half a dozen counsel often sought recognition to make the same point. Relations between the prosecuting attorneys and the defense attorneys were poisonous. Defense lawyers disputed among themselves, although their clients did not; indeed, some of the defendants who had not previously met were now planning future ventures. Eicher, whose evidentiary rulings favored the government, faced hundreds of motions to disqualify himself, for directed verdicts, or to declare a mistrial. The judge levied fines against lawyer after lawyer for contempt. Following revelations that one of the lawyers had filed a petition with the House of Representatives for Eicher's impeachment, Eicher dismissed him from the case and barred him from the courtroom. The Court of Ap-

---

30. *United States v. McWilliams*, 54 F. Supp. 791 (1944).

peals, petitioned for mandamus to order Eicher to reinstate the attorney, twice divided 2–2 and finally denied it, 3–2, Stephens and Groner dissenting.[31]

During the night of November 29–30, in the eighth month of the trial, after 18,000 pages of testimony had been taken and 1,100 documents introduced—but only thirty-nine of the 100 witnesses produced—Edward Eicher died of a heart attack. "Solomon himself could not have survived the trial," one senator commented.[32]

A mistrial was declared. For nearly two years the case was on the docket with neither prosecution, defense, nor judges of the District Court anxious to see it tried. Finally, on November 22, 1946, the new Chief Justice of the District Court, Bolitha Laws, dismissed the indictments, essentially on speedy-trial grounds. The Court of Appeals affirmed the dismissal by a vote of two to one.[33] The "great sedition trial" did nothing for the reputations of any of its participants: the government, the defense lawyers, the defendants, or the trial judge. The government's reliance upon conspiracy charges and perennial witnesses and undercover agents foreshadowed their use in Cold War trials, as did the disruptive tactics of the defense attorneys.

In the years immediately after the war, the courts of the District were involved in a "mopping-up operation" connected with the loyalty of Americans during the Second World War. Contempt cases related to the "great sedition trial" were disposed of. The courts reviewed orders of deportation of enemy aliens. Several treason prosecutions were brought in the District Court against American nationals, including the poet Ezra Pound (see below) and Mildred Gillars, the infamous "Axis Sally," who had made radio broadcasts intended to lower the morale of allied troops.[34]

After the war, the District Court for the District of Columbia became an appropriate forum for review by way of habeas corpus on behalf of those convicted of war crimes by tribunals constituted under the authority of the U.S. armed forces. *Eisentrager v. Forrestal*, decided by the Court of Appeals

---

31. *Laughlin v. Eicher*, 145 F.2d 700 (1944) (*Edg*-JMil-Arn/*Ste*-Gro).

32. In the even more acrimonious trial of eleven Communist leaders in 1949, Judge Harold Medina had Eicher's fate much in mind. Medina, however, would live to be over 100 years old. Judge Medina's opinion in that trial, in the District Court for the Southern District of New York, is given at *United States v. Foster*, 9 F.R.D. 367 (S.D.N.Y. 1949).

33. *United States v. McWilliams*, 69 F. Supp. 812 (1946), aff'd, 163 F.2d 695 (1947) (*Gro*-WMil/*Edg*).

34. *Gillars v. United States*, 182 F.2d 962 (1950) (*Fahy*-Cla-WMil). In a suit brought by 159 German aliens threatened with deportation, the Court of Appeals upheld the Alien Enemy Act, passed at the same time as the Alien and Sedition Acts. *Citizens Protective League v. Clark*, 178 F.2d 703 (1949) (*Pre*-WMil-Edg).

in 1949, concerned German nationals who had been tried for war crimes in China by a U.S. military commission, then taken to Germany. The court held that habeas corpus lay to any person, including enemy aliens, arguably deprived of their liberty by officials of the United States acting under purported authority of government. Jurisdiction lay in the district court with territorial jurisdiction over those officials who possessed directive power over the immediate jailer. The Supreme Court, however, reversed, holding that enemy aliens not physically present in U.S. territory do not enjoy access to our courts.[35] While there were suggestions that the *Eisentrager* path taken by the Court of Appeals could be used by those convicted of war crimes by international tribunals that included American officials, and efforts were made to achieve this, such judicial review in the District of Columbia never occurred.[36]

Ezra Pound, one of the great poets of the twentieth century, was a creative genius marred by personality defects that included virulent anti-Semitism and an obsession with extreme political views. Living in Italy while Mussolini was in power, Pound became a fascist. During the war he made pro-fascist, anti-American radio broadcasts for the Italian government—some 300 in all—full of scurrilous vituperation.

In 1943, Pound was indicted for treason by a grand jury in the District of Columbia. Seized by partisans a few days before the war in Europe ended, Pound was eventually brought back to Washington, where he was arraigned on November 23, 1945. Pound's lawyer, Julien Cornell, developed a strategy, in concert with a network of concerned writers including Ernest Hemingway, T.S. Eliot and Robert Frost, in which Pound acquiesced. The first step in the strategy was to argue that Pound was unfit to stand trial because of mental illness. Chief Justice Bolitha J. Laws of the District Court ordered Pound transferred to Gallinger Hospital for observation. The panel of examining psychiatrists, concerned that this great man of letters might face execution, issued a diagnosis pronouncing Pound unfit for trial and in need of care in a mental hospital. At the formal sanity hearing requested by the

---

35. *Eisentrager v. Forrestal*, 174 F.2d 961 (1949) (*Pre-Pro-Edg*), rev'd sub nom. *Johnson v. Eisentrager*, 339 U.S. 763 (1950).

36. See *Flick v. Johnson*, 174 F.2d 983 (1949) (*Pro-WMil-Ste*), affirming *Ex parte Flick*, 76 F. Supp. 979 (1948) (Holtzoff) (an unsuccessful attempt by a German citizen, imprisoned in the American zone of Germany but tried by international military tribunal, to get judgment reversed by the District Court); *Nash v. MacArthur*, 184 F.2d 608 (1950) (*Fahy-Pre-Ste*) (denial of a petition to proceed *in forma pauperis* by the attorney of Japanese nationals convicted of war crimes by U.S. military commissions).

government, held on February 13, 1946, Laws charged the jury in such a way that it took only three minutes for them to concur that Pound was of "unsound mind." A highly publicized trial, and a possible death sentence, were avoided.

The second part of attorney Cornell's strategy was to have Pound declared not only incurably insane but also harmless, so that he could be released from St. Elizabeths Hospital, where he had been committed. This goal would not be realized for over a decade. At a hearing on January 29, 1947, Laws refused to go along, although he did order that Pound be transferred to more comfortable quarters. The initial diagnosis, that Pound was mentally unfit, was not confirmed by a single physician during the twelve years Pound spent in St. Elizabeths. Changes in the law governing the insanity defense that would have made Pound's conviction even more difficult, as well as changes in public opinion, finally made his release possible. Pound appeared once again before Laws on April 18, 1958, this time represented by Thurman Arnold. On the motion of the federal government, the treason indictment was nolle prossed. Pound left the hospital for good on May 6, 1958. His last fourteen years were marked by depression and even remorse. "I lost my head in the storm," he wrote.

$$\sim$$

On Thursday afternoon, April 12, 1945, the President was sitting for a portrait in Warm Springs, Georgia. Just before 2:15 p.m. he said quietly, "I have a terrific headache." His arm dropped; his body slumped; his head fell to the left. He was pronounced dead at 4:55. In Washington, the Vice President was driven without police escort down Pennsylvania Avenue through rush-hour traffic. At 7:09 p.m. Chief Justice Harlan Fiske Stone administered the oath of office to Harry Truman.

Franklin Roosevelt's impact and that of his administration would be felt directly in the courts of the District of Columbia Circuit until 1970, the year of the death of Henry W. Edgerton. The effect of the changes Roosevelt wrought in American governance continues to this day.

Chapter 5

"Questions of National Magnitude"
The Truman Years, 1945–52

For Americans, the years that followed victory in the Second World War were tortured. The United States had emerged from the war as the world's greatest power, unrivaled in its national prosperity. Americans ought to have been able to take pride in the success of their great republican experiment. Instead, their freedom and wealth seemed threatened—from without, by still another totalitarian enemy apparently seeking world domination, and from within. The excitement of victory soon gave way to strikes, political witch hunts, bitter partisan politics, and, later, to an unpopular and stalemated war in Korea.

In Harry Truman, who had inherited the presidency on the eve of victory in the war, the American people did not see another Franklin Delano Roosevelt. His lack of dignity, blunt directness, and desire to get into the fray rather than remain above it, as well as his excessive loyalty to cronies and tolerance of mediocrity and corruption, made the public suspicious of the man from Missouri. These traits also eclipsed his strengths: integrity, personal and political bravery, and, eventually, mastery of the most profound series of foreign policy challenges the nation had ever faced.

The most pressing domestic issues Truman encountered in office—civil rights, loyalty and security questions, and labor relations—were reflected in some of the most significant work of the District of Columbia Circuit in the years 1945 to 1952. In each of these areas, the President and the courts operated in an environment in which political factors and public opinion played a powerful role. In the area of racial civil rights, where progress was often more symbolic than real, the courts of the District of Columbia Circuit lagged behind both the President and the Supreme Court. In loyalty-security matters, both the D.C. courts and the High Court tended to defer to the government.

For the city of Washington, the eight years of Truman's presidency were years of enormous growth and profound change. The huge population influx that began during the war continued, and while private restoration of old homes attracted the wealthy to previously rundown neighborhoods like Georgetown and Capitol Hill, the District as a whole became increasingly black and increasingly poor, as whites continued to move out of the city. As Constance McLaughlin Green noted in her history of the capital, during this period the District was "a geographically confined, racially divided, politically impotent area threatened by economic strangulation from the uncontrolled expansion of a surrounding megalopolis."

Yet the nationwide postwar euphoria also generated great optimism that the problems of Washington and other large cities could be solved by government through metropolitan planning and urban renewal. That optimism was reflected in the District of Columbia Redevelopment Act of 1945, which envisioned a vast new highway system, additional parks and playgrounds, and the rebuilding of all of Washington's slum-ridden areas. Redevelopment was executed boldly, if not always wisely. Almost every structure within Washington's southwest quadrant was condemned and replaced by new housing (more for the rich than for the poor), as well as by parks, governmental and commercial buildings, and highways. For over a generation the federal courts of the District were the forum in which neighborhood groups fought the construction of highways and the destruction of homes.

For many former New Dealers the excitement of government service gave way to different challenges—and higher incomes. One of the foremost of these was Thurman Arnold, who was restless on the bench and convinced Abe Fortas to leave the Department of the Interior and join him in private practice. Paul Porter, former head of the Federal Communications Commission, would become their partner.

Before and during the war, the District had had a relatively intimate bar, for the most part concerned with local issues and specialized governmental matters such as public land titles, veterans' pensions, and patents. Now, as the nation returned to peacetime, the city's legal community was transformed in both size and scope. These changes came above all in response to the growing size and power of the administrative agencies. The regulatory state demanded attorneys to fertilize and coordinate it—lawyers for the government and lawyers for those affected by federal regulation. As a large administrative law bar developed in Washington, appeals from the rulings of the agencies were increasingly brought in the courts of the District of Columbia Circuit.

The most important development in judicial administration during this period was the building of a new courthouse for the Court of Appeals and the District Court. The Court of Appeals had been housed separately since

1910, but the District Court was scattered over nine different buildings. As early as 1938 a committee of the Bar Association of the District of Columbia had been formed to address the problem, but action was postponed during the war. Congress approved the acquisition of the site, on Constitution Avenue at the foot of Capitol Hill, in May 1947 and authorized construction a year later. The cornerstone was laid on June 27, 1950, in a ceremony attended by President Truman and Chief Justice Vinson. In words that presaged the great constitutional battle he would wage with the steel companies less than two years later, Truman declared, "Nowhere else, outside the Supreme Court of the United States, will so many legal questions of national magnitude be decided as in the building before us."

During these years there was growing recognition of the importance of the litigation coming before the courts of the Circuit. Indeed, in the postwar period, the Court of Appeals was hard pressed by the increase in the size and difficulty of its cases. The caseload was high for the time: 264 cases were filed in fiscal 1947 and 350 in 1948, when the per-judge caseload of fifty-eight ranked third highest among the federal circuits. The median time from docketing to disposition was nine and a half months. However relaxed such a docket seems by today's standards, it was sufficiently crowded to convince Congress, prodded by Chief Judge Harold M. Stephens, to add three judgeships in 1949.[1] Indeed, both Chief Judges during this period—Duncan Lawrence Groner (until 1948) and Harold Stephens—while relatively conservative jurisprudentially, were activists in matters of judicial administration both within and outside the circuit.[2]

The local jurisdiction of both federal courts was still an important factor in their work, with divorce, estate, and criminal cases regularly coming before them. That jurisdiction was also responsible for some of the courts' most important and nationally prominent cases, especially those involving racial civil rights—a struggle that was visible in the streets as well as the courtroom.

---

1. Act of August 3, 1949, 63 Stat. 493. Stephens' prodding included a letter to Attorney General Tom Clark, enclosing a "Statement concerning the need for additional judges in the United States Court of Appeals for the District of Columbia Circuit."

The title "Justice" had been changed to "Judge" in the Act of June 25, 1948, 62 Stat. 869. That Act also provided for the Chief Judgeship, which had previously been a presidential appointment, to pass automatically to the most senior judge under seventy.

2. Stephens, in particular, in pushing for higher judicial salaries and annuities for the widows of federal judges, attempted to use the power and influence of the Attorney General and the President, the American Bar Association, and the news media.

The federal part of the docket of the D.C. Circuit courts, the jurisdiction they shared with other federal courts—admiralty, bankruptcy, patent, and copyright cases—proved not to generate much law of importance, constricted as the circuit was by its narrow geographic and economic base. However, more and more cases of importance were coming to the circuit in its role as a "national" court. Many more petitions to review the actions of administrative agencies were brought in the Court of Appeals, not only because of increased activity by the agencies but also because the District's growing administrative law bar was generally pleased with the manner in which the Court was handling those cases. During this period, suits brought in the District Court to contest the actions of federal officials would also prove of considerable importance.

Near the beginning of Truman's presidency, and again in his last year in office, the courts of the District were called upon to deal with legal conflicts involving great matters of state. Both cases typified the personal battles fought by the man who sat where, as he believed, the buck ought to stop. In one, the battle with the United Mineworkers Union and their president, John L. Lewis, Truman won a mighty victory. In the other, the owners of the nation's large steel producers successfully used the courts to deal the President a stunning defeat. In both cases, doughty, idiosyncratic district judges stood up to powerful forces. In both cases, expedited procedures were used to circumvent review by the Court of Appeals and assure rapid consideration by the Supreme Court, which in both cases upheld the District Court. From both cases, judicial power emerged greatly strengthened.

Truman's Judicial Appointments

In less than five years after assuming the presidency, Harry Truman virtually reconstituted the Court of Appeals, appointing eight of its nine regular members. Truman's appointees to the Court of Appeals reflected the polarities so evident in his administration as a whole. They were almost equally divided between liberal and conservative, mediocre and distinguished. Roosevelt had made the Court of Appeals a first-rate national court; Rutledge, Edgerton, and Arnold were all outstanding, and each of his remaining appointees—Stephens, Justin Miller, and Fred Vinson—had considerable ability.[3] While the caliber of Truman's appointees was not as

---

3. He tried to place Dean Acheson there as well, and two others he passed over, Charles Clark and Jerome Frank, would have honored any bench in America.

high, on average, they would leave more of a mark on the Court of Appeals: four would serve for over twenty-five years, during which time the Court earned much of its present national reputation. Most influentially, Truman's last three appointees, named in 1949, would constitute the heart of the strong liberal faction that emerged in the mid-1950s and dominated the Court in the 1960s.

During his two terms as President, Truman also made ten appointments to the District Court. On the whole, his appointees to that court were less distinguished and more conservative than those he named to the Court of Appeals.

The Court of Appeals

When Truman became President, one of the Court of Appeals' six judge-ships had been vacant since Fred Vinson's resignation in 1943. Harold Stephens had been lost to the Court for over a year, trying a complex antitrust case that was expected to last another year. Soon after Truman took office, Thurman Arnold and Justin Miller announced their resignations — Arnold to return to private practice and Miller to become president of the National Association of Broadcasters. This threatened to leave the Court of Appeals in the autumn of 1945 with only two active judges. Albert Lee Stephens, a judge of the Court of Appeals for the Ninth Circuit, was called upon to fill the three-judge panels in a number of cases. To fill the vacancies, Truman appointed E. Barrett Prettyman, Wilbur K. Miller, and Bennett Champ Clark.

Prettyman was well regarded by the local bar and would make a judicial career of distinction. Born in 1891 in Lexington, Virginia, he grew up in and around Washington and practiced law there, specializing in corporate, tax and public utility work. He had taught tax law at Georgetown Law School and had written on administrative law. A personal friend of Roosevelt, Prettyman served as the first General Counsel of the Bureau of Internal Revenue in 1933–34, later as Corporation Counsel of the District of Columbia, and during the Second World War, as a dollar-a-year man, he acted as hearing officer considering claims of conscientious objectors. Prettyman chaired the President's Conference on Administrative Procedure in 1953–54, and later chaired the Administrative Conference of the United States and the President's Advisory Commission on Narcotics and Drug Abuse.

While on the bench, Prettyman would make important contributions to administrative law, not only by his opinions but also through other writings and as a moving force in the revision of the Administrative Procedure Act. An influential moderate on the Court of Appeals, Prettyman would support some of the experimental jurisprudence in the criminal area crafted by the Court's liberals in the 1950s. Ultimately, he joined its conservatives in opposition, although he never joined in their rhetoric.

Wilbur K. Miller, the second Truman appointee, was born in Owensboro, Kentucky, in 1892. The major part of Miller's career prior to his appointment to the Court of Appeals was spent in private practice in Owensboro, although he also served as county attorney, chairman of the state Public Service Commission (1934–35), and judge of the Kentucky Court of Appeals (1940–41). Never a strong figure on the Court, Miller would become one of its most conservative members; as the years passed, he often simply noted his dissent without filing an opinion.

The third of Truman's 1945 appointments to the Court of Appeals, named to replace Arnold, came as a shock. Bennett Champ Clark, born in 1890 in Bowling Green, Missouri, was the son of Champ Clark, who had served as Speaker of the U.S. House of Representatives. The younger Clark was appointed in 1933 to fill the unexpired term of U.S. Senator Harry B. Hawes and elected twice in his own right, but was defeated for reelection in 1944. His appointment to the Court of Appeals was surprising because, although Clark had been Truman's Missouri colleague in the Senate, he was neither a political ally nor a friend of Truman, who thought him lazy and given to excessive drinking. Of the appointment, Truman is reputed to have said, "I thought as a judge he couldn't do too much harm, and he didn't.... [H]e wasn't the worst court appointment I ever made. By no means the worst. [But] I'm none too proud of it."

Truman's first three appointees brought to the Court of Appeals considerable experience at the bar and in public affairs. Nevertheless, few would say that they were the equal of the men whose seats they filled: Vinson, Rutledge, and Arnold. Each of these appointees was also more conservative on the bench than the judge he replaced.

Early in 1948, Chief Justice Groner retired because of ill-health. Truman elevated the senior judge on the Court of Appeals, Harold Stephens, then sixty-one years old, to the Chief Judgeship and promoted sixty-six-year-old James M. Proctor from the District bench to what had been Stephens' seat.[4] Proctor thus replaced Groner as the only Republican sitting on the Court of Appeals in a regular, active capacity. The appointment was made at least partially in response to pressure from the Bar Association of the District of Co-

---

4. Truman chose him over Chief Justice Robert G. Simmons of Nebraska, who, in a letter to the President on January 31, 1948, had offered his own candidacy as a "dehorned Republican from the Middle West."

lumbia for an appointee with experience practicing law in Washington. Proctor did add strength in local cases. Born in Washington in 1882, he worked for eight years in the U.S. Attorney's office and engaged in private practice in the District for almost two decades; at the time of his appointment to the Court of Appeals he had been a district judge for seventeen years.

The elevation of Stephens and the appointment of Proctor did not greatly change the ideological composition of the Court of Appeals. However, the three appointments Truman made in 1949 to fill the three additional judgeships created by the Act of August 3, 1949— David L. Bazelon, Charles Fahy, and George T. Washington—did. These three appointments brought to the bench strong civil libertarians (especially Bazelon and Fahy) with a dynamic view of the law. Their impact would, by the mid-1950s, transform the Court of Appeals.[5]

Fahy arrived with the strongest credentials. Georgia-born in 1892, he was the son of a Jewish mother and a Catholic father (whose religion he adopted). His brilliant career had included service as General Counsel of the National Labor Relations Board, as Solicitor General, and as a member of the legal committee of the U.N. General Assembly. Fahy had argued the *Jones and Laughlin Steel* case before the Supreme Court and had helped to draft the "Bombers for Bases" agreement with Great Britain and the U.N. Headquarters Agreement. Several times he had been seriously considered for appointment to the Supreme Court. Fahy was a gentle, lovable man, but under attack was made of steel. He developed into a staunch ally of Bazelon and Edgerton and in his own right was a strong and creative judge, who contributed pathbreaking opinions in the areas of mental health and the right to travel.

George T. Washington was a direct sixth-generation descendent of Samuel Washington, brother of George Washington, and a descendent of Bushrod Washington, who served on the U.S. Supreme Court from 1798 to 1829. Born in Ohio in 1902, Washington practiced in New York then taught at Cornell before the war called him to the capital in 1942. His notable career of government service included heading the U.S. Lend Lease Mission to Iran during the war and stints as Special Assistant to the Attorney General and Assistant Solicitor General. Washington would never fully realize his potential on the bench; illness forced his retirement in 1965 at the age of fifty-seven.

---

5. All three men received recess appointments on October 21, 1949. Washington was the first to take the judicial oath (October 25), followed by Bazelon (November 1) and Fahy (December 15); however, the lifetime appointments were rendered in such a way that Bazelon was first in seniority (commissioned on February 10, 1950), Fahy second (April 7) and Washington third (May 1).

Truman's third 1949 appointee, David L. Bazelon, was just past his fortieth birthday when he received his recess appointment and far less known in the legal community than Fahy and Washington. But he would leave the greatest mark on the Court of Appeals, especially as Chief Judge from 1962 to 1979. Bazelon had been active in Illinois politics and had served five years as an Assistant U.S. Attorney for the Northern District of Illinois. During the three years prior to his appointment to the Court of Appeals, Bazelon had served in the Department of Justice, first as Assistant Attorney General for the Lands Division and then as head of the Office of Alien Property.

It did not take long for Bazelon to begin contributing major opinions in the field of administrative law,[6] where he continued to be a seminal figure during a tenure of over thirty years. Almost from the beginning of his judicial career, Bazelon was a staunch ally of Judge Edgerton in loyalty-security and civil rights cases. More than any other member of the Court of Appeals, Bazelon was responsible for the Court's reputation in the 1960s and 1970s as a visible, influential, activist, and controversial tribunal, employing the law as a dynamic instrument for change.

The District Court

Five of President Truman's ten additions to the D.C. District Court can be viewed as "locals": men born or educated in Washington, and whose legal experience—in the office of the U.S. Attorney or of the Corporation Counsel, or in private practice—primarily (though not exclusively) involved local matters. They were Henry A. Schweinhaut, Edward M. Curran, Richmond B. Keech, James R. Kirkland, and Walter M. Bastian. Curran was also a local Police Court judge from 1936 to 1940, and Kirkland briefly served on the Municipal Court of Appeals.

Two others had spent much of their careers in Washington, but in the Department of Justice, where their concerns were national in nature. Alexander Holtzoff had been Special Assistant to the Attorney General for some twenty years and was a nationally known authority on federal practice and procedure. Edward A. Tamm had been for eighteen years one of the highest-ranking officials in the FBI. Another, Burnita Shelton Matthews, although she had been in private practice in Washington, was best known as counsel to the National Women's Party.

Charles F. McLaughlin and Luther Youngdahl were appointed to the District Court after political careers in the Midwest. McLaughlin had

---

6. See, e.g., *Washington Gas Light Co. v. Baker*, 188 F.2d 11 (1950) (*Baz-Edg-Fahy*).

served four terms in the House of Representatives representing Nebraska. Youngdahl had been Governor of Minnesota, as well as a justice of the Minnesota Supreme Court. Youngdahl, Kirkland, and Bastian were Republicans. Most of these district judges would line up sturdily against the Court of Appeals' decisions in the 1950s and 1960s expanding the rights of criminal defendants.

Although two of Truman's appointments to the District Court—Bastian and Tamm—would be elevated to the Court of Appeals, the district judges of greatest historical interest are Holtzoff, the most brilliant and the most difficult, and Burnita Shelton Matthews, the first woman District Judge in the United States.

Alexander Holtzoff was the first Jew named to the U.S. District Court for the District of Columbia. He was born in 1896 in New York City, and practiced law there before going to Washington in 1924. He served as Special Assistant to Supreme Court Justice Harlan Fiske Stone, then for two decades in the Department of Justice. There he helped write the Federal Rules of Civil Procedure and co-authored what became the standard work on federal practice. As aide to Attorney General Homer Cummings, Holtzoff was a central figure in the search for a plan to limit the Supreme Court, discouraging suggestions to strip the High Court of much of its appellate jurisdiction.

A small man of five feet four, Holtzoff was a terror in the courtroom and the bête noir of the Court of Appeals. An exceptionally pro-prosecution judge, he intervened often to ask questions of witnesses and defendants during criminal trials. He had limited patience for criminal defendants' lawyers and gave heavy sentences to persons convicted of violent crimes. No trial judge in two centuries in the District of Columbia was reversed in as many important cases as Holtzoff; in some, the appellate court ordered that the case be retried before a different judge.

Yet it should also be noted that Holtzoff was a workhorse who contributed mightily to reducing the backlog of the District Court. He could listen to complex legal arguments and then rule in an hour-long oral opinion without notes, dealing with complex arguments and even producing complete citations. If harsh with the lawyers who practiced before him, he was also known for spending hours in chambers educating the same (often young) attorneys. Appointed in 1945, Holtzoff served until his death of a heart attack in 1969.

With her appointment in 1949, Burnita Shelton Matthews became the first female U.S. District Judge. Born in Mississippi in 1894, she was the daughter of a plantation owner who objected to her ambitions for a law ca-

reer and insisted that she prepare for a career in music. She studied voice
and piano at the Conservatory of Music in Cincinnati and taught piano in
Georgia before moving to Washington, where she studied law at night while
working in the Veterans Administration. On Sundays, she picketed for
women's suffrage.

After receiving her L.L.B. and L.L.M. from National (later George Washington) University Law School, but unable to find any job as a lawyer in the
public or private sector in Washington, Matthews began practice on her own.
She became a legal advisor to the National Women's Party, drafting laws to
remove barriers to women in areas such as jury service, inheritance rights,
and equal pay. Matthews represented the Women's Party and others in their
battle with Chief Justice William Howard Taft over the condemnation of
their properties to clear the land for the new U.S. Supreme Court building.
Though unable to persuade the Court or Congress to abandon the plans,
she won a record condemnation award from the federal government.

In 1948, endorsed by the D.C. Bar Association (from which she had been
rejected years before because of her gender) and by Mississippi's two senators, as well as the formidable Democratic National Committeewoman
India Edwards, Matthews was appointed to the newly created District Court
judgeship. Matthews' initial reception by her judicial colleagues was mixed.
Some, such as Judge T. Alan Goldsborough, expressed outright hostility to
the idea of a woman judge.

Matthews served for seventeen years before taking senior status in 1966,
and continued to sit in the District Court until the age of eighty-eight. She
presided over trials involving Jimmy Hoffa, Paul Robeson, and A. Ernest
Fitzgerald, the Defense Department whistle-blower. At the request of Chief
Judge Bazelon, Matthews also sat for nine years by designation on the Court
of Appeals, as well as on the Court of Customs and Patent Appeals. She died
of a stroke in 1988 at the age of ninety-three. She was, then-Judge Ruth
Bader Ginsburg wrote in a posthumous tribute to her, "a southern gentle
woman of high mind and indomitable spirit, a 'role model' before that term
was coined," who, "while engaged in a traditional practice,...devoted her
talent and will, simultaneously, to then untraditional activity—advance-
ment of the equal stature of women and men under the law."

The United Mine Workers Case

As the nation converted from a total war to a peacetime economy, industry,
eager to take advantage of the availability of capital and pent-up consumer

demand, sought the removal of wartime price and production controls. At the same time, labor, freed from the wartime freeze on hourly wages and ban on strikes—but now confronting inflation, the reduced need for overtime, and the downgrading of jobs and unemployment—sought wage increases averaging thirty percent. After a labor-management conference called by the President broke down, strikes broke out like a contagion. By early December 1945 half a million American workers were off the job. During the year following the end of the war, five million workers were involved in 4,630 work stoppages.

Truman was sorely tested. In May 1946, 400,000 soft-coal miners were on strike. The government seized control of the coal mines on May 21, but the miners ignored the order. A few days later the United Mine Workers won a wage increase from the government, a guaranteed work week with overtime pay, and a welfare and retirement fund to be financed by a royalty of five cents on every ton of coal mined. However, in the fall of 1946 the UMW leader, John L. Lewis, sought to reopen the agreement. When Secretary of the Interior Julius A. Krug refused, Lewis announced, on November 15, that the agreement would end five days later.

The mercurial leader of the mine workers—a forbidding, hulking lion of a man with dark, baleful eyes, menacing eyebrows, a scowl of "Olympian ferocity," and a white mane—was a veteran of many a labor war. Never forgetting that he was the son of a miner, Lewis had no fear of the President of the United States. He was a man of remarkable oratorical ability and a talent for vilification, and was revered by those he led.

In 1946 the prospect of a coal strike in the winter was a very serious matter. Coal heated more than half the houses in the United States, produced a majority of all electric power, powered the nation's locomotives, and fired its great steel-making furnaces. With control of the production of coal, Lewis said, "we hold the vitals of our society right in our hands." But Lewis misread Truman's political needs and his toughness, and overreached. Public opinion was strongly against the labor leader. Truman directed Attorney General Tom C. Clark to ask for a temporary injunction, to keep the UMW from striking, and for a declaratory judgment that termination of the contract was illegal. He then left for a vacation in Key West, refusing to take any phone calls from Lewis, saying that he would not confer with that "son of a bitch."

On November 18, 1946, because the union headquarters were located in Washington, Clark applied for the injunction from the D.C. District Court. The case came before Judge Thomas Alan Goldsborough. Goldsborough, then sixty-nine, was a Marylander by birth and education. He had served in Congress for twenty years before resigning to accept Franklin Roosevelt's appointment to the District Court. He would remain on the bench until his death in 1951.

Goldsborough issued a temporary restraining order commanding Lewis to cancel the strike on the ground that he was violating the War Labor Disputes Act of 1942, which barred strikes against government-seized facilities until the President formally proclaimed an end to hostilities. Lewis was thrown off balance by the legal proceedings, but the miners still walked off their jobs on November 20. Goldsborough then held that the anti-injunction provision of the Norris-LaGuardia Act did not prevent the government from enjoining a union in order to prevent "a public calamity." The government pressed for a contempt citation. Summoned before the District Court to show cause why he should not be held in contempt, Lewis said he would not acquiesce in "government by injunction."

On December 3 Lewis was found guilty of contempt. The government asked for a fine of $3,500,000, based upon daily losses of $250,000. Lewis's lawyers denounced the request, saying it was intended to put the United Mine Workers out of business. The next day Judge Goldsborough rendered judgment, first stating, "This is not the act of a low law-breaker, but it is an evil, demoniac, monstrous thing that means hunger and cold and unemployment and destitution and disorganization of the social fabric.... [I]f actions of this kind can be successfully persisted in, the government will be overthrown." Holding the UMW and Lewis in civil and criminal contempt, Goldsborough fined the union the full $3,500,000 and Lewis $10,000.[7]

Three days later Lewis retreated, announcing that he had called off the strike to avert a national coal shortage and to permit the Supreme Court to hear the appeal without economic pressure. For its part, the government requested an end to the criminal contempt proceedings. There was no doubt that Truman had won a great victory.

To hasten a final decision, the government joined the union in petitioning the Supreme Court to hear the case immediately, bypassing the Court of Appeals. The High Court announced its decision on March 6, 1947. In the leading opinion, Chief Justice Vinson characterized Lewis's defiance of the court order as "the germ center of an economic paralysis which was rapidly extending itself... into practically every other major industry of the United States."[8]

---

7. *United States v. United Mine Workers of America*, 70 F. Supp. 42 (1946).
8. *United States v. United Mine Workers of America*, 330 U.S. 258 (1947).

The Court sustained the fine against Lewis but ordered the fine against the union cut to $700,000 on the condition that Lewis withdraw the notice of termination of the Krug-Lewis agreement. The Court upheld the government's position that the War Labor Disputes Act superseded the Norris-LaGuardia anti-injunction provision in situations in which the President as Commander-in-Chief issued an executive order pursuant to the declaration of national emergency; injunctions could, therefore, issue against work stoppages at properties seized by the government.

The case had three important results. First, it revealed what a weapon federal seizure could be against fractious union leaders. Second, the outcry against Lewis' tactics contributed to one of the most important conservative triumphs of the postwar era, the Taft-Hartley Act, which curtailed union power in emergency disputes, allowed states to enact "right-to-work" laws outlawing the closed shop, and reinstated the use of the injunction to restrain strikes and other union actions. Third, the controversy gave Truman a short-term boost in opinion polls, rid him of the image of being "soft on labor," and enabled him for the first time to come out from under the shadow of F.D.R.

Racial Civil Rights

As the war came to an end, tensions between the races rose. A struggle was brewing in the District between advocates of civil rights—who included among their number many white religious leaders, social workers, labor officials, and a few small businessmen—and those who wanted the status quo maintained, such as the representatives of banks and insurance companies on the Board of Trade and the real estate board. In less than a decade, after a nonviolent struggle employing sit-ins, picketing, litigation, and appeals to the court of public opinion, many of the formal barriers of segregation would be eliminated.

The President played no small role in this transformation. Truman's actions and policies, driven as much by political necessity as moral imperative, embraced the use of federal power to promote civil rights. The report of his Committee on Civil Rights, released in 1947, had a significant impact upon public opinion with its indictment of segregation and discrimination in Washington as a "graphic illustration of the failure of democracy." The following year, after unsuccessfully urging Congress to pass a ten-point civil rights program, the President ended formal discrimination within the federal government by executive order.[9]

The report *Segregation in Washington*, published in 1948 by the National Committee on Segregation in the Nation's Capital, a private group which included Eleanor Roosevelt and other luminaries in its membership, contributed importantly to breaking the hard core of racism in Washington. Not the least of those who led the battle for racial equality in Washington and elsewhere were the lawyers: blacks like Charles Houston, William Hastie, Louis L. Redding, Spottswood Robinson, and Thurgood Marshall; whites like Charles Fahy, Jack Greenberg, Louis Pollack, and Charles L. Black Jr. Finally, the courts themselves would prove critical in the battle against segregation in housing, public accommodations, and schools, although usually it was not until a case reached the Supreme Court of the United States that a civil rights claimant would actually win a favorable result.

Public Accommodations

In 1907, a black woman, Mary Church Terrell, observed, "I may walk from the Capitol to the White House, ravenously hungry and abundantly supplied with money with which to purchase a meal, without finding a single restaurant in which I could be permitted to take a morsel of food, if it was patronized by white people, unless I was willing to sit behind a screen." Forty years later that was still true. But in the postwar years, segregation in public accommodations was subjected to a two-pronged attack, by demonstration and litigation.

During Reconstruction the Legislative Assembly of the District had passed laws guaranteeing equal accommodations in public facilities. Those laws, passed in 1872 and 1873, had never been repealed, although they had been left out of the 1901 codification of the laws governing the District and had not been enforced in the twentieth century.[10] In the spring of 1949 a biracial coalition of sixty-one civic, religious, and charitable organizations was able to convince the Corporation Counsel of the District that the laws were valid and should be enforced.

To help convince Washington's restaurants to comply, the District Commissioners had the Corporation Counsel undertake a test case. Thompson's restaurant, at 725 14th Street, N.W., was prosecuted under the Reconstruc-

---

9. Executive Orders 9980 and 9981, July 26, 1948.

10. The Act of June 20, 1872 (Comp. St. 1894 c.16 Sec. 48 et seq.) made it a misdemeanor for any restaurant keeper to refuse to serve "any respectable well-behaved person" without regard to race, color, or previous condition of servitude. A similar law was enacted on June 26, 1873 (Comp. St. 1894 c.16 Sec. 151 et seq.).

tion ordinances for denying service to three blacks (one of whom was Mary Terrell, now eighty-seven years old) and a white. In July 1950 Judge Frank Myers of the Municipal Court quashed the prosecution, holding that the Reconstruction acts had been repealed by implication. The Municipal Court of Appeals held that the Act of 1872 was no longer in effect but that the prosecution could be maintained under the Act of 1873.[11]

The appeal to the U.S. Court of Appeals in the case titled *John R. Thompson Co. v. District of Columbia* was heard *en banc* and attracted *amicus* briefs from the Solicitor General and the American Civil Liberties Union. On January 22, 1953, the Court of Appeals, by a 5–4 vote, held the Reconstruction laws invalid.[12] Writing for four members of the majority (Clark, Miller, Proctor, and himself), Chief Judge Stephens took the position that the 1872 and 1873 laws were of the character of "general legislation" which Congress could not constitutionally have delegated to the Legislative Assembly, and that they had not done so. Furthermore, the laws had been repealed *de facto* when the D.C. Code was enacted in 1901. As the laws had lain unenforced for seventy-eight years, the decision to enforce them was one that was legislative in character and therefore better left to Congress rather than the municipal authorities. Furthermore, since various municipal state regulations *requiring* segregation were valid because they were in accord with the local custom of segregation, enactments in conflict with the local custom, such as these District laws, could not be justified.

Judge Prettyman concurred in the judgment, taking the position that the neglected regulations should have been deemed as having been abandoned by the municipal licensing authority. Judge Fahy wrote the dissent, in which he was joined by Judges Edgerton, Bazelon and Washington. His studied lack of passion gave way only in the final paragraph:

> We have not separately discussed the [Thompson] Company's suggestion that the equal service provisions have become unenforceable by reasons of obsolescence. It is enough to point out that custom has not moved away from equal treatment, leaving these regulations derelicts of the past. Custom has moved toward equal treatment, as is shown by developments of recent years in the Government, in the armed services, in industry, in organized labor, in educational institutions, in sports, in the theater, and in restaurants in this community.

---

11. *District of Columbia v. John R. Thompson Co.*, 81 A.2d 249 (1951).
12. *District of Columbia v. John R. Thompson Co.*, 203 F.2d 579 (1953) (Ste-Cla-WMil-Pro-Pre/Fahy-Edg-Baz-Was).

In June 1953 a unanimous Supreme Court reversed, Justice Douglas writing. The local ordinances remained valid.[13] A few days later, Mary Church Terrell, by then ninety years old, and her three colleagues revisited Thompson's restaurant and were served. Following the *Thompson* decision, public accommodations in Washington were rapidly desegregated.

School Desegregation

The U.S. District Court for the District of Columbia was directly a party to segregation of Washington's schools. Under a 1906 act of Congress, the power to appoint the members of the school board was vested in the judges of the D.C. Supreme Court, a responsibility that continued after the Court's name was changed.

Segregation in Washington schools had begun before the end of the Civil War. In 1864 Congress had provided schools for African-Americans; while segregation was not mandatory, it was assumed that it would be preferable. By the end of the Second World War segregation was so rigid that a white child could "go through seventeen years of public school training without ever seeing a colored child in classroom or inter-mural or extracurricular activities." Although for many years the District of Columbia had some of the best schools for blacks among segregated school systems in the United States, they were not tangibly equal to the white schools. The buildings were older and less well equipped, and less money was available for teachers' salaries. Meanwhile, the city's demographic changes produced a critical classroom shortage in black schools, while some white schools were half empty.

In the autumn of 1947, Marguerite Daisy Carr was denied a transfer from her grossly overcrowded black junior high school to a thinly attended white school. Marguerite's school, Browne Junior High, had two sessions a day compared to a single, longer session at the white school to which she sought admission. Her father sued the Superintendent of Schools. The Browne School PTA also sued, arguing that if the unequal accommodations could not be ended, the races had to be mixed. However, after space was found in an abandoned building to accommodate the overflow from the Browne school, the District Court held for the Superintendent.

The Court of Appeals decided *Carr v. Corning* and *Browne Junior High School PTA v. Magdeburger* on February 14, 1950. Judges Prettyman and Edgerton refused to dismiss the case as moot. Judge Clark dissented on that issue but, on the merits, joined Prettyman (who wrote for the Court) in

---

13. 346 U.S. 100 (1953).

upholding the position of the school system. The judges held that, on the record before the Court, the black plaintiffs were receiving the same treatment that they would have received if they had been white. The double sessions at the black school were viewed as "temporary expedients" which had at other times had been used for white students.[14]

In his dissent, Edgerton became the first judge in the United States to subscribe in an opinion to the view that segregated schools amounted to a violation of due process of law. He wrote:

> Instead of serving a public purpose it fosters prejudice and obstructs the education of whites and Negroes by endorsing prejudice and... preventing mutual acquaintance.... The education required for living in a cosmopolitan community, and especially for living in a humane and democratic country and promoting its ideals, cannot be obtained on either side of a fence that separates a more privileged majority and a less privileged minority.

The next attack on school segregation, a frontal challenge, was brought against Melvin Sharpe, president of the Board of Education, by James M. Nabrit Jr., a professor of law at Howard University, who taught the first full-scale course in civil rights ever offered by an American law school. *Bolling v. Sharpe* grew out of efforts to have eleven black children admitted to a white school, the new and lavishly equipped John Philip Sousa Junior High School, which faced a golf course. One of those children was twelve-year-old Spottswood T. Bolling Jr., who attended a school that was forty-eight years old, dingy, ill-equipped, and located across the street from a pawn shop. Judge Walter M. Bastian dismissed the suit in April 1951 on the ground that as the Court of Appeals had, in *Carr v. Corning*, upheld the constitutionality of segregation, and as no claim of unequal school facilities was being made by Bolling, there was no ground upon which relief could be granted.

The Court of Appeals never heard *Bolling v. Sharpe*. In October 1952 the Supreme Court combined cases from Kansas, South Carolina, and Virginia (a Delaware case was added later) that raised the constitutionality of school segregation. The High Court then took the unique step of asking Nabrit to file a petition for certiorari in *Bolling*, bypassing the Court of Appeals. In December 1952 the five cases were heard by the Supreme Court. Robert L. Carter argued for the plaintiffs in the Kansas case, Thurgood Marshall argued the South Carolina case, Louis L. Redding and Jack

---

14. *Carr v. Corning*, 182 F.2d 14 (1950) (*Pre-Cla/Edg*).

Greenberg the Delaware case, and Nabrit and George E. C. Hayes, who had once served on the D.C. school board, the D.C. case; Milton D. Korman represented the D.C. school board). The Virginia case, from Prince Edward County, was argued by a soft-spoken, ascetic-looking black lawyer, Spottswood W. Robinson III. Within a generation Carter would sit as a federal district judge in the Southern District of New York, Marshall on the Supreme Court, and Spottswood Robinson, first as judge of the District Court for the District of Columbia and then on the U.S. Court of Appeals.

As the justices were divided, the Court decided to hold the cases over for reargument during the October 1953 term. By time the Court reconvened, Chief Justice Vinson had died and Earl Warren had been named his successor. The decisions were handed down on May 17, 1954. The new Chief Justice first read the opinion in *Brown v. Board of Education of Topeka*, which disposed of the state cases. He then turned to *Bolling v. Sharpe*, which was handled in just a few paragraphs. As segregation in public education was not reasonably related to a proper governmental objective, the Court held that it imposed upon the black children a burden which constituted denial of due process of law.[15]

In Washington, unlike the South, formal compliance with the segregation decision was immediate. Four months after the Supreme Court decision, all of Washington's public schools opened on an integrated basis.

Urban Renewal

Outside the area of civil rights, perhaps the most important local case decided by the courts of the District of Columbia during these years arose from the District's postwar urban renewal boom, and dealt with the constitutionality of the 1945 District of Columbia Redevelopment Act. The law authorized the condemnation of property on land where slums were located or where "blight" had occurred and provided for compensation to be paid the owners of the property, after which the property might be sold to private developers. In 1953, several small businessmen challenged the Act as an unconstitutional delegation of power by the Congress to the D.C. Commissioners and as a violation of the Takings Clause of the Fifth Amendment.

In a decision that anticipated the failure of much redevelopment of the 1950s and 1960s, the three-judge District Court of Prettyman (writing),

---

15. 47 U.S. 497 (1954).

Keech, and Curran upheld the statute, but limited its reach. Clearance of a slum was clearly for a public purpose, the Court ruled, adding that the government probably could have condemned without even paying compensation. However, the Court was considerably more reserved about the use of condemnation to deal with "blight" rather than slums. The court held that Congress lacked the power to authorize the seizure of property by eminent domain "for the sole purpose of redeveloping the area according to its, or its agents', judgment of what a well-developed, well-balanced neighborhood would be.... That the Government may do whatever it deems to be for the good of the people is not," the Court said, "a principle of our system of government," adding that "[t]here is no general power in government, in the American concept, to seize private property."[16]

The following year, a unanimous Supreme Court affirmed the District Court, but took a much broader view of the government's police power and a much narrower view of the judiciary's role in reviewing such an exercise. "We do not," Justice Douglas wrote, "sit to determine whether a particular housing project is or is not desirable." It was, the Supreme Court said, "within the power of the legislature to determine that the community should be beautiful as well as healthy, spacious as well as clean, well-balanced as well as carefully patrolled." An area-wide solution to redevelopment which even eliminated buildings that did not themselves contribute to the making of the slum was constitutional. It was not for the courts to substitute the landowner's standard of public need for that prescribed by the Congress.[17]

Administrative Law

The battle over the future of the administrative agencies, loudly waged during the New Deal days, was resolved by passage of the Administrative Procedure Act of 1946.[18] The product of the differing views of business, the American Bar Association, scholars of the administrative process, F.D.R., and the Congress, the Act preserved the agencies but imposed upon them a variety of procedural requirements and expanded judicial review. As a result, the agencies became less free-wheeling, but also more legalistic, judge-like, and prone to delays.

---

16. *Schneider v. District of Columbia*, 117 F. Supp. 705 (1953).
17. *Berman v. Parker*, 348 U.S. 26 (1954).
18. 60 Stat. 237.

Most of the important administrative cases decided by the Court of Appeals during this period were more notable for their economic significance or for the complexity of the issues involved than for the black-letter law they left. For example, the Court reviewed awards by the Civil Aeronautics Board of lucrative overseas passenger and cargo routes,[19] as well as upholding entry into the field by two new types of air commerce. One of these involved freight forwarders, a proceeding in which the CAB had before it some seventy-eight applications, and the other, concerning cargo-only transportation, came to the Court of Appeals with a 30,000-page record and nineteen briefs on appeal.[20]

The Truman years were a period of particularly ineffectual performance by the Federal Communications Commission. Although it threatened in 1946 not to renew the licenses of radio stations that violated their public service responsibility and succumbed to advertising excesses, the FCC was thwarted by congressional opposition aroused by the industry. The Commission mishandled the potential of FM by moving its frequencies to a higher band, thereby making all existing FM receivers and transmitters obsolete. The FCC first capitulated to the pressures of the fledgling television industry to permit commercialization, then endorsed a technical system, VHF, with an inadequate number of television channels to allow that commercial service to be totally competitive, at the same time consigning UHF and cable television to the economic hinterlands for a generation.

In reviewing communications policy, the Court of Appeals did not, in a number of important cases, support FCC decisions, and in those it was often reversed by the Supreme Court. This was true, for example, in a case involving a Detroit radio station, WJR, in which the Court of Appeals had held that a petitioner for intervention in an administrative hearing is entitled to an oral hearing as a matter of constitutional right. In another case, when the Court of Appeals held that a license renewal could not be denied purely because a station had made a false statement in its application, the Supreme Court unanimously reversed, declaring that it was for the FCC rather than the Court to make that determination.[21]

Two other significant cases from the late 1940s, however, did not generate review by the High Court. In *Easton Publishing Co. v. FCC*, the Court of

---

19. See, e.g., *Seaboard & Western Airlines v. CAB*, 181 F.2d 777 (1949) (*Pre*-Edg-Pro).

20. *National Air Freight Forwarding Corp. v. CAB*, 197 F.2d 384 (1952) (*Baz-Was/Pre*); *American Airlines v. CAB*, 192 F.2d 417 (1951) (*Pre*-Fahy-Was).

21. *WJR, The Goodwill Station v. FCC*, 174 F.2d 226 (1948) (*Ste*-Cla-WMil/*Pre*-Edg); rev'd, 337 U.S. 265 (1949); *WOKO v. FCC*, 153 F.2d 623 (1946) (*WMil*-Pre/*Gro*), rev'd, 329 U.S. 223 (1946).

Appeals ruled that when awarding a broadcast license to an FM radio station, the Commission was not limited by the pattern of AM broadcasting and did not first have to fill in the gaps in existing service. However, in *Simmons v. FCC,* the Court upheld a Commission ruling that a licensee who makes no effort to structure its programs to the particular needs of the community does not satisfy the public service responsibility of a broadcast licensee.[22]

Loyalty-Security Cases

With the exception of the momentous United Mine Workers and Steel Seizure cases, the cases that focused most national attention on the District of Columbia Circuit in this period were those involving loyalty and national security. Because most prosecutions for contempt of Congress involved hearings held in Washington, and because a large number of federal employees affected by the federal loyalty program worked in the capital, between 1945 and 1970 more loyalty-security cases arose in the D.C. District Court than in any other federal district. More than 125 generated opinions in the Court of Appeals. In the loyalty-security area, the courts of the District have made more law than any other court.

In the uneasy postwar atmosphere, the courts of the D.C. Circuit handled loyalty cases cautiously, tending to defer to the political branches, a stance for which there was ample support from both case law and public opinion. The issues before the Court in the most important cases heard during this period involved challenges to the subpoena and contempt powers of House investigatory committees and the legitimacy of dismissals of federal employees on disloyalty charges, including the validity of the Attorney General's list of subversive organizations.

Congressional Investigatory Powers

During the wave of contempt-of-Congress prosecutions resulting from the investigations of the House Un-American Activities Committee (HUAC),[23] one of the most influential federal cases dealing with the limits of the investigatory power of Congress—and the first important postwar loyalty case heard by the D.C. courts—was *United States v. Barsky.* Once the war ended, the Committee, formed in 1938, had begun to investigate alleged

---

22. *Easton Publishing Co. v. FCC,* 175 F.2d 344 (1949) (*Pre-*Pro-Ste); *Simmons v. FCC,* 169 F.2d 670 (1948) (*Edg-*Cla-*WMil*(c)).
23. Formally, the House Committee on Un-American Activities.

Communist-front organizations. One of these was the Joint Anti-Fascist Refugee Committee, which provided medical care and other services to Spanish refugees in France but which was also a source of anti-Franco propaganda. When HUAC subpoenaed the organization's records, its chairman, Dr. Edward K. Barsky, and other members of the executive board refused to produce them. In March 1946, with only four dissenting votes, the House of Representatives cited Barsky for contempt. Later, contempt citations were voted against all the members of the board and the group's executive secretary.

Barsky was tried early in 1947 and found guilty. His appeal before the Court of Appeals was not argued until November 24, 1947, and was decided March 18, 1948. Between Barsky's citation for contempt and the Court of Appeals' decision, events in Eastern Europe transformed the atmosphere in the United States. Soviet-inspired operations crushed the democratic opposition in Poland and Bulgaria and ousted the governments of Hungary, Rumania, and Czechoslovakia.

In one of the first federal appellate opinions in the postwar period to carefully study the congressional power to investigate, the Court of Appeals upheld Barsky's conviction. Joined by Judge Clark, Judge Prettyman wrote a long (by the standards of the era — it was nine pages) and thoughtful opinion. The court viewed the power of inquiry by the legislature as "coextensive with the power of legislation" and "not limited to the scope or the content of private legislation." Inquiry into threats to the existing form of government by extra-constitutional processes of change was a legitimate congressional power. While recognizing that the "Congressional power of inquiry is not unrestricted," the Court affirmed that the Committee did not have to wait until there was a clear and present danger to the government. The court went on to uphold the resolution creating the House Un-American Activities Committee. Although the Committee's performance — its circus-like atmosphere, pandering to fear, and inability to produce constructive legislation — was subject to criticism, the remedy for that, Prettyman and Clark held, was political, not judicial.[24]

In the early years of the Cold War, Judge Edgerton stood almost alone among lower federal court judges throughout the nation in his willingness to curb congressional power. For Edgerton the insensitivity of the Committee to individual rights was central. In this case, Edgerton concluded,

---

24. *United States v. Barsky*, 72 F. Supp. 58 (1947), aff'd, 167 F.2d 241 (1948) (*Pre-Cla/Edg*).

the entire investigation by the Committee "was unconstitutional both as abridging freedom of speech and as attempting to punish without trial."

Among the loyalty cases that came before the courts of the District of Columbia Circuit during this period, perhaps the most notorious were the contempt-of-Congress convictions of screenwriters Dalton Trumbo and John Howard Lawson, members of the "Hollywood Ten" who refused to answer questions at a HUAC hearing in October 1947. Their convictions were affirmed in a single memorandum opinion by an Appeals Court panel which included neither Edgerton nor Prettyman, who had begun to have reservations about the use of congressional power. The panel, composed of Bennett Champ Clark, Wilbur Miller, and visiting District Judge George C. Sweeney of Massachusetts, stood on *Barsky* and specifically upheld Congress's power to inquire into membership in the Screen Writers Guild. Judge Clark's opinion was based on the conviction that "in the current ideological struggle between communistic-thinking and democratic-thinking people of the world" the power of the motion picture industry to influence public opinion made it a legitimate target of congressional investigators seeking to discover if the authors of screenplays harbored Communist sympathies.[25]

There were a very few cases in the Truman era in which the Court of Appeals did reverse a contempt-of-Congress conviction, but it was always on very narrow grounds. The conviction of Ernestina G. Fleischman, for example, who had also refused to produce the records of the Joint Anti-Fascist Refugee Committee, was reversed on appeal because the Court found that a factual question—whether a quorum of the Committee was present—should have been determined by the jury.[26] On the whole, in the early years of the Cold War neither the courts of the District of Columbia nor the Supreme Court attempted to restrain the activities of congressional investigatory committees.

Executive Powers

A second line of loyalty-security cases involved the methods used by the executive branch to assure the loyalty of its employees. On March 21, 1947, under considerable political pressure, President Truman issued Executive Order 9835, which barred from federal employment anyone who belonged

---

25. *Lawson v. United States*, 176 F.2d 49 (1949).

26. *Fleischman v. United States*, 174 F.2d 519 (1949). Judges Edgerton and Proctor made the majority for the reversal, although Proctor and Prettyman were the majority for another aspect of the decision. This decision was in turn reversed by the Supreme Court, which held that the absence of a quorum could not be raised in the trial court for the first time. *United States v. Fleischman*, 339 U.S. 349 (1950).

to any political party or organization which advocated overthrow of the constitutional form of government. The order instituted a federal loyalty program that seemed to be based on the assumption that even a single potentially disloyal person was a serious threat to the security of the nation. It established boards in each federal agency to review investigative reports from the FBI—reports often based on the casual statements of acquaintances or fellow workers. Employees charged with disloyalty would have a hearing before the board, and could appeal an adverse finding to a central Loyalty Review Board.

The first person dismissed from government service under the program was Dorothy Bailey, a supervisor in the training section of the U.S. Employment Service with fourteen years of government experience. On March 28, 1949, Bailey received an interrogatory from the Civil Service Commission containing allegations that she had been a member of the Communist Party, attended its meetings, and associated with Communists on numerous occasions. She was also accused of having belonged to two other organizations on the Attorney General's list. Bailey denied any Communist activity, but admitted to brief membership in one of the other leftist organizations. She offered in the record affidavits from some seventy persons attesting to her loyalty. At her hearing, not a single person appeared to testify against her, nor was any evidence openly introduced against her, although Bailey was informed that there were unfavorable statements in her file. Her request to know the particulars and the identity of her accusers was denied. The hearing board found against Bailey. The Loyalty Review Board sustained the finding, although its members knew neither the particulars of the charges in her file nor the identity of her accusers, just that they were informants the FBI believed were experienced and reliable. Bailey was dismissed from government service.

She brought suit in the District Court, represented by Thurman Arnold, Abe Fortas, and Paul Porter. On October 17, 1949, Arnold wrote to Attorney General J. Howard McGrath, "The use of a secret document as evidence in the Dorothy Bailey case seems to us identical with the use of a secret document in the famous Dreyfus case." Bailey's suit was dismissed by Judge Holtzoff on the ground that the President's authority over government employees was absolute, unless checked by Congress.

A divided panel of the Court of Appeals affirmed. The crux of the majority opinion, written by Judge Prettyman (joined by Judge Proctor) was that the responsibility for the executive branch was the President's, that responsibility for its personnel belonged both to the President and to Congress, and that the President's removal power was not restricted by due process of law. In the first paragraph of his dissent, Judge Edgerton went to the essence of the case: "Without trial by jury, without evidence, and without even being allowed to confront her accusers or to know their identity, a citizen of the United States has been found disloyal to the government of the United States."[27]

The Supreme Court granted certiorari, but divided evenly 4–4 (former Attorney General Tom C. Clark not sitting), thereby affirming the decision of the Court of Appeals.[28] Dorothy Bailey thus could not regain her government position. So that she would have a job, Arnold, Fortas, and Porter made her their office manager.

A few months after its *Bailey* decision, the Court of Appeals pulled back somewhat in *Deak v. Pace*, where Judge Proctor (writing) joined Edgerton in holding the removal of two government employees improper because the Loyalty Review Board had not indicated the ground for removal in enough detail to give the employees an opportunity to oppose the removal order and apply for reinstatement. And two years later, in *Kutcher v. Gray*, a unanimous Court of Appeals held that the Veterans Administration had improperly removed a government employee who held a non-sensitive position, simply because he belonged to the Socialist Workers Party, an organization on the Attorney General's list.[29]

Under Truman's Executive Order 9835, the Attorney General was authorized to designate an organization as "totalitarian, fascist, communist or subversive." Membership in one of these organizations was to be one evidentiary factor (out of six) in determining disloyalty. The first Attorney General's list of eighty-two subversive organizations was sent to the central Loyalty Review Board in November 1947 and made public on March 20, 1948. The list would become enormously important because it would be used not only to judge the loyalty of federal employees, but also in federal proceedings concerning would-be immigrants, foreign visitors, and U.S. passport holders, as well as by state and municipal governments in their own loyalty proceedings.

The Joint Anti-Fascist Refugee Committee sued to have Executive Order 9835 declared unconstitutional as well as to restrain Attorney General Tom C. Clark from placing the Committee on the list. The District Court dismissed the complaint and the Court of Appeals affirmed the dismissal. Writing for himself and Judge Clark, Judge Proctor held that the Attorney

27. *Bailey v. Richardson*, 182 F.2d 46 (1950) (*Pre-Pro/Edg*).
28. 341 U.S. 918 (1951).
29. *Deak v. Pace*, 185 F.2d 997 (1950) (*Pro-Edg/Pre*); *Kutcher v. Gray*, 199 F.2d 785 (1952) (*Pro-WMil-Pre*).

General was only providing information. "The Executive Order imposes no obligation or restraint upon the Committee. It commands nothing of the Committee. It denies the Committee no authority, privilege, immunity or license. It subjects the Committee to no liability, civil or criminal." Any injury suffered by the Committee was indirect and incidental; there was, therefore, no justiciable controversy.[30]

Once again dissenting, Judge Edgerton had no doubt that the matter was justiciable. The wide publicity given to the list, Edgerton argued, would cause an organization to lose reputation, members, supporters, contributions, speakers, and meeting places. The members of the organization might be subjected to ridicule. obloquy, and economic loss.

The Supreme Court consolidated the *Joint Anti-Fascist Committee* case with two similar cases appealed from the D.C. Circuit, both of which had also been won by the government. The Court of Appeals was reversed, 5–3.[31] Four justices agreed with Judge Edgerton on the constitutional question, while the fifth agreed with the way Edgerton had interpreted the pleadings as obviating the need to reach the constitutional question. The three cases were sent back to the District Court for retrial and were subsequently tossed back and forth between the District Court and the Court of Appeals for some time.

While Harry Truman was President, the Court of Appeals decided some two dozen loyalty cases and the District Court a number more. In most, judgment was rendered for the government. In the first years of the Cold War, neither the courts of the D.C. Circuit nor the Supreme Court anticipated the excesses to come sufficiently to create enough black-letter law to ward them off. Alone in dissent in these years, Judge Edgerton picked up some support with the three Truman appointees of 1949, Bazelon, Fahy, and Washington. Nevertheless, during the Truman presidency there was generally a six-man majority on the Court willing to defer to government power.

Attempted Presidential Assassination

The fourth attempt on the life of a President in Washington occurred on November 1, 1950. With the residential part of the White House closed for

---

30. *Joint Anti-Fascist Refugee Committee v. Clark*, 177 F.2d 79 (1949) (*Pro-Cla/Edg*).

31. *Joint Anti-Fascist Refugee Committee v. McGrath*, 341 U.S. 123 (1951). The two other cases were *International Workers Order v. McGrath*, 182 F.2d 368 (1950) (*WMil-Pro/Edg*), rev'd, 341 U.S. 123 (1951), and *National Council of American-Soviet Friendship v. McGrath*, 339 U.S. 956 (1950) (the U.S. Court of Appeals decision is unreported).

structural repairs, President Truman was living in the Blair House, diagonally across the street. At 2:19 p.m., Truman was taking a nap in a second-floor room when two slim, neatly dressed men approached Blair House from different directions. Gunfire exploded—twenty-seven shots in two minutes. The President was not harmed, but three White House policemen were hit, one fatally. As for the assailants—fanatical Puerto Rican nationalists seeking attention for their cause—twenty-five-year-old Griselio Torresola was dead and thirty-six-year-old Oscar Collazo was wounded.[32]

Although it was Torresola who had fired the fatal bullet, Collazo stood trial for murder before Judge T. Allen Goldsborough beginning February 26, 1951. Contending that his views were relevant as to intent and the prosecution's claim of motive, Collazo testified for hours about the history of what he saw as Puerto Rico's "oppression" by the United States. However, Judge Goldsborough instructed the jury that "the defendant's views about the situation in Puerto Rico have absolutely nothing to do with this case, and when I say absolutely nothing, I mean exactly what I say."

Collazo was convicted. On appeal, the Court of Appeals (Judge Prettyman writing, joined by Judges Fahy and Kimbrough Stone, visiting from the Eighth Circuit) agreed that Collazo was legally responsible for his cofelon's act and that the views of the two men concerning Puerto Rico "were irrelevant or immaterial or both" to the issue whether their contemplated demonstration did or did not include an intended killing. The Supreme Court denied certiorari.[33]

At sentencing, Collazo said: "Anything that I had done I did it for the cause of liberty of my country, and I still insist, even to the last, that we have the right to be free." Judge Goldsborough remarked, "The Court has no reason to believe that you are not sincere. The Court doesn't think you are an inherently evil man. The Court, as an individual, is sorry for you." Goldsborough sentenced Collazo to death, but Truman commuted the sentence to life imprisonment. After twenty-nine years in Levenworth, Collazo was pardoned in 1979 by President Carter.

The cause of Puerto Rican independence inspired another shooting incident in the District early in the Eisenhower administration. On the after-

---

32. Two days before the attempt on Truman's life, another nationalist had attacked the Governor's mansion in San Juan. The attacks in the two cities led to a nationalist uprising in Puerto Rico in which thirty-two people died.

33. *Collazo v. United States*, 196 F.2d 573 (1952) (*Pre*-Fahy-Stone), cert. denied, 343 U.S. 968 (1952). Judge Goldsborough's admonishment to the jury is quoted in the Appeals Court opinion.

noon of March 1, 1954, four Puerto Rican nationalists seeking to attract attention to their cause opened fire in the House of Representatives. Five members of Congress were slightly wounded. All four nationalists were found guilty of five counts of assault with a dangerous weapon; three of the four were convicted of assault with intent to kill. The Court of Appeals panel—Judges Miller (writing), Washington, and Danaher—affirmed.[34]

The Steel Seizure Case

In his final year in office, Truman once again, as he had six years earlier with the United Mine Workers, challenged powerful players on the national stage. Once again he seized control of a major industry. And once again the setting for the legal battle was the D.C. Circuit. But this time, Truman was badly beaten both in the District Court and the U.S. Supreme Court.

By the spring of 1952 the Korean War was stalemated on the battlefield and unpopular at home. In its wake had come inflation, an unpopular draft and an increase in the domestic concern over communist subversion. The Truman administration had been badly weakened by revelations of corruption, some of it in the Department of Justice, which functioned without an Attorney General during the battle over the steel seizures. Truman's popularity was at an all-time low. On March 29, he announced that he would not run for reelection.

1952, like 1946, was a year of widespread labor unrest. In December 1951 the steel workers' union had asked for a sizable wage increase, which the steel companies claimed they could not grant without higher prices. Truman's Wage Stabilization Board had recommended the wage increase. However, the head of the Office of Defense Mobilization agreed with the industry that sizable price increases would be necessary if wages were increased and believed it would destabilize the economy.

The United Steel Workers of America voted to strike. After postponing the deadline several times, union president Philip Murray informed the steel companies that a strike would commence at 12:01 a.m. on April 9. Truman was in a difficult position. He did not want to grant the wage increase, nor did he wish to employ the machinery of the Taft-Hartley Act, a law he had publicly called unjust and repressive and which had been passed over his veto. On the other hand, the nation needed steel. After his Wage Stabilization Board tried unsuccessfully to resolve the conflict, Truman acted.

---

34. *Lebron v. United States*, 229 F.2d 16 (1955).

On the evening of April 8, the President issued Executive Order 10340, directing Secretary of Commerce Charles Sawyer to take possession of the steel mills of eighty-five companies. The War Labor Disputes Act, which Truman had used to seize the coal mines in 1946, had now expired with the formal end of the Second World War. The Taft-Hartley Act did provide for courts to enjoin strikes, but did not provide for Presidential seizure of an industry to end or prevent a walkout. So Truman based his order on constitutional rather than statutory grounds — on "the authority vested in me by the Constitution and laws of the United States, and as President of the United States and Commander-in-Chief of the armed forces of the United States."

An hour after Truman issued his executive order, attorneys for the Youngstown Sheet and Tube and Republic Steel companies knocked on Judge Walter Bastian's door and handed him a motion for a temporary restraining order and an application for a permanent injunction. Bastian would not act without hearing from the government and set a hearing for 11:30 the next morning. By that time similar motions had been filed by other steel companies.

The motion for the restraining order was heard by Alexander Holtzoff, sitting as motions judge. For the government, Holmes Baldridge, Assistant Attorney General in charge of the Claims Division and an antitrust expert, argued that Article II of the Constitution was sufficiently broad that it gave the President "the power to protect the country in times of national emergency." Holtzoff was concerned that, even though an injunction would technically run against the Secretary of Commerce, it would have the effect of nullifying an order of the President of the United States "promulgated by him to meet a nation-wide emergency problem." For this reason, and the fact that the steel companies could continue to operate during the seizure and ultimately recover damages, Holtzoff denied the temporary restraining order.[35] Nevertheless, the suits for permanent injunctions were still pending. Judge Bastian, who owned thirty shares of Sharon Steel (not a party to the suits), referred that part of the case to Judge David A. Pine. Pine informed the parties that his wife owned some shares in Bethlehem Steel, but neither party objected to his hearing the case.

Pine, sixty years old, Washington-born, had served in the Justice Department during the Wilson and Roosevelt administrations, beginning as confidential clerk to Attorney General James McReynolds and working his

---

35. *Youngstown Sheet & Tube Co. v. Sawyer*, 103 F. Supp. 569 (1952).

way up to be U.S. Attorney for the District of Columbia before being appointed to the District Court by Roosevelt in 1940. Hard-working, conservative, mild-mannered, and slightly stooped in appearance, Pine had a bit of a reputation for absent-mindedness, gained one day when he almost sentenced a lawyer, instead of the lawyer's client, to jail.

Because the government opposed an early hearing on the permanent injunction, the steel companies, on Pine's advice, filed motions for preliminary injunctions. At the hearing—at which twenty-one attorneys appeared for seven steel companies—Pine did not focus upon the questions of equity that are traditionally at issue in such hearings, but rather seemed to be concerned with the constitutional issues. Perhaps the most telling moment of the hearing came when Baldridge, again arguing for the government, stated that "we read Article II of the Constitution" as placing no limits on the powers of the Executive. That assertion, pounced on by opponents of the seizure, greatly damaged the President in the battle for public opinion, even though he disavowed it.

On April 29 Pine rendered judgment.[36] In his fifteen-page opinion, Pine stated that the administration's claim "spells a form of government alien to our constitutional government of limited powers." He held the acts of the government "illegal and without authority of law." He then granted the applications for injunctive relief:

> Under these circumstances I am of the opinion that, weighing the injuries and taking the last-mentioned considerations into account, the balance is on the side of plaintiffs. Furthermore,...I believe that the contemplated strike, if it came, with all its awful results, would be less injurious to the public than the injury which would flow from a timorous judicial recognition that there is some basis for this claim to unlimited and unrestrained Executive powers.

Government attorneys worked through the night on an appeal brief, and all the next day the Court of Appeals heard argument *en banc* on the government's motion to stay Pine's decision. The Court adjourned at 6:09 and reconvened forty-one minutes later. Chief Judge Stephens announced a forty-eight-hour stay, essentially so that the Supreme Court would be able to consider petitions for certiorari. Although every member of the Court of Appeals save Judge Edgerton had been appointed by Truman, the Court divided 5–4 on the stay petition. Those voting for the stay were Edgerton, Prettyman, and the three 1949 appointees; Miller, Clark, Proctor, and Stephens opposed

---

36. 103 F. Supp. 569 (1952).

it. The stay did not, however, prevent the government from granting the wage increases during the period of time it was controlling the industry.

Before Stephens had a chance to leave the courtroom after announcing the stay, attorneys for the steel companies buttonholed him and pointed out that the Court had imposed no conditions with the stay. The upshot was that the lawyers worked through another night. The next morning formal application was filed to attach a condition to the stay stating that no changes could be made in the terms or conditions of employment while it was in effect, unless the companies agreed to the changes or a collective bargaining settlement was reached. This was followed by more argument before the Court *en banc*. By the same 5–4 vote, the application was denied.[37]

The Supreme Court granted certiorari on May 3, setting the case down for argument on May 12 and telling the government not to take any action to change any term or condition of employment. On June 2, by a 6–3 vote, the Supreme Court ruled the steel seizure unconstitutional. There were seven opinions, one by each of the justices in the majority and a single dissenting opinion, written by Chief Justice Vinson. The opinion of the Court, by Justice Black, held that the seizure of property is a lawmaking task and that Congress had not provided Truman authorization for the seizure. The dissenters emphasized the nature of the emergency, the importance of steel as a war material, and the many past actions taken by presidents in emergencies.[38]

Truman immediately complied with the Court's decision and withdrew government control from the steel mills. A fifty-three-day steel strike followed, ending in sizable wage and price hikes that accelerated inflation and destroyed the system of economic stabilization. In the longer run, the Steel Seizure case became a central precedent for dealing with claims of Presidential power, giving the courts some authority to resist claims of inherent executive power.

Pine's opinion in this case is remembered as part of a long line in which judges of the District of Columbia Circuit have held the executive branch accountable under the rule of law, dating back to Judge Cranch's stand against President Jefferson in the *Bollman and Swartwout* case and Judge Merrick's in the *Lyons* case during the Civil War. The Steel Seizure case also presaged other blockbuster separation-of-powers cases yet to come in the D.C. Circuit, among them the *Pentagon Papers* case and *United States v. Nixon*.

---

37. *Sawyer v. United States Steel Co.*, 197 F.2d 582 (1952) (*Edg*-Pre-Baz-Fahy-Was/Ste-Cla-WMil-Pro).

38. *Youngstown Sheet and Tube Co. v. Sawyer*, 343 U.S. 579 (1952).

Chapter 6

Crucial Controversies

The Eisenhower Years, 1953–60

The years Dwight D. Eisenhower was President of the United States were years of consolidation, not crusade. After the upheavals of the Depression and the New Deal, the horrors of the Second World War, and the disruptions of the early postwar years, the American people seemed to need time to rest and absorb the developments of the previous two decades. That is what the Eisenhower presidency offered.

The Eisenhower administration was conservative (but not strongly partisan) and cautious, preferring state to national regulation, private over public initiatives, the status quo to change. However, it proved unable to hold back the growth of the welfare state or to disperse expectations that the federal government would take a leading role in responding to social and economic problems. If the administration made no real effort to dismantle the regulatory structures put in place by the New Deal, it also did little to prevent the regulatory agencies' penetration and capture by private enterprise.

The President himself, a man who sought to be a grand national harmonizer, did not offer strong leadership on two of the great issues of his day — "McCarthyism" and racial equality. The courts, particularly the Supreme Court, would attempt to fill the vacuum in both areas. Ironically, a relatively passive President contributed to a more activist federal judiciary.

Although silent about civil rights nationally, Dwight Eisenhower came to the presidency pledged to end segregation in the District of Columbia, and he helped to do so. Within four months of the first decision in *Brown v. Board of Education*, a desegregated school system opened without violence. Public accommodations and recreational facilities were also rapidly desegregated. However, integration in the schools triggered massive white flight. While the Washington metropolitan area grew steadily during the 1950s, the population of the District itself declined; by 1960 a majority of the city's population was black. Nonetheless, as late as 1957, there was not a single black police lieutenant, and the city's craft unions were exclusively white.

Support for home rule grew in the District of Columbia and was endorsed by both national political parties. It was stymied, however, by the Board of Trade and the House Committee on the District of Columbia. Lacking authority to deal with many local problems, denied the power to raise taxes, unable to effectively attack problems such as pollution, sewage disposal, and increased traffic without more metropolitan area cooperation, the D.C. Commissioners were frustrated and ineffectual.

During the years of Eisenhower's presidency, the federal courts of the District of Columbia wrestled repeatedly with volatile, highly visible cases whose political content was only partially hidden by the legal questions they addressed. These struggles, most notably in the areas of loyalty and security and the criminal law, opened gaps between the District Court judges and the Court of Appeals and, more visibly, among the judges of the Court of Appeals.

Eisenhower's Judicial Appointments

Dwight Eisenhower's impact on the courts of the District of Columbia Circuit was not as great as that of his predecessor. Not only did the Eisenhower administration spawn fewer constitutional conflicts, but Eisenhower's appointments to the Court of Appeals and District Court — seven in all — were on average less distinguished than F.D.R.'s, or Truman's of 1949. Nevertheless, two — Warren E. Burger and John J. Sirica — would achieve great renown during judicial careers of almost thirty years each.

The Court of Appeals

Eisenhower replaced three conservative members of the Court of Appeals — James M. Proctor, Bennett Champ Clark, and Harold M. Stephens — with three men who would develop into sturdy pro-government judges. Proctor died in September 1953 at the age of seventy-one, after twenty-two years on the bench, five of them on the Court of Appeals. Just two weeks later, John A. Danaher was appointed in his place. Clark died the next year, aged sixty-four, and his seat was filled by elevating Walter M. Bastian from the District Court. When Stephens died in 1955, after almost twenty years on the Court, the Chief Judgeship passed automatically to Henry W. Edgerton, pursuant to the 1948 law under which the most senior judge under seventy years of age would succeed to the post. To the vacant judgeship Eisenhower appointed Warren E. Burger, who took his seat in April 1956.

John A. Danaher, the first U.S. Senator in almost fifty years to become a judge of the Court of Appeals, was born in Meriden, Connecticut, in 1899. Active in Republican state politics, he ran successfully for the U.S. Senate in 1938, vowing to oppose Franklin D. Roosevelt.[1] Danaher was defeated for reelection in 1944, after which he practiced law in Washington with the firm of Danaher, Poole & Levy (with which Charles Fahy was briefly associated) and continued to be active in politics.

After working effectively for Eisenhower's election in 1952, Danaher hoped to be named to the U.S. Court of Appeals for the Second Circuit, but there was strong opposition from Chief Judge Charles E. Clark and members of the Yale Law School faculty. Attorney General Herbert Brownell convinced Danaher to accept appointment to the D.C. Circuit, knowing he could be confirmed there and predicting that he would become an effective counterweight to Judges Edgerton and Bazelon. An active member of the D.C. Circuit until 1969, Danaher began as a moderate conservative and developed into a strong conservative. He proved to be of special value to his colleagues in cases involving statutory interpretation, but perhaps his most important legacy was his leadership in the reform of bail practices in the District of Columbia during the 1960s. Danaher died in 1990.

Walter Maximillian Bastian, born in Washington in 1891, spent his entire pre-judicial career in private practice in the city, serving as president of the Bar Association of the District of Columbia (1936) and later as treasurer of the American Bar Association, and lecturing at the National School of Law. Although he was a Republican, Truman appointed Bastian district judge in 1950. Brownell had also been instrumental in Bastian's appointment, and came to see him as "the essence of reason." Bastian wrote brief, common-sense decisions with limited resort to scholarly apparatus. Deferential to the other branches of the federal government, to the administrative agencies, and to the District Court, he was, with Wilbur K. Miller, one of the most conservative judges on the Court of the late 1950s and the 1960s. Bastian died in 1975.

Neither Bastian, who took senior status in 1965, nor Danaher, who did so in 1969, left an important mark on American law. However, Eisenhower's third appointee, Warren E. Burger, who was a judge of the D.C. Circuit from 1956

---

1. As he recalled in a 1968 interview, "I certainly had no intention whatever of seeing bureaucracy increase and its leadership vested in the hands of appointees of the President with scarcely any accountability to the public."

to 1969, did. Burger was forty-eight years old at the time he was appointed to the bench. Minnesota born and educated, Burger impressed leaders of the Dewey-Eisenhower wing of the Republican Party at the 1948 and 1952 conventions. Brownell appointed him Assistant Attorney General in charge of the Claims (later Civil) Division of the Department of Justice in 1953.

As Brownell described it almost forty years later, Burger's appointment to the D.C. Circuit was "a fluke." After two years in the Justice Department, Burger intended to return to his law practice in St. Paul. But the health of his wife, Elvira, was frail and Minnesota's climate was judged insalubrious for her. When Brownell heard of this, he quickly arranged for Burger's appointment to the bench. Burger accepted the position with some hesitation, perhaps because he felt his temperament was more that of an advocate than a judge, or perhaps because in twenty-three years in practice his total experience in criminal justice had been two straightforward cases as court-appointed counsel. A strong, forceful man with considerable administrative talent, Burger would have an important influence on the direction of the Court of Appeals.

In 1958 Edgerton, having reached the age of seventy, was obliged to retire as Chief Judge and exercised his option of remaining on the Court as an associate judge. The Chief Judgeship passed automatically to Prettyman, the most senior associate judge under seventy. Two years later, under the same mechanism, Wilbur K. Miller took over the Chief Judgeship when Prettyman turned seventy.

The District Court

During the 1950s, the District Court was conservative, undistinguished, and tending to the parochial. Eisenhower made four appointments to the District Court: Joseph C. McGarraghy in 1954, John J. Sirica in 1957, George L. Hart Jr. in 1958, and Leonard P. Walsh in 1959. All were local attorneys and three had been very active in local Republican politics. McGarraghy had spent almost forty years in private practice and had served as president of the Washington Board of Trade and chairman of the Republican Committee for the District. Sirica (see also chapter nine), the son of an Italian immigrant, had spent many years as a solo practitioner in the District before joining Hogan & Hartson in 1949 as their leading litigator. Hart, who had also been Republican Committee chairman in the District, would become an able Chief Judge of the District Court. In the 1960s his voice would be perhaps the loudest among the district judges who were publicly critical of the "liberal" decisions of the Court of Appeals. Walsh, born in Wisconsin, had practiced in Washington from 1933 to 1953, had been president of the Bar Association of the District of Columbia, and had served as Chief Judge of the Municipal Court from 1953 to 1959.

The Chief Judge of the District Court from 1945 to 1958 was Bolitha J. Laws. Born in Washington in 1891, he spent his entire career in the city and was appointed to the District Court by Franklin D. Roosevelt in 1938. He was designated judge of the U.S. Emergency Court of Appeals in 1943 and appointed Chief Judge in 1945. Laws was a vigorous advocate for the needs of his court before the Judicial Conference of the United States. He was followed as Chief Judge by F. Dickinson Letts (1958–59) and David A. Pine (1959–61).

Jurisprudence

During the Eisenhower years, in contrast with the Truman period, it was the Court of Appeals that was the more visible of the two federal courts of the D.C. Circuit and the one that produced the most important jurisprudence. Although it encountered no "blockbuster" cases comparable to those of the Truman era, during these years one can observe the Court of Appeals beginning to take advantage of the richness of its jurisdiction. Consistently confronted with cases raising important issues of administrative law, criminal procedure, and separation of powers, the Court of Appeals made significant contributions in each of these areas. This activity began to attract considerable attention from judges outside the jurisdiction as well as from law professors and other shapers of opinion.

The D.C. Circuit's unique jurisprudential mix overlapped that of the other circuits primarily in diversity cases and cases brought from the National Labor Relations Board and the U.S. Tax Court. It is unsurprising, therefore, that the most important case lines in the 1950s were "local" cases, primarily criminal, and "national" cases arising from the courts' location in the capital, mainly loyalty-security and administrative cases. By the end of this period, largely because of its work in these three areas, the Court of Appeals had developed a reputation for innovation, boldness, and controversy, characteristics that not every observer found admirable. By the end of the 1950s the U.S. Court of Appeals for the District of Columbia Circuit had become one of the nation's most closely watched courts.

During the 1950s, the courts of the D.C. Circuit were still doing a healthy local business, hearing cases involving violent crimes as well as tort, family law, and commercial matters—cases that in other jurisdictions would have come before state courts. The local criminal cases repeatedly raised difficult problems—questions of oversight of police conduct, the proper role of court-appointed counsel for the indigent on appeal, and the scope of the insanity defense. In the latter case line in particular, the boldness of some of the judges and their willingness to rethink old problems and face new ones, with the risk of criticism that entailed, raised the profile of the Court, as did thoughtful criticism of these new directions by some other members of the Court. The Court's consideration of the insanity defense also produced what is arguably the most important decision in the D.C. Circuit during this period, *Durham v. United States.*

The Court's location at the seat of the government brought it appeals in prosecutions growing out of congressional investigations, suits over the dismissal of federal employees under the government's loyalty program, and cases involving review of the regulatory commissions. Two important categories of cases, involving the FCC and the Subversive Activities Control Board (the latter treated in chapter seven), could have been brought *only* in the D.C. Circuit. Although the Court of Appeals had not yet emerged as the nation's major administrative tribunal, it would leave a legacy of important administrative law. During a time of burgeoning economic growth—a period characterized not by cozy relationships between the regulators and the regulated—the Court of Appeals repeatedly stressed the duty of the regulators to protect the public interest.

Of the traditional concerns of the D.C. Circuit, only one—racial civil rights—generated few cases. But even here, an appreciation of the District's history of racial discrimination surely affected the way in which some of the judges approached their criminal law docket. Beginning in the 1950s, and increasingly during the sixties and early seventies, the liberal wing of the Court of Appeals saw itself as a sort of ombudsman to a disenfranchised black municipality.

Many of the most important issues facing the District of Columbia Circuit during the 1950s—especially the loyalty-security and criminal cases— raised questions of how much discretion the courts would allow government officials and how vigorously judicial power would be wielded to oversee governmental conduct which impacted upon civil liberties. During the 1950s, the Court of Appeals was consistently, and often bitterly, divided over these issues. While a strong civil-liberties wing coalesced toward the end of the decade, the majority of the Court—made up of Eisenhower's three appointees and the two most senior Truman appointees—took a position of much greater deference to the political branches. Virtually all of the District Court judges belonged to this camp, although they were less publicly vocal about it in the fifties than they would become in the sixties. Within the Court of Appeals, stresses around these issues, especially those involving the rights of criminal defendants, increased dramatically during the decade, resulting in a bitterly fractured bench, not only jurisprudentially but personally as well.

Loyalty-Security Cases

Public anxiety about subversive activities reached its peak early in the 1950s, but loyalty matters occupied the courts well into the 1960s. During the years of the Eisenhower presidency, the D.C. Circuit handled more loyalty-security cases than any other American court. The cases arose in a number of contexts, including prosecutions for contempt of Congress and perjury before congressional committees, challenges to the federal loyalty program, and denials of applications for passports.

Like most American courts, those of the D.C. Circuit generally upheld the contentions of the government in these cases—about seventy-five percent of the time during the Eisenhower era. In part this was because the Supreme Court under Chief Justice Vinson had not left much black-letter law that was helpful in cabining congressional investigations or in assuring procedural due process for government employees faced with security investigations. In its early years, the Warren Court was badly divided in loyalty-security matters and often cautious, although even then it placed some limits on governmental conduct. Without guidance or support from the High Court or from more moderate forces in the political branches, the judges of the D.C. Circuit approached internal security questions from the position of judicial restraint. When interests were balanced, they ordinarily found the scales tipping to the government's need for security. Virtually none of the judges of the District Court save Luther Youngdahl, a Truman appointee and a Republican, were sympathetic to claims of individual rights in this area. While loyalty-security issues divided the Court of Appeals, only Judges Edgerton and Bazelon consistently refused to defer to the government, although occasionally they picked up support from Judges Fahy and Washington.

Contempt of Congress

The courts of the circuit were particularly reluctant to curb the abuses of congressional investigatory committees, which bullied witnesses and often limited the right to use counsel and to cross-examine witnesses. Perhaps no case better illustrates the abuse of investigatory power than that of Owen

Lattimore. Lattimore was director of the School of International Relations at Johns Hopkins, an Asian specialist who had acted as a political advisor to Chiang Kai-Shek during the Second World War at the request President Roosevelt. When China was "lost" to the Communists in 1949, the search for scapegoats began. In 1950 Senator Joseph McCarthy named Lattimore "one of the top Communist agents in the country." After extensive hearings, a Senate subcommittee concluded that the charges against him were a fraud.

However, the following year another subcommittee, chaired by Senator Pat McCarran of Nevada, held six months of hearings with Lattimore as its principal target. Lattimore was on the witness stand for a total of twelve days, grilled about incidents that had occurred almost a decade earlier. His recollections were then compared with documents the subcommittee would not allow him to see. Prodded by McCarran, the Department of Justice prosecuted Lattimore on seven counts of perjury.

The case was assigned to District Judge Luther Youngdahl. Born in 1896 in Minneapolis, Youngdahl had become a municipal court judge at the age of thirty-four and, twelve years later, a justice of the Minnesota Supreme Court. He was elected governor of Minnesota in 1946 and served until 1951, when, although he was a Republican, Harry Truman appointed him to the District Court for the District of Columbia.

Youngdahl dismissed four of the seven counts against Lattimore and indicated serious doubts about the other three. The government appealed, and a badly divided Court of Appeals sitting *en banc* affirmed as to two counts and reversed as to the other two.[2] The government obtained a new indictment and sought unsuccessfully to have Youngdahl disqualify himself. Youngdahl dismissed all of the new charges, stating that "to require defendant to go to trial for perjury under charges so formless and obscure would be unprecedented and would make a sham of the Sixth Amendment and the Federal Rule requiring specificity of charges." The dismissal was affirmed, but again the Court of Appeals was closely divided. Five years after he had originally been cleared by the first Senate subcommittee, Lattimore was formally exonerated.[3] Nevertheless, the fractures evident in the Court of Appeals over this issue hardly inspired the Congress to curb this sort of behavior.

---

2. *United States v. Lattimore*, 112 F. Supp. 507 (1953) (Youngdahl), aff'd in part, rev'd in part, 215 F.2d 847 (1954).

3. *United States v. Lattimore*, 127 F. Supp. 405 (Youngdahl 1955), aff'd, 232 F.2d 334 (1955). Two years later, in the case of a foreign service officer accused, like Lattimore, of "losing China," the Supreme Court reversed the Court of Appeals for the District of Columbia Circuit and held his firing invalid because the Secretary of State had acted

In 1956, eight years after its panel decision in *Barsky v. United States* upholding broad congressional power to investigate the loyalty of citizens, the full Court of Appeals came to grips with the constitutionality of that power in *Watkins v. United States*. John T. Watkins, a labor organizer, was accused of having been a member of the Communist Party. Testifying before the House Un-American Activities Committee, he freely answered questions about his own past activities but refused to speak about individuals who, to his knowledge, had long since removed themselves from the Communist movement. A divided panel of the Court of Appeals — Judges Edgerton and Bazelon in the majority, Judge Bastian in dissent — overturned Watkins' conviction for contempt of Congress.

There was sharp criticism of the panel decision in *Watkins* and the full court granted the Justice Department's petition for rehearing *en banc*. Upon rehearing, Watkins' conviction was upheld 7–2. Writing for the Court, Judge Bastian held that Congress had the power to investigate the Communist Party, the Committee had been properly authorized by the House to investigate, the purpose of its investigation was valid, and the questions put to Watkins had been pertinent to the Committee's legislative purpose.

In dissent, Judge Edgerton (joined by Bazelon) stated, "If we were obliged to decide what the Committee's purpose was in asking the questions Watkins would not answer, we might be forced to conclude that the Committee asked them for the sole purpose of exposure." It was, he continued, "very questionable whether exposure of individuals to public contempt or hostility is a 'valid legislative purpose.'"[4]

At the end of its 1956 term, the Supreme Court reversed by a vote of 6–1.[5] Chief Justice Warren, speaking for the Court, administered a lengthy scolding to the Congress, reminding that body that it had no general authority to expose the private lives of individuals. However, the actual holding in *Watkins*, which was limited to the question of pertinency, could be — and was — read both by the Congress and by the lower courts not as a limitation on the prerogatives of congressional committees but merely as a requirement to explain to a witness the subject of its inquiry and how its questions were pertinent to that subject.

---

arbitrarily. *Service v. Dulles*, 354 U.S. 363 (1957), reversing 235 F.2d 215 (1956) (*Bas-Was-WMil*).

   4. *Watkins v. United States*, 233 F.2d 681 (1956) (*Bas-Pre-WMil-Fahy-Was-Dan/Edg-Baz*).

   5. 354 U.S. 178 (1957).

The same day the Supreme Court decided the *Watkins* case, it granted
certiorari in another contempt of Congress case coming out of the D.C. Circuit, *Barenblatt v. United States*, then remanded it to the Court of Appeals
for consideration in light of *Watkins*. Lloyd Barenblatt, a former University
of Michigan student who had been called before a HUAC subcommittee investigating Communism in higher education, had refused to answer the
Committee's questions because he disputed the Committee's underlying authority. He was convicted of contempt of Congress and an Appeals Court
panel of Bastian (writing), Burger, and Washington affirmed.[6]

On remand, the Court of Appeals, sitting *en banc*, sustained Barenblatt's
conviction by a vote of 5–4. Judge Bastian, writing for the majority, held that
"Barenblatt was made fully aware of the subject under inquiry and was in a
position to judge the pertinency of the questions relating to that subject. We
are further of the opinion that the questions were in fact relevant and pertinent to that subject." Judges Edgerton, Bazelon, Fahy and Washington dissented. The Supreme Court, also by a 5–4 vote, agreed with the majority of
the Court of Appeals.[7] Eight cases had been held for *en banc* consideration
by the Court of Appeals pending the resolution of *Barenblatt*. After the
Supreme Court decision, they were instead referred to the same Appeals
Court panel of Bastian, Burger, and Washington, which upheld six of the eight
convictions.[8]

The Federal Loyalty Program

A number of important cases heard by the courts of the District of Columbia Circuit involved challenges to the constitutionality and scope of the
federal loyalty program instituted by President Truman and expanded
under Eisenhower, as well as questions of procedural due process in the dismissal of employees. The Court of Appeals generally defended the program,
while the Supreme Court tended to limit it.

President Truman's Executive Order 9835, issued in 1947 (see chapter
five), had been supplemented by Congress with the Summary Suspension
Act of 1950,[9] which gave the heads of eleven federal agencies with especially
close links to national security the authority to suspend any employee sus-

6. *Barenblatt v. United States*, 240 F.2d 875 (1958).
7. *Barenblatt v. United States*, 252 F.2d 129 (1958) (*Bas*-Pre-WMil-Dan-Bur/*Edg*-Baz-*Fahy*-Was), aff'd, 360 U.S. 109 (1959).
8. See *Gojack v. United States*, 280 F.2d 678 (1960), and the seven other cases that follow directly in 280 F.2d.
9. 64 Stat. 476.

pected of disloyalty. Soon after taking office, the Eisenhower administration extended the federal loyalty program with Executive Order 10430. The Eisenhower program was predicated on the notion that the American Communist Party, in cooperation with the Soviet Union, was engaged in a gigantic conspiracy to penetrate the government. It encompassed jobs with no connection to national security, allowed the removal of employees as "security risks" for infractions having nothing to do with loyalty, and severely restricted the possibility of review of a dismissal. At the time the Eisenhower loyalty program was adopted, the leading judicial authority on its constitutionality was the 1950 Court of Appeals decision in *Bailey v. Richardson*, which upheld a dismissal on loyalty grounds through procedures which made a mockery of due process (see chapter five).

The first important case testing the Eisenhower program was *Cole v. Young*.[10] Kendrick Cole, a Food and Drug Administration inspector in a nonsensitive, non-policy-making position, had been terminated after declining to answer charges that he had associated with Communists and was connected with an organization on the Attorney General's list. In 1954 Judge Alexander Holtzoff upheld the new loyalty program against constitutional attack in Cole's case. The Court of Appeals—Prettyman (writing), Bastian, and Edgerton (dissenting)—affirmed, upholding the extension of summary dismissal procedures beyond the agencies authorized in the Summary Suspension Act. The extension, the Court said, was "a pronouncement by the President that in his judgment it is advisable in the interest of the national security under present circumstances that no employee be retained unless his retention is clearly consistent with the interests of the national security."

The Supreme Court agreed with Edgerton, holding as a matter of statutory interpretation that Congress had intended to have the Act applied only to sensitive positions or agencies. If the law was to be invoked, the agency first had to make the determination that the position held by the employee was in fact related to national security.[11]

In *Cole* and at least two other cases challenging the loyalty program,[12] the Court of Appeals upheld the government and the Supreme Court re-

---

10. 125 F. Supp. 284 (1954), aff'd, 226 F.2d 337 (1955) (*Pre-Bas/Edg*).

11. 351 U.S. 536 (1956).

12. In *Peters v. Hobby*, 349 U.S. 331 (1955) (the case in the Court of Appeals is not reported), a consultant to the U.S. Public Health Service, charged with Communist affiliations, was discharged as a security risk and barred from federal employment for three years; the government's argument before the Supreme Court, given by Warren Burger, then Assistant Attorney General for the Civil Division, is reported in *Peters v.*

versed each time. In none of these decisions, however, did the High Court come to grips with the constitutional issues inhering in the loyalty program itself.

Denial of Passports

Under the Internal Security Act of 1950, known as the McCarren Act,[13] members of the Communist Party or Communist-front organizations were prohibited from applying for or using passports. During the 1950s hundreds of persons, illustrious and obscure alike, were denied passports by the State Department. Among the prominent left-wingers refused passports were the author Howard Fast, the painter Rockwell Kent, the actor-singer Paul Robeson, the lawyer Leonard Boudin, and the scientist Linus Pauling. On this issue, the D.C. courts and the Supreme Court were notably bolder than in other loyalty-security areas, largely abandoning the almost unlimited discretion they had recognized in the State Department since passports had been first required of Americans in 1914. The Court of Appeals made important contributions to the evolution of the law in this area.

An early example of the courts' resolve concerned the revocation of the passport of Anne Bauer, a naturalized American citizen who was working as a journalist in Paris. The only explanation given for the cancellation was that "her activities are contrary to the best interests of the United States." A three-judge District Court of the District of Columbia held that the revocation constituted a deprivation of personal liberty under the Due Process clause. Writing for the Court, Judge Richmond Keech acknowledged that the Secretary of State had wide discretion; however, as with "other curtailments of personal liberty for the public good, the regulation of passports must be administered, not arbitrarily or capriciously, but fairly, applying the law equally to all citizens without discrimination, and with due process adopted to the exigencies of the situation."[14]

Hobby, 99 L.Ed. 1133–34 (1955). *Vitarelli v. Seaton*, 253 F.2d 338 (1958) (*Was*-Dan-Fahy), rev'd, 359 U.S. 535 (1959), concerned an Interior Department employee discharged under the loyalty program, although it was later revealed that the real reason for dismissal was his poor job performance, not his past left-wing connections. See also *Greene v. McElroy*, 254 F.2d 944 (1958) (*Was*-WMil-Dan), rev'd, 360 U.S. 474 (1959), in which the Supreme Court likewise reversed a Court of Appeals ruling that upheld the revocation of the security clearance of a private citizen whose company did business with the Defense Department. In all these cases, the accused had no access to the purported evidence nor the opportunity to confront their accusers.

13. 78 Stat. 168.
14. *Bauer v. Acheson*, 106 F. Supp. 445 (1952) (*Keech-Curran*(c)/*Fahy*).

The State Department responded to the decision by establishing regulations defining the scope of its authority, categories of persons who were to be denied passports (including members of the Communist Party and those who supported its goals or whose activities abroad would advance the Communist movement), and machinery for hearing and appeal.

While Eisenhower was President, the Court of Appeals five times overturned passport denials or prodded action after long delays. In one of these cases, concerning the denial of a passport to the chairman of the Independent Socialist League, the Court further articulated the concept of a right to travel. As Judge Fahy wrote, "The right to travel, to go from place to place," is a "natural right subject to the rights of others and to reasonable regulation under law."[15]

In 1956, in the District Court, Judge Youngdahl overturned the State Department's refusal to grant a passport to Leonard Boudin on the basis of confidential information to which Boudin had not had access. The full Court of Appeals, Washington writing, unanimously upheld Youngdahl's ruling and the case was remanded to the State Department for further consideration.[16]

However, the following year the Court of Appeals, sitting *en banc*, decided two high-profile cases — involving Walter Briehl, a psychoanalyst, and Rockwell Kent, the painter — 5–3 for the government. The Briehl case generated the principal opinions. Judge Prettyman wrote for four judges and signaled that judicial review in these cases would be limited, citing "the exceedingly broad boundaries within which [the Secretary of State] is free to act without judicial review." He then concluded:

> In the international situation of the present, the reasonable requirements of national security and interest and the delicate characteristics of foreign relations outweigh the needs or desires of an individual to travel, when the Secretary finds the facts to be such as to preclude grant of a passport under the regulation.

Judge Washington concurred only in the result, and Judges Bazelon, Edgerton, and Fahy, each writing an opinion, dissented. Edgerton said, "We have temporized too long with the passport practices of the State Department. Iron curtains have no place in a free world." Bazelon argued, "The word 'Communist' is not an incantation subverting at a stroke our Constitution and all our cherished liberties."[17]

---

15. *Shachtman v. Dulles*, 225 F.2d 938 (1955) (*Fahy-Edg*(c)-Was).
16. *Boudin v. Dulles*, 235 F.2d 532 (1956), aff'g 136 F. Supp. 218 (1956).
17. *Briehl v. Dulles*, 248 F.2d 561 (1957) (*Pre-WMil-Dan-Bas-Was*(c)/*Edg-Baz-Fahy*).

A closely divided Supreme Court reversed in both cases. The High Court sharply curtailed the wide-ranging discretionary authority of the State Department in the absence of statutory authority, holding that the right to travel is part of every American's "liberty" and cannot be deprived without due process of law.[18] The State Department issued the passports in the outstanding cases, and for its pains was criticized by the Chairman of the Un-American Activities Committee for complying so speedily with the Supreme Court decision. Some commentators suggested that the Supreme Court had come close to legalizing treason.

Administrative Law

Although the Court of Appeals was not yet viewed as the nation's principal administrative tribunal, during the 1950s it produced a body of important administrative law. The Eisenhower years were a time of enormous economic and technological growth, and the federal regulatory commissions were called upon to oversee mushrooming industries, including television, transcontinental airlines, electric power, and natural gas. Review of the Federal Power Commission and the Federal Communications Commission generated the greatest number of important administrative decisions. The conduct of the FCC also yielded the most important political corruption cases in the Circuit during the era.

The regulatory agencies were heavily criticized during these years. Informed observers castigated them for declining to use their regulatory authority, as well as for their arbitrariness, sluggishness, expense, and susceptibility to political pressures. Staffed for the most part by undistinguished patronage appointees, the commissions tended to equate the public interest with the private interests of the groups they were regulating. Toward the end of the decade, congressional hearings publicly revealed the lack of vigor of the regulators and the unhealthy coziness between the regulators and those they regulated.

In the 1950s the courts were no longer seen as a threat to the continued existence of the agencies, as they had been by some in the 1930s. They did attempt to promote consistency in agency decision making while leaving the agencies a good deal of discretion in formulating and implementing policies, and without disturbing informal communication and negotiation processes. During these years the U.S. Court of Appeals seemed to see itself

---

18. *Kent v. Dulles*, 357 U.S. 116 (1958), rev'g *Briehl*.

as a counterweight to the capture of the agencies by the regulated industries, constantly reminding them of their duty to protect the public interest.

The courts also served as a spur that often prodded less-than-vigorous regulators to act. A notable example of this involved the Federal Power Commission. *Wisconsin v. FPC* concerned the regulation of the price of natural gas at the wellhead. The Natural Gas Act of 1938 was unclear on whether the FPC had authority over the field prices paid by pipeline companies to independent gas producers and gatherers. Northern gas-using states sought such regulation; southern states opposed it. After a 1947 Supreme Court decision holding that all sales in interstate commerce were subject to federal regulation,[19] an unsuccessful attempt had been made in the Congress to limit FPC jurisdiction.

Then, in 1951, in a case involving the Phillips Petroleum Company brought by the State of Wisconsin and several midwestern cities, the FPC ruled that it had no power to fix the field prices of independents. The Court of Appeals for the District of Columbia Circuit, dividing 2–1, reversed the agency, stating that the Act and governing Supreme Court decisions "permit only one answer"—that the FPC should have fixed the rates. The Supreme Court held, by a 5–3 vote, that while Philips's production activities could not be regulated by the FPC, its sales to pipelines intending to resell did fall within the Natural Gas Act and FPC jurisdiction.[20] In the wake of the decision, the FPC was deluged with thousands of rate applications from producers—so many that it finally abandoned the attempt to regulate rates on a case-by-case basis and established regional producer rates and ceiling prices.[21]

Precedent-Setting Decisions

In the 1950s the Court of Appeals made important black-letter law on such matters as the finality of an administrative order, the factors governing the issuance of a judicial stay of an administrative proceeding, and standing and intervention.

Isbrandtsen v. United States involved the question of what kind of administrative order is "final" for purposes of judicial review. At issue was a

---

19. *Interstate Gas Co. v. FPC*, 331 U.S. 682 (1947)

20. *Phillips Petroleum Co. v. Wisconsin*, 347 U.S. 672 (1954), aff'g *Wisconsin v. FPC*, 205 F.2d 706 (1953) (*Edg*-Pre/*Cla*). See also discussion in *Shell Oil Co. v. FPC*, 520 F.2d 1061 (5th Cir. 1975).

21. In *Wisconsin v. FPC*, 303 F.2d 380 (1961) (*Pre*-Dan/*Fahy*(c/d)), the Court of Appeals upheld the Commission's establishment of area rates.

Federal Maritime Board order which had permitted, on a temporary basis, eighteen common-carrier shipping lines to charge lower rates to shippers using them exclusively and higher rates to others, thus "encouraging" exclusive use of those eighteen companies. Isbrandtsen, the only other shipping line competing for the Japanese-Atlantic trade, requested an immediate hearing and suspension of the system prior to the hearing. The Board denied the request, and when Isbrandtsen sought review in the Court of Appeals, argued that its order was merely interlocutory and therefore unreviewable. A majority of Judges Bazelon and Prettyman (Judge Fahy dissented) held that the order was final for purposes of review because "[whether or not the statutory requirements of finality are satisfied in any given case... depends not upon the label affixed to its action by the administrative agency but rather upon a realistic appraisal of the consequences of such action."[22]

In *Virginia Petroleum Jobber's Ass'n v. FPC*, the Court of Appeals denied a stay sought by a petroleum distributor pending the Court's review of an FPC order denying intervention in a competitor's application to market natural gas in its territory. The decision, outlining the factors governing issuance or denial of a stay order, became a leading case cited by the lower federal courts, and occasionally by the Supreme Court.[23]

A recurring issue for the Court of Appeals was whether a party was "aggrieved" by an order issued by an agency and therefore had standing to appeal the order. In *Cincinnati Gas & Electric Co. v. FPC*, the Court held that retail distributors of natural gas were not aggrieved by an order of the Commission permitting natural-gas wholesalers to demand long-term contracts from local power companies, despite the possibility of drastic economic changes during that term, and therefore that they had had no right of review. The Court held that for purposes of Section 19(b) of the Natural Gas Act, "a petitioner's aggrievement must be present and immediate, or at least must be demonstrably a looming unavoidable threat" or "immediately pressing."[24]

The Federal Communications Commission was a major battleground where the issue of intervention in administrative proceedings was fought out. During this decade *competitive interest* came more frequently to be considered a sufficient interest to justify intervention, as exemplified by two cases from the late fifties.

---

22. 211 F.2d 51 (1954) (*Baz-Pre/Fahy*). See also *Federal Maritime Board v. Isbrandtsen Co.*, 239 F.2d 933 (1956) (*Fahy-Pre-Was*(c)), aff'd, 356 U.S. 481 (1958).

23. 259 F.2d 92 (1958) (*per curiam* WMil-Bur-Baz).

24. 246 F.2d 688 (1957) (*WMil-Dan-Bas*).

In 1958 the Court of Appeals held that the FCC must allow an existing broadcaster to oppose a license application by showing that the grant of another license would make operation of both the existing and the new station economically infeasible and thus deprive the public of service.[25] In the same year, Philco, a manufacturer of radio and television equipment, was held to be a "party in interest" statutorily entitled to demand a hearing in a television station license-renewal application, even though it was not in the business of television broadcasting. The station involved was an affiliate of NBC, a wholly owned subsidiary of RCA, with which Philco competed in the sale of radios and televisions. The station was inserting the phrase "a service of RCA" during station breaks, giving undeserved news coverage to RCA, and advising the public that RCA was the pioneer and developer of compatible color. The Court, Judge Fahy writing, thought this constituted "a direct economic effect" on Philco. Judge J. Warren Madden of the Court of Claims, sitting as a visiting judge, dissented.[26]

The Public Interest

One constant theme runs through the work of the Court of Appeals in administrative law during the 1950s: the public interest, on behalf of which the Court constantly impelled the agencies to act. Judge Bazelon, perhaps the most eloquent but certainly not the only spokesman for this position, wrote,

> The [Federal Communications] Commission's role is not merely that of a referee in an adversary proceeding who scores points only upon issues selected by the individual contestants and gives the decision to the highest scorer. While this might assure a "right" decision between the contestants, it does not assure a "right" decision in the public interest. The latter decision requires exploration and evaluation of factors vital to such interest, whether or not they have been raised by the parties.[27]

Part of what was troubling the judges of the Court of Appeals was the growing coziness between the regulators and the regulated. This was exemplified by a case in 1960 involving the Federal Maritime Board's denial — overruling its hearing examiner — of an application by Pacific Far East Line to operate unsubsidized vessels between the Pacific coast and Hawaii. The application had been opposed by Matson Navigation Company, which car-

25. *Carroll Broadcasting Co. v. FCC*, 258 F.2d 440 (1958) (*Pre-Baz-Bur*).
26. *Philco Co. v. FCC*, 257 F.2d 656 (1958).
27. *Pinellas Broadcasting Co. v. FCC*, 230 F.2d 204, 211 (1956) (*Pre-Was/Baz*).

ried ninety-eight percent of the cargo in the West Coast-Hawaii trade. The Maritime Board explained its denial with a finding that Pacific might be able to "skim the cream" of the trade, even though the actual diversion of tonnage might have been less than ten percent. The Court of Appeals sharply rebuked the Board, stating that it had "practically equated unfair competition with effective competition." In language undoubtedly intended to recall the Eisenhower cabinet official who had declared, "What is good for General Motors is good for the country," Judge Edgerton wrote, "[W]hat is bad for Matson is not necessarily bad for the country."[28]

The commissions' conflicts of interest were most strikingly revealed by the history of the Federal Communications Commission's awarding of the license for Channel 10 in Miami, a matter that ended up as a lengthy administrative proceeding in the D.C. Circuit and also in prosecutions in the District Court for political corruption. The Channel 10 hearings demonstrated the pressures the commissioners were under from nationally famous politicians, local political sponsors, influence-peddling lawyers, and friends bearing gifts.

After a four-year administrative proceeding, the FCC, overruling its hearing examiner, awarded Channel 10 to Public Service Television, a subsidiary of National Air Lines. Commissioner Richard A. Mack of Florida, without hearing argument, cast what proved to be the decisive vote. The application of Public Service Television, one of four applicants, had been strongly supported by a lifelong friend of Mack, Miami attorney Thurman Whiteside, who, while the application was pending, loaned and gave Mack a considerable amount of money. Another applicant had tried unsuccessfully to hire Whiteside; a third applicant had employed a childhood friend of Mack as a lobbyist and had applied senatorial muscle.

After the FCC decision, but before its circumstances were exposed, WKAT, the fourth unsuccessful applicant, appealed to the Court of Appeals. After the scandal was revealed (and Mack had resigned), the Court of Appeals remanded the case to the FCC at the Commission's request, asking it to make full findings of fact.[29] The FCC did not reopen the proceedings for any further applications, but instead disqualified three of the four applicants for their conduct and awarded the station to the fourth.[30]

---

28. *Pacific Far East Lines v. Federal Maritime Board*, 275 F.2d 184 (1960) (*Edg*-Bas-WMil).

29. *WKAT, Inc. v.* FCC, 258 F.2d 418 (1958) (*per curiam* Pre-Was-Dan).

30. See *WKAT, Inc. v. FCC*, 296 F.2d 375 (1961) (*Pre*-Was-Dan). In the 1960s, in the wake of this and other influence-peddling scandals, the Commission generally

Mack and Whiteside were prosecuted separately for conspiracy and bribery—the most notable political corruption trials in the District of Columbia during this period. Whiteside was found not guilty and shortly thereafter committed suicide. The prosecution of Mack before Judge Matthews ended in a hung jury.[31] Mack died before he could be retried.

Criminal Cases

During the 1950s the D.C. Circuit, especially the Court of Appeals, gained a considerable reputation—some might say notoriety—for its work in the criminal law. Because of its local jurisdiction, this circuit heard more criminal cases than any other lower federal court, and far more cases involving violent crimes. Some controversial decisions of the Court of Appeals were reported in the national press and were the subject of law review notes. The heated divisions among its judges and criticism of the decisions by law professors, politicians, and other judges attracted attention far beyond the District of Columbia. These controversies were part of the broad national debate over judicial recognition of the rights of criminal suspects and, for the most part, anticipated similar decisions and divisions in the Supreme Court.

Two important criminal case lines will be examined here, both involving factious issues: a suspect's right to a prompt arraignment after arrest, and the insanity defense.

The Mallory Line

The most volatile of these case lines within the Court of Appeals, and the one that attracted the most vigorous criticism outside, concerned the rule which held that evidence was to be suppressed if it was obtained during an "unnecessary delay" in bringing an arrestee before a magistrate to be informed of his rights and the charges against him. The seminal case, *McNabb*

---

sought to award licenses to those remaining applicants in each city who had not been disqualified for unethical conduct, while the Court wanted proceedings reopened and new applicants considered. See, e.g., *WORZ, Inc. v. FCC,* 345 F.2d 85 (1965) (*per curiam* Fahy-Bur-McG); *Consolidated Nine, Inc. v. FCC,* 403 F.2d 585 (1968) (*Bur-Bas-Tamm*); *Jacksonville Broadcasting Corp. v. FCC,* 348 F.2d 75 (1965) (*Fahy-Bas/Bur*(c/d)). See also *Sangamon Valley Television Corp. v. United States,* 294 F.2d 742 (1961) (*Edg-Fahy-Bas*); *Fort Harrison Telecasting Corp. v. FCC,* 324 F.2d 379 (1963) (*Was-Baz/Wri*).

31. See *Mack v. United States,* 274 F.2d 582 (1959) (*per curiam* Edg-Pre-WMil), upholding Judge Matthews' denial of a motion to acquit.

22222

2222

v. United States, had arisen in the Sixth Circuit and was decided by the Supreme Court in 1943.[32] The *McNabb* rule was codified the following year, in Rule 5(a) of the Federal Rules of Criminal Procedure. Rule 5(a) provided that an arrested person be taken "without unnecessary delay before the nearest available commissioner or before any other nearby officer empowered to commit persons charged with offenses against the United States," who was to inform the defendant of the complaint against him, of his right to retain counsel, of his right to have a preliminary examination, and that "he is not required to make a statement and that any statement made by him may be used against him."

In *McNabb* the High Court used its supervisory power over the lower federal courts to formulate a non-constitutionally based rule of evidence: detention of a defendant beyond the time when a committing magistrate was readily accessible constituted "wilful disobedience" of law, rendering inadmissible incriminating statements elicited from defendants during the period of unlawful detention. If arrests were not followed by a prompt preliminary hearing, any confessions which resulted would be inadmissible as evidence.

The *Mallory* case involved a particularly brutal rape, which had occurred in the basement of the apartment house in which Andrew Mallory lived. Mallory and his two nephews were arrested on April 8, 1954, taken to police headquarters and questioned about the crime. After seven hours of detention and interrogation, Mallory confessed and then, represented by court-appointed counsel, William B. Bryant (who would be appointed to the D.C. District Court in 1965), was brought before the committing magistrate. Judge Alexander Holtzoff admitted the confession into evidence and Mallory was convicted.

The Court of Appeals affirmed the conviction on June 26, 1956.[33] Judges Prettyman and Bastian thought the delay had not been unreasonable, as "it is inconceivable that [the police] should be required to lodge charges against any suspect until their investigation had developed." Judge Bazelon dissented, seeing a *McNabb* violation and objecting to a police policy of arresting several suspects and grilling them all until one confessed. Bazelon contended that "[t]he law's requirement of arraignment without unnecessary delay is grounded upon the theory that, where policemen are judges, individual liberty and dignity cannot long survive." That probably just one

---

32. *McNabb v. United States*, 318 U.S. 332 (1943).
33. *Mallory v. United States*, 236 F.2d 701 (1956) (*Pre-Bas/Baz*).

other member of the Court, Judge Edgerton, shared Bazelon's views at the time is suggested by the *en banc* decision in *Green v. United States*, decided the same day as *Mallory*.[34]

On June 27, 1957, the Supreme Court unanimously reversed *Mallory*.[35] Justice Frankfurter, who had written the opinion in *McNabb*, also wrote the *Mallory* opinion. The Court held that once an arrest had been made on probable cause, the next step was arraignment "as quickly as possible." Frankfurter suggested that the rule was not to operate mechanically, that there might be circumstances, such as verification of a defendant's story by a third party, which might justify a brief delay. But a delay would not be permitted if its purpose was to extract a confession.

Although the *McNabb-Mallory* rule was not the handiwork of the Court of Appeals, that court would become closely identified with the criticism of it. In the years after the Supreme Court decided *Mallory*, the Court of Appeals rendered many decisions resting on it. Although such decisions, by the nature of the test, had to be fact-specific, nevertheless there was a great deal of inconsistency and it did not take long before more heat than light was generated.

The judges of the Court of Appeals were deeply divided on philosophical grounds over the manner in which *Mallory* was to be applied. To use the terminology of Herbert L. Packer's "Two Models of the Criminal Process," one wing of the Court adhered to a "Due Process Model," the other to a "Crime Control Model." The first model held actors representing the state — police, prosecutors, and judges — to high standards of conduct and insisted that factual determinations of guilt had to be made in a procedurally correct fashion. During the Eisenhower years, Judges Edgerton, Bazelon, and Fahy (who, as Solicitor General, had been on the government brief in *McNabb*) adhered to this approach, as, to a somewhat lesser degree, did Judge Washington. The "Crime Control Model" emphasized factual guilt over legal guilt and social control over individual justice, sought efficiency through rational administration, and allotted wide discretion to the police, prosecutors, and trial judges. Judge Burger would emerge as the leader of this wing of the Court, which also included Judges Miller, Danaher, Bastian, and, ordinarily, Judge Prettyman.

---

34. *Green v. United States*, 236 F.2d 708 (1956) (*WMil*-Bas-Dan-Bur-Was-*Pre*(c)/*Baz*-Edg-*Fahy*). The majority held that statements by an accused to police while in a hospital and before arraignment are admissible where there was neither coercion nor illegal detention and no suggestion of inducement through promises. Fahy's dissent was on a different issue from the question of admissions of confessions.

35. 354 U.S. 449 (1957).

The *Mallory* line of decisions in the District of Columbia Circuit attracted widespread publicity and political criticism. Southern politicians used them as a way to fight civil rights and attack the Supreme Court. Certainly, the struggles of the judges of the courts of the District of Columbia Circuit in attempting to apply the *McNabb-Mallory* rule attracted far more attention than ordinarily is the lot of lower court judges attempting to apply Supreme Court decisions.

The Court of Appeals weakened *Mallory* for the first time in *Metoyer v. United States*.[36] This was also the occasion for Judge Burger's first strong attack on the direction the Court's liberal wing appeared to be taking. The case involved a defendant who had been picked up in Maryland for a murder committed in the District of Columbia the preceding day. Held for an hour until the D.C. police arrived, Metoyer then readily admitted the crime, and within two hours had signed a written statement. After being arraigned in Maryland, he was extradited to Washington, where he was finally arraigned late in the day. Judge Edgerton, who dissented, would have admitted the oral, but not the written, statement. The panel majority—Judges Burger and Prettyman—saw nothing wrong with the police delaying the return to Washington by an hour in order to get the written confession, which would be useful for minimizing later disputes over what was said. Burger added, "Every citizen has a right to insist that the police make some pertinent and definitive inquiry before he may be arraigned on a criminal charge."

The discord on the bench over this issue began to boil over in *Trilling v. United States*, which was argued before the Court *en banc* on December 11, 1957, and decided on April 17, 1958.[37] John E. Trilling had been implicated in a warehouse robbery and arrested in the early hours of the morning. Initial interrogation proved unsuccessful, but he later made some admissions to another policemen, a friend of Trilling's family. Since he was also suspected of some other crimes, Trilling was held for further questioning about those crimes and confessed to some of them. Trilling was eventually arraigned about ten hours after his arrest.

The five opinions of the nine-judge court in *Trilling* fill thirty-five pages, a great deal for the era. Writing for the Court for part of the case and for himself as to part (Judge Burger wrote as to the rest), Judge Danaher emphasized

36. 250 F.2d 30 (1957) (*Bur-Pre/Edg*).
37. 260 F.2d 677 (1958). See also *Watts v. United States*, 278 F.2d 247 (1960) (*Bur-Dan-Bas*), involving a co-defendant of Trilling who may have pleaded guilty when he was confronted with Trilling's confession.

that the reasonableness of the delay depended upon the circumstances. The admissions Trilling made to the family friend were admissible, but not those made subsequently. Writing for himself and Judges Miller and Bastian, Judge Prettyman thought that all of the evidence should have been admitted. The term "unnecessary delay," Prettyman wrote, has "a content of substance, embodying allowance for proper police procedures." The police had their case already proven before Trilling confessed; the police were in the middle of a busy day and had other things to worry about besides Trilling's hearing.

Judge Burger reluctantly concurred with Danaher, since he believed the result in *Trilling* was compelled by *Mallory*. But his heart was really with Judge Prettyman's dissent. Burger urged reexamination of Rule 5(a), either by the rule-making process or by Congress. Writing for himself and for Judge Edgerton, Judge Bazelon agreed with Judge Danaher on the inadmissibility of the later confession, but also thought the confession to Trilling's family friend inadmissible. An "ignorant and friendless prisoner," Bazelon wrote, should be treated in the same manner as a "prisoner who is not ignorant and friendless." While not joining in Bazelon's language, Judges Fahy and Washington stated, in a one-sentence opinion, that they would reverse on all counts and remand for new trials on the authority of *McNabb* and *Mallory*.

By 1958 the differences within the Court of Appeals, and the tensions resulting from those differences, were such that the Court began resorting to *en banc* hearings to overturn fact-specific panel decisions a majority did not like.[38] One of the earliest public indications of the strong differences between Judges Bazelon and Burger in criminal cases occurred in *Heideman v. United States*, decided on September 25, 1958.[39] In *Heideman*, Judge Holtzoff had admitted into evidence a confession which had occurred during a one-hour delay between the arrest and the preliminary hearing—an hour largely consumed by the preparation of papers, booking, photographing, fingerprinting and transportation. Burger held that this was "necessary" rather than "unnecessary" delay. He also suggested that a delay after confession is less crucial than a delay before confession. In dissent, Bazelon responded, "My brethren 'protect' the accused by authorizing the police to question him secretly and induce him to confess while he is ignorant of his rights and is in the state of fear produced by police control and domination."

38. See, e.g., *Starr v. United States*, 264 F.2d 377 (1958) (WMil-Pre-Dan-Bas-Bur/*Baz*-Edg-Fahy-Was).

39. 259 F.2d 943 (1958) (*Bur*-Madden(Ct.Cl.)/*Baz*), aff'g 21 F.R.D. 335 (1958) (Holtzoff).

The differences among the judges of the Court of Appeals in dealing with *Mallory*'s progeny were far from resolved at the end of the decade. And the most explosive case of all, *Killough v. United States,* had yet to reach the Court.

The Insanity Defense

Perhaps the single most important case decided by the courts of the D.C. Circuit during the 1950s was *Durham v. United States,* in which the Court of Appeals recast the test for criminal insanity used in many American jurisdictions. As the first serious attempt by a U.S. appellate court to address the discrepancy between modern psychiatric theory and the law of criminal responsibility, *Durham* generated intense interest from judges, lawyers, law reviews, and even the popular press. The dialogue stimulated by *Durham* led to the reconsideration of existing tests for criminal insanity throughout the United States, and increased respect for the District of Columbia Circuit outside of Washington.

In the long run *Durham* was rejected both inside and outside the Circuit, but the ferment initiated by the decision led many jurisdictions to adopt more modern formulations of the insanity test. Within the Circuit, most judges gave *Durham* some time to succeed, although by the early 1960s most of the district judges and several members of the Court of Appeals had had enough and even some of its strong proponents were greatly disturbed by the problems which had surfaced. Nevertheless, before the courts of the D.C. Circuit lost most of their criminal jurisdiction in 1971, and formally abandoned *Durham* in 1972 in *United States v. Brawner*[40] (see chapter seven), the District of Columbia Circuit had become a laboratory for consideration of a great many aspects of the relationship between mental health and the law.

In 1954 the prevalent test for criminal insanity in the United States was that defined by the Court of King's Bench in 1843 in a case that involved a defendant who had attempted to assassinate the British prime minister, Robert Peel. The test stated in *M'Naghten's Case* was whether "the party accused was labouring under such a defect of reason, from disease of the mind, as not to know the nature and quality of the act he was doing; or as not to know that what he was doing was wrong."[41]

Virtually every American jurisdiction, following Supreme Court decisions from the 1890s,[42] followed some variant of the *M'Naghten* rules. The

---

40. 471 F.2d 969 (1972).
41. 10 Cl. & Finn. 718 (1843).
42. See *Davis v. United States,* 160 U.S. 469 (1895), 165 U.S. 373 (1897).

District of Columbia Circuit, with a heritage of concern with the insanity defense and with greater freedom than the other circuits because it was the equivalent of a state supreme court, employed the right-wrong test as it had been laid out by Justice Cox at the trial of President McKinley's assassin, Charles Guiteau (see chapter two):

> If you find from the whole evidence that, at the time of the commis-
> sion of the homicide, the prisoner in consequence of disease of mind,
> was laboring under such a defect of his reason that he was incapable
> of understanding what he was doing, or that it was wrong...then he
> was not in a responsible condition of mind, and was an object of com-
> passion, and not of justice, and ought to be now acquitted.[43]

A number of states used an additional test, sometimes labeled the "irre-sistible impulse test," under which the accused would not be held crimi-nally responsible if, at the time of the crime, he or she had been suffering from such an extreme mental disorder as to produce conduct that had prac-tically nothing in common with that of an ordinary person.[44]

After the Second World War, the *M'Naghten* rules came under increas-ingly sharp criticism from psychiatrists and judges throughout the nation. Over-stressing the cognitive and underemphasizing the emotional, the rules in most judicial hands limited the testimony the jury could hear on the ac-cused's mental condition, and conscientious psychiatrists rarely felt that they were replying honestly to questions based on the rules.

Monte Durham, a strange and pathetically confused twenty-three-year-old man, was arrested on July 13, 1951, while burglarizing a Georgetown home. Durham was no newcomer to trouble with the law. He had committed other burglaries, stolen a car, passed bad checks, and violated parole twice. He also had a psychiatric history. While in the Navy he had been diagnosed as hav-ing a "profound personality disorder" and in two judicial proceedings he had been pronounced of unsound mind. He had attempted suicide twice, had suf-fered from hallucinations, and had been confined three times to St. Elizabeths for a total of sixteen months. After this attempted burglary, Durham was judged mentally incompetent for trial and returned to St. Elizabeths.

When Durham was finally found competent to stand trial, it was before Alexander Holtzoff, whose relations with the Court of Appeals were already

---

43. *United States v. Guiteau*, 10 Fed. 161, 186 (1882). See also *United States v. Lee*, 15 D.C. (4 Mackey) 489 (1886); *Snell v. United States*, 16 App. D.C. 501 (1900).
44. The Court of Appeals had tacked "irresistible impulse" onto the right-wrong test in *Smith v. United States*, 36 F.2d 548 (1929).

strained. His rigid application of the District of Columbia Circuit's version of the *M'Naghten* rule offered to the Court of Appeals an excellent opportunity to make law.

At trial, Durham's only defense was that he was not guilty by reason of insanity. His own testimony was confused and aimless. The one expert witness, Joseph G. Gilbert, Chief Psychiatrist at Gallinger Hospital, was of the opinion that Durham was "of unsound mind." But for Holtzoff the issue was simple. The only question was whether Durham knew the difference between right and wrong in governing his own actions. The judge found that there was "no testimony concerning the mental state of the defendant as of July 13, 1951, and therefore the usual presumption of sanity governs."[45] Durham's psychiatric history was disregarded because the defense psychiatrist was unwilling to testify in terms of a legal fiction that Durham could not tell right from wrong on the date of the crime. Durham was sentenced to three to ten years in prison.

After the case on appeal was briefed by Durham's first counsel, Mason B. Leming, the Court of Appeals designated Abe Fortas to represent the indigent defendant. Oliver Gasch, then in the U.S. Attorney's office, advised the U.S. Attorney, Leo Rover, to confess error in *Durham*, but Rover declined, saying, "If we go down, we go down with our battle flag nailed to the mast." Durham's appeal was argued twice before the panel of Edgerton, Bazelon, and Washington. Fortas (with Abe Krash) argued that the right and wrong test was "an inappropriate, inadequate and unjust yardstick for ascertaining criminal responsibility," and recommended that "a test for criminal responsibility should focus...upon the total competence of the accused, both rational and emotional to regulate his conduct in accordance with the norms of society."[46]

The opinion of the Court of Appeals in *Durham*, written by Judge Bazelon, was rendered on July 1, 1954.[47] Durham's conviction was reversed: there had been enough evidence to have shifted the burden to the government of proving sanity beyond reasonable doubt, and the trial judge had not weighed the whole evidence on the insanity question. The court then turned to the question of the test of criminal responsibility. As an exclusive criterion, the *M'Naghten* test was found inadequate. *M'Naghten* did not take suf-

---

45. The record of the trial of Monte Durham, March 19–20, 1953, otherwise unreported, was preserved on microfilm by the Unit in Law and Psychiatry of Temple University. He was retried in the District Court, *United States v. Durham*, 130 F. Supp. 445 (1955).

46. Supplemental brief on behalf of appellant in *Durham v. United States*, 4.

47. *Durham v. United States*, 214 F.2d 862 (1954) (*Baz-Edg-Was*).

ficient account of psychiatric realities and scientific knowledge. It was based
"upon one symptom and so cannot be validly adopted in all circumstances."
The irresistible impulse test was also found inadequate, "in that it gives no
recognition to mental illness characterized by brooding and reflection."

The new and broader test announced by the Court of Appeals was not
original. It bore a close resemblance to what had been used in New Hamp-
shire since 1870.[48] As Bazelon restated that test, "It is simply that an accused
is not criminally responsible if his unlawful act was the product of mental
disease or mental defect." Under *Durham*, when there was some evidence
that the accused was suffering from a disease or a defective mental condition, that condition was to be a question of fact for the jury. The jury was
to be permitted to hear expert psychiatric testimony as to all the defendant's
symptoms but was left with the basically moral question of guilt. The opinion closed with a moving peroration:

> The legal and moral traditions of the Western World require that those
> who, of their own free will and with evil intent,... commit acts which
> violate the law, shall be criminally responsible for those acts. Our tra-
> ditions also require that where such acts stem from and are the prod-
> uct of a mental disease or defect... moral blame shall not attach, and
> hence there will not be criminal responsibility.

The *Durham* decision provoked an enormous response in the press and
in the law reviews. The lines were drawn at once in the feuding editorial
pages of the District's two major newspapers. On July 5, 1954, the conservative *Evening Star* expressed concern "for the rights of the people of Washington," while on the sixteenth the liberal *Washington Post* declared that the
decision's "fusion of law and psychiatry will do much to enlighten justice."

In the first year and a half after the decision, twenty-nine notes on
Durham appeared in various legal periodicals, and four symposia were de-
voted to it. Some of the most prominent men at the bar, on the bench, and
beside the couch engaged in the debate. Supporting the rule were Solicitor
General Simon E. Sobeloff, Justices Douglas and Brennan, Judge Roger B.
Traynor, and psychiatrists Manfred Guttmacher and Gregory Zilboorg.

---

48. *State v. Jones*, 50 N.H. 369 (1871) held that the defendant should be held not
guilty by reason of insanity "if the killing was the offspring or product of mental disease." The "product" test was the work of Judge Charles Doe, who did not write the
opinion in *Jones* but had advanced the test in dissent in *Boardman v. Woodman*, 47 N.H.
120 (1866) and in *State v. Pike*, 49 N.H. 399 (1870).

Those who were dubious about *Durham* included Judge Learned Hand and Professor Herbert Wechsler of Columbia University School of Law.

Wechsler's views were of particular importance, for as reporter for the American Law Institute's Model Penal Code he, more than anyone else, would create the standard which would ultimately prevail. In a 1955 law review article, Wechsler said he was disturbed by the vagueness of the terms "disease" and "defect" in *Durham*, and by the problem of causality posed by the requirement that the unlawful act be the *product* of mental disease or defect. He believed that the opinion did not "face the question of how extensively capacity must be impaired to call for holding the defendant irresponsible."

Because of its local jurisdiction, the Court of Appeals was provided a constant supply of cases involving the insanity defense. Indeed, between 1954 and 1967 the Court of Appeals adhered to, enforced, explained, or expanded the *Durham* rule in over 150 opinions. But *Durham*'s impact in the Circuit was even greater than that, leading the courts to reform procedures for competency hearings for defendants standing trial. During this time, Judge Bazelon's deep concern with cases raising problems in the area of forensic psychiatry and mental health achieved a specialization rarely equaled by an American judge in any area of law. Of this, more will be seen later.

The Court of Appeals' first important clarification of *Durham* was delivered in its opinion in *Carter v. United States* on October 24, 1957.[49] Writing for himself, Burger, and Bazelon, Judge Prettyman, who had been a strong supporter of *Durham* (he later claimed to be its "granddaddy"), explained that *Durham* had been the means of escape from the sloganized use of the right-and-wrong and irresistible-impulse tests. Prettyman stated that *Durham* merely extended the established rule to apply the insanity defense to all acts which would not have been committed except for a mental illness of the accused. The role of the expert witness was not to label, but rather to explain the disease and its dynamics.

To ease fears that those found not guilty by reason of insanity would be back on the streets in a short time, the Court of Appeals, in *Overholser v. Leach*, made it clear that the standard for release of such a person was not to be the same as for a civilly committed person. Rather, that person would have to show "freedom from such abnormal mental condition as would make the individual dangerous to himself or the community in the reasonably foreseeable future."[50]

---

49. 252 F.2d 227 (1957) (*Pre*-Bur-Baz).
50. 257 F.2d 667 (1958) (*Was*-Edg-Bur).

Reservations about the *Durham* rule were expressed publicly by members of the Court for the first time in *Wright v. United States*, heard *en banc* on February 1, 1957, but not decided until October 30.[51] In *Wright* a conviction for second-degree murder was reversed and remanded with instructions to enter the judgment of not guilty by reason of insanity not withstanding the verdict of the jury. Judge Miller, dissenting with Judges Danaher and Bastian, wrote of the "confusion already engendered by the *Durham* rule, as given *ad hoc* interpretations in subsequent opinions of the Court," and noted that the rule had been pressed upon and rejected by the Fifth and the Ninth Circuits and the high courts of six states. Judge Burger's growing wariness about *Durham* is suggested by his one-sentence concurrence in the result.

Only a week later, in *Catlin v. United States*, decided *per curiam*, Judge Miller, dissenting, essentially said that *Durham* was unsound and ought to be overruled: "One who knows that what he is doing is wrong but chooses freely and voluntarily to do it, should be held criminally responsible for his act even though he thinks the moon is made of green cheese." Miller argued that *Durham* was too abstract, making difficulties for trial judges and confusing juries. Burger, concurring, seemed still sympathetic to *Durham's* aims:

> These are complicated, difficult and trying problems for the law enforcement officers, for the profession and for the courts, and solutions are often elusive. As with all difficult legal problems the pronouncements [of Judge Prettyman in *Carter*] require concentrated, thoughtful study, and where that is given improved understanding and better administration of justice will follow.[52]

Even though *Durham* stimulated reconsideration of the standard of criminal responsibility by almost every state supreme court and federal court of appeals, it was specifically followed in just a few. Instead, among those jurisdictions that abandoned *M'Naghten*, the formulation of the Model Penal Code (§4.01) prevailed, according to which a person suffering from a "mental disease or defect" is not held responsible for criminal conduct if it deprives him or her of "substantial capacity" to tell right from wrong or to resist wrongful behavior.

In the two decades following the *Durham* decision, the District Court and the Court of Appeals of the District of Columbia Circuit would become a laboratory for consideration of an extraordinary number of aspects of the relationship between mental health and the law. An example is found

---

51. 250 F.2d 4 (1957) (*Baz-Pre-Fahy-Was-Edg-Bur*(c)/*WMil*-Dan-Bas).
52. *Catlin v. United States*, 251 F.2d 368 (1957) (*per curiam* Fahy-Bur(c)/*WMil*).

in *Durham*'s companion case, *Stewart v. United States,* when the Court of
Appeals rejected a defense based on the claim of diminished capacity.[53] The
Stewart case reached the Court of Appeals twice more before a conviction
was finally affirmed, by a 5–4 vote, in 1960. By that time, the majority was
quite skeptical of the extent to which judges could contribute to the mesh-
ing of law and psychiatry. Writing for the Court in *Stewart,* Judge Burger
declared, "The problem of classifying, assessing and analyzing the results of
the application of modern psychiatry to administration of criminal law as
it relates to gradations of punishment according to the relative intelligence
of the defendant is beyond the competence of the judiciary."[54]

Monte Durham, too, was tried again (before Judge Pine) and convicted.
The Court of Appeals again reversed, holding that Pine had erred by informing the jury that if Durham was found not guilty by reason of insanity, he would probably be released in a short time.[55]

The *Mallory* and *Durham* case lines hardly exhaust the rich criminal jurisprudence of this period. For example, the Court of Appeals gave thoughtful consideration to the constitutional command of a speedy trial and considered safeguards for defendants in prosecutions connected with
homosexuality. There were rape cases in which the more conservative
judges demonstrated more than their liberal colleagues a solicitude for the
rights of the rape victim — a consideration that is now widely accepted —
and cases in which members of the Court of Appeals were troubled by what
appeared to them to be prosecutions brought simply to punish narcotics
addicts for their addiction.[56]

With a large population of indigent, uneducated defendants, the courts
of the D.C. Circuit were also called upon repeatedly to define the meaning

---

53. The conviction was overturned on other grounds. 214 F.2d 879 (1954) (*Baz-
Edg-Was*).

54. *Stewart v. United States,* 275 F.2d 617 (1960) (*Bur*-Pre-Dan-Bas-WMil/*Fahy*-Edg-
Baz-Was), rev'd, 366 U.S. 1 (1961). The second appeal is reported at 247 F.2d 42 (1957)
(*Baz*-Edg-Was-Bur-*Fahy*/*Bas*-WMil-Dan-Pre).

55. *Durham v. United States,* 237 F.2d 760 (1956) (*Baz*-Edg-Was).

56. The speedy-trial issue was considered in *King v. United States,* 265 F.2d 567
(1959) (*Pre*-WMil-Dan-Bas-Bur/*Baz*-Edg-Fahy-Was). The homosexuality case was
Guarro v. United States, 237 F.2d 578 (1956) (*Was*-Edg-WMil). On rape cases, see, e.g.,
Walker v. United States, 223 F.2d 613 (1955) (*Dan*-WMil/*Baz*); *Farrar v. United States,*
275 F.2d 868 (1960) (*Edg*-Fahy/*WMil*). On narcotics cases, see, e.g., *Trent v. United States,*
284 F.2d 286 (1960) (*Bur*-Bas/*Baz*); *Hawkins v. United States,* 288 F.2d 122 (1960) (*per
curiam* Pre-WMil-*Baz*(c)).

of "the right to counsel." While the Court of Appeals' "Crime Control Model" majority limited the right of appeal *in forma pauperis* in several cases,[57] in the latter half of the decade the Court extended the right of counsel to juvenile proceedings, to parole revocation proceedings (in a strong opinion by Judge Danaher), and even to appeals from the Municipal Court in which a fine as low as $25 was at issue.[58]

Relations among the Judges of the Court of Appeals

During the 1950s differences among the judges of the D.C. Circuit disturbed the workings of the Court of Appeals more seriously than any court in the Circuit had been affected since the time of the Cranch court. In the early 1950s, dissents were relatively infrequent and heated dissents rare. The Appeals Court bench had not yet hardened into discernible blocs. Judge Bazelon, his judicial philosophy still evolving, had not yet clearly joined Judge Edgerton as the Court's other strong civil libertarian. Judges Clark, Stephens, Proctor, and Miller were more conservative than Edgerton and Bazelon, but so, it appeared at the time, were Judges Fahy and Washington. At the time of their appointment, President Eisenhower's appointees, Danaher, Bastian, and Burger, did not appear to be discernibly more conservative than the judges they replaced—Proctor, Clark, and Stephens. For months, perhaps years, after taking their seats, their contributions were moderate and collegial.

Even more than the loyalty-security cases, it was the criminal cases that caused the most friction between members of the Court. The first of the judges to publicly indicate strong dissatisfaction with pro-defendant decisions was Judge Miller. By 1958 two separate wings of four judges each had emerged. Their differences could be measured not only in *Mallory*'s progeny, loyalty cases, and to some degree in insanity cases, but also in areas

---

57. See, e.g., *Ellis v. United States*, 249 F.2d 478 (1957) (*Bur*-Pre-WMil-Dan-Bas/*Was*-Edg-Baz-Fahy), vacated, 356 U.S. 674 (1958); *Cash v. United States*, 261 F.2d 731 (1958) (*Pre*-Bur/*Edg*), vacated, 357 U.S. 219 (1958); also *Cash v. United States*, 265 F.2d 346 (1959) (*per curiam* Pre-Edg-Bur).

58. *Shioutakon v. District of Columbia*, 236 F.2d 666 (1956) (*Baz*-Pre/*Bas*(c); *Moore v. Reid*, 246 F.2d 654 (1957) (*Dan*-Edg-WMil); *Wildeblood v. United States*, 278 F.2d 73 (1959) (*Bur*-Bas-*Edg*(c)).

which ought to have been less highly charged, such as the right to counsel on appeal and municipal tort liability.[59]

By 1958, personal relations on the Court of Appeals had undergone a severe rupture. The number of dissents in panel decisions had enormously increased. Symptoms of disagreement and disarray were also evident in the number of times rehearing *en banc* was used to reverse panel decisions and in the registering of dissents from denial of rehearing *en banc*. Further, the *tone* of dissenting opinions had become far more strident.

The public manifestations of the rupture can be traced in 104 U.S. App. D.C., covering 1958–59. The first forty-four cases of this volume, covering a period of just over four months, contain fifteen dissenting opinions and another five concurring opinions or separate statements. The public discord portrayed in vol. 104, unusual in state supreme courts of the time and unique in the lower federal courts, degenerated into outright insult and name-calling. In *United States v. McElroy*, Judge Burger characterized the ruling of the majority (Fahy and Edgerton) as "an invitation to larceny and every other one of the vast array of crimes within the reach of human ingenuity."[60] In *Heideman v. United States*, Bazelon, dissenting from a Burger-Madden affirmance of a conviction raising a *Mallory* problem, stated that the result "makes a farce out of the carefully designed procedures prescribed by Rule 5."[61] Volume 104 also contains the *en banc* decision in *Trilling v. United States*, already discussed, in which there were six opinions.

Confronting, as these judges did, important and difficult issues during a time of great ferment in the law, working together in the same courthouse in the highly charged atmosphere of the capital, and living within a few miles of each other, it is hardly surprising that differences in principle between strong personalities grew into personal differences. Yet the Court appeared to thrive on controversy. If the performance of the Court of Appeals during the 1950s was often unseemly, it cannot be said that its judges hid from difficult issues. This combination of boldness and unruliness would continue to mark the Court during the next decade, one in which the District Court would emerge as an influential national court and the Court of Appeals would increasingly be viewed as the nation's second most important court.

---

59. On right to counsel, see, e.g., *Ellis v. United States*, cited above; on tort liability, see, e.g., *Stone v. District of Columbia*, 237 F.2d 28 (1956) (*Was*-WMil-Bas-*Edg*(c)-Fahy-Baz(c)/*Dan-Pre*).

60. 259 F.2d 927, 940 (1958).

61. 259 F.2d 943, 949 (1958)

Figure 1. William Cranch, Circuit Court of the District of Columbia 1801–55; Chief Judge 1806–55.

Figure 2. The Dunlop Circuit Court 1855–63.

176

Figure 3. Old City Hall (circa 1850), which served as the federal courthouse from 1850–1950.

Figure 4. The Shepard Court of Appeals for the District of Columbia (1905).
C. H. Duell, Seth Shepard, Louis E. McComas.

Figure 5. The Groner Court of Appeals for the District of Columbia (circa 1939), including future Chief Justice of the United States Vinson and future Justice Rutledge. Standing: Henry W. Edgerton, Frederick M. Vinson, Wiley Rutledge; seated: Harold M. Stephens, D. Lawrence Groner, Justin Miller.

Figure 6. The Bazelon Court of Appeals for the District of Columbia Circuit (circa 1963), including future Chief Justice of the United States Burger. Standing: Carl McGowan, Warren Burger, John A. Danaher, George T. Washington, Walter M. Bastian, J. Skelly Wright; seated: Wilbur K. Miller, Henry W. Edgerton, David L. Bazelon, E. Barrett Prettyman, Charles Fahy.

Figure 7. The Robinson Court of Appeals for the District of Columbia Circuit (circa 1983), including future U.S. Supreme Court justices Scalia and Ginsburg. Standing: Antonin Scalia, Ruth Bader Ginsburg, Abner J. Mikva, Harry T. Edwards, Robert H. Bork, Kenneth W. Starr; seated: Malcolm R. Wilkey, J. Skelly Wright, Spottswood W. Robinson III, Edward A. Tamm, Patricia M. Wald.

Figure 8. The Wald Court of Appeals for the District of Columbia Circuit (circa 1990), including future U.S. Supreme Court justices Thomas and Ginsburg. Standing: Karen LeCraft Henderson, David B. Sentelle, Stephen F. Williams, James L. Buckley, Douglas H. Ginsburg, Clarence Thomas, A. Raymond Randolph; seated: Ruth Bader Ginsburg, Abner J. Mikva, Patricia M. Wald, Harry T. Edwards, Laurence H. Silberman.

Figure 9. The Laws District Court (circa 1952), including Judge Matthews, first woman federal district judge in the nation. Standing: Walter M. Bastian, Burnita Shelton Matthews, Charles F. McLaughlin, Edward M. Curran, Richmond B. Keech, Edward A. Tamm, James R. Kirkland, Luther W. Youngdahl; seated: Henry A. Schweinhaut, Matthew F. McGuire, James W. Morris, Thomas Jennings Bailey, Bolitha J. Laws, F. Dickinson Letts, David A. Pine, Alexander Holtzoff.

Figure 10. The Sirica District Court (circa 1971). Standing: Charles R. Richey, June L. Green, Gerhard A. Gesell, Aubrey E. Robinson Jr., William B. Bryant, Howard F. Corcoran, William B. Jones, Oliver Gasch, John Lewis Smith Jr., Joseph C. Waddy, John Helm Pratt, Barrington D. Parker, Thomas A. Flannery; seated: Leonard Walsh, Luther W. Youngdahl, Charles F. McLaughlin, Richmond B. Keech, John J. Sirica, Edward M. Curran, Burnita Shelton Matthews, Joseph C. McGarraghy, George L. Hart Jr.

Figure 11. Women judges of the D.C. Circuit courts (1997). Left to right: Magistrate Judge Deborah Robinson, District Judge Colleen Kollar-Kotelly, Circuit Judge Karen LeCraft Henderson, Chief District Judge Norma Holloway Johnson, Circuit Judge Judith Rogers, Circuit Judge Patricia Wald, Senior District Judge Joyce Hens Green, Senior District Judge June Green. (District Judge Gladys Kessler absent from photo.)

Figure 12. E. Barrett Prettyman United States Courthouse (circa 2000).

Chapter 7

"A Collectivity of Fighting Cats"
The D.C. Courts in the Sixties

Throughout the history of the D.C. Circuit courts, a major reason for their importance has been their location in the "two Washingtons"—Washington the beautiful and majestic Federal City, the nerve center of national politics and capital of the Western world, and Washington the urban municipality, mostly black and poor. The windows of the U.S. Courthouse facing south, east, and west overlook the grand buildings symbolizing the size and power of the federal government. But to the north, within walking distance of the Courthouse, lie large pockets of poverty and despair. For 170 years the jurisdiction of the federal courts of the District of Columbia Circuit—both a federal (indeed, a "national") court and the equivalent of a state supreme court—embraced the two Washingtons almost equally. Although at the end of the decade the federal courts of the District of Columbia Circuit would lose their local or "state" jurisdiction, this dual responsibility was perhaps never more important than during the 1960s.

The prudent conservatism of the Eisenhower years was succeeded in this decade by more dynamic government. If the two men who occupied the White House had very different personalities and styles of leadership, their administrations shared an impatience with traditional rhetoric and were willing to attack problems energetically. Under John F. Kennedy and Lyndon B. Johnson, the waters of reform, dammed for almost a quarter of a century, flowed again onto the political plain. They poured into renewed regulation of the economy and a burst of social legislation. All this vigorous activity affected the work of the D.C. courts.

During the 1960s, the United States Court of Appeals for the District of Columbia Circuit was rapidly emerging as the nation's second most important court, a significance attributable to the caliber of its judges and the quality of its jurisprudence, as well as to the variety of its docket. In a rich

187

administrative-law docket, the Court's greatest impact was on the Federal Communications Commission, as it issued important rulings on standing and the Fairness Doctrine. Although in the 1960s it saw considerably fewer loyalty-security cases than in preceding years, the Court of Appeals made an important contribution to the evisceration of the Subversive Activities Control Board. In the areas of criminal law, mental health law, and what then was referred to as "poverty law," encompassing landlord-tenant and consumer issues, the Court of Appeals, in its "state" court role, used its common-law prerogatives to serve as the high court of a poor, disenfranchised black municipality. In both roles, it was in the vanguard of liberal judicial activism, and as such was often at the center of angry controversies.

Notwithstanding the quality, importance, and frequent controversy of its work, it was less the jurisprudence of the Court of Appeals in this period than the sometimes bitter divisions among its judges that gained the Court the widest attention in this decade. The ideological split was personified—and exacerbated—by two able, strong-willed judges. The Court's liberal wing was led by Chief Judge David L. Bazelon, who advanced his agenda imaginatively and stubbornly; its more conservative side was headed by Warren E. Burger, an intelligent, hard-working judge, equally tenacious and unafraid of controversy.

The beautification of downtown Washington made headway during this decade, spurred by President Kennedy and the First Lady, Jacqueline Kennedy. Washington no longer resembled a sleepy Southern city, but had become a troubled Northern one. Whites continued to flee to the suburbs and blacks continued to migrate into the city; by 1970, Washington was seventy-one percent black and the National Capital Planning Commission reported that nearly a quarter of the capital's residents were living in "abject poverty." In addition to the social problems bred by Washington's dismal slums—high rates of drug addiction, infant mortality, functional illiteracy, and one-parent families—the city had substandard schools and other public facilities and suffered from problems of water supply, pollution, and transportation which demanded a metropolitan-wide solution.

Many of the ills of urban life found their way into the courts of the District of Columbia: deteriorated housing, consumer fraud, unequal educational facilities, inadequate treatment for the mentally ill, and high crime rates. In confronting these problems, majorities on the Court of Appeals often sought to replace, in Chief Judge Bazelon's words, "outmoded abstract doctrines that keep the real world at bay" and to craft remedies that could not be provided by the impotent municipal government or by the Congress. To this end, they reexamined Anglo-American common law and equity principles which had evolved over the centuries, generally without the benefit of legislation. It was these decisions—especially those in criminal cases—that proved contentious, incurring the wrath of other judges within and outside the circuit, law professors and politicians. The decisions were criticized as result-oriented, unrealistic, impractical and belonging to the domain of the legislative branches.

By the mid-sixties, Washington had been without home rule for almost a century. Effective control of the affairs of the city lay largely with congressional committees, many of whose members represented constituencies which were anti-urban and racist. Progress toward home rule began with the ratification, in 1961, of the Twenty-third Amendment, which enfranchised the residents of the District in presidential elections. In 1967, using his power to reorganize the agencies of the federal government, Lyndon Johnson created a new government for the District, ending eighty-nine years of government by commission. The new government was headed by a single commissioner (known popularly as "Mayor") and a nine-person City Council, both appointed by the President and intended to be "broadly representative of the community." (This structure remained in place until 1973, when the District of Columbia Self-Government Act created a home-rule charter which provided for an elected Mayor and City Council.) Johnson named Walter Washington, who had been active in the New Negro Alliance and executive director of the National Capital Housing Authority, the first Mayor. The Mayor, however, was basically an administrative functionary with heavily encumbered powers, and the new City Council's authority was similarly limited. Lacking an executive responsive to the electorate, a consistent and responsible rule-making body, and the typical interplay of group interests, the District continued to struggle with numerous local problems. That many of them would find their way into the courts did not come as a surprise; what was unexpected was the willingness of the U.S. Court of Appeals to abandon or modify old doctrines to apply more fairly to modern urban life.

Judicial Administration

President Kennedy made but one appointment to the District Court, the able William B. Jones; President Johnson made ten. Four of Johnson's appointees were African-Americans: Spottswood W. Robinson III, William B. Bryant, Aubrey E. Robinson Jr., and Joseph C. Waddy. Johnson also appointed one woman, June L. Green. Of Johnson's appointees, William Bryant is deserving of particular mention here; Spottswood Robinson is profiled later in this chapter and two others, Aubrey E. Robinson Jr. (appointed in 1966) and Gerhard A. Gesell (appointed in 1967), are treated in later chapters.

William Benson Bryant was born in Wetumpka, Alabama, in 1911. A graduate of Howard University and Howard University Law School, Bryant as a young man participated in the early stages of Gunnar Myrdal's study of race in the South under the supervision of Ralph Bunche. He was later associated with Charles Houston in the practice of law and was an Assistant U.S. Attorney for the District of Columbia from 1951 to 1954. From then until his appointment to the District Court in August 1965, Bryant was in private practice, representing such notable criminal defendants as Andrew Mallory and James W. Killough and serving as executor for the estate of Daddy Grace. His appointment to the District Court was supported by A. Philip Randolph, Ralph Bunche, and Abe Fortas, among others.

During the mid-sixties, the performance of the U.S. District Court, as well as the "inferior" local courts — the D.C. Juvenile Court and the Court of General Sessions — came under considerable scrutiny from the press and the Congress, largely as a result of the rising crime rate in the District. A series of official commissions and committees focused on aspects of the relationship between crime in the city and the way the courts did business. These efforts (as well as conservative criticism of the Court of Appeals' liberalism) kept the courts in the public eye and contributed to the dramatic recasting of the court system in 1970, when the U.S. District Court and the Court of Appeals would lose the local jurisdiction they had exercised since 1801.

Thus, the 1960s was the last decade in which the work of the D.C. federal courts was composed of the unique mix of local, federal, and national cases that had defined it for over a century and a half. The local cases included, most notably, felony prosecutions arising in the District Court, but also appeals from the local Court of Appeals and from local administrative agencies such as the Washington Metropolitan Area Transit Commission. The "national" cases included petitions to review decisions of the regulatory commissions, suits to mandamus executive officials, and litigation arising from the exclusive jurisdiction of the Court of Appeals — especially the review of certain proceedings of the FCC and the Subversive Activities Control Board. The much less significant "federal" docket included diversity, immigration, and labor cases.

The Voting Rights Act of 1965[1] was the first of many statutes that added to the "national" jurisdiction of the circuit in the sixties and seventies.

---

1. 79 Stat. 437.

Under that law, three-judge panels of the U.S. District Court for the District of Columbia, appointed by the Chief Judge of the Court of Appeals, were given sole jurisdiction to review government actions concerning voting rights, for example, determinations of the Attorney General and the Director of the Census that less than fifty percent of voting-age citizens were registered to vote in a state with a literacy test. They were also authorized to decide whether a literacy test had been used in the previous five years to deny the right to vote for reasons rooted in race.

By today's standards, the caseload of the Court of Appeals during the early sixties appears very light. For example, during the judicial year ending June 30, 1964, 735 cases were commenced in the Court of Appeals (compared with 717 in the Second Circuit and 621 in the Ninth) and 713 were terminated. Later in the decade, however, filings in the Court of Appeals grew sharply—to 935 by the 1968 judicial year. Criminal filings, only eighteen per cent of the docket in 1950, comprised a third in 1964. The backlog of the Court of Appeals more than doubled between 1965 and 1969. During these years, when the caseload demanded, the nine regular judges of the Court of Appeals had the assistance of its own senior judges, judges from the District Court sitting by designation, retired U.S. Supreme Court justices, and judges visiting from other circuits.[2]

If the Court of Appeals was challenged by the increase in its docket, a rising backlog of cases nearly sank the District Court. The number of filings in the District Court, both civil and criminal, had actually dropped between 1950 and 1960, from 10,000 to 8,000. While civil filings dropped even more sharply between 1961 and 1968, from 7,000 to 4,500, criminal filings increased from 1,077 to 1,756. Nevertheless, delays and backlog in the District Court continually rose—to 610 in 1965 and to 1,374 in 1968. The interval from filing to trial in civil cases rose from seventeen months in fiscal 1962 to twenty months in fiscal 1969. The District Court's fifteen regular judges required assistance from half a dozen senior judges as well as visiting judges; circuit judges Bastian and Burger also sat as district judges several times during this period. According to one critical report, at least part of the reason for the increased delays was a "lack of management expertise."

---

2. The workload of the Court of Appeals during the 1960s continued to be varied, as Chief Judge Spottswood Robinson reflected in a law review article a generation later: "On a typical sitting day, a panel would hear oral argument in a local criminal case, a private civil appeal, and a review of action of some federal regulatory agency. It was not at all unusual for a panel to complete the day's sitting without any agency review. We devoted a great deal of time and energy to local cases, and to that extent we were a general law court."

Adoption of the Individual Calendar

Until the 1960s, a Master Calendar system was used for assigning cases in most multi-judge federal trial courts, including the U.S. District Court for the District of Columbia. Judges were given assignments every day by an Assistant Commissioner, who tried to even the judges' loads and, whenever possible, to give them the kinds of cases they preferred. The system worked, but it had its faults. A single case passing through the process might come before six or eight different judges; when the case neared trial, a knowledgeable attorney could repeatedly seek continuances until he was assigned the judge he wanted.

As civil litigation became more complex, the weaknesses of the Master Calendar system came under scrutiny. Reform efforts focused on various forms of an Individual Calendar system under which criminal and civil cases would be assigned to a single judge from the outset of the case and remain that judge's responsibility through all phases of pretrial and trial. While the Individual Calendar system made judges more accountable, the idea was resisted by some members of the bar who enjoyed the flexibility and tactical advantages of the existing system. Some judges, too, felt that an Individual Calendar would mean more work.

In March 1966, the Judicial Council of the D.C. Circuit appointed a Committee on the Administration of Justice, made up of practicing lawyers, to make recommendations on all aspects of the work of the courts. Gerhard A. Gesell, then still at Covington & Burling, was appointed to chair it.[3] After Gesell was made a judge of the District Court in December 1967, the chairmanship was taken over by one of his law partners, Newell W. Ellison. Among those who served on the committee at various times were Patricia M. Wald, John H. Pratt, Thomas Flannery, June Green, and Barrington Parker, all of whom later became federal judges.

The Individual Calendar was recommended by the committee in a preliminary memorandum in January 1967, and promptly vetoed by Chief Judge Curran. It was decided that a detailed management study of the U.S. Court of Appeals and U.S. District Court would be necessary before the idea would get serious attention. Early in 1969, with the study still pend-

---

3. Gesell's private, unpublished memoranda on the process of introducing the Individual Calendar system— "The Individual Calendar" (September 1990) and "Re: Chronology of District Court Individual Calendar Reform" (undated), in the possession of this author—provide a fascinating insight into the struggles for reform in judicial administration. The author also interviewed Judge Gesell on May 21, 1990, and April 4–6, 1991.

ing, an impatient Gesell urged the District Court to take control of the criminal calendar away from the U.S. Attorney's office. The broad outlines of Gesell's proposal were approved by the Executive Committee of the District Court (Judges Hart, Jones and Corcoran) and by Chief Judge Curran. On June 16, 1969, after long debate and by a vote of 8–7, the judges of the District Court agreed to initiate an Individual Calendar for criminal cases only. Support came almost entirely from the junior members of the Court. Judge Walsh, then almost blind, cast the tie-breaking vote. Eight judges agreed to take on the Court's entire criminal calendar.[4]

The Criminal Individual Calendar Plan was formally approved by the Court on September 8 and the first criminal trial under the new system was held in October. The new system was a great success. Criminal business moved. Calendar calls got rid of old cases. A defendant indicted at the same time for separate offenses came before the same judge. Prosecutors were assigned to individual judges so they were always available to the Court. Civil cases went on Individual Calendar assignment in April 1970, although the four senior judges — Pine, Youngdahl, Keech and McGarraghy — continued, as was their preference, under the old system.

In his private memorandum on the process, Gesell termed the adoption of the Individual Calendar "the spark that transformed the District Court into a true federal status. Judges felt they were now truly federal judges. They could determine the cases needing attention and guide their preparation for trial and be held solely accountable for the result." When Watergate arose, the Individual Calendar system provided two essential ingredients. First, it assured that a single judge would manage each step of the proceedings. Second, the Court's rules allowed the Chief Judge, who was not in the assignment draw, to assign a protracted matter specially, either to himself or another judge.

Bail Reform

In 1962, deeply dissatisfied by the bail system in the District of Columbia, Chief Judge Bazelon appointed a committee of the D.C. Judicial Conference, headed by Judge Danaher, to consider bail reform. This led to the creation of the D.C. Bail Project, which established a system for pre-sentence release of accused persons on non-financial conditions. The success of the project (and of a similar effort begun earlier in New York) was a major fac-

---

4. They were Walsh, Gasch, Bryant, Smith, Aubrey Robinson, Gesell, Pratt, and June Green.

tor in congressional passage of the Bail Reform Act of 1966, the purpose of which was "to assure that all persons, regardless of their financial status, shall not be needlessly detained...when detention serves neither the ends of justice nor the public interest."[5] Danaher marshaled support for its passage and was involved in formulating the legislation establishing the District of Columbia Bail Agency to help realize the purpose of the Act.

The Bazelon Court

The judges who served on the Court of Appeals during the 1960s were, on the whole, an unusually able and strong-minded group. When John F. Kennedy became President, the Court of Appeals was made up of one Roosevelt appointee (Henry W. Edgerton, seventy-two years old), five Truman appointees (Chief Judge Wilbur Miller, sixty-eight; E. Barrett Prettyman, sixty-nine; David L. Bazelon, fifty-one; Charles Fahy, sixty-eight, and George T. Washington, fifty-two) and three Eisenhower appointees (John Danaher, sixty-two, Walter Bastian, sixty-nine, and Warren Burger, fifty-three). As expected, the older judges took senior status during the 1960s and, with the exception of Fahy, played a diminishing role in the life of the Court. Less expected was the departure of Washington, who retired in 1965 because of ill health and never sat with the Court again.

President Kennedy appointed two judges to the Court of Appeals—J. Skelly Wright and Carl McGowan—and President Johnson named three— Edward Tamm, Harold Leventhal and Spottswood Robinson. All save Leventhal would serve a full generation on the Court and all would make important contributions to its work.

During the sixties, the Court of Appeals was often sharply divided, especially over criminal, landlord-tenant, and mental-health issues. The court was effectively split into "liberal" and "conservative" wings. Judges on the liberal side were Bazelon, Fahy, Washington, Robinson, Wright, and Leventhal; the conservatives were Burger, Danaher, Bastian, Miller, and Tamm. From the beginning of his tenure, Carl McGowan sought consensus and was not, during this period, allied with either faction of the Court. Retirement to senior status and new appointments changed the chemistry of the Court somewhat, but throughout the decade the ideological balance hardly shifted.

---

5. 80 Stat. 214.

Wright

Of all the appointments by presidents Kennedy and Johnson, the one with the greatest impact on the Court during the 1960s was the first, J. Skelly Wright. Wright took his seat on April 6, 1962, replacing E. Barrett Prettyman. After a brief period of adjustment, he emerged not just as David Bazelon's strong right arm but as one of the nation's most influential appellate judges.

When he joined the Court of Appeals, Wright was already a legend—the district judge who had desegregated the New Orleans school system, the largest in the South, in the face of strong official resistance. Born in New Orleans in 1911, Wright, a Catholic, attended Loyola University for college and law school. After a stint in the Coast Guard during the Second World War, Wright practiced in Washington, arguing two cases before the U.S. Supreme Court.[6] In 1948 President Truman appointed Wright U.S. Attorney for the Eastern District of Louisiana. After Truman's reelection, Wright sought appointment to the Court of Appeals for the Fifth Circuit, but instead, in 1949, he was appointed as a judge of the Eastern District of Louisiana, the youngest federal district judge in the nation. Although his renown as a district judge came from his work on civil rights cases, Wright was also a superb manager of his docket, and his use of pretrial procedures was widely imitated. In 1959 he handled the greatest number of cases of any district judge in the nation.

Four years before the Supreme Court decided *Brown v. Board of Education*, Wright wrote the opinion for a three-judge District Court, holding that admission to Louisiana State University's whites-only law school (the university maintained a separate law school for African-Americans) could not be denied solely on the basis of race or color.[7] It was, however, Wright's effort to desegregate the New Orleans school system that gained him national attention. From 1951 to 1962, Wright issued forty-one rulings in the litigation titled *Bush v. Orleans Parish School Board*. Wright and fellow Louisianan Herbert Christenberry held forty-four Louisiana laws uncon-

---

6. See especially *Louisiana ex rel. Francis v. Resweber*, 329 U.S. 429 (1949), the "Willie Francis" case, which involved the constitutionality of attempting to execute a prisoner after the electric chair failed to work the first time.

7. *Wilson v. Board of Supervisors*, 92 F. Supp. 986 (E.D. La. 1950), aff'd per curiam, 340 U.S. 909 (1951). The next year, in *Foister v. Board of Supervisors*, no. 52-937 (E.D. La. 1952), Wright ordered L.S.U. to admit blacks to its graduate and medical schools. He also ordered desegregation of the New Orleans bus and streetcar system and used the 1957 Civil Rights Act to protect black voters.

stitutional and issued injunctions against dozens of officials, from the Governor to mayors and chiefs of police, as well as the entire state legislature. In the end, Wright prevented the closing of the New Orleans public schools and upheld federal supremacy under the Constitution. He was the first district judge to place a school board under an injunction and the first to draw up a plan of his own after a board dragged its feet.[8]

The Kennedy administration intended to elevate Wright to the U.S. Court of Appeals for the Fifth Circuit, but opposition by both of Louisiana's U.S. senators deflected the promotion to the D.C. Circuit. Thus, unexpectedly, the Court gained a judge every bit as activist as David Bazelon. As District Court judge Louis F. Oberdorfer later recalled, in his memorial tribute to Wright, Wright himself had confessed:

> I guess I am an activist, but I want to do what's right. When I get a case,...the first thing I think of [is] what should be done—and then you look at the law and see whether or not you can do it.... [I]f you don't take it to extremes, I think that it's good to come out with a fair and just result and then look for law to support it.[9]

Wright started out as a harmonizer on the badly divided Court of Appeals. Shortly after his arrival, in the spring of 1962, he successfully mediated differences over the administration of the insanity defense by forging a compromise that led to a unanimous *en banc* decision defining "mental disease or defect."[10] However, Wright's decision to join the Bazelon wing in *Killough v. United States,* the quintessential *Mallory*-line case (discussed below), provoked the greatest demonstration of internecine bitterness of the entire period. It took little time to recognize that Wright's concern for the poor and underprivileged would make him a firm ally of Bazelon, Edgerton, and Fahy. "Even if the courts cannot solve the problems that beset the inner city," Wright wrote in the *New York Times Magazine* in 1969, "they and the legal system as a whole should play a significant part in that endeavor."

By appointment of Bazelon, Wright presided as a district judge over the litigation desegregating Washington's schools (the case, *Hobson v. Hansen,*

---

8. For his pains, Wright was denounced as "Smelly Wright" and "Judas Scalawag Wright" and ostracized socially. The members of the Louisiana House of Representatives rose and applauded when his blackened effigy was brought into their chamber.

9. In fact, in his own tribute to Judge Bazelon on the twenty-fifth anniversary of Bazelon's appointment, Wright claimed to be even more of an activist than the Chief Judge.

10. *McDonald v. United States*, 312 F.2d 847 (1962).

is discussed later in this chapter). He also made important contributions to First Amendment, environmental, administrative, communications and separation of powers law, contributions that are discussed in later chapters. In what was perhaps his most activist decision, Wright, acting as a one-person motions panel, in the absence of formal papers and lacking a clear-cut case or controversy, granted a hospital's request and ordered an emergency blood transfusion at the bedside of a dying Jehovah's Witness who for religious reasons was unwilling to consent to it.[11]

Bazelon did not make way for Wright to serve as Chief Judge until 1978, which may have contributed to the breach between the two men that appeared to exist during their later years on the Court. Although the two shared courage, compassion, stubbornness, and "a passion for doing what's right" (as well as a reliance upon their law clerks for the details of their opinions), they affected people differently. Wright tended to make friends where Bazelon made enemies. Perhaps it was Wright's "sweet sincerity," his gentleness, his lack of pomp or arrogance; whatever the reason, Wright, as Judge Gerhard Gesell observed in a memorial tribute, "did not allow his burning sense of injustice to override or disrupt the work of the circuit as a whole."

McGowan

Carl McGowan, President Kennedy's second appointee to the Court of Appeals, reached the bench in 1963 at the age of fifty-two, after a distinguished career in academia, corporate law and politics. McGowan had been a professor at Northwestern Law School, counsel to the Chicago and Northwestern Railroad, and, from 1949 to 1952, counsel to Governor Adlai Stevenson of Illinois—Stevenson's closest advisor and perhaps his closest friend.[12] McGowan had hoped for appointment to the Seventh Circuit, in Illinois, but he was named to the District of Columbia Circuit, where it was hoped that this gentle man would calm the tensions on the Court. As Felix Frankfurter put it in a letter to University of Chicago Law School professor Philip B. Kurland at the time of McGowan's nomination, "[T]he Court of Appeals for the District is a collectivity of fighting cats and it needs nothing as much as just the kind of human being as Carl McGowan." It was not

---

11. *Application of the President & Dirs. of Georgetown College*, 331 F.2d 1000 (1964), reh'g en banc denied, 331 F.2d 1010, cert. denied sub nom. *Jones v. President & Dirs. of Georgetown College*, 377 U.S. 978 (1964).

12. It is quite possible that had Stevenson reached the White House, McGowan would have been elevated to the Supreme Court, perhaps as Chief Justice.

for want of trying that McGowan was unsuccessful in his role as a concil-
iator in these years. McGowan did not write a single dissenting opinion, a
modern record for the Court of Appeals, nor did he even publish a concurring opinion. From the beginning, however, his ability to deal effectively
with long and complex rate-regulation cases proved invaluable to this demanding aspect of the D.C. Circuit's jurisprudence.

Tamm

The elevation of Edward A. Tamm on March 17, 1965, brought to the Court
of Appeals a seasoned trial judge, whose appointment to the District Court
in 1948 had, ironically, been opposed for lack of trial experience. Born in
St. Paul in 1906, Tamm received his law degree from Georgetown in 1930.
For eighteen years he served in the FBI, rising from Special Agent to Assistant to the Director, the agency's third highest position.

In his early years on the Court of Appeals, Tamm added weight to the
conservative wing of the Court, opposing initiatives in criminal and mental health law. More important, as the Court of Appeals evolved into the
national court of administrative appeals Tamm would contribute a series
of important administrative opinions. By appointment of his close friend
Warren E. Burger, Tamm served as Chief Judge of the Emergency Court of
Appeals from 1971 to 1982, where he was primarily responsible for the
Court's operation and procedures (he was succeeded as Chief Judge by J.
Skelly Wright). He also served on three U.S. Judicial Conference committees, his major contribution coming as chairman of the Ethics Review Com-
mittee, where, from 1978 to 1985, he personally reviewed more than 2,000
annual financial reports submitted by judges and other court personnel.
Tamm died in 1985, while still serving.[13]

Leventhal

Harold Leventhal, appointed to replace Wilbur Miller, arrived on the Court
of Appeals with Tamm; their appointments were perceived as an attempt
to keep the Court balanced. A hard-nosed liberal activist in whom practi-
cality was joined with compassion, Leventhal brought to the Court a quick-
witted, superbly analytical and cultivated mind and a ready pen. Born in
New York City in 1915, Leventhal attended Columbia College and Colum-

---

13. Tamm's major opinions included *American Airlines, Inc., v. CAB*, 365 F.2d 939
(1966); *Red Lion Broadcasting Co. v. FCC*, 381 F.2d 908 (1967), aff'd, 395 U.S. 367 (1969);
Medical Committee for Human Rights v. SEC, 432 F.2d 659 (1970), vacated, 404 U.S. 403
(1972); *NAB v. FCC*, 554 F.2d 1118 (1976).

bia Law School. He then clerked for both Harlan Fiske Stone and Stanley Reed. In the years just before and during the Second World War, Leventhal became one of the nation's leading experts on price regulation, drafting the basic statute governing the Office of Price Administration, serving as its General Counsel from 1940–43, and later writing a book about the experience of the OPA lawyers. He drew upon those experiences when he wrote the leading opinion upholding the Economic Stabilization Act of 1970.[14]

After the war, Leventhal was a member of the staff of Justice Robert Jackson, the chief American prosecutor at the Nuremberg War Crimes trials. He then continued his legal career in Washington with his own firm, Leventhal & Ginsburg, and as head of the first Hoover Commission task force on independent regulatory commissions. In addition to this experience, Leventhal was also a visiting lecturer on regulated industries for the Yale Law School.

Leventhal's knowledge of government regulation, together with his writing skill, sensitivity to the views of others, and talent for weaving a compromise, made him well equipped to contribute to a court dealing with novel questions of administrative law on the advancing frontiers of science and technology. He also demonstrated an unusual ability to manage cases with huge administrative records, pioneering a variety of devices, such as the pre-argument conference and the organization of oral argument issue by issue.

Although he had philosophical affinities with Bazelon, Leventhal was nobody's surrogate. He was more pragmatic than Bazelon, and relations between the two were often strained. Their intellectual disagreements stimulated important opinions on the proper approach to oversight of agency decisions, jury nullification, and the insanity defense (see chapter 9). He died prematurely at the age of sixty-four in 1979.

Robinson

Spottswood W. Robinson III, the first African-American to serve on the District Court and the first to serve on the Court of Appeals, was one of the great legal figures of the civil rights movement. Born in Richmond in 1916, Robinson received his law degree from Howard University; Richard Kluger, in his history of *Brown v. Board of Education*, called him the "finest legal technician Howard Law School had ever produced." Robinson taught at Howard Law School and from 1960 to 1963 was its dean, but spent much of his career in private practice in Richmond. During this period, he also tried cases for the NAACP Legal Defense and Education Fund. Robinson

---

14. *Amalgamated Meat Cutters v. Connally*, 357 F. Supp. 737 (1971).

worked on the restrictive covenant cases with Charles Houston (see chapter four) and argued the Prince Edward County, Virginia, school desegregation case, one of the companion cases to *Brown v. Board of Education* (see chapter five). President Kennedy appointed Robinson to the U.S. Commission on Civil Rights in 1961 and two years later, making a recess appointment, chose him for the District Court for the District of Columbia. Lyndon Johnson made the permanent appointment and in 1966 elevated Robinson to the Court of Appeals.

Robinson was a conscientious man of balanced judgment and great good will, but his appellate court career was marked by serious delays in getting out opinions—five times the Court's average—at least partially because of his penchant for footnotes. Some of his most important decisions came in the *Ricks* cases, holding sections of the D.C. vagrancy statutes unconstitutional (see below). He also made major contributions to the interpretation of the Equal Pay Act and the treatment of sexual harassment under Title VII of the 1964 Civil Rights Act.[15] Robinson took senior status in 1989.

Bazelon as Chief Judge

On October 9, 1962, David L. Bazelon, then fifty-two years old, became Chief Judge of the Court of Appeals. For sixteen years he was the dominant force, not just on the Court of Appeals, but in the D.C. Circuit. Bazelon's impact cannot be measured by victories, for he was just as often on the dissenting side of decisions. Nor could it be said that Bazelon "intellectually dominated" a court well provided with powerful intellects and strong personalities. Bazelon's impact, especially during the period considered here, came from his power to set an important part of the Court's agenda, a power deriving largely from his rare ability to identify in seemingly ordinary cases important legal issues—often never before dealt with in the circuit (and sometimes nowhere else, either)—and, by effort and will, to persuade his colleagues to deal with them.

A judge who inspired veneration and dislike almost equally among his judicial colleagues and attorneys practicing in the District, Bazelon was a compound of extraordinary paradoxes. Possessed of one of the most creative legal minds of any generation, he left the details of his opinions to his law clerks. Accused by critics of being a theorist whose head was in the clouds, Bazelon, more than any judge of his generation, worked to shed light upon the real-

---

15. See, e.g., *Laffey v. Northwest Airlines*, 567 F.2d 429 (1976); *Vinson v. Taylor*, 753 F.2d 141 (1985), aff'd and remanded sub nom. *Meritor Savings Bank v. Vinson*, 477 U.S. 57 (1986).

ities of law in action—what being in the police station meant for an ignorant suspect, in the ghetto for an African-American child, in a mental hospital for an involuntarily committed patient. A man of extraordinary tenac-
ity, forcing his colleagues to look at issues time and time again, Bazelon
nevertheless was almost uniquely willing to identify and accept the failures
of his own jurisprudence and to try a different approach. Bazelon used the
Chief Judgeship as effectively as any chief judge of his day to advance his substantive agenda, but he also fueled resistance to it by his sometimes abrasive
personality. Judge Abner Mikva, a friend, noted that Bazelon "could be stubborn as a bear when he thought he was right." One lower court judge re-
members Bazelon as "difficult to have a rational discussion with." On his own
court, Bazelon's relations with colleagues holding different views were tense,
and even his relations with judicial allies could be testy; his open disdain of
the District Court was reciprocated by many of its judges.

The controversy and strong passions aroused by Bazelon's tenure were
due, more than anything, to the results of his decisions. Although his judicial craft was fertile and creative, more than a few times he gave the appearance of scrambling to overturn precedent in order to reach results he
had already decided. His critics were particularly outraged by the many
criminal convictions reversed or remanded on appeal. Nonetheless, it can
be argued that Bazelon was one of the great generalist judges of all time.
He made seminal contributions in at least six major areas to the development of the law throughout the nation.

First, he articulated as powerfully as any American judge the relationship
between law, politics, and crime, giving somewhat different reasons for
stricter judicial oversight of police treatment of suspects than the Warren
Court and advancing doctrinal approaches to achieve that oversight. Second, he rekindled the modern debate over the insanity defense and explored
the legal and practical problems with the administration of the defense.
Third, he advanced more fully than any judge of the sixties the position that
those in custody "for their own good"—especially those in mental hospitals and juvenile facilities—have a right to treatment, and he developed the
corollary concept that those detainees are entitled to the least restrictive
placement available. Fourth, he articulated an approach to review of administrative agencies which scrutinized the fairness, regularity, and reasonableness of the decision-making process. Fifth, Bazelon was the first jurist to
systematically explore First Amendment issues in government oversight of
radio and television. Finally, Bazelon, to a greater degree than any other
judge, explored the problem of the low quality of counsel available to poor
criminal defendants. Although he was never able to convince his brethren

to establish a test for ineffective assistance of counsel which would lead to wholesale reversals of criminal convictions, because of his efforts the problem at least was not hidden in the District of Columbia Circuit.

At his roots, Bazelon bore more than a passing resemblance to those Old Testament prophets—reformers of the moral and social order who fought to raise the standards of personal conduct, opposed iniquity and injustice wherever they saw it, and brooked no argument or compromise. Bazelon, after all, believed that "courts should and must reveal to society the reality that often festers behind" legal euphemisms.

The Bazelon/Burger Duel

Interviewed in 1983, Edward Tamm commented that collegiality was "nonexistent" on the Court of Appeals at that time. But the Court in that era was positively harmonious compared to the 1960s, when relations between the two wings of the Court were poisonous. Carl McGowan, appointed in the hope that he would be a harmonizer, often lunched at the Federal Trade Commission to avoid the unpleasantness that prevailed among his colleagues. Until the late 1950s, disagreements on the Court had been intellectual and largely confined to the *Mallory* line of cases, appeals *in forma pauperis*, and loyalty-security cases. In the early sixties, they spread over a wider variety of issues and became personal. The principal battle was between David Bazelon and Warren Burger.

Even before Bazelon became Chief Judge in 1962, Burger had emerged as the leader of the conservative wing of the Court. Burger was younger and more energetic than his colleagues Miller and Bastian (whose contributions to dialogue on the Court of Appeals would increasingly be brief and splenetic dissents), more disenchanted with the direction of the Bazelon-Edgerton wing than Prettyman, and temperamentally more of a leader than Danaher. Neither an intellectual nor a scholar, Burger nevertheless more than held his own on the Court of Appeals. He was smart, outspoken and quotable. Like Bazelon, he was not absorbed by the craft of judging. By temperament more advocate than judge, with strong administrative talents and interests, Burger needed an outlet for his energy and desire to lead.

In many respects, Bazelon and Burger resembled each other. Both were born poor, were largely self-made, and had been involved in politics without having run for office. Neither had demonstrated much interest in criminal law before reaching the bench. Both were open to ideas from outside the law. Both were strong warriors, willing to do battle for their views, in and out of court. Both were conversant with the media and well connected in the legal and political communities. Both were criticized for being more result-oriented judges than legal craftsmen. Both were activists in oversight of the administrative agencies and both were interested in the relationship between science and law. As heads of a court—Bazelon, the Court of Appeals, and Burger, the Supreme Court—both men saw the link between their efforts as administrators and their jurisprudential goals and made powerful use of their positions.

In matters of substantive law, however, there was a yawning gulf between the two. Bazelon was a liberal Democrat who sympathized with the poor and disadvantaged, Burger a moderately conservative Republican who believed that the beauty of the American system lay in the opportunity it affords to unleash one's talents and improve one's lot.

In the duel between Bazelon and Burger, which lasted thirty years, their jurisprudential differences were magnified by the dynamics of their relationship. Both were emotional, strong-willed men. As the personal rift widened, each discovered more profound disagreements with the other. Bazelon was deeply concerned about the plight of the poor, Burger deeply concerned about crime. Bazelon was disturbed by physicians' lack of expertise in dealing with mental illness, Burger thought doctors far better qualified to deal with it than judges. Increasingly, Burger adhered to the philosophy of free will and Bazelon to a sort of environmental determinism. Even when they appeared to agree on the diagnosis, they disagreed on the prescription; for example, both found the average attorney ill-equipped, but Burger called for the certification of trial advocates, while Bazelon sought to overturn convictions on the grounds of "ineffectiveness" of counsel.

Possessing a paper-thin majority on the Court of Appeals, but with the Warren Court behind him and considerable sympathy in the political branches, Bazelon won many of the important battles with Burger in the 1960s. However, the election of Richard Nixon in 1968 and his own elevation to the Supreme Court the following year shifted the balance to Burger. During Burger's seventeen-year Chief Justiceship, the Supreme Court adopted his point of view in Fourth Amendment and confession cases and rejected Bazelon's approach to agency review and his doctrine of the "right to treatment."

Criminal Law

The Court of Appeals began the decade deeply divided over two major decisional lines: the *Mallory* issue, involving police treatment of suspects, which had been "inflicted" on the Court of Appeals by the Supreme Court; and the *Durham* line, dealing with the insanity defense. Because the D.C.

Circuit encompassed such a small area so heavily populated by the urban poor, over and over again appeals from convictions for violent crimes came before the Court of Appeals. Many of these raised issues pertaining to the *Mallory* and *Durham* rules.

By the middle of the 1960s, the number of major crimes committed in the Washington metropolitan area was growing at an alarming pace. In 1963, for example, the major-crime rate grew by twenty-two percent, and in 1964 by twenty-five percent. By 1965 Washington ranked third among major cities in wilful homicides, third in robberies and fifth in aggravated assaults. The police, the press, and members of Congress played up—and often exaggerated—the extent of crime in Washington compared to other cities. Indeed, in the Congress, reference to crime in the District became a politically acceptable way to attack the civil rights movement and the Supreme Court.[16]

The response of the Kennedy and Johnson administrations was, for the most part, the one strongly advocated by Chief Judge Bazelon and Judge Wright. That was to attack what were thought to be the underlying causes of crime—unemployment, poor schools, inadequate housing, and functional illiteracy—and to try to achieve better treatment of the poor in the criminal justice process. Such policies were unlikely to bring rapid results. In the meantime, the media and politicians gave Washington's crime national visibility. Law and order were central issues in the presidential campaigns of 1964 and 1968.

Such was the atmosphere in which the Court of Appeals was hearing appeals of convictions for violent crimes. The court was deeply divided between those who sought to hold police, prosecutors, and lower court judges to high standards of procedural correctness, and those who were concerned about decisions that appeared to exalt "technicalities" over law and order. The latter position was most effectively articulated by Judge Burger, who had the support of Judges Miller, Bastian, Danaher, and Prettyman and most of the district judges. The former approach was forcefully argued by Chief Judge Bazelon and Judge Wright, who had strong support from Judges Fahy, Washington, and Edgerton, support tempered with skepticism from Judge Leventhal and, in these years, more cautious support from

---

16. While emphasizing the areas in which Washington's crime rate stood near the top in national rankings of major cities, critics overlooked or wilfully ignored other statistics: the District was only sixteenth in burglaries, twenty-second in forcible rapes, and thirty-first in larcenies of $50 or more.

Judges Robinson and McGowan.[17] Bazelon and Wright were particularly concerned with the plight of poor people caught up in the criminal justice system, a concern that sometimes led them to dramatic flights of rhetoric. Wright, for example, took the part of a defendant who "stated that he stole because he was poor," seeing him as "a modern Jean Valjean, who was convicted of burglary for stealing bread for his starving children."[18]

In the early 1970s, Chief Judge Bazelon waged a major campaign to raise the standards of counsel appearing for impoverished defendants. As he complained in a 1973 law review article, "I come across these 'walking violations of the Sixth Amendment' week after week in the cases I review." He sought to have the courts promulgate standards for effective counsel and insisted that defendants have different counsel on appeal than at trial. In *United States v. DeCoster*, the case which would become the major vehicle for Bazelon's efforts, counsel for someone convicted of aiding and abetting an armed robbery had filed the bond review motion late and in the wrong court. He proceeded to trial, but without alibi witnesses and unaware that the defendant's accomplices had been tried before the same judge. The Court of Appeals held that "a defendant is entitled to the reasonably competent assistance of an attorney acting as his diligent conscientious advocate" and listed the duties of such an attorney. After the trial judge denied a motion for a new trial, the panel reversed once again. The case was then considered *en banc*, and the full court upheld DeCoster's conviction, holding that to reverse a conviction, defense council must demonstrate a serious incompetency measurably below the performance expected of fallible lawyers.[19]

Mallory's Progeny

The most explosive case line handled by the Court of Appeals was that involving the application of the *Mallory* rule, which held that a confession extracted during an unreasonable delay in the period between arrest and ar-

17. Washington, however, would hear cases for only part of the period, and Edgerton was sitting and writing less.

18. *Everett v. United States*, 336 F.2d 979, 984 (1964) (*Bur-WMil/Wri*). In *Robinson v. United States*, 335 F.2d 975, 978 (1964) (*Bur-Dan/Baz*), a case involving a motion to modify or vacate a ten-year-old sentence for second-degree murder, Bazelon began his dissent in this manner: "The case presents the familiar story of an appellant whose ignorance, indigence and incarceration foreclosed appellate review of his conviction."

19. *United States v. DeCoster*, 487 F.2d 1197 (1973) (*Baz-Wri/MacK*(c/d)), "*DeCoster* I"; 624 F.2d 196 (1976), "*DeCoster* II."

raignment was inadmissible (see chapter six). Here the Court was so divided that the composition of the panel, rather than any consistent principle, appeared to dictate the result in each decision. One case, the 1962 *en banc* decision in *Killough v. United States*, brought to a boil all the internecine bitterness that had accumulated on the Appeals Court bench and left a poisonous heritage in its wake.

Killough was a murder case. In October 1960, James W. Killough, enraged at discovering that his wife had a lover, strangled her and disposed of the body in a secluded spot. Five days later he reported to the police that his wife was missing, and then left town. A police investigation led to the discovery of Mrs. Killough's abandoned car, with traces of blood in it. Killough was arrested at his girlfriend's house and taken to police headquarters.

Questioning began at 9:30 in the morning and continued until 10 p.m. Killough responded evasively to questions, stated that he knew his constitutional rights and asked twice for an attorney, although after being given the opportunity he did not call one. The interrogation was resumed the next morning; after several hours, Killough confessed and was charged with murder. He then led the police to the body. Back at police headquarters, Killough gave a written statement, which he finished at 2 p.m. Only then, at 3:43 p.m., more than thirty hours after his arrest, was he given a preliminary hearing. Still undecided about counsel, Killough was committed without bail to the D.C. jail. The following afternoon, discussing the disposition of his wife's body, he made inculpatory statements to the officer to whom he had confessed the previous day.

Judge Luther Youngdahl suppressed all the statements made before the preliminary hearing and the defendant's on-the-scene identification of his wife's body. However, Youngdahl admitted the inculpatory statements made after the preliminary hearing—even though the defendant had been without counsel and the statements might have been the fruit of an illegal chain of events—because he believed that exclusion of that evidence would go beyond limits which had been set by the Court of Appeals.[20]

Initially, a panel of Burger, Bastian and Fahy (dissenting) affirmed. The case was reheard *en banc* and the full court reversed by a vote of 5–4. The swing vote was that of freshman Judge J. Skelly Wright. Writing for himself and Judges Edgerton, Bazelon and Washington, Judge Fahy held that the inculpatory statements, made while Killough was in jail and without counsel, and obtained so soon after the illegally procured and inadmissible con-

---

20. *United States v. Killough*, 193 F. Supp. 905 (1961).

fessions, were not admissible because they were the "fruit of the poisonous tree." In his concurring opinion, Judge Wright tried to take a moderate position, stating that both deterrence of the police and public safety were relevant considerations in attempting to correct police wrongdoing and advocating a rebuttable presumption that, if a confession is either coerced or the result of illegal detention, a later confession would be presumed the fruit of the first.

The four dissenters—each of whom wrote an opinion—were outraged. Judge Bastian spoke of "a grievous blow at the administration of criminal justice." Judge Miller called *Killough* another example "of what I think is this court's tendency unduly to emphasize technicalities which protect criminals and hamper law enforcement." Judge Danaher indicated that Rule 5(a) of the Federal Rules of Criminal Procedure, which required evidence to be suppressed if it was obtained during an "unnecessary delay" in bringing an arrestee before a magistrate to be informed of his rights and the charges against him, demanded only that the accused be advised of his rights, as Killough had been.

Judge Burger's dissent was so vigorous that Judge Danaher would not join him, and Judge Fahy tacked on to his majority opinion a nine-point rebuttal. Burger felt that the admissibility of the second confession was controlled neither by Rule 5(a) nor by any of the cases in the *Mallory* line, "for that Rule and every case which has ever construed it relates to statements made during unlawful detention and prior to preliminary hearing and its judicial warnings."[21]

Killough was again convicted after a jury trial and sentenced to serve five to fifteen years. At issue in the second appeal was an incriminating statement Killough had made in jail to an intern who routinely interviewed inmates about their personal backgrounds. This account of how Mrs. Killough met her death was later put in writing and signed by Killough. This statement at least had not been tainted by the earlier confessions, for the intern had not discussed Killough's case with anyone. A panel of Washington (writing), Wright, and Danaher (dissenting) nevertheless held the statement inadmissible because Killough had given it after he had been promised that the information would be kept confidential.[22] Ultimately, Killough went free.

21. *Killough v. United States,* 315 F.2d 241 (1962) (*Fahy*-Edg-Baz-Was-Wri(c)/Bur-Bas-WMil-Dan).

22. *Killough v. United States,* 336 F.2d 929 (1964) (*Was*-Wri(c/d)/*Dan*), rev'g 218 F. Supp. 339 (1963).

The raw sore that was *Mallory* would ultimately begin to heal only because it was largely supplanted by the Supreme Court decision in *Miranda v. Arizona*, which required that a confession made by a suspect who was the focus of a police investigation would be admissible in evidence only if the suspect had been previously advised of the rights to counsel.[23] In 1968, Congress resolved the delay problem in *Mallory* by requiring prompt arraignment.

Durham's Progeny

While there were practical reasons which explained, at least in part, why *Mallory* had festered in the D.C. Circuit, *Durham* (see chapter six) continued to suppurate even though its practical effects were limited. Acquittals by reason of insanity occurred in only about two percent of the criminal cases that went to trial, and about two-thirds of those acquittals went uncontested by the government. Moreover, most of those committed spent as much if not more time in St. Elizabeths than they would have spent in jail. Furthermore, even those sympathetic to the experiment recognized disturbing problems with the administration of the insanity defense: the difficulty of presenting meaningful information about the defendant through the adversary process; the unreliability of "expert" testimony; the discrepancy between legal and psychiatric thinking on responsibility; the inadequacy of many defense counsel in the subtle area of medical symptoms and the inability of defendants to afford psychiatric experts of their own.

In *Blocker v. United States*, decided *en banc* in 1961, Judge Burger, by no means initially hostile to *Durham*, delivered a searching analysis of the problems spawned by it. Burger argued that *Durham* was "a wrong step but in the right direction." Although it had given the jury valuable information from the expanding knowledge of the human mind, Burger saw serious problems with *Durham*'s "disease-product" test. He argued that the use of the term "disease" was misleading, for it had "no fixed, agreed or accepted definition in the discipline...called upon to supply expert testimony." The jury was not getting what it needed from the expert witnesses, namely, "lucid explanations of the forces, drives and compulsions which affect the controls of an abnormal personality which has become separated from reality."[24]

The following year, in *McDonald v. United States*, a unanimous *en banc* court tried to cure the problem by providing a legal definition of "mental disease or defect" for the jury: "any abnormal condition of the mind which

---

23. 384 U.S. 436 (1966).
24. 288 F.2d 853 (1961) (*Edg*-Pre-Baz-*Fahy*(c)-Was-Dan-*Bur*(c)/*WMil*-Bas).

substantially affects mental or emotional processes and substantially impairs behavior controls." The purpose of the new definition was to emphasize that it was for the jury, not the psychiatrists, to determine the question of criminal responsibility. In addition, the Court made clear in *McDonald* that before the burden of proof switched to the government to prove sanity, the defendant had to come forward with some substantive evidence of insanity. Acquittals by reason of insanity diminished for a time after *McDonald*, appeasing some of the critics of *Durham* in the press and Congress.[25]

But *McDonald* did not cure *Durham's* ills, and by the end of the 1960s the Court of Appeals appeared ready to jettison it. In 1967, for instance, Bazelon himself had indicated that he was "deeply troubled by the persistent use of labels and by the paucity of meaningful information presented to the jury." In January 1971 he suggested that he might abandon the label of "mental illness" altogether, as well as the question of product. The following year, Bazelon declared that "the responsibility defense is nothing more than a public ritual, maintained to satisfy the public's need for the image—and only that—of fairness and justice."[26] After eighteen years, the Chief Judge was prepared to give up on *Durham* "because in practice it had failed to take the issue of criminal responsibility away from the experts."

However, if the test itself had not been a success, the *Durham* experiment had many benefits. The attention of judges, attorneys, and scholars had focused upon a rich variety of issues related to the intersection of mental health and the law.[27] Moreover, not only had psychiatrists' discomfort with the law been demonstrated, but also the limits of their knowledge about the workings of the mind. The litigation spawned by *Durham* also yielded a small but growing specialized bar of attorneys knowledgeable in the ways of psychiatric treatment; psychiatrists who were more savvy about

---

25. 312 F.2d 847 (1962) (*per curiam* Edg-Baz-Fahy-Was-Wri-Bur-*Dan*(c)-*Bast*(c)/ W*Mil*).

26. *Washington v. United States*, 390 F.2d 444, 446 (1967); *United States v. Eichberg*, 439 F.2d 620 (1971); *United States v. Alexander*, 471 F.2d 923, 957 (1972).

27. These included, for example, the procedures of the hearing to test the competence of a defendant to stand trial, *Thornton v. Cameron*, 407 F.2d 695 (1969) (Baz-Rob/*Bur*); *Leach v. United States*, 353 F.2d 451 (1965) (Baz-Wri-*Bas*(c)); the rights of those committed after voluntarily and successfully raising the insanity defense, *Bolton v. Harris*, 395 F.2d 642 (1968) (Baz-Edg-Rob); and whether a defendant found not guilty by reason of insanity, who had not raised the defense himself, had to be mandatorily committed (the Court of Appeals said yes, the Supreme Court, 6–3, said no), *Overholser v. Lynch*, 288 F.2d 388 (1961) (*Bas*-WMil-Pre-Was-Dan-Bur/*Fahy*-Edg-Baz), rev'd, 369 U.S. 705 (1962).

the possibilities and limitations of litigation; and judges impatient with the legal fictions that shielded the treatment of involuntarily committed persons from judicial review. *Durham* proved to be the tip of the iceberg. During the 1960s the Court of Appeals began to deal with the iceberg itself— the treatment of the mentally ill in psychiatric hospitals. The court's engagement with that issue will be taken up later in this chapter.

The insanity defense was redefined in 1972 by the Court of Appeals in the case of Archie W. Brawner, who was suffering from a psychiatric abnormality related to epilepsy. After a quarrel at a party, he walked out, then came back with a gun and fired shots through a closed door, killing a man. He was convicted in a trial before Judge Aubrey Robinson. On appeal, the *en banc* Court of Appeals unanimously adopted the rule of the Model Penal Code's Section 4.01, which had in essence been adopted by all the other federal courts of appeals:

> A person is not responsible for criminal conduct if at the time of such conduct as a result of mental disease or defect he lacks substantial capacity either to appreciate the criminality (wrongfulness) of his conduct or to conform his conduct to the requirements of the law.

The Court did so not only because of the problems discovered in *Durham* but also because it saw the value of uniformity of approach by the circuits. The Court, however, retained the D.C. Circuit's definition of "mental disease or defect," set forth in the 1962 *McDonald* decision as "any abnormal condition of the mind which substantially impairs mental or emotional processes and substantially impairs behavior controls."[28] In his opinion for the Court, Judge Leventhal emphasized that courts should be aware "how justice in the broad may be undermined by an excess of compassion as well as passion."

In his concurring opinion, which read more like a dissent, Bazelon expressed concern that "the change... is primarily one of form rather than substance" and that the Court's attitude was "sharply at odds with the spirt of experimentation, inquiry, and confrontation that have characterized so much of our work in this field." Bazelon would have preferred that the jury instruction provide that a defendant is not responsible "if at the time of his unlawful conduct his mental or emotional processes or behavior controls were impaired to such an extent that he cannot justly be held responsible for his act." Such a test would "focus the jury's attention on the legal and

---

28. *McDonald v. United States*, 312 F.2d 851 (1962).

moral aspects of criminal responsibility" and "make clear why the determination of responsibility is entrusted to the jury and not the expert witness."[29]

Status Offenses

In 1962, the Supreme Court held, in *Robinson v. California*, that narcotics addiction is an illness and that punishing it per se constitutes cruel and unusual punishment.[30] Following *Robinson*, the Court of Appeals was among the first American courts to subject status offenses — "victimless crimes" — to close scrutiny. In 1966, the Court of Appeals for the District of Columbia Circuit held *en banc*, in *Easter v. District of Columbia*, that chronic alcoholism was a defense to a charge of public intoxication. Employing its supervisory powers, the Court rested its decision, not on the Cruel and Unusual Punishment Clause of the Eighth Amendment, but on the premise that a chronic alcoholic lacked the *mens rea* necessary to be held criminally responsible for being drunk in public.[31] Thus, when the Supreme Court, two years later, refused to extend its ruling on narcotics addiction in *Robinson* to encompass alcoholism,[32] the D.C. Circuit's *Easter* ruling survived.

In 1968, a panel made up entirely of Johnson appointees — Robinson (writing), Leventhal and Tamm — addressed other status offenses. In two cases involving a drug addict named Hattie Mae Ricks, the Court held unconstitutional five sections of the District of Columbia General Vagrancy and Narcotics Vagrancy statutes.[33] In his opinion for the Court in the first case, Judge Spottswood Robinson criticized vagrancy enforcement as "a device utilized not only to inflict punishment for suspected but unprovable violations in progress but also, through preventive conviction and incarceration, to suppress one in the future." In the second decision he called the

---

29. *United States v. Brawner*, 471 F.2d 969 (1972) (Lev-Wri-McG-Tamm-Rob-MacK-RRobb-Wilk-*Baz*(c)).

30. 370 U.S. 660 (1962).

31. 361 F.2d 50 (1966) (*Fahy*-Baz-Wri-Lev-*McG*(c)/*Dan*-Bur-Tamm).

32. *Powell v. Texas*, 392 U.S. 514 (1968).

33. *Ricks v. District of Columbia*, 414 F.2d 1097 (1968) (*Rob*-Tamm-Lev); *Ricks v. United States*, 414 F.2d 1111 (1968) (*Rob*-Tamm-Lev). As early as 1952, in *Beail v. District of Columbia*, 201 F.2d 156, Judges Edgerton and Bazelon (Proctor dissenting) had indicated that the term "not giving a good account of oneself" in the definition of vagrancy was vague and inadequate. This position was reinforced nine years later in *Kelley v. United States*, 298 F.2d 310 (1961) (*Dan*-Bas-Was). The *Ricks* cases had been tried by Judge Harold Greene, then of the Court of General Sessions, who personally believed the two statutes to be unconstitutional, but who felt bound by the precedents of the D.C. Court of Appeals (see *Ricks v. District of Columbia* at 1100).

Narcotics Vagrancy law "a blunderbuss statute without a bead-sight enforcement policy."

In matters involving such status offenses, as in other areas involving poor, disenfranchised defendants, Judges Bazelon and Wright were the most sympathetic and outspoken members of the Court. Bazelon joined Wright in a 1969 decision declaring that a ten-year mandatory sentence for a nontrafficking, addicted narcotics purchaser was cruel and unusual punishment.[34] And in *United States v. Moore*, argued by Patricia Wald by appointment of the Court and decided in May 1973, Bazelon joined in Wright's dissenting opinion that a drug addict may not be held criminally responsible if, by reason of his use of drugs, he lacks substantial capacity to conform his conduct to the requirements of the law. While Judge Robb objected that such a doctrine "would license an addict to commit any criminal act... that he considers necessary to support and maintain his habit," Wright wrote of the "misery, alienation and despair" of the addict, insisting that "no matter how low he sinks, he cannot lose his right to justice; and the lower he sinks, the greater his claim to our concern."[35]

Members of the District Court were sharply critical of the criminal decisions of the Court of Appeals during this period. Under fire for their own management practices from the President's Commission on Crime in the District of Columbia and the D.C. Circuit Judicial Council's Committee on the Administration of Justice, the district judges pointed their fingers at the decisions of the Court of Appeals, where the rate of appeal in criminal cases skyrocketed from thirty-six percent in 1960 to ninety-three percent in 1966, before settling at eighty-one percent in 1968.

Judges Pine, Holtzoff, and Hart were particularly outspoken critics of the Court of Appeals. Pine, a member of the President's Commission on Crime in the District of Columbia, slashed away at the Court of Appeals in his minority report. That court, Pine said, had created "a climate hospitable to the belief that punishment of the guilty is far from certain and may be avoided by technicalities in the law." Pine criticized the Court for "a quest for 'error'

---

34. *Watson v. United States*, 439 F.2d 442 (1969) (*Wri-Baz/RRobb*). The case was reargued *en banc* and decided on other grounds.

35. 486 F.2d 1139 (1973) (*per curiam Wilk-MacK*(c)-*RRobb*(c)-*Lev-McG/Wri*(d)-*Baz*(c/d)-Tamm-Rob). Bazelon was even willing to permit a jury to consider addiction a defense to armed robbery or drug trafficking, on the question as to whether the defendant was, because of his addiction, under such duress or compulsion that he was unable to conform his conduct to the requirements of law.

in order to find grounds for reversal," and for conflict of opinion in panel decisions, which "tended to create a belief that the law is unequally administered
and uncertain and weak." Even though Pine's criticisms did not accurately reflect the Court of Appeals' record,[36] there is no question that he was expressing the views of a majority of his colleagues. In the end, these concerns contributed to improved management in the District Court (see chapter nine)
and influenced the content of the Court Reform Act of 1970, which overturned the *Mallory* decision, limited the achievements in bail reform, and deprived the District Court and the Court of Appeals of their local jurisdiction.

Civil Cases

Both before and after its reorganization by President Johnson in 1967, the
District of Columbia government lacked an accountable executive and a
consistent and responsible law-making body. Thus hampered, it was unable to deal adequately with a range of local problems, many of which,
consequently, found their way into the D.C. courts. Given the background,
experience, and forceful personalities of many of the judges of the D.C.
Circuit, it might have been expected that they would willingly fill the vacuum left by the weakness of local institutions. It could not, however, have
been foreseen that many of the judges would be as activist as they proved
to be, nor so solicitous toward the residents of the "other Washington."

Indeed, among all federal and local officials, it was the life-tenured judges
of the D.C. Circuit who were the most responsive to the needs of a majority of the residents of the District of Columbia during these years. In an era
when most American courts continued, as Judge Wright claimed in his 1969
New York Times article, "to apply ancient doctrines which merely compound the plight of the poverty stricken," the Court of Appeals was one of
the pioneers (along with the California and New Jersey Supreme Courts)
in reshaping civil law to take account of the problems faced by the poor,
modifying or abandoning older judge-made common-law or equity doctrines and replacing them with new ones which seemed to Court majorities more in tune with prevailing philosophies of fairness.

---

36. For example, only three and one-half percent of all defendants before the District Court had their convictions reversed by the Court of Appeals; the percentage of
reversal in criminal cases was lower than in civil cases (and only one percent higher than
the average in the other circuits) and had declined from twenty-nine percent in 1955 to
fifteen percent in 1968.

Though these efforts were spurred by the Bazelon-Wright wing of the
Court, they caused considerably less discord than changes in criminal law
and procedure. The Court of Appeals recast the common law of contracts
to equalize the bargaining power of seller and buyer, reformed the law of
landlord-tenant relations, discarded much of what was left of the doctrine
of municipal sovereign immunity, and radically changed mental health law.
In addition, Judges Wright and Bazelon came close, in the acrimonious litigation over the ill-fated Three Sisters Bridge project, to articulating the
view that it was within the province of the federal courts to protect a disenfranchised black municipality from what they perceived as vindictive government by congressional committees.

The Court of Appeals was also, in this period, one of the leading American courts engaged in re-crafting antique common-law tort doctrines to fit
the needs of a different era, with results that often tended to favor the underprivileged. The court chipped away at the doctrine of interspousal immunity
under which a wife could never sue her husband in tort.[37] Some members of
the Court also sought to reduce the formidable hurdle plaintiffs had to overcome in medical malpractice actions.[38] And both the Court of Appeals and
the District Court were chipping away at the doctrine of sovereign immunity.[39] In *Elgin v. District of Columbia*, a case involving a public school student
injured during a required recreation program, the Court of Appeals took a
giant step towards elimination of the principle.[40] In a thoughtful opinion,
Judge McGowan questioned the centuries-old distinction that granted mu-

---

37. Judge Wright, who was particularly impatient with what he deemed outmoded
tort doctrines, called for the judicial abrogation of the interspousal immunity doctrine
in his dissent in *Mountjoy v. Mountjoy*, 347 F.2d 811 (1965) (*per curiam* WMil-
Wash/*Wri*). But even the more cautious Danaher appeared fed up with the doctrine. In
Roscoe v. Roscoe, 379 F.2d 94 (1967) (*Dan*-Edwards(6th Cir.)-Tamm), the Court, in a diversity case, denied interspousal immunity applying North Carolina law. Nevertheless,
undoubtedly disturbed by the absurd result that a wife injured in an automobile accident could not sue (to provide a basis for insurance company liability) even though her
husband had died, Danaher devoted considerable space in his opinion to further undermining the doctrine.
38. For example, dissenting in *Brown v. Keaveny*, 326 F.2d 660 (1963) (*per curiam*
Was-Dan/*Wri*), Judge Wright urged that the doctrine of *res ipsa loquitur* apply at least
in those cases where the conditions that caused the injury were completely under the
control of the doctor.
39. See *Calomeris v. District of Columbia*, 125 F. Supp. 266 (1954) (Holtzoff), aff'd,
226 F.2d 266 (1955) (*Pre*-Was-WMil). See also Judge Wright's dissent in *Urow v. District
of Columbia*, 316 F.2d 351 (1963) (*per curiam* Was-Bur/*Wri*).
40. *Elgin v. District of Columbia*, 337 F.2d 152 (1964) (*McG*-Bas-*Baz*(c)).

nicipalities immunity from torts growing out of "governmental" functions but not from those in which the municipality was performing a "proprietary" function. In his concurrence, Chief Judge Bazelon called for the outright abandonment of the elaborate categorizations of the common law and their replacement with a single rule: "that the existence and extent of the defendant's duty to the plaintiff is to be determined in the context of all the circumstances of the action of which the plaintiff complains." Five years later, an *en banc* Court of Appeals unanimously interred the governmental-proprietary test.[41]

Landlord-Tenant Relations

During the 1960s the Court of Appeals, in its common-law, state-court role, strengthened the position of tenants with a series of tort decisions which had the effect of imposing greater liability upon the owners of substandard property. As early as 1952, Judge Bazelon had criticized the common-law rule that absent a statutory or contractual duty a lessor was not responsible for an injury resulting from a defect occurring during the term of the lease, calling it "an anachronism which has lived on through stare decisis alone."[42] In a 1960 case, he and Judge Washington found a way around the rule, holding that the D.C. Housing Regulations imposed a duty on the landlord for maintenance and repair of residential property, neglect of which might be remediable in tort.[43]

The following year, in *National Bank v. Dixon*, the Court of Appeals held that the owner of rental property—in this case, a bank—should not be able to shield itself from tort liability despite the fact that the bank was not managing the property and had no actual knowledge of either the defect or the sublessee.[44] In a series of negligence cases following *Dixon*, the Court of Appeals—sometimes badly divided—placed a greater duty of care on the landlord.[45]

In *Edwards v. Habib*, the first "tenants' rights" case in the D.C. Circuit during the 1960s to get national attention, the Court of Appeals addressed

41. *Spencer v. General Hospital*, 425 F.2d 479 (1969) (*McG*-Baz-Tamm-Lev-Rob-RRobb-*Pre*(c)-Dan-*Wri*(c))

42. *Bowles v. Mahoney*, 202 F.2d 320, 325 (1952) (*WMil*-Stone(8th Cir., ret.)/*Baz*).

43. *Whetzel v. Jess Fisher Management Co.*, 282 F.2d 943 (1960) (*Baz*-Was/*WMil*).

44. 301 F.2d 507 (1961) (*Pre*-Was/*WMil*). Judges Miller, Burger, and Bastian would have reheard the case *en banc*.

45. E.g., *Morgan v. Garris*, 307 F.2d 179 (1962) (*Edg*-Fahy(c)-Baz-Was-Wri/*WMil*-Dan-Bas-Bur*); *Gould v. DeBeve*, 330 F.2d 826 (1964) (*McG*-Edg/*WMil*); *Kanelos v. Kettler*, 406 F.2d 951 (1968) (*Rob*-Wri-*WMil*(c)).

a problem faced by month-to-month tenants in slum housing, who were not protected by long-term leases. If they complained about the conditions in their buildings their tenancies could be summarily terminated, with the assistance, if need be, of the courts.

In 1965, Yvonne Edwards complained to the Department of Licenses and Inspection about sanitary code violations in her building. The department found more than forty violations, which it ordered the landlord, Nathan Habib, to correct. Habib brought an action in the Court of General Sessions to evict Edwards, but Judge Harold Greene set aside a default judgment, stating that Edwards had proved *prima facie* that the eviction was purely retaliatory. However, at trial, before a different judge, the tenant's defense was not permitted to go to the jury. Verdict was directed for the landlord and eviction was ordered. The D.C. Court of Appeals affirmed.[46]

The U.S. Court of Appeals issued the stay. Writing for the Court, Judge Wright (joined by Judge McGowan) held that eviction as punishment for alerting the authorities to unsanitary conditions was illegal.[47] On the merits, the local Court of Appeals held that the tenant had no statutory protection against the landlord for the right to report violations of law. On review, the U.S. Court of Appeals (Judge Wright, writing, and Judge McGowan) found that right in the housing and sanitary codes of the District of Columbia, because of the "strong and pervasive congressional concern to secure for the city's slum dwellers decent, or at least safe and sanitary, places to live." To permit retaliatory evictions, the Court ruled, would clearly frustrate the effectiveness of the Housing Code as a means of upgrading the quality of housing in Washington.[48]

Another significant case dealing with the habitability of rented housing was *Javins v. First National Realty Corp.*, decided in 1970 and called at the time "the most scholarly and far-reaching decision" in that field to date. Here the Court of Appeals, Wright again writing, discarded an age-old assumption of landlord-tenant law, that a lease primarily conveys an interest in land and contains no implied warranty that the premises are fit for occupancy. Such a rule, Wright said, might have been "reasonable in a rural agrarian society," but not for the modern apartment dweller. The court held that it was not the law of property, but the law of contracts, that should

---

46. 227 A.2d 388 (D.C. App. 1967).

47. *Edwards v. Habib*, 366 F.2d 628 (1965) (*Wri-McG/Dan*).

48. *Edwards v. Habib*, 397 F.2d 687 (1968) (*Wri-McG/Dan*), rev'g 227 A.2d 388 (1967). Danaher dissented on the ground that the result could be achieved only through legislation, not by judicial action alone.

govern the construction of leases for urban dwelling units: contracts with an implied warranty of habitability measured by standards set out in the D.C. Housing Code.[49]

Consumer Protection

In *Williams v. Walker-Thomas Furniture Co.*, the Court of Appeals confronted the frequent problem of stores employing the court system to take advantage of the poor by enforcing unfair, one-sided contracts. Ora Lee Williams, an uneducated black woman with seven children, had over a considerable period of time made fourteen purchases from a retail furniture store, totaling $1,800, to be paid for in installments. With each purchase Ms. Williams signed a lengthy contract containing a long paragraph in fine print. That paragraph provided that the full amount would continue to be due on *all* the items she purchased, and title to all of them would remain with the company, until the full balance was paid. Having reduced her debt to $164, Ms. Williams purchased a stereo for $515. She then defaulted. The store came to the Court of General Sessions to repossess not only the stereo but everything it had sold her.

The Court of General Sessions granted judgment for the store. The local Court of Appeals recognized that Ms. Williams had been victimized by a sharp business practice, but affirmed because it was unable to find a statute or decision providing authority for declaring the contract void.[50] The decision was in line with contract law then prevailing throughout the nation, which viewed businesses and their customers as trading as equals. However, under Section 2-302 of the Uniform Commercial Code (1963), which was not yet widely in effect, courts could refuse to enforce contracts deemed "unconscionable."

Reviewing the decision of the D.C. Court of Appeals, the U.S. Court of Appeals, Judge Wright writing, concluded that "when a party of little bargaining power, and hence little real choice, signs a commercially unreason-

---

49. 428 F.2d 1071 (1970) (*Wri-McG-RRobb*(c)).

In the 1960s the Court began to move away from the traditional classifications of trespasser, invitee, and licensee as a means of determining a landowner's standard of care. These distinctions, rooted in a culture closely connected to the land, seemed to some of the judges quite inappropriate in a more complex urban society, particularly as the courts had become increasingly occupied with creating new subclassifications, making fine gradations in standards of care or employing subtle verbal distinctions. See Bazelon's opinion in *Daisey v. Colonial Parking*, 331 F.2d 777 (1963) (*Baz-Bur*(c)/*WMil*); see also Bazelon's concurring opinion in *Levine v. Katz*, 407 F.2d 303 (1968) (*Pre*-Bur-*Baz*(c)).

50. *Williams v. Walker-Thomas Furniture* Co., 198 A.2d 914 (1964).

able contract with little or no knowledge of its terms, it is hardly likely that his consent, or even an objective manifestation of his consent was ever given to all the terms."[51] The court held that it could, through the exercise of its common law and equity authority, adopt a rule similar to that of the Uniform Commercial Code, and remanded to the trial court to consider whether in this case the terms of the contract were so unfair that enforcement should be withheld. Judge Danaher dissented, but not sharply, preferring to see Congress provide protection from exploitative contracts.

The *Walker-Thomas* case did not in practice provide a "bill of rights" for the poor protecting them from unscrupulous business practices. Indeed, the D.C. Court of Appeals did not hold a single contract unconscionable during the first decade after the *Walker-Thomas* decision. Nevertheless, the decision had influence throughout the nation and stimulated a rethinking of the role of courts as collection agencies.

Unequal Facilities in Education

Although *de jure* school desegregation in Washington's schools ended with the District's rapid compliance with the 1954 Supreme Court decision in *Bolling v. Sharpe*, *de facto* segregation was widespread and grew as whites left the District. In 1965 only twenty-seven of Washington's 129 public elementary schools were integrated, and eighty-seven were more than ninety percent black. In 1966, Julius W. Hobson, a government statistician and civil rights activist, brought suit against the Superintendent of Schools, the Board of Education, and the judges of the District Court, who were responsible for appointing the board. Hobson argued that the school board was purposely sheltering white students from blacks by not busing or reassigning pupils from overtaxed black schools to underused white schools, by setting up "optional attendance zones" which let whites avoid schools too black for their taste, by using a tracking system which segregated students by the results of test scores, and by keeping teaching faculties largely segregated. Hobson also argued that the appointment of the school board by the judges of the U.S. District Court was unconstitutional.[52]

---

51. *Williams v. Walker-Thomas Furniture Co.*, 350 F.2d 445 (1965) (*Wri-Baz/Dan*).

52. A three-judge District Court, over Wright's dissent, upheld the constitutionality of the method of selection of the school board. *Hobson v. Hansen*, 265 F. Supp. 902 (1965)) (*Fahy*-WMil/*Wri*). See also *Hobson v. Hansen*, 252 F. Supp. 4 (1966) (Wright). At the request of the D.C. Circuit Judicial Conference, Congress eliminated the anachronism by providing for an elected school board in the District of Columbia Board of Education Act of 1968.

Because the entire District Court bench were parties defendant and thereby effectively disqualified, that court requested Chief Judge Bazelon to assign a member of the Court of Appeals to hear the case. Bazelon assigned the judge most familiar with litigation over school segregation, Skelly Wright, even though Wright was already on record as believing that *de facto* segregation was unconstitutional.

At the time Wright rendered his principal opinion in the *Hobson* case, in 1967, the Supreme Court had not dealt with northern *de facto* segregation and the lower federal courts were divided on it. Wright's one-hundred-page opinion, ruling against the school board, was the broadest attack on northern school segregation up to that time. The judge had no trouble finding violations of the Constitution. He found that the neighborhood school policy had in some instances been intentionally manipulated to increase segregation, and that tracking as then practiced in Washington was a denial to blacks of equal educational opportunity. Wright ordered that African-American students be bused to under-capacity white schools and put an end to tracking, optional attendance zones, and segregated school staffs.[53]

When the newly elected Board of Education refused to appeal Wright's decision, Superintendent of Schools Carl Hansen resigned and joined with a group of white parents in bringing an appeal. By a 4–3 vote the Court of Appeals generally upheld Wright, although the Court construed narrowly his order abolishing tracking.[54] Retaining control of the litigation, Wright held in 1971 that the Board had to equalize per-pupil teacher expenditures in most elementary schools. No appeal was taken from that decision.[55]

Over time, the *Hobson* decision has had few admirers. Like busing orders elsewhere, it neither stemmed white flight nor led to an upgrading of the substandard school system. Although the District's experience in this area was similar to that of other major cities where federal courts ordered desegregation through busing,[56] *Hobson* is a prime example of the kind of case that attracted criticism of the Bazelon Court.

---

53. *Hobson v. Hansen*, 269 F. Supp. 401 (1967).

54. *Smuck v. Hobson*, 408 F.2d 175 (1969) (*Baz-Lev-Rob-McG*(c/d)/*Dan*-Bur-Tamm).

55. *Hobson v. Hansen*, 327 F. Supp. 844 (1971).

56. See *Morgan v. Kerrigan*, 401 F. Supp. 216 (D.Mass 1975), aff'd, 530 F.2d 401 (1st Cir. 1976), ordering busing in Boston; *Morgan v. Nucci*, 620 F. Supp. 214 (D.Mass. 1985), aff'd in part/vacated in part, 831 F.2d 313 (1st Cir. 1987), ending court jurisdiction over busing in Boston.

Mental Health: The Right to Treatment

By the 1960s medical professionals were beginning to doubt that, for many of the mentally ill, large institutions were the best treatment option. Public mental hospitals throughout the country were overcrowded, understaffed and underfunded. Because of these conditions, the intractability of their ailments, or both, most patients, including those who had been involuntarily committed, were not receiving meaningful treatment. This was certainly true of St. Elizabeths Hospital, the major public mental health facility in Washington. For many patients, St. Elizabeths offered little more than custodial care, although such care was given the high-sounding title "environmental therapy."

Courts throughout the nation shielded themselves from the problem by deferring to the expertise of doctors or by using the fiction that what was being provided was the "best available treatment." The U.S. Court of Appeals for the D.C. Circuit would be the first American court to confront head-on the conflict between the rationale for commitment (treatment) and the reality of treatment (inadequate or nonexistent).

The rationale for a right to treatment was first articulated by Judge Fahy in 1960 in a concurring opinion in *Ragsdale v. Overholser*. Noting the heavy burden of proof placed on a patient who had been committed to a mental hospital after being found not guilty by reason of insanity, Fahy remarked that the mandatory commitment provision of the statute then in force "rests upon a supposition, namely, the necessity for treatment of the mental condition which led to the acquittal by reason of insanity. And this necessity for treatment presupposes in turn that treatment will be accorded."[57]

In 1966, in his opinion in *Rouse v. Cameron*, Judge Bazelon identified a statutory right to treatment. The case involved eighteen-year-old Charles Rouse, who had been stopped by a police officer in the middle of the night carrying a small suitcase with several hundred rounds of ammunition and burglary tools. At trial the examining physician testified that Rouse was mentally ill, dangerous, and treatable. While Rouse himself wanted to argue that the police search was unconstitutional, Rouse's attorney waived the defense because, he believed, with the U.S. Attorney and Rouse's mother, that "this man needs treatment." Rouse was found not guilty by reason of insanity. Pursuant to statute, he was committed to St. Elizabeths without a hearing and held under maximum security for three years.

Rouse sought relief three times in the District Court by way of habeas corpus. When he petitioned for the third time, he argued both that there

---

57. 281 F.2d 943, 950 (1960) (*Bur*-Reed(Sup.Ct., ret.)-*Fahy*(c)).

was no longer a need for treatment of his mental condition, and that in fact he had received no treatment for approximately six months. The trial judge, Alexander Holtzoff, took the position that his jurisdiction was limited to determining whether Rouse had recovered his sanity, not whether he was receiving treatment. Holtzoff decided that Rouse would benefit from a further stay in the hospital.[58]

On appeal, Judges Bazelon (writing) and Fahy (Judge Danaher dissented) saw incarceration without treatment. "The purpose of involuntary hospitalization," Bazelon wrote, "is treatment, not punishment." Rouse's summary commitment was permissible only if there were "humane therapeutic goals." Had Rouse been convicted of the crime he had been charged with—carrying a dangerous weapon, a misdemeanor—he would have served no more than a year in jail; instead, he had already spent four years in the asylum.

Bazelon found the statutory right to treatment in Section 21-562 of the D.C. Hospitalization of the Mentally Ill Act of 1965, which provided that every mental patient in a public hospital "be entitled to medical and psychiatric care and treatment."[59] A hospital would not be required to show that the treatment it was administering would cure or improve an involuntarily committed patient, Bazelon wrote, but it did have to demonstrate that it was making a bona fide effort to do so. If a court found that a mandatorily committed patient was in custody in violation of a statute or the Constitution, the hospital might be allowed a reasonable opportunity to initiate treatment; however, conditional or even unconditional release might be ordered if the opportunity for treatment had been exhausted or the treatment was otherwise inappropriate.[60]

On remand, Judge Joseph C. McGarraghy denied Rouse's petition for habeas corpus. In the appeal, heard *en banc*, the Court of Appeals avoided the treatment issue by holding that Rouse's original commitment had been improper.[61] In other cases decided the same day, the full court declined to endorse a right to treatment. Concurring in one of the cases, Judge Burger indicated "grave doubts that we are qualified to oversee mental hospitals in

---

58. Holtzoff's opinion is printed as an appendix to Judge Danaher's dissent in *Rouse v. Cameron*, at 467 (see below).

59. 79 Stat. 758.

60. *Rouse v. Cameron*, 373 F.2d 451 (1966) (*Baz*-Fahy/*Dan*). In a case decided the same day, the Court of Appeals held that the same principles applied to a person involuntarily committed as a sexual psychopath. *Millard v. Cameron*, 373 F.2d 468 (1966) (*Baz*-Wri/*WMil*).

61. *Rouse v. Cameron*, 387 F.2d 241 (1967) (*Baz*-Wri-Lev-Rob/*Dan*-Bur-Tamm).

cases of civil commitments," adding that "obviously judges have no competence to evaluate the quality of a given choice of treatment."[62]

Although the Court of Appeals in 1967 had no desire to initiate another major case line that would plunge it into the morass of psychiatry and the law, the impact of the first *Rouse* case was considerable. It was the seminal case that pierced the veil of discretion previously allowed mental hospitals and recognized that involuntarily committed patients had rights. The case provoked almost as much law review commentary as *Durham*, much of it favorable.[63]

Bazelon created a second influential doctrine, that of the right to "an alternative course of treatment." The case in which Bazelon first articulated it, *Lake v. Cameron*, is a testament to his persuasiveness. At issue was the habeas corpus petition of Catherine Lake, who had been committed to St. Elizabeths because she was suffering from a senile brain disease. After Judge Leonard P. Walsh denied her petition for habeas, a panel of the Court of Appeals (Edgerton, Danaher, Burger) affirmed. Mrs. Lake's petition for rehearing *en banc*, submitted *pro se*, was virtually unintelligible. Eight judges voted to deny rehearing, but a dissent by Bazelon swung four votes for reconsideration. On the merits, Bazelon, writing for the Court, looked again to the D.C. Hospitalization of the Mentally Ill Act and found that even where some kind of confinement was proper, the decision maker was obligated to explore alternatives other than those conventionally expected and attempt to place the individual in the least restrictive alternative.[64]

In the D.C. Circuit, the right enunciated by Bazelon was subsequently applied to fashioning the conditions of bail, the place of juvenile confinement, and even the particular place of confinement within St. Elizabeths.[65] By the mid-1970s, the ongoing involvement of the Court of Appeals in mental health issues had produced a public-interest mental health bar. In 1974, in the wake of the right-to-treatment decisions, Patricia Wald and Benjamin W. Heineman Jr. filed a class action against a number of officials, including Secretary of Health, Education and Welfare Casper Weinberger

---

62. *Dobson v. Cameron*, 383 F.2d 519 (1967) (*per curiam* Baz-McG-Wri-Lev-Rob-Bur(c)-Dan(c)-Tamm).

63. The *Harvard Law Review*, for example, noted that "the changes envisioned for the District of Columbia are comparable to the changes set in motion by *Brown v. Board of Education*."

64. *Lake v. Cameron*, 364 F.2d 657 (1966) (*Baz*-Edg-Fahy-Lev-*Wri*(c)/*Bur*-Dan-Tamm-*McG*).

65. See *Vauss v. United States*, 365 F.2d 956 (1966) (*per curiam* Baz-Lev-Bur); *Creek v. Stone*, 379 F.2d 106 (1967) (*per curiam* Baz-Lev-McG); *Covington v. Harris*, 419 F.2d 617 (1969) (*Baz*-McG-*Fahy*(c)).

and Luther Robinson, the Superintendent of St. Elizabeths Hospital. The hospital had become a dumping ground for patients whose families were unable to care for them. The attorneys argued that all those subject to confinement in St. Elizabeths had a statutory right to treatment in the least restrictive, most appropriate setting and that, if those facilities did not exist, responsible authorities were obliged to create them.

In handling the litigation known as *Dixon v. Weinberger,* Judge Aubrey Robinson's approach was not to micro-manage mental health care in the District himself but rather to encourage the parties to agree on a detailed plan. Such cooperation was not easy to achieve; throughout the litigation, the District government fought the suit, largely because of its own tenuous financial situation. It was not until five years after Robinson had entered partial summary judgment in favor of the class[66] that the parties agreed on a consent order and final plan to implement the 1975 decision. That order and plan, with a targeted completion date of December 31, 1985, required that the District of Columbia develop a comprehensive system of community-based care. However, the District was consistently unable to meet its obligations, forcing the plaintiffs to seek or threaten to seek findings of contempt and the appointment of a special master. At the end of the 1990s the matter remained under the Court's supervision, twenty-five years after the complaint was filed, with the *Dixon* goals expected to be accomplished by 2003.

The Three Sisters Bridge Case

As already noted, David Bazelon's sympathy with the poor and oppressed, and his judicial activism on their behalf, were matched by Skelly Wright. In matters affecting the District of Columbia, both men were also deeply disturbed by the extent to which congressional committees and their chairmen appeared to be exercising undue influence over the government of the District of Columbia. Although they were most roundly and regularly criticized for their stands on issues of criminal law, Bazelon and Wright's activism can be just as clearly seen in their decisions in a civil matter: the drawn-out litigation over the Three Sisters Bridge, the climax of the bitter battles over the "concretizing" of Washington that occurred after the Second World War.

A crossing of the Potomac at the Three Sisters rocks was first designated as part of the interstate highway system in 1960; a preliminary design was proposed in 1964. Two years later, an action was brought by a coalition of citizens' groups to enjoin the government from building three freeways and

---

66. *Dixon v. Weinberger,* 405 F. Supp. 974 (1975).

the Three Sisters Bridge, which were to cost $182 million and would have displaced 800 poor families and 100 businesses. In October 1967 Judge Alexander Holtzoff upheld the government, dismissing the actions against the federal authorities and granting standing to some, but not all, of the parties against the D.C. authorities. Early in 1968, a panel of the Court of Appeals unanimously reversed. Much of the opinion rested on the District's failure to hold a public hearing in order "to protect property rights by insuring that the highway plans are evolved democratically rather than arbitrarily." Construction of the bridge and highways was enjoined until the District had complied with the planning provisions of the law.[67]

It appeared that the bridge project would be abandoned. The District government and the Johnson administration both opposed it. Some members of Congress, however, wanted the bridge built and kept the project alive. Congress inserted into the 1968 Federal Aid Highway Act a mandate to build the bridge, and Rep. William H. Natcher of Kentucky, chairman of the House Appropriations Subcommittee on the District of Columbia, announced his intention to withhold appropriations for building the much-needed D.C. Rapid Transit System until the bridge project was underway. In September 1969, the District let the first contracts for building the bridge.

On October 3, several citizens' groups, represented by Covington & Burling, sought injunctive relief from the District Court. Judge John J. Sirica held that work on the bridge should continue. However, in April 1970 a divided panel of the Court of Appeals reversed him.[68] A majority of Wright (writing) and Bazelon held that to go forward would deprive "an already voiceless minority of its important personal right to contest disruptive highway projects enjoyed by citizens generally." Judge George E. MacKinnon dissented strongly. He argued that the panel had created a "monstrous result" that "completely frustrates the expressed will of Congress." Referring to the representation of the citizens' groups by Covington & Burling, but ignoring the fact that the District was not represented in Congress, he added:

> [I]t should be recognized that plaintiffs here and their lawyers are actually some of the most articulate and politically powerful individuals in America. Their success in obstructing this project now for onto four years is mute testimony that they are not "voiceless."

---

67. *D.C. Fed'n of Civic Ass'ns v. Airis*, 391 F.2d 478 (1968) (*per curiam* Baz-Wri-Tamm), rev'g 275 F. Supp. 540 (1967) (Holtzoff).

68. *D.C. Federation of Civic Associations v. Volpe*, 434 F.2d 436 (1970) (*Wri-Baz*(c)/*MacK*), rev'g 308 F. Supp. 423 (1970) (Sirica).

On remand, Judge Sirica dismissed many of the procedural contentions, but enjoined construction of the bridge until there was complete compliance with the applicable federal highway statutes and Department of Transportation policy and procedures. Because the present design of the bridge was so substantially different from that proposed in 1964, he ruled, the public should be given an opportunity to present their views on the revised proposal.[69]

The Court of Appeals affirmed in part and reversed in part, holding that the Secretary of Transportation's approval of the project had been "entirely premature." In a remarkable section of his opinion, Chief Judge Bazelon suggested that the decision of the Secretary approving the project "would be invalid if based in whole or in part on the pressures emanating from Representative Natcher." Although the Court insisted it was not saying "the bridge cannot be built," as a practical matter that is exactly what it did.[70] The Supreme Court denied certiorari, and in 1972 the unfinished framework of the bridge was swept away in a wild storm. The bridge was never built.

Review of the Administrative Agencies

Although not yet seen as the nation's principal administrative tribunal, the Court of Appeals made important contributions to the development of administrative law during the Kennedy and Johnson administrations. This was an era in which the regulatory commissions were more forceful, the most visible indication of which was FCC Chairman Newton Minow's well-publicized pressure on broadcasters to provide better programming. In this period, too, well-organized consumer groups emerged that were capable of monitoring the agencies.

The Court exercised its greatest influence over the Federal Communications Commission, where it had special jurisdiction not entrusted to the

---

69. *D.C. Fed'n of Civic Ass'ns v. Volpe*, 316 F. Supp. 754 (1970).

70. *D.C. Fed'n of Civic Ass'ns v. Volpe*, 459 F.2d 1231 (1971) (*Baz-Fahy*(supp. op.)-*MacK*(c/d)). Judge Sirica refused to award attorneys' fees to Covington & Burling, whose lawyers had invested 4,000 hours in the litigation. 71 F.R.D. 206 (1976).

While there were many who disagreed with the Court's treatment of Rep. Natcher's actions, calling it naive, in 1994 a unanimous panel of the Court of Appeals—Judges Henderson (writing), Wald, and Williams—treated the Three Sisters Bridge case as authority for the proposition that an otherwise valid administrative decision may be rendered invalid if based in whole or in part on congressional pressures. *ATX, Inc. v. Department of Transportation*, 41 F.3d 1522 (1994).

other U.S. courts of appeals. But it did important work in oversight of the other agencies as well, often prodding the commissions to regulate vigorously but fairly, promote competition, and protect the consumer. For example, the Court cautiously upheld the Federal Trade Commission's policy of putting out a press release when it issued a complaint, weighing the public's right to know about dubious practices against the possibly harmful effects of such pre-adjudication publicity.[71] But in *Texaco v. FTC* (one of the longest-running cases in American history, having begun with an investigation in the 1930s), it twice dismissed charges of collusive, coercive and restrictive business practices by an oil company and a tire manufacturer, for lack of proof and because the undue protraction of the administrative process constituted a denial of due process.[72]

In the Federal Power Commission's highly complex area of responsibility, which included regulation of the generation, delivery, and cost of electric power and natural gas, the Court of Appeals tended to give the Commission its head, deferring to its technical work while remaining skeptical of its level of dedication to the consumer.[73] The Court was also generally supportive of the Civil Aeronautics Board, backing, for instance, the Board's decision to permit both scheduled and nonscheduled airlines to operate individual charter flights, its approval of United Airlines' takeover of the bankrupt Capital Airlines (a decision that made United the country's largest carrier but which retained competition on Capital's routes), and its granting to all-cargo air freight carriers the right to set discount rates for high-volume business, thus increasing their competitive edge over the passenger carriers in this arena.[74] The last decision had implications beyond compe-

---

71. *FTC v. Cinderella Career & Finishing Schools, Inc.,* 404 F.2d 1308 (1968) (*Tamm-McG(c)-Rob(c)*).

72. 336 F.2d 754 (1964) (*WMil-Bur/Was*), vacated, 381 U.S. 739 (1965); *Texaco, Inc. v. FTC,* 383 F.2d 942 (1967) (*Bur-WMil-Baz*).

73. In *Wisconsin v. FPC,* 303 F.2d 380 (1961) (*Pre-Dan-Fahy(c/d)*), Judge Prettyman, among the most able judges in the field of administrative law in the history of the D.C. Circuit, needed only ten pages to approve the Commission's approach to natural gas regulation. But in another case, Judge Bazelon, writing for the Court, reminded the Commission that "Congress created the FPC to pro*tect* the consumer from the market place, not simply to reflect it." *Public Service Commission v. FPC,* 373 F.2d 816 (1967) (*Baz-Tamm/WMil*). See also Judge Wright's opinion in *Northern Natural Gas Co. v. FPC,* 399 F.2d 953 (1968) (*Wri-Rob-Bas*).

74. *American Airlines v. CAB,* 348 F.2d 349 (1965) (*Bur-WMil-Baz(c)*); *Northwest Airlines v. CAB,* 303 F.2d 395 (1962) (*Pre-WMil-Fahy*); *American Airlines v. CAB,* 359 F.2d 624 (1966) (*Lev-Baz-Fahy-Wri-McG-Was/Bur-Dan-Tamm*).

tition in the air industry; the actual issue before the Court involved the Board's rule-making process, and Judge Leventhal's opinion for the *en banc* court (among the earliest of his major opinions in administrative law) also held that rulemaking is a vital part of the administrative process and should not be shackled by the formalities developed for the adjudicative process.

The Federal Communications Commission entered the 1960s badly tainted by the influence-peddling scandals of the 1950s and with a reputation for being bureaucratic, timid and institutionally conservative in regulating an industry with a history of constant technological change. Responsible for awarding valuable franchises to syndicates with the power to influence public policy through news broadcasts, the FCC was the constant object of all kinds of political pressures and a continual storm center.

With broad power to review Commission decisions, the Court of Appeals could take responsibility for producing, in the words of FCC Chairman Richard E. Wiley, "more careful and thorough Commission consideration of proposed decisions...better legal analysis, increased sensitivity to procedural rights of parties and, finally, greater responsiveness to [the Commission's] ultimate mandate to serve the public interest." The Court was not, however, alone in its power to influence the Commission in making communications policy; it shared the field with Congress, the White House and, from time to time, the Supreme Court. Unable to dominate the process, its "victories" were rarely permanent.

Of the many contentious questions addressed by the Court of Appeals in its oversight of the FCC in the 1960s, two stand out: the participation of citizen groups in license-renewal proceedings, and the application of the Fairness Doctrine. In the first category, the Court issued a precedent-setting ruling that conferred standing in license-renewal proceedings on representatives of viewers; in the second, the rules requiring equal time for opposing points of view were tested in a pair of important cases involving political and commercial messages.

The Court of Appeals' decision in *Office of Communication of United Church of Christ v. FCC*, as Fred W. Friendly later wrote, "opened the door to a new era in which blacks, Chicanos, women's groups and all organizations interested in improving television had standing to petition the Commission, and if dissatisfied with its ruling, to seek review in the courts.... For the first time the public could make the broadcaster account directly for his stewardship of the airwaves." But this seminal 1966 decision was even more important than that, for it greatly influenced the expansion of standing throughout the federal administrative process and in the federal courts as well.

The case involved WLBT, a white-owned television channel in Jackson, Mississippi, which regularly used the words "nigger" and "nigra" on the air. Parts of national telecasts which treated civil rights sympathetically were blacked out with a "Sorry, cable trouble" sign. For ten years the FCC had received complaints about WLBT, and had begun an investigation which was continuing in March 1964, when the channel filed an application for license renewal. The United Church of Christ, a Protestant denomination whose Office of Communication was principally concerned with minority access to the airwaves, filed a petition to intervene in the WLBT renewal proceeding on its own behalf and as representative of "all other television viewers in the state of Mississippi." The petition's primary complaint was that WLBT did not give a fair and balanced presentation of controversial issues, especially those involving African-Americans.

Under the Communications Act of 1934, standing to intervene in FCC cases was limited to persons "aggrieved or whose interests are adversely affected" by Commission action. Thus far, the Commission and the courts had read this language as providing for intervention only by those alleging electrical interference and those alleging economic injury.[75] Accordingly, the FCC denied the petition but granted WLBT just a one-year license renewal, conditioned upon immediate cessation of discriminatory programming and compliance with the Fairness Doctrine. Two of the seven commissioners dissented bitterly.

Judge Burger, writing for himself, McGowan, and Tamm, reversed the FCC decision. As this was an agency case, he wrote, the constitutional limits on standing to sue in federal courts did not apply. Burger viewed standing in agency proceedings as a "practical and functional" concept. There was no reason to "exclude those with such an obvious and acute concern as the listening audience," nor was the legal fiction that the Commission itself represented the public's interest sufficient grounds for denial of standing. The court held the grant of the one-year license renewal erroneous and remanded to the Commission for a hearing.[76]

Although the Court of Appeals minimized the path-breaking nature of its decision, stating that "there is nothing unusual or novel in granting the consuming public standing to challenge administrative actions," the deci-

---

75. *NBC v. FCC*, 132 F.2d 545 (1942) (*Rut*-Ste-Vin-*Gro*(c)/*JMil*-Edg), aff'd, 319 U.S. 239 (1943); *FCC v. Sanders Bros. Radio Station*, 309 U.S. 470 (1940).

76. *Office of Communication of United Church of Christ v. FCC*, 359 F.2d 994 (1966) (*Bur*-McG-Tamm).

sion was momentous. Along with the Second Circuit's decision in the *Storm King Mountain* case some weeks earlier,[77] it spurred the work of public interest groups throughout the nation and inspired the creation of new ones.

The second *United Church of Christ* case was brought after the FCC, in 1968, granted a three-year license renewal to WLBT, over the dissents of two commissioners. That decision was handed down in June 1969, on the eve of Warren Burger's taking office as Chief Justice. The Court—Burger, again writing, McGowan and Tamm—castigated the Commission for its deference to the station's owner, Lamar Life Broadcasting, and its prejudicial treatment of the public-interest representatives. The FCC was ordered to vacate the grant of the license and to open a new application process; Lamar could still seek the license, but only as an equal applicant on a level playing field.[78]

For ten years, while the FCC's comparative proceeding inched slowly forward, WLBT was operated on an interim basis by a nonprofit, racially mixed group of local residents. The eighteen-year dispute finally ended in 1979 when the license was granted to a local group headed by Aaron Henry, an African-American who had been one of the appellants in the original case. The case marked one of the first times that a U.S. court had ordered the termination of a license in any regulated field. It sent a message that license renewal should not be considered automatic (although in practice nonrenewals would be extremely rare) and it gave listener groups leverage to negotiate with broadcasters on matters of hiring and program content. Indeed, for some years public interest organizations and the Court of Appeals acted reciprocally to nudge the FCC toward a greater concern for the listeners.

Cases involving the Fairness Doctrine were an important concern of the Court of Appeals in the late 1960s and 1970s, and stimulated some of the most interesting thinking from members of the Court in this period. The Fairness Doctrine required broadcasters to afford reasonable opportunity for the discussion of conflicting views on issues of public importance. It grew out of an evolutionary process, through rulings of the Federal Radio Commission and the FCC over several decades, and was written into Section 315

---

77. *Scenic Hudson Preservation Conference v. FPC*, 354 F.2d 608 (2d Cir. 1965), holding that parties with a non-economic interest have standing to question decisions of the FCC.

78. *Office of Communication of United Church of Christ v. FCC*, 425 F.2d 543 (1969).

of the Federal Communications Act in 1959.[79] Under the doctrine, which rarely had been challenged by licensees in the courts for fear of provoking the Commission, broadcasters were permitted to editorialize, as long as they sought reasonably balanced presentations of all viewpoints on important and controversial public issues. Prior to the mid-1960s, a letter of admonition was the only direct sanction the FCC had employed to enforce the Doctrine, although the threat of license nonrenewal was always present.

The Fairness Doctrine finally confronted the Constitution in *Red Lion Broadcasting Co. v. FCC*, decided by the Court of Appeals in 1967. Reverend John M. Norris, a strong-minded conservative, owned a radio station in the small town of Red Lion, Pennsylvania, which broadcast the Reverend Billy James Hargis's "Christian Crusade." After Hargis sharply criticized Fred J. Cook for articles he had written in *The Nation* attempting to expose extreme conservative broadcasters, including Hargis, Cook recorded a reply which he asked the station to air. When the station offered to sell him time but refused to provide free air time, Cook filed a complaint with the FCC. The Commission ordered the station to air Cook's reply. Norris—who had unsuccessfully sought to sue Cook in the District Court for the District of Columbia[80]—petitioned for review of the order by the Court of Appeals.

The Court of Appeals upheld Cook and the FCC. At the core of Judge Tamm's opinion was the view that "[t]he broadcasters, as public trustees, have an obligation in a democratic society to inform the beneficiaries of the trusteeship, i.e., the public, of the different attitudes and viewpoints which are held by the various groups which make up the community." Unlike other modes of expression, radio and television were subject to governmental regulation, Tamm thought, because of the limited availability of space on the broadcast band. Tamm held the Fairness Doctrine "a vehicle completely legal in its origin which implements by the use of modern technology the 'free and general discussion of public matters [which] seems absolutely essential to prepare the people for an intelligent exercise of their rights as citizens.'"[81]

---

79. 73 Stat. 557. A touchstone of the doctrine was the FCC's *Report on Editorializing by Broadcast Licensees*, 13 FCC 1246 (1949).

80. He had sought damages of five million dollars, a declaration that the Fairness Doctrine was unconstitutional, and an injunction against its enforcement. Chief Judge Bazelon, whose views in this area would evolve considerably, refused to convene a three-judge District Court, calling the action "frivolous." *Red Lion Broadcasting Co. v. FCC*, case no. 2331-65 (1965).

81. *Red Lion Broadcasting Co. v. FCC*, 381 F.2d 908 (1967) (*Tamm-Fahy*(c)). Tamm was quoting from a citation in *Grosjean v. American Press Co.*, 297 U.S. 233, at 249.50

A month after that decision was handed down, the FCC announced new rules governing political editorializing by broadcasters and the right of reply for those criticized on the air. The rules were criticized by virtually the entire broadcast industry as, among other things, violations of the First Amendment, and challenged by the Radio-Television News Directors Association (RTNDA) in a suit brought in the Seventh Circuit. In that case, decided in 1968, the Court rejected the view that the broadcast media were entitled to a lower order of First Amendment protection than the print media and held the FCC's new rules unconstitutional.[82]

The Supreme Court granted review of both the *RTNDA* and *Red Lion* cases and unanimously upheld the D.C. Circuit.[83] Justice Byron White's opinion for the Court reflected in many respects the views expressed by Judge Tamm, holding the Fairness Doctrine constitutional "[i]n view of the scarcity of broadcast frequencies, the Government's role in allocating those frequencies, and the legitimate claims of those unable without governmental assistance to gain access to those frequencies for expression of their views." *Red Lion* was not the end, but rather the beginning of an exploration of the problem, which would involve the Court and the Commission for years.

Loyalty-Security: The Subversive Activities Control Board

The nation's anti-Communist hysteria was largely spent by the time John F. Kennedy was elected President. In the 1960s the Court of Appeals heard far fewer loyalty-security cases than it had in the 1940s and 1950s and, for the most part, was more likely to side with the individual against the government in this area than it had previously been. It also imitated the Supreme Court's approach of straining to avoid decisions on constitutional grounds. During this period, the Court of Appeals' most important con-

---

(1936) to Cooley's *Constitutional Limitations,* 8th ed., 2:886 (Boston: Little, Brown, 1927). Because Judge Miller did not participate in the panel ruling and Judge Fahy concurred only in the result, the formal impact of Tamm's opinion for the Court was limited. It was, nevertheless, an important beginning for what would become an intense judicial debate over the Fairness Doctrine.

82. *Radio Television News Directors Ass'n v. United States,* 400 F.2d 1002 (7th Cir. 1968).

83. *Red Lion Broadcasting Co. v. FCC,* 395 U.S. 367 (1969).

tribution in the loyalty-security area was its role in curbing the Subversive Activities Control Board.

The SACB had been created by the Internal Security Act of 1950, known as the McCarran Act, which required "Communist-action" and "Communist-front" organizations to register with the Board and to furnish it with complete membership lists and financial statements. Another category, "Communist-infiltrated organizations," was added by the Communist Control Act of 1954.[84] Noncompliance with the Act was punishable by fines or imprisonment. The Court of Appeals for the District of Columbia Circuit was given exclusive jurisdiction over orders of the SACB (although the Court could, at its discretion, transfer cases to the home circuits of petitioners).

During the 1950s, the Court had several times upheld the legality of SACB orders against challenges by the Communist Party of the United States, the most obvious target of the Act. Judge Bazelon, concerned about Fifth Amendment problems, dissented in whole or in part from these decisions.[85] Then, in 1963, a panel of Bazelon (writing), Washington, and McGowan reversed, on Fifth Amendment grounds, a District Court conviction of the Communist Party for failure to register. The ruling held that since the statutes under which the SACB operated made Party membership a crime, its officers had a valid claim of the privilege against self-incrimination. On appeal from a second conviction on retrial, the Court (McGowan, Prettyman, and Danaher) held that Congress had erred by seeking at the same time to compel disclosure by the Party and incrimination of its members. The statutory scheme, viewed as a whole, was "hopelessly at odds with the protections afforded by the Fifth Amendment." That decision essentially put an end to the Subversive Activities Control Board.[86]

---

84. 68 Stat. 775.

85. *Communist Party of the United States v. Subversive Activities Control Board*, 223 F.2d 531 (1954) (*Pre-Dan/Baz*), rev'd, 351 U.S. 115 (1956); *Communist Party of the United States v. Subversive Activities Control Board*, 254 F.2d 314 (1957) (*Pre-Baz-Dan*); *Communist Party of the United States v. Subversive Activities Control Board*, 277 F.2d 78 (1959) (*Pre-Dan(c)/Baz*), aff'd, 367 U.S. 1 (1961). Bazelon began his dissent from the 1954 decision thus: "Suppose an Act of Congress required bands of bank robbers to file with the Attorney General statements of their membership and activities, and imposed criminal penalties upon their leaders and members for failure to do so.... No argument could reconcile such an Act with the Fifth Amendment."

86. *Communist Party of the United States v. United States*, 331 F.2d 807 (1963) (*Baz-Was-McG*); *Communist Party of United States v. United States*, 384 F.2d 957 (1967) (*McG-Pre-Dan*).

Reform of the District of Columbia Court System

The District of Columbia Court Reform and Criminal Procedure Act of July 29, 1970,[87] was the result of diverse pressures: the political need to do something about crime in the District; the trend toward greater home rule, which had awakened the need for a stronger local court system; criticism of the management of the courts dealing with criminal cases; and a desire in the Nixon administration and among congressional conservatives to remove criminal cases from David Bazelon and Skelly Wright — "Judge Babble-on and Judge Wrong," as some frustrated prosecutors dubbed them.[88]

During the 1960s, congressional hearings and several commission reports had underscored the media image of Washington as a crime-infested city and had drawn attention to the serious backlog of cases in the District Court and Court of General Sessions and to the mismanagement of the local Juvenile Court. Indeed, during the late sixties the crime rate in the District rose exponentially; a headline in the January 12, 1970, issue of *Newsweek* dubbed the city "Capital of Crime."[89] The mounting backlog, combined with the extremely liberal approach to bail emanating from the Court of Appeals, meant that very few serious offenders were going to jail.

In this period, too, the District Court had not been well managed, and had been widely criticized for its refusal in 1965 to permit a study of its management for the D.C. Crime Commission. Until 1969 the Court was still operating with a Master Calendar, allowing the U.S. Attorney to control its criminal calendar and the attorneys in civil cases to control the civil

---

87. 84 Stat. 473.

88. Almost a generation later, Judge Wald wrote in the *Administrative Law Review*, "[I]t is no secret that a major motivation for the 1970 District of Columbia Court Reorganization Act...was the Nixon administration's fierce opposition to many of these rulings, although the reason formally asserted for the legislation...was the administration's dismay at the serious backlog of crime cases in the federal district court."

89. During the twelve-month period ending November 30, 1969, serious crime in Washington rose by twenty-nine percent, homicides by a third, and robberies by forty percent; aggravated robberies in Washington grew from 2,881 in 1965 to 12,366 in 1969. In 1968, 65,982 index crimes were committed, and 14,125 arrests were made for serious crimes. In 1969, with 8,000 cases pending, only 255 adults had been convicted. From fiscal 1964 through fiscal 1968 only 910 suspects were convicted of robbery in the District Court; the time between indictment and disposition more than doubled, to nine months, between 1965 and 1969; those released on bail reportedly had a thirty percent rate of recidivism.

calendar. There were no regular meetings between the U.S. Attorney and the Chief Judge of the District Court. A lot of paper shuffling went on, but no one was in command.

Richard Nixon had come to office having pledged to "restore freedom from fear to the nation's capital." His proposals went to Capitol Hill on July 11, 1969, and he signed the Court Reform Act just over a year later. The law coupled a dramatic reorganization of the courts of the District with stiffer criminal penalties, greater latitude for the police in apprehending suspects, and other measures designed to readjust the balance between the government and the criminal defendant, including provisions that effectively overturned the *Mallory* rule and shifted the burden of proof of an insanity defense from the prosecution to the defense.

Though it was clear that the Court of Appeals' liberal wing was a primary target of the reorganization plan, this was never fully ventilated in the Senate hearings on the legislation. Bazelon himself, unwilling to oppose home rule, testified in favor of it, stating that his court was "in full agreement with those who pointed to the substantial benefits which will accrue to the citizens of the District of Columbia in the establishment of a vigorous local court system equal in power and prestige... to that of any state in the country."[90] Chief Judge Curran also supported the bill, but admitted that his view was "not shared by all the Regular Judges of the District Court."

By the Court Reform Act, which took effect on February 1, 1971, the federal courts of the District of Columbia lost the expressly local jurisdiction they had held since their creation in 1801. The judiciary in the District was divided into federal courts—the U.S. District Court and the U.S. Court of Appeals for the District of Columbia Circuit (Article III courts)—and local courts—the Superior Court and the District of Columbia Court of Appeals (Article I courts).

---

90. Among the few to suggest the jurisprudential implications was Professor Addison Bowman of Georgetown Law School, who testified in the Senate hearings that the U.S. Court of Appeals "has earned a nationwide reputation because of the competence and the intelligence of its judges, and most importantly, because of its willingness to view the law as a dynamic instrument in the context of social change." However, in his written statement, Bowman said this of the judges of the "inferior" courts that were to become the local courts in the reorganized court system: "Time and time again, lawyers representing the poor and the powerless expect to lose (and sometimes to be personally abused) at the trial level and in the D.C. Court of Appeals. Though there are a few exceptions, generally the judges there seem determined to stick rigidly to the law as laid down in the past, despite the obvious new social realities of the present."

The Superior Court was a trial court, created from the consolidation of the Court of General Sessions, the Juvenile Court and the D.C. Tax Court. The new judges of the Superior Court were to be appointed by the President, subject to Senate confirmation, for terms of fifteen years. The District of Columbia Court of Appeals, formerly an intermediate appellate court, was recognized as the highest court of the District of Columbia, possessing jurisdiction over cases from the Superior Court and from orders and decisions of any agency of the District of Columbia.

After a transition period of thirty months, the U.S. District Court completely lost its local jurisdiction—criminal, civil, family and probate—and became solely an Article III court. The U.S. Court of Appeals for the D.C. Circuit, which was barely mentioned in the legislation, now more closely paralleled the regional circuit courts of appeals. In a series of decisions interpreting the Court Reform Act, the new system in the District of Columbia was made almost exactly parallel to that in each of the states.[91]

Although the federal courts of the District of Columbia Circuit had lost an important part of their traditional jurisdiction, their influence was about to grow significantly. The District Court and the Court of Appeals would become the major forum for the adjudication of cases precipitated by the burst of legislation, passed during the Johnson and Nixon administrations, that greatly enlarged the role of the federal government. Within a few years, there would be no doubt that the Court of Appeals was the nation's chief administrative tribunal. Freed of many of its local responsibilities, the District Court would be called upon far more than before to oversee the executive branch of the federal government. And soon it would become involved in the most profound test of judicial power in the nation's history.

---

91. In *Palmore v. United States*, 411 U.S. 389 (1973), the Supreme Court upheld the power of the Superior Court, a non-Article III court, to try criminal cases, and held that the federal courts of the District were without jurisdiction to entertain collateral attacks by way of habeas corpus on convictions of persons in prison as a result of convictions in the D.C. local courts. In *United States v. Henson*, the U.S. Court of Appeals held that, absent an unmistakable indication of congressional intent, the D.C. Circuit would not apply a rule for its federal courts which differed significantly from that of the other federal courts. 486 F.2d 1292 (1973) (*McG*-Wri-Tamm-Lev-Rob-MacK-RRobb-Wilk-*Baz*(c/d).

Chapter 8

Separation of Powers
The Nixon Era, 1969–74

Nothing in the history of the D.C. Circuit prepared its courts for the torrent and variety of cases involving basic principles of the separation of powers that occurred during the Nixon administration. In the space of a few short years, the American constitutional system was repeatedly tested by actions of the government and events in the streets. In responding to such stresses, the federal courts would be challenged as never before. Nowhere were they challenged so often or so significantly as in the District Court of the District of Columbia.

It was during this period that the District Court, which for most of its history had been an essentially local court manned by judges with essentially local experience, became the focal point for some of the great tests of American constitutionalism. In these years the District Court came of age as a visible and influential national court, for a time placing its superior, the Court of Appeals, in the shadows. More than any other American court, the District Court demonstrated that the judiciary would not flinch from making the separation of powers work. The large number of cases in the District Court testing the constitutional powers of the three branches of government were made possible by doctrinal changes which broadened standing to sue and by a more assertive approach to reaching the merits in constitutional litigation brought about by the Supreme Court.

The judges of the District Court were equal to the occasion, establishing the standard for the courts of the nation. Major contributions were made by a number of judges, notably Gerhard Gesell, William Jones, June Green, and Aubrey Robinson. The most visible was, of course, John Sirica, who handled the major Watergate cases.

This chapter will focus on the separation-of-powers issues faced by the D.C. federal courts in this period, particularly the challenges from the

Nixon administration over the Pentagon Papers, Watergate, and other matters, as well as the courts' relations with the Congress in this area. Other issues confronted by the courts in the early 1970s will be considered in the next chapter, as will the three judges Richard Nixon appointed to the Court of Appeals in 1969–70 — Roger Robb, George MacKinnon, and Malcolm Richard Wilkey.

Relations with the Congress

Separation-of-powers cases involving the prerogatives of congressional committees had appeared regularly in the courts of the D.C. Circuit, especially in the 1940s and 1950s, when most of them grew out of prosecutions for contempt of Congress. Now members of Congress, congressional committees, and even functionaries such as the Doorkeeper were often unwilling defendants in actions to enjoin hearings or the publication of committee reports. Sometimes, too, members of Congress were willing plaintiffs, seeking the help of the courts in policy struggles with the executive. Constitutional issues always lurked in these battles, and the questions of immunity, standing, and the "political question" doctrine that often arose in these cases would come up repeatedly in litigation over the Watergate affair.

During the late 1960s and early 1970s, the U.S. Supreme Court made several modifications to doctrines restricting access to the federal courts. These decisions greatly contributed to the geometric increase in the number of important separation-of-powers cases in the D.C. Circuit. The High Court relaxed some of the rigors of the "case or controversy" limitation of Article III of the Constitution[1] and showed itself willing to deal with questions it had previously left to the executive and legislative branches. During this period, therefore, federal judges, especially in the D.C. Circuit, were less likely to use "gate-keeping doctrines" as a reason not to decide cases on their substantive merits.

In addition, the Supreme Court demonstrated greater willingness to ignore traditionally prudential limitations upon review and to risk more collisions between the judiciary and the political branches. One of the most important steps along this road, *Powell v. McCormack*, arose in the D.C. Circuit. Adam Clayton Powell was a charismatic, flamboyant and aggressive politi-

---

1. In *Flast v. Cohen*, 392 U.S. 83 (1968), the Court allowed taxpayer standing to challenge expenditures on grounds that they violated the Establishment Clause of the First Amendment.

cian, and a legend in the black community. He had represented Harlem in the House of Representatives since 1944 and had fought energetically for civil rights, but had become increasingly erratic and irresponsible. After his reelection in 1966, the House of Representatives refused to seat him. Powell and eighteen voters from his congressional district brought suit in the District Court for the District of Columbia, seeking injunctive relief, a declaratory judgment and mandamus to force the House to seat him.

The case was assigned to Judge George L. Hart Jr., who handled many important cases during this period. Born in Roanoke in 1905, Hart had been appointed to the bench by President Eisenhower in 1958. He was esteemed by his colleagues as a man of courage and many talents, a doer who always did for the institution. Although formally Chief Judge of the District Court only during the years 1974–75, Hart is considered one of the finest chief judges of modern times—an excellent administrator, open, efficient, and inspiring loyalty. Well-respected in Congress, Hart was a conservative judge and one of the strongest critics of the Bazelon Court.[2]

Refusing to convene a three-judge court, Hart held that the subject matter of the suit embraced a "political question" and dismissed the complaint for want of subject-matter jurisdiction.[3] When the Court of Appeals acted on Powell's appeal, on July 30, 1968, the panel of Warren Burger, Carl McGowan, and Harold Leventhal was unanimous that the case was not justiciable, though each man reached his conclusion by a different route.[4] In the final opinion Earl Warren rendered as Chief Justice, the Supreme Court reversed. Finding that the House had "excluded" but not "expelled" Powell, the Court held that the Constitution left the House without authority to exclude any duly elected person who met the constitutional requirements of age, residence, and citizenship, as Powell did.[5]

Members of Congress fussed and fumed, disagreed and defied, but a true confrontation between the branches was averted. The Supreme Court de-

2. Hart was especially critical of the Bazelon court over the *Cannikin* case, the cases dealing with demonstrations in Lafayette Park (see below), and the Three Sisters Bridge case (see chapter seven). The view reflected here of Hart as a man and a judge was gained from interviews the author had with Judges Thomas Flannery, June Green, Oliver Gasch, and Gerhard Gesell and Clerk of Court James F. Davey in 1990 and 1991.

3. *Powell v. McCormack*, 266 F. Supp. 354 (1967). The political question doctrine concerns questions over which courts have jurisdiction, but which are regarded as nonjusticiable and inappropriate for judicial resolution because they are better left to the "political branches" of government.

4. *Powell v. McCormack*, 395 F.2d 577 (1968) (*Bur-McG*(c)-*Lev*(c)).

5. 395 U.S. 486 (1969).

cision had provided for only declaratory relief—an order that Powell had been unconstitutionally excluded from his seat—leaving the shaping of further relief to the lower court. Hart dismissed Powell's claim for back pay, the reestablishment of his seniority and the recovery of his fine. On February 2, 1970, the Supreme Court refused to hear the appeal. Powell had already settled much of the suit, agreeing to be seated as a freshman member and to have a fine of $25,000 deducted from his salary. He was defeated for reelection in 1970 (by 150 votes) and died a year and a half later.

For the next few years the Powell case stood as an example to the lower federal courts that they need not always dismiss, on grounds of justiciability, lawsuits requiring interpretation of the prerogatives of the other branches of the federal government. By mid-decade, the Burger Court would tighten the rules governing standing and ripeness, and, for the most part, counsel judicial self-restraint in separation-of-powers cases. However, while Richard Nixon was President, the lower federal courts were operating under these more liberalized rules of access to the federal courts.

Congressional Immunity

The courts of the D.C. Circuit were not always as willing as the Supreme Court to go to the merits in litigation seeking to enjoin actions of congressional committees; in the early 1970s the Court of Appeals affirmed the District Court's rejection of several suits claiming improper use of the subpoena power by congressional committees.[6] But in several cases involving areas outside traditional "legislative action," decisions of the D.C. Circuit suggested that some of its judges doubted the capacity of the political process to protect the rights of those caught in the vise of congressional investigations.

In this regard, a recurrent issue was that of congressional immunity from suit under the Speech and Debate Clause of Article I. Two such cases con-

6. For example, *Davis v. Ichord*, 442 F.2d 1207 (1970) (*Fahy*-McG-*Lev*(c)) (affirming Hart), which challenged an investigation by the House Committee on Internal Security into the demonstrations at the 1968 Democratic National Convention in Chicago; *Cole v. McClellan*, 439 F.2d 534 (1970) (*per curiam* Lev-RRobb-Wilk) (affirming Corcoran), which challenged the validity of a *subpoena duces tecum* served on colleges and universities and seeking to enjoin the use of information obtained by the subpoenas; *Ansara v. Eastland*, 442 F.2d 751 (1971) (*per curiam* Tamm-Lev-Wilk) (affirming Smith), a case brought by anti-war activists contesting a subpoena as overbroad, thereby inhibiting speech, assembly, and association; and *Sanders v. McClellan*, 463 F.2d 894 (1972) (*Fahy*-McG-Rob) (affirming Corcoran and Jones), a suit to enjoin enforcement of a Senate subcommittee subpoena seeking to force an editor of an African-American underground periodical to name the author of articles about black terrorism and sabotage.

cerned attempts to enjoin the publication of reports issued by committees of the House of Representatives. In *Hentoff v. Ichord*, which sought to enjoin the House Committee on Internal Security from publishing what was essentially a list of political radicals, Judge Gerhard Gesell held that the members of Congress were protected by the Speech and Debate Clause but the Public Printer and Superintendent of Documents were not; he enjoined publication on the ground that the report did not fulfill a legitimate legislative purpose but was a blacklist intended to inhibit speech.[7]

In *Doe v. McMillan*, on the other hand, Judge John J. Sirica twice refused to enjoin publication of a report by the House Committee on the District of Columbia that contained the names and addresses of students charged with disciplinary and other infractions, as well as copies of test papers of named students. The Court of Appeals affirmed Sirica's dismissal, holding that the District Court was without jurisdiction because all of the defendants were immune from suit. The Supreme Court, while agreeing with the lower courts that the Committee's actions were protected in this case, also warned that the Speech or Debate Clause did not immunize those who publish and distribute otherwise actionable material beyond the reasonable requirements of the legislative function.[8]

However, when a split Court of Appeals, in *United Servicemen's Fund v. Eastland*, tried to follow the Supreme Court down the path it appeared to have taken in *Doe v. McMillan*, it was rebuffed. After Judges John Pratt and Oliver Gasch had both denied applications for preliminary injunctions against the Senate Judiciary Committee's Subcommittee on Internal Security, which had subpoenaed the bank records of an anti-war organization, the Court of Appeals reversed. It thought the issue justiciable under *Powell*, and ruled that the Speech or Debate Clause did not protect those who issued or served the subpoena. Judge MacKinnon dissented vigorously and the Supreme Court, by a vote of 8–1, agreed with him.[9] Chief Justice Burger,

---

7. *[Nat] Hentoff v. Ichord*, 318 F. Supp. 1175 (1971). The House then overwhelmingly passed a resolution ordering the Public Printer and Superintendent of Documents to print and distribute a "new committee report" (which was a restatement of the previous one) and warning all persons "to refrain from molesting, intimidating, damaging, arresting, imprisoning, or punishing any person because of his participation" in publishing the report. That report was printed without judicial interference.

8. *Doe v. McMillan*, 442 F.2d 879 (1971) (*per curiam* Fahy-Lev-Tamm); 459 F.2d 1304 (1972) (*MacK*-WMil/*Wri*), aff'd in part, rev'd in part, 412 U.S. 306 (1973).

9. *United Servicemen's Fund v. Eastland*, 488 F.2d 1252 (1973) (*Tuttle*(5th Cir.)-Baz/*MacK*); rev'd, 421 U.S. 491 (1975). Though the vote was 8–1, three justices concurred with reservations.

who had been in dissent in the Supreme Court decision in *Doe v. McMillan*, wrote the opinion for the Court, holding that the power to investigate and use compulsory process pursuant to an authorized investigation was an indispensable ingredient of lawmaking. The members of Congress were absolutely protected; the Speech and Debate Clause trumped even the First Amendment.

Congressional Standing

If some members of Congress resented the intrusion of the courts into the legislative branch, some also used the courts to try to keep the executive in line. One of the most interesting developments of this period was the willingness of the D.C. Circuit to accord members of Congress standing to challenge executive acts. In the first of these cases, *Mitchell v. Laird*, thirteen members of Congress sued the President and the secretaries of State and Defense, contending that for seven years the United States had prosecuted a war in Vietnam without obtaining a declaration of war or an explicit, discrete authorization of war, and that this, therefore, impaired their constitutional right as members of Congress to decide whether the U.S. should fight a war. They sought to enjoin prosecution of the war and/or a declaratory judgment.

District Court Judge William B. Jones dismissed the action. The Court of Appeals decided that the members of Congress had standing, though it did not linger over the issue. What seemed more important about the case at the time was that it was the closest the courts of the Circuit had come to penetrating the barrier of the political question doctrine in an action over the constitutionality of the Vietnam War.

On the merits, the panel, composed of visiting judge Charles Wyzanski of the District of Massachusetts (writing), Chief Judge Bazelon and Judge Tamm, agreed that, under the Constitution, the President may initiate some types of war without congressional approval, that Congress may employ a means other than a formal declaration of war to give its approval, and that the courts cannot require Congress to employ one means rather than another. At that point, the unity of the panel ended. While Judge Tamm would have relied upon appropriations, the draft extension and cognate laws to signify congressional assent, Wyzanski and Bazelon did not believe that Congress had, in fact, given its assent to the war in Vietnam: "An honorable, decent, compassionate act of aiding those already in peril is no proof of consent to the actions that placed and continued them in that dangerous posture."

Nevertheless, the plaintiffs did not prevail. Even if his predecessors *had* exceeded their constitutional authority in waging war, President Nixon's present duty, as the Court saw it, was to try in good faith to bring the war to an end as promptly as was consistent with the safety of those fighting and with the durable interests of the nation. Whether the President had so proceeded was a question, absent a case of clear abuse, which a court could not answer.[10]

At issue in *Kennedy v. Sampson* was the so-called pocket veto. Under Article I, Section 7 of the Constitution, a bill can become law without the President's signature, "unless the Congress by their adjournment prevent its return." During the six-day Christmas recess in 1970, President Nixon exercised a pocket veto by not signing the Family Practice of Medicine Act, which had passed 64–1 and 346–2; a return veto would almost certainly have been overridden. Senator Edward Kennedy sued to overturn the pocket veto and argued the case *pro se*.

The case came to Judge Joseph C. Waddy, who first held that Kennedy, like the Congressmen in *Mitchell v. Laird* (which had been decided by the Court of Appeals five months before), had standing. His injury in fact was that the pocket veto rendered his vote in the Senate ineffective and deprived him of his constitutional right to vote to override. On the merits, Waddy held that the short recess had not prevented the return of the bill. The pocket veto was invalid and the bill had become law.[11] Shortly after Nixon's resignation in 1974, the Court of Appeals affirmed on the issue of standing and on the merits. The relationship between the Senator and his claim, Judge Tamm wrote for the Court, was one which assured that the issues would be litigated with the vigor and thoroughness necessary to assist the Court in rendering an informed judgment.[12]

A major confrontation between members of Congress and the courts was averted in *Schlesinger v. Reservists Committee to Stop the War*, a suit challenging whether members of Congress could also belong to the armed forces reserves. It also proved to be the case in which the Supreme Court reversed the trend toward liberalized standing.

---

10. *Mitchell v. Laird*, 488 F.2d 611 (1973) (*per curiam* Wyzanski-Baz-Tamm). Judges MacKinnon, Tamm, Robb, and Wilkey would have reheard the case *en banc*, arguing that the "annual multi-billion dollar appropriations over an eight-year period reflect a clear Congressional assent to the war."

11. *Kennedy v. Sampson*, 364 F. Supp. 1075 (1973).

12. *Kennedy v. Sampson*, 511 F.2d 430 (1974) (*Tamm-Fahy*(c)-Baz). In 1976 the Department of Justice announced that President Ford would use the return veto rather than the pocket veto during intrasession and intersession recesses and adjournments of Congress.

The suit was brought by an association of present and former members of the reserves who opposed the war in Vietnam and by five of its members, as taxpayers and citizens, reservists and persons opposed to the war. At the time the suit was filed in the District Court (as *Reservists Committee to Stop the War v. Laird*), 130 members of Congress were also members of the reserves. Plaintiffs sought a declaratory judgment and injunction against the Secretary of Defense holding that members of Congress could not constitutionally hold a commission in the armed forces because of the Incompatibility Clause of Article I of the Constitution, which states that "no Person holding any Office under the United States, shall be a Member of either House during his continuance in Office."

The case came before Judge Gesell, who found standing in the plaintiffs' status as citizens. Every citizen, he thought, had an interest in maintaining independence among the branches. On the merits, he found the potential conflict between an office in the military and an office in Congress "not inconsequential." Once again, a declaratory judgment rather than an injunction issued, holding that, under the Constitution, a member of Congress was ineligible to hold a commission in the armed forces during his continuance in office. The Court of Appeals affirmed on the basis of Gesell's opinion.[13]

The Supreme Court reversed by 5–4 on the standing issue. In one of the opinions he was most proud of, Chief Justice Burger held that "standing to sue may not be predicated upon an interest of the kind alleged here which is held in common by all members of the public, because of the necessarily abstract nature of the inquiry all citizens share. Concrete injury, whether actual or threatened, is that indispensable element of a dispute which serves in part to cast it in a form traditionally capable of judicial resolution."[14]

Confrontations with the Executive Department

The nation Richard M. Nixon was called upon to lead in 1969 was deeply divided—by the war that had driven his predecessor from office, rebellious college campuses, random political violence, high racial tensions, painful

13. *Reservists Comm. to Stop War v. Laird*, 323 F. Supp. 833 (1971), aff'd, 495 F.2d 1074 (1972).
14. *Schlesinger v. Reservists Comm. to Stop War*, 418 U.S. 208 (1974). The author discussed this case with Chief Justice Burger in the spring of 1979. See also *United States v. Richardson*, 418 U.S. 166 (1974).

memories of recent assassinations, and skepticism of the government itself. The central task was, as he defined it the day after his election, to bring the nation together.

Richard Nixon was not well cast for such a role. An infinitely complicated man of enormous courage and humorless energy, his efforts succeeded, more often than not, in further dividing the nation rather than unifying it. Almost from the beginning, the Nixon administration made bold, often unnecessary, claims of presidential power and privilege, in domestic matters as well as in the areas of national defense and foreign affairs. Well before the Watergate break-in, the administration's approach to the constitutional powers of the executive was largely in place: the contention that the Constitution gave the President virtually plenary powers in military and foreign affairs; rapid, even cavalier, resort to the shield of "national security," not only to keep information secret but to operate against domestic opponents; an adversarial, even hostile attitude toward the establishment press; and extensive use of executive privilege to prevent embarrassing revelations.

One of the D.C. Circuit's first confrontations with the Nixon White House came about because of the administration's penchant for secrecy. The result helped set the tone for future clashes, and would be cited as a precedent during the battle over the Nixon tapes. *Soucie v. David* was a suit under the Freedom of Information Act (FOIA) for release of a report evaluating the federal program for development of a supersonic transport aircraft. Dismissing the case with a brief order, Judge John H. Pratt held that the Office of Science and Technology, from which the document had been requested, was part of the Office of the President and therefore protected by executive privilege.

The Court of Appeals reversed. Writing for himself and visiting judge Francis Van Dusen of the Third Circuit, Chief Judge Bazelon held that the trial court ought first to have determined whether the exemptions in FOIA permitted nondisclosure. In a footnote, Bazelon made it clear that should the government assert executive privilege on remand, the Court would not thereby be deprived of jurisdiction, "for the judicial power extends to resolving the questions of separation of powers raised by the constitutional claim." In the very next footnote, Bazelon indicated that, even if the President ordered the Director of the Office of Science and Technology not to release the report, the Court nevertheless had the power to compel its release.[15]

---

15. *Soucie v. David,* 448 F.2d 1067 (1971) (*Baz*-Van Dusen-*Wilk*(c)).

Rights of Demonstrators

Throughout the Vietnam War, Washington was the focus of demonstrations, and the D.C. courts were faced with legal issues surrounding them, from the extent of the First Amendment right "peaceably to assemble" to the legality of mass-arrest procedures.[16] There was persistent litigation over allowing demonstrations at some of the most symbolically appealing locations in Washington—the sidewalk in front of the White House, Lafayette Park, the Mall, the Ellipse and the Capitol grounds. The most significant example of such litigation, brought by a Quaker action group, reached the Court of Appeals four times. In that case, the Court of Appeals had some success in persuading the National Park Service—and Judge Hart—that concern for the safety of the President must be tempered by the constitutional right to assemble and present grievances at the seat of government.[17]

The arrests of hundreds of antiwar demonstrators in Washington in the spring of 1971 raised serious questions as to the constitutional sensitivities

---

16. As early as May 1967, the Court of Appeals reversed the conviction of demonstrators who marched up the Mall and staged a sit-in on the Capitol grounds, because "they were entitled to know with some precision what law they allegedly violated." *Feeley v. Dist. of Columbia*, 387 F.2d 216 (1967) (*Pre*-Wri-Lev). See also Bazelon's opinion in *Dixon v. Dist. of Columbia*, 394 F.2d 966 (1968) (*Baz-McG*(c)-*WMil*(c result). Other examples include *Lange v. United States*, 443 F.2d 720 (1971) (*Lev*-Baz-Rob), reversing a conviction stemming from an arrest during the Poor People's Campaign of 1971, and *[Abbie] Hoffman v. United States*, 445 F.2d 226 (1971) (*Fahy-MacK*(c)-*RRobb*(c)), reversing a conviction for flag desecration.

Judge Pratt tried another case that gained considerable attention, the prosecution of antiwar activists, some of them priests and nuns, who had ransacked the Washington office of Dow Chemical to protest the company's manufacture of napalm for use in Vietnam. Pratt refused to allow the defendants to use the trial as an antiwar forum and was reversed by the Court of Appeals for not permitting them to represent themselves. Pratt unsuccessfully pressed contempt and disbarment actions against the attorney who did represent them, Philip J. Hirschkop. The Dow group ultimately pleaded guilty to misdemeanor charges. *United States v. Meyer*, No. 872-69 (1970); *United States v. Dougherty*, 473 F.2d 1113 (1972),(*Lev*-*Baz*(c/d)/*Adams*(3rd Cir.)); 462 F.2d 827 (1972) (*McG*-*Tamm*(c)/*WMil*).

17. *Quaker Action Group v. Hickel*, 421 F.2d 1111 (1969) (*Baz*-Rob), modifying injunction of Judge Bryant; *Quaker Action Group v. Hickel*, 429 F.2d 185 (1970) (*per curiam* Lev-McG/*MacK*), rev'd, remanded (to Hart); *Quaker Action Group v. Morton*, 460 F.2d 854 (1971) (*Lev*-McG-*MacK*(c)), remanded (to Hart); *Quaker Action Group v. Morton*, 515 F.2d 717 (1975) (*Lev*-McG/*MacK*), aff'g Hart with qualif. See also *Women Strike for Peace v. Morton*, 472 F.2d 1273 (1971) (*per curiam Wri-Lev-RRobb*), in which the Court held that a protest group could erect an antiwar display in a park near, but not in, the Ellipse, where a Christmas pageant was held.

of the Nixon administration. Prime responsibility for keeping public order during these "May Day" demonstrations belonged to the District of Columbia Police Chief, Jerry Wilson, but the Department of Justice and the White House were closely involved. Ten days of protests by tens of thousands of antiwar demonstrators culminated on Monday, May 3, when the marchers intended to block access to the city during rush hour. With all available police reserves ordered to duty, the D.C. National Guard called out, and 4,000 federal troops deployed to protect the bridges and main traffic arteries of the city, Chief Wilson suspended the normal field arrest procedures.

Nearly 8,000 persons were taken into custody and trucked to detention centers that day—in many cases, without a scintilla of evidence that they had committed a crime. Neither field arrest forms nor Polaroid photographs were prepared at the time of apprehension, nor were many of those arrested aware of the identity of the officer arresting them or of the charges intended to be filed against them. No records were kept of the time, location or circumstances of the arrests; instead, special booking procedures were later used to make sketchy records of the arrests. President Nixon expressed wholehearted support of the work of the police and the Department of Justice.[18]

The judges of the D.C. Circuit were less pleased with the dragnet arrests. On May 26, a panel of Bazelon, Tamm, and Wilkey, reversing Judge Howard Corcoran, enjoined further prosecution of those cases in which the government did not "reasonably believe that they have in their files and records adequate evidence to support probable cause for arrest and charge."[19] In the principal decision dealing with the episode, delivered on April 16, 1973, Judge Leventhal, writing for himself and for Judges Bazelon and Spottswood

---

18. The expedient procedures worked. Disruptions were frustrated, traffic snarls limited; the rate of federal employee absenteeism was lower than that of an average workday.

It appears that at one point Nixon was concerned that the police response to the demonstrations might have been too strong, but, seeing the protestors as "vandals and hoodlums"—tire slicers who blocked traffic and terrorized innocent bystanders—he ultimately said he was "very pleased with the job Chief Wilson has done." White House aide Patrick Buchanan had counseled Chief of Staff H. R. Haldeman not to provoke a confrontation with the antiwar Vietnam veterans demonstrating the first weekend, stating that "the 'crazies' will be in town soon enough...if we want a confrontation, let's have it with them—not with the new Bonus Army. This is not a recommendation that we not be tough, but that we pick the most advantageous enemy from our point of view."

19. *Sullivan v. Murphy*, 444 F.2d 840 (1971).

Robinson, held that almost every element of the expedited arrest procedures violated the Fourth Amendment.[20]

Rights of Government Employees

The Nixon administration's propensity to view those who spoke out against governmental policies as "enemies" was manifestly illustrated by the case of A. Ernest Fitzgerald. At stake was the right of Congress to require testimony from government officials about government mismanagement. The litigation would last over a decade and further expose the Nixon administration's intolerance of dissent and predilection for secrecy.

Fitzgerald had been a Pentagon procurement specialist whose responsibility was cost analysis of major weapons systems acquisition. In 1968, against the wishes of his superiors, he testified before the Joint Economic Committee of the Congress, giving the first in a long series of disclosures of serious cost overruns and mechanical flaws in key weapons programs. The Pentagon, which had yet to acknowledge the problems, took away Fitzgerald's civil service protection, assigned him menial tasks, and searched his private life for incriminating evidence. Almost a year after his testimony, the Defense Department announced that Fitzgerald's post had been abolished as a budgetary measure—a "reduction-in-force." The same day, however, a consultant was hired to perform Fitzgerald's duties.

Fitzgerald challenged his treatment in a civil service proceeding and sought to open his civil service hearing to the press and public, although under Civil Service Commission rules it was supposed to be closed. On June 25, 1971, Judge William Bryant gave him the injunction he requested.[21] On appeal the government contended that there was no valid constitutional claim to a hearing with all the attributes of due process because constitutional rights are not violated when reduction-in-force is the stated ground for termination. The Court of Appeals, Senior District Judge Burnita Shel-

---

20. *Sullivan v. Murphy*, 478 F.2d 938 (1973). The decision held that the Fourth Amendment required a declaration holding presumptively invalid any arrest that was unaccompanied by a contemporaneous Polaroid photograph and a field arrest form executed by the arresting officer. The Court also held that the Constitution does not permit arrests made at the scene of demonstrations without probable cause but in the hope that during detention evidence would be uncovered; that the "gravest constitutional problems" were presented by the withdrawal of a probable cause judicial hearing; and that the broad and flexible powers of the federal court permitted an order limiting the maintenance and dissemination of arrest records and of all materials obtained from persons during the May Day protest.

21. *Fitzgerald v. Hampton*, 329 F. Supp. 997 (1971).

ton Matthews writing, held that this was not a routine reduction-in-force matter and Fitzgerald was entitled to a fair opportunity, including a public hearing, to show that the governmental action was unwarranted.[22]

The prevailing view in the White House seems to have been that of Deputy Assistant to the President Alexander P. Butterfield, who called Fitzgerald "a basic nogoodnick" who "must be given very low marks in loyalty.... We should let him bleed, for a while at least. Any rush to pick him up and put him back on the Federal payroll would be tantamount to an admission of earlier wrong-doing on our part."[23]

After extensive hearings, the Civil Service Commission ordered Fitzgerald's reinstatement, but he was assigned to a different position. Early in 1974 he brought suit for alleged conspiracy to deprive him of his job in retaliation for the testimony before the congressional committee. Judge Gesell threw out the lawsuit on statute-of-limitations grounds. More than two years later, the Court of Appeals affirmed the dismissal of the suit against all but one of the defendants.[24] At the end of the decade Fitzgerald amended his complaint, this time suing ex-President Nixon and his closest aides. Before this case reached the Supreme Court, Nixon settled in part with Fitzgerald for $142,000. When the Supreme Court decided the case, in 1982, it held, 5–4, that the President had absolute immunity from damage liability predicated on his official acts. Then, by a vote of 8–1, the High Court held that presidential aides were entitled to qualified immunity, "insofar as their conduct does not violate clearly established statutory or constitutional rights of which a reasonable person would have known."[25]

The Delegation Doctrine

In the fall of 1971, in what was arguably the most important opinion in decades on the delegation doctrine, a three-judge District Court gave the administration a major victory, while also defining limits on the delegation of powers to the President. The Economic Stabilization Act of 1970,[26] the

---

22. *Fitzgerald v. Hampton,* 467 F.2d 755 (1972) (*Matthews*-Baz-Tamm).

23. Quoted in *Fitzgerald v. Seamans,* 553 F.2d 220 (1977) at 225.

24. *Fitzgerald v. Seamans,* 384 F. Supp. 688 (1974); 553 F.2d 220 (1977) (*Lev*-Wilk-Bryan(D. Va.)). The Appeals Court upheld the dismissal of Fitzgerald's suit against the Department of Defense officials, but remanded as to Butterfield, whose involvement Fitzgerald had not known about when the statute of limitations began to run.

25. *Nixon v. Fitzgerald,* 457 U.S. 731 (1982); *Harlow v. Fitzgerald,* 457 U.S. 800 (1982).

26. 84 Stat. 799.

epitome of post-New Deal delegation to the President, authorized the Chief Executive to issue orders and regulations that he deemed "appropriate" to stabilize prices, rents, wages and salaries at levels not less than those prevailing on May 25, 1970. Under considerable pressure to fight inflation, Nixon invoked the Act, which he had opposed. The President's order, which froze wages and prices for a ninety-day period, was challenged by a union, the Amalgamated Meat Cutters and Butcher Workmen, whose members had been deprived of a 25-cent-an-hour wage increase by the action. The suit contended that the Act was an unconstitutional delegation of power and lacked procedural safeguards such as notice, hearing, and judicial review. Judge Aubrey Robinson declined to issue an injunction, but ruled that the case should be considered by a three-judge panel.

Harold Leventhal, an expert in price regulation,[27] wrote the opinion for a court that included Aubrey Robinson and Charles Richey.[28] While upholding the delegation to the President, the Court rejected the government's broadest contentions. Leventhal rejected the union's claim that the law vested "unbridled legislative power in the President" and was a "naked grant of authority." The Constitution, he wrote, does not "forbid a Congress concerned with controlling inflation from coping with escalating expectations by calling on the shock of a general presidential freeze to check the inflationary psychology." Leventhal thought the rule of law might have been "beleaguered but not breached" by the delegation, but that this was not a "legislative initiation of control by bare executive fiat."

This much might have been expected, for no law had been successfully challenged on delegation grounds since 1935. But Leventhal went on to indicate limits on presidential discretion. These, he said, could be not only found in the statute but also derived from the historical context and the expressions of legislative purpose. The President's powers had been limited in time; furthermore, once standards were developed in the administration of the law, those standards would limit the latitude of subsequent executive action. Even though the Act did not contain language that the regulations be "fair and equitable," the Court thought that "there is fairly implicit in

---

27. During the Second World War Leventhal had been an attorney with the Office of Price Administration. He had also clerked for, and greatly admired, Chief Justice Harlan Fiske Stone, who had written the leading precedent, *Yakus v. United States* (321 U.S. 414 (1944)), which had upheld price controls during the war.

28. *Amalgamated Meat Cutters & Butcher Workmen v. Connally*, 337 F. Supp. 737 (1971).

the Act the duty to take whatever action is required in the interest of broad fairness and avoidance of gross inequity."

Executive Privilege

In October 1971, the same month the Economic Stabilization Act decision came down, courts of the Circuit went "eyeball to eyeball" with the executive branch over the legality of an underground nuclear test explosion in Alaska, code-named Cannikin. If eventually the courts blinked, the litigation proved critical, not only in establishing the relationship between nuclear testing and the National Environmental Policy Act (NEPA) but in further defining the parameters of executive privilege that would be tested in the Watergate cases.

In two related lawsuits, members of Congress and several conservation groups sought to prevent a test the government considered essential to the Strategic Arms Limitation Talks. One of the suits went through seven judicial hearings — three each in the District Court and the Court of Appeals and one in the Supreme Court — which made it clear that the decision to test was reviewable by the courts. The litigation demonstrates how members of Congress used NEPA and the Freedom of Information Act to fight the executive in the courts, as well as how dubious many of the judges of the Court of Appeals had become of the Nixon administration's good faith and of the validity of its constitutional positions.

In *Committee for Nuclear Responsibility v. Seaborg*, several environmental groups brought suit to enjoin the test, primarily on the ground that the environmental impact statement rendered by the Atomic Energy Commission had not satisfied the National Environmental Policy Act of 1969. At the same time, in *Mink v. Environmental Protection Administration*, thirty-three members of Congress sued under FOIA to obtain documents relating to the test — documents dealing with environmental matters as well as national defense and foreign relations issues, and which might have indicated the quality of environmental advice the President was receiving. In both cases, Judge Hart granted summary judgment for the government.

With the test less than a month away, the Court of Appeals reversed the *Seaborg* decision, rejecting what it said was Hart's holding — that congressional passage of authorization and appropriation bills constituted a conclusive determination of Congress's acceptance of the environmental impact statement — and said the case was not appropriate for summary judgment. If the ultimate responsibility to go forward with the test was the President's, the judiciary nevertheless had the authority to determine whether the President had been clearly informed of the environmental facts, as Congress intended him to be. The Court of Appeals further held that Congress must be free to provide authorizations and appropriations for projects proposed by the executive without those actions prejudging claims of noncompliance pending in the courts.[29]

Ten days later, Judges Fahy and Leventhal overturned Hart's ruling of summary judgment in the *Mink* case. One of the ten documents at issue, a memorandum from the Council on Environmental Quality, was unclassified, but the executive contended that it, too, was secret because it had been incorporated into a secret file. The Court of Appeals stipulated that the district judge was to consider *in camera* the possible separation of the documents for purposes of disclosure.[30] Nevertheless, the Court "tempered somewhat" the rule of *Soucie v. David* that exemptions from disclosure of FOIA must be construed narrowly, for at issue in *Mink* was the national defense and the conduct of foreign relations.

On remand in the *Seaborg* case, Judge Hart ordered the government to provide *in camera* inspection of documents related to that case. This was met by a government contention of executive privilege. Hart certified to the Court of Appeals the question as to whether executive privilege precluded *in camera* screening. The government argued before the Court of Appeals that the claim of privilege by the executive was conclusive and that the Court had no judicial authority to require the production of documents of executive privilege once the head of an executive department had made the claim. The court (Bazelon, Leventhal, and Robinson) rejected the claim of absolute privilege for a document upon the bald assertion of a department head. In words that would take on deeper meaning in the next few years, the Court stated that

> no executive official or agency can be given absolute authority to determine what documents in his possession may be considered by the court in its task. Otherwise the head of an Executive department would have the power on his own say so to cover up all evidence of fraud and corruption when a federal court or grand jury was investigating malfeasance in office, and this is not the law.

Nevertheless, the Court of Appeals did not stay the test, for it was "the responsibility of the Executive to take into account both the considerations

---

29. *Committee for Nuclear Responsibility v. Seaborg,* 463 F.2d 783 (1971) (*per curiam* Baz-Lev-Rob).

30. *Mink v. EPA,* 464 F.2d 742 (1971) (*per curiam* Fahy-Lev).

of national security and the serious issues of legality identified by the opinions of this Court."[31]

On second remand, Judge Hart directed the release of some of the documents, but declined to enjoin the test. Two days later, on November 3, the Court of Appeals left Hart's order intact, even though it believed there were substantial questions as to the test's legality. Given the $120 million already put into the test, and the fact that enjoining the test would delay it a year and might jeopardize the SALT talks, the Court of Appeals was unwilling to take such a grave step. On November 6, the Supreme Court denied an application to enjoin the Cannikin test. The test took place that day.[32]

When it decided the *Mink* case a year later, the Supreme Court upheld the executive by a vote of 5–3. FOIA was not, the High Court said, intended to subject the soundness of executive security classification to review at the insistence of any objecting citizen, nor did it permit *in camera* review of a classified document. The role of the Court was limited to determining whether the executive had asserted that the matters were classified. While the trial judge might order *in camera* inspection, such examination was not a necessary or inevitable tool in every case.[33] In the first Watergate tapes case, *Nixon v. Sirica*, the Special Prosecutor would argue that the *Mink* case "established the proposition that the constitutional separation of powers does not give the Executive any constitutional immunity from judicial orders for the production of evidence."[34] In 1974, a year after the *Mink* decision, Congress overrode it with legislation authorizing federal courts to examine sensitive records *in camera*.[35]

Military Surveillance of Civilian Political Activity

In *Tatum v. Laird*, the Nixon administration sought to defend a discredited program of its predecessor that was aimed at keeping an eye on political dissenters. The program, initiated by the Johnson administration, used military intelligence agents to gather information on civilian political activists. The program, which directly contravened federal law, was exposed by a

31. *Committee for Nuclear Responsibility v. Seaborg*, 463 F.2d 788 (1971) (*per curiam* Baz-Lev-Rob). Hart's order is set out after the Court of Appeals ruling.

32. *Committee for Nuclear Responsibility v. Schlesinger*, 404 U.S. 917 (1971).

33. *EPA v. Mink*, 410 U.S. 73 (1973).

34. The Special Prosecutor's brief in *Nixon v. Sirica* is reprinted in "Separation of Powers and Executive Privilege: The Watergate Briefs," *Political Science Quarterly* 88 (1973): 612, 623.

35. 88 Stat. 1561 (1974).

whistle blower, former Army Intelligence Captain Christopher H. Pyle, who
wrote in the *Washington Monthly*, "Today the Army maintains files on the
membership, ideology, programs, and practices of virtually every activist
political group in the country."

Caught with egg on its face, the Army announced it was ending the program and destroying the data bank of information it had gathered. Critics
of the program thought it wise not to rely upon the Army's representations,
and asked the District Court for a declaratory judgment holding the program unconstitutional or illegal, and for an injunction ordering the cessation of the program and the destruction of all data. But the plaintiffs in the
case faced perplexing problems at the threshold. There were no clear and
apparently no continuing First or Fourth Amendment violations. The
plaintiffs had indeed been under surveillance, but had been exercising their
First Amendment rights vigorously.

Judge Hart had this litigation as well. He granted Secretary of Defense
Melvin Laird's motion to dismiss prior to trial for lack of subject-matter
jurisdiction. A "conservative" panel of the Court of Appeals reversed. Writing for himself and Judge Tamm, Judge Wilkey held that there was jurisdiction and had little trouble finding standing. Wilkey then turned to the
problem of justiciability. Against the government's contention that no harm
had been done to the plaintiffs, or was contemplated, or would be justiciable even if it had been contemplated, Wilkey weighed the plaintiffs' contention that the existence of the program constituted an impermissible burden on them and exercised a present inhibiting effect on the full expression
and utilization of their First Amendment rights. That was, for Tamm and
Wilkey, enough to make the case ripe for adjudication. The court then remanded for amplification of the record.

Judge MacKinnon dissented. He believed that "such indefinite claims...
do not present a case involving facts of sufficient realism and definiteness
to confer jurisdiction on the court to make a sweeping constitutional decision affecting important activities of the federal Government."[36]

The Supreme Court, by a vote of 5–4, agreed with Judge MacKinnon.
Allegations of a subjective "chill" were not, the High Court thought, an adequate substitute for a claim of present objective harm or a threat of specific harm. To permit what plaintiffs seemed to be seeking, a broad-scale
investigation into Army misconduct, carried to its logical end, "would have
the federal courts as virtually continuing monitors of the wisdom and

---

36. *Tatum v. Laird*, 444 F.2d 947 (1971) (*Wilk*-Tamm/*MacK*).

soundness of Executive action."[37] Justice Brennan's dissent—he was joined by Justices Stewart and Marshall (Justice Douglas dissented separately)—essentially consisted of a quotation almost two pages long from Judge Wilkey's opinion.

Presidential Power to Appoint and Impound

In 1973 the Nixon administration was beginning to unravel under the pressure of the Watergate scandal. Even in non-Watergate matters, judges of the D.C. District Court were much less deferential. Three judges in particular—William B. Jones, June Green, and Gerhard Gesell—handed the administration major setbacks in cases involving presidential powers—the power of appointment and the President's right to impound congressionally authorized funds.

High on the conservative side of the Nixon agenda was the dismantling of the Office of Economic Opportunity, which had been created as part of Lyndon Johnson's anti-poverty program. Though OEO had been authorized by the Congress through June 1974, the fiscal 1974 budget submitted by the President in early 1973 contained no funds for OEO's community action programs and proposed transferring the agency's other programs to existing agencies and departments. A young lawyer, Howard J. Phillips, was appointed "acting director" of OEO by the President and charged with terminating the agency. The administration was essentially taking the position that once the President submitted his budget, Congress would have to act affirmatively to preserve legislative programs from extinction.

Several community action organizations and labor unions representing OEO employees brought suit against Phillips. On April 11, Judge Jones, who had been appointed by President Kennedy, enjoined termination of the OEO funding as unlawful. He held that Congress had made clear its intent that OEO should exist at least through June 1974, and that the proper way to abolish an agency was to submit a reorganization plan to Congress, which that body could approve or disapprove. Jones wrote that if the administration's position were declared valid, "no barrier would remain to the executive ignoring any and all congressional authorizations if he deemed them...contrary to the needs of the nation."[38] Two months later, in a lawsuit brought by four members of Congress, Judge Jones held that Phillips's

---

37. *Laird v. Tatum*, 408 U.S. 1 (1972).
38. *Local 2677, American Fed. of Gov't Employees v. Phillips*, 358 F. Supp. 60 (1973).

appointment had been an attempt to circumvent the Senate's power to confirm and that he could no longer serve as acting director.[39]

Before the second of Jones' OEO decisions, Judge June Green, who had been appointed to the bench by Lyndon Johnson, also spoke to the appointment issue—and in even stronger terms—as well as to the issue of impoundment. At issue in *Minnesota Chippewa Tribe v. Carlucci* was the administration's impoundment of eighteen million dollars in funds allocated for the education of American Indians, and the President's recommendation of its rescission to the Congress. Nixon had also chosen not to make any appointments to the National Advisory Council on Indian Education, without which it appeared the Indian Education Act of June 23, 1972 (which he had signed), could not be implemented.

The government moved to dismiss on the ground that the suit was directed against the person of the President, which was barred by the separation-of-powers doctrine. Although ordinarily the President is not sued directly, because a member of the Cabinet with statutory responsibility can be used in his stead, in this case only the President had the power to appoint the advisory council and he had neither employed nor delegated it. "The President of the United States is not completely immune from judicial process for the sole reason that he is President," Judge Green declared; nor would she dismiss the case under the political question doctrine. Although the President clearly had discretion to choose whomever he wanted to appoint to the council, "he apparently has no discretion to decide if the Council should or should not be constituted," for the statute provided that "appointments *shall* be made by the President."[40]

Two weeks later, Nixon appointed all fifteen members of the council. A later, unpublished order by Judge Green forced the release of the impounded money and required the appointment of a Deputy Commissioner of Indian Education.[41]

Impoundment was also at issue in a case decided the same year by Judge Gesell. Here, the Secretary of Health, Education and Welfare had impounded $52 million in grants for the staffing and construction of mental health treatment centers. Gesell made little effort to hide his impatience with the threshold boiler-plate defenses raised by the government:

---

39. *Williams v. Phillips*, 360 F. Supp. 1363 (1973), stay denied, 482 F.2d 669 (1973) (*per curiam* Wri-Lev-Rob).

40. *Minnesota Chippewa Tribe v. Carlucci*, 358 F. Supp. 973 (1973).

41. *Minnesota Chippewa Tribe v. Carlucci*, Civ. No. 628-73 (1973).

To say that the Constitution forecloses judicial scrutiny in these circumstances is to urge that the Executive alone can decide what is best
and what the law requires. To say that persons immediately and seriously affected by failure to commit funds authorized by the Legislature
cannot go to court is to ignore the democratic base of our society.

Then, on the merits, Gesell held, "At least with respect to the programs involved here, there is no basis for defendants' assertion of inherent constitutional power in the Executive to decline to spend in the face of a clear
statutory intent and directive to do so."[42]

By the end of 1973, three more district judges had decided against the
administration in impoundment cases.[43] The clashes over impoundment
between the executive and the judiciary were greatly eased the following
year by the resignation of the President, by the Impoundment Control Act
of 1974, which established procedures for congressional consent to impoundments, and by a decision of the Supreme Court in a case that had
arisen in the D.C. Circuit, requiring the administrator of a regulatory
agency to allot congressionally authorized funds.[44]

---

42. *National Council of Community Mental Health Centers v. Weinberger*, 361 F. Supp.
897 (1973).

43. In *Commonwealth of Pennsylvania v. Lynn*, Judge Charles Richey, the only Nixon
appointee to the District Court, held that the Secretary of Housing and Urban Development had acted improperly in suspending certain subsidized housing programs. 362
F. Supp. 1363 (1973), stayed, 414 U.S. 809 (1973), rev'd, 501 F.2d 848 (1974) (*McG-
Tamm-Lev*). In *Pennsylvania v. Weinberger*, a case involving aid under the Elementary
and Secondary Education Act, Judge Aubrey Robinson decided against the administration on statutory grounds. 367 F. Supp. 1378 (1973). And in *Guadamuz v. Ash*, concerning the expenditure of funds under the Rural Environmental Assistance Program
and the Federally Assisted Code Enforcement Program, Judge Thomas Flannery rejected
the government's broad contentions that the President had inherent power to impound
to "protect the economic stability of the nation, the national position in Foreign Affairs
and the needs of the National Defense" and that to limit the President's prerogative in
this area would substantially undercut his authority to combat inflation and unemployment. 368 F. Supp. 1233 (1973).

44. *New York v. Train*, 494 F.2d 1033 (1974) (*Tamm*-Rob-Wilk), aff'd, 420 U.S. 35
(1975). In *Train*, the Court of Appeals (reversing Judge Oliver Gasch) read a federal
water pollution statute to require the EPA Administrator to make the full allotment of
the authorized funds. No constitutional issue was involved.

Four years after the 1983 Supreme Court decision in *INS v. Chadha*, 462 U.S. 919,
holding the legislative veto unconstitutional, the Court of Appeals declared the Impoundment Control Act of 1974 unconstitutional. *City of New Haven v. United States*,
809 F.2d 900 (1987) (*Edw*-Bork-Swygert(7th Cir.)).

The Pentagon Papers

On Sunday June 13, 1971, the *New York Times* published the first of what was intended to be a series of articles based on the "Pentagon Papers," a forty-seven-volume Pentagon study of the origins and conduct of the war in Vietnam, which had been leaked by a former Pentagon staff member, Daniel Ellsburg. Although the litigation over their publication began in New York City, and the title of the Supreme Court decision was *New York Times v. United States,* crucial scenes in the drama took place in the District of Columbia Circuit.

The Pentagon Papers case, among the most dramatic in U.S. history, was the climax of the Nixon administration's feud with the national media. It may also be seen as the seminal point in the chain of events that eventually led to President Nixon's downfall. In its wake, the administration became more proactive in its attempts to silence its enemies, taking ever more illegal steps in the name of national security.

Even now, one cannot be entirely sure why the Nixon administration reacted as strongly as it did to the publication of the Pentagon Papers. They were history, commissioned and completed before President Nixon took office, offering perspective on decisions long made and potentially embarrassing only to previous administrations. The Nixon administration's rationalizations for suppression of the articles—national security, damage to the conduct of ongoing diplomatic negotiations, the threat to America's code-breaking potential—did not immediately surface. Indeed, in the first days after publication, White House discussions largely revolved around how the publication of the papers could be used to smear liberals. Undoubtedly, the *Times*'s position at the pinnacle of the eastern, liberal media was a factor in the decision to seek to enjoin publication, as was the fact that the classified document had been obtained illegally. Uncertainty as to the exact contents of the papers (at the time no one in the U.S. government had read the entire 3,000 pages of analysis and 4,000 pages of documentary evidence) and as to whether the *Times* possessed the most sensitive parts of them (it appears it did not) also played a role.

In any event, after the *Times* refused to heed Attorney General John Mitchell's cabled request to stop publication of the series, the government brought suit in the Southern District of New York seeking a permanent injunction against publication. It was the first time in U.S. history that the federal government had asked the courts for a prior restraint on publication. The case came before Murray I. Gurfein, a judge only recently appointed by President Nixon. Gurfein issued a temporary restraining order so that he could consider the matter. On June 18 he held a hearing on the request for a permanent injunction, and the following day denied the government's request for an injunction.

Meanwhile, on June 18, the *Washington Post* had published the first of its own series of articles based on the Pentagon Papers. The government could have brought action against this publication in New York, where the *Post* had offices, and consolidated it with the *Times* litigation. But the Justice Department, apparently unhappy with the U.S. Attorney there, the independent Whitney North Seymour Jr., decided to bring suit in the District of Columbia. The case was randomly assigned to Judge Gerhard Gesell.

Gesell, then sixty-one years of age, had been appointed to the bench four years before by Lyndon Johnson and was in the early years of what would prove to be a brilliant judicial career. He was the son of Arnold Gesell, one of the great figures in the history of American pediatrics. Gesell's legal career had been spent primarily at Covington & Burling, where he had become one of the nation's leading antitrust defense attorneys. He knew something about national defense, having been counsel to the Joint Congressional Committee on Investigation of the Pearl Harbor Attack, and about newspaper publishing, having at one time represented the *Washington Post*. Reflecting on the Pentagon Papers case almost exactly two decades later, Gesell would say, "There is [and ought to be] a tendency in this court to *believe* the government, to respect the government. Many of us have been in the government. We don't like to disbelieve the government any time."[45]

But Gesell was quick to admit that he could not have viewed the actions of the Nixon administration with utter detachment. Two experiences in particular had raised his level of skepticism about the administration's motivations in its use of the courts. In May 1969, Gesell had handled some of the litigation over student riots at Howard University; although he had held the students in contempt for violating temporary restraining orders issued by his colleagues McGuire and Jones, he found some of the government's behavior provocative and inflammatory, and was left with the "distinct impression that the administration was "'hyping up' the crisis for political reasons." And when dealing with *Hentoff v. Ichord* in 1971, Gesell had come to the conclusion that the administration was not resisting "this red-baiting [by a congressional committee] very hard."

---

45. This and subsequent reflections by Gesell are from an interview with the author, April 4–6, 1991.

Immediately after the suit was filed, Gesell held a conference in his chambers, where the *Post* refused his request to voluntarily withhold publication for two or three days while he weighed the case. He then held a brief public hearing and shortly afterward orally delivered a 600-word opinion. The case presented, he said, "a raw question of preserving the freedom of the press as it confronts the efforts of the Government to impose a prior restraint on publication of essentially historical data." While regretting that the *Post* would not delay publication, and reminding the paper that it stood "in serious jeopardy of criminal prosecution," Gesell denied the government's request for a temporary restraining order.[46] Of the twenty-eight judges in the Second and D.C. circuits who dealt with the Pentagon Papers litigation, Gesell was the only one to refuse to grant even a temporary stay of publication.

Later that same evening, Friday, June 18, as the presses were about to roll with the second *Post* story, a panel of the Court of Appeals — Judges Wright, Robinson and Robb — heard argument on issuing a restraining order. The three judges were divided, Robb and Robinson forming the majority which summarily reversed Gesell as to the TRO and ordered him to hold an evidentiary hearing the following Monday to determine whether publication could "so prejudice" U.S. defense interests or result in "such irreparable injury" that prior restraint was justified.

The majority noted that freedom of the press was not "boundless." In the leading prior restraint case, *Near v. Minnesota*, decided in 1931, the Supreme Court had recognized a narrow area, primarily national security, in which a prior restraint on publication might be appropriate.[47] "We do not understand," the Appeals Court's *per curiam* opinion stated, "how it can be determined without even a cursory examination" that the Pentagon Papers are "nothing but 'historical data' without present vitality."

Judge Wright began his dissent,"This is a sad day for America." The government, he said, had not shown even one specific harm that would result from publication of anything in the Pentagon Papers. "As if the long and sordid war in Southeast Asia had not already done enough harm to our people, it now is used to cut out the heart of our free institutions and system of government."[48]

At the hearing on Monday morning, the government insisted that parts of the hearing be secret; black plastic was placed over the windows and

---

46. *United States v. Washington Post Co.*, Civ. No. 1235-71, 1971.

47. 283 U.S. 697 (1931).

48. *United States v. Washington Post Co.*, 446 F.2d 1322 (1971).

doors of the courtroom during those times. However, Gesell permitted all defendants and additional *Post* reporters with national security expertise to remain in the courtroom. Already on his guard from previous encounters with the Nixon administration, unsettled by some of the tactics used by the government in this case, and "instinctively against the idea of suppression," Gesell heard the government out and ruled against it.[49]

In his opinion (delivered from the bench and never published)[50] Judge Gesell stated that the "wide-ranging and often vitriolic debate" which had been taking place over the war in Vietnam had to be taken into account in weighing the equities. Democracy depends for its future, Gesell declared, "on the informed will of the majority, and it is the purpose and effect of the First Amendment to expose to the public the maximum amount of information on which sound judgment can be made by the electorate." Thus, the equities favored disclosure, not suppression. Further, no contemporary military or diplomatic plans would be compromised, nor was there a "showing of an immediate grave threat to the national security which in close and narrowly-defined circumstances would justify prior restraint of publication." Gesell even refused to grant a long enough stay to guarantee appellate review. "You have twenty minutes," he told the government. "I am sure they [the Court of Appeals] are waiting for you upstairs."

The Court of Appeals granted an immediate stay to permit an appeal. The case was set down for argument *en banc* at two the next afternoon. The same day, a three-judge panel of the Second Circuit extended its restraining order and ordered argument of the appeal *en banc* from Judge Gurfein's ruling allowing the *Times*'s publication of the Pentagon Papers. This was

---

49. According to Gesell's later recollections, the government had attempted to bar the defendants from the courtroom; had sent armed National Security Administration guards to the first hearing in Gesell's courtroom and later to "protect" his house while he was meeting with lawyers in the case; and had sent "public relations people...all over Capitol Hill saying that Gesell would release war plans and young men will die." (However, at the Monday hearing a general with knowledge of war plans testified that the plans published in the Pentagon Papers were out of date, even quipping that it would therefore be great to announce to the Russians that these were indeed war plans.)

The theatrical show of secrecy made by the government increased as the proceedings went on. In New York, the government originally refused to tell its own lawyers which specific documents would jeopardize the national security. In Washington, the government refused to turn over its secret affidavits to the *Post*'s lawyers until Gesell ordered it, and even then, Assistant Attorney General Robert Mardian told the *Post*'s chief lawyer that he could not take notes on them.

50. A transcript is in the possession of this author.

only the second time in the history of that more tranquil circuit in which a case was heard *en banc* before panel consideration.

On Tuesday, June 22, both courts of appeal heard oral argument *en banc* simultaneously, and their decisions were announced at the same time the next day. Chief Judge Henry J. Friendly and Chief Judge Bazelon coordinated the timing. Law clerks for judges in the two cities exchanged calls and members of each court were aware in advance that the two courts would reach conflicting decisions.

On four hours' notice, Solicitor General Erwin N. Griswold argued the case in the Court of Appeals for the D.C. Circuit. Appearing before that court for the first time in forty years, Griswold had a rocky time. While listing examples of "analogous situations," including unauthorized publication in England of photographs of Queen Victoria, he was interrupted by Judge Wright, who asked him to direct his comments to the First Amendment. During a discussion about the effect of press disclosures on foreign governments, Judge Leventhal observed that "many foreign governments were upset to learn after World War I that our treaties have to be approved by the Senate." Noting the publication of extracts from the Pentagon Papers that day in the *Boston Globe*, Nixon appointee Roger Robb, who had voted for the temporary restraining order, asked whether the government was "asking us to ride herd on a swarm of bees."

Following the public argument, the Court of Appeals held a one-hour *in camera* session. A top-ranking aide to the director of the National Security Administration appeared before the bench and handed Chief Judge Bazelon a double-locked briefcase containing, he declared, an instance of a threat to the security of the United States' code-breaking ability. Inside the briefcase was a copy of a cable, included in the Pentagon Papers, which was said to reveal that the NSA had the capability of intercepting North Vietnamese communications and breaking their code. Bazelon passed it to the prosecution. Then it was given to the *Post's* lawyers, who handed it to the newspaper's defense correspondent. The cable looked familiar to him; as the hearing continued, he paged through a collection of published legislative hearings until he found the place the cable had already been printed.

The Second Circuit split 5–3, remanding once again to Judge Gurfein for reconsideration of his refusal to grant the government a permanent injunction. No opinions were written, so as not to delay an appeal to the Supreme Court. The D.C. Circuit, by a vote of 7–2, affirmed Gesell.[51] No

----

51. *United States v. Washington Post Co.*, 446 F.2d 1327 (1971).

longer members of an emergency motions panel, Spottswood Robinson and Roger Robb changed their earlier positions. Edward Tamm also joined with Bazelon, Wright, Leventhal and McGowan. The one-page *per curiam* was businesslike, simply stating that having examined the record made in the District Court, the Court of Appeals agreed with the trial judge's conclusion that the government's proof did not justify an injunction. Judges MacKinnon and Wilkey dissented, the former emphasizing that "courts are not designed to deal adequately with national defense and foreign policy." Wilkey indicated that "on careful detailed study of the affidavits in evidence I find a number of examples of documents which, if in the possession of the *Post* and published, could clearly result in great harm to the nation... the death of soldiers, the destruction of alliances, the greatly increased difficulty of negotiation with our enemies." He urged a remand to the District Court to produce an immediate release of the great bulk of the documents and permit the government to pinpoint its objections to each of the remaining documents.

On the following day, the government petitioned for rehearing and modification of the D.C. decision to read like that of the Second Circuit, for reasons of comity as well as on the partial ground that it had less time to prepare its case in Washington. Remarkably, the government also argued that the result would be unfair to the *Times*: the *Post* would be able to publish, but not the *Times*. The Court of Appeals reaffirmed its decision, stating that "considerations of comity may not properly be stretched unduly when what is involved is a prior restraint on the press we do not find constitutionally authorized." The matter, the Court said, "is now ripe for presentation to the Supreme Court."[52]

Both the Second and the D.C. Circuits continued the stays of publication until Friday June 25 at 6 p.m. On that date, the Supreme Court granted certiorari and agreed to hear argument the following day. The restraining order was continued, over the dissents of four justices. On June 30 the Supreme Court, by a vote of 6–3, upheld the right of the *New York Times* and the *Washington Post* to publish articles based on the Pentagon Papers. There were ten opinions—a brief *per curiam* and nine separate opinions. The next day both newspapers resumed publication of their series.

---

52. Ibid.

Watergate

The ultimate focus of the Watergate affair was one of the most successful American politicians of the twentieth century, a President who had carried forty-nine states when reelected in 1972, a well-organized, energetic man with a clear capacity for the dispatch of public business and considerable personal courage. Yet Richard M. Nixon was also a professional politician who was strangely uncomfortable with people and who had difficulty confronting the truth publicly and privately.

With very few exceptions, the cases dealing with Watergate were brought in the D.C. Circuit. The list of the Watergate-related proceedings in the District Court between January 1972 and January 1975 runs to thirty-six pages. It includes forty-seven criminal and thirty-six civil cases, as well as nineteen miscellaneous proceedings. The District Court was at center stage, and almost nothing done by that court in Watergate matters was overturned on appeal.[53]

The Watergate cases were assigned and controlled by John J. Sirica, Chief Judge of the District Court, who allocated the central matters to himself. He was responsible for the grand juries investigating Watergate matters, handled the pleas, trials, and sentencing of the Watergate burglars, decided the litigation over the President's taped conversations, and tried the prosecution of those accused of the cover-up. George Hart handled the cases involving corporate contributions in violation of the campaign expenditure laws; Gerhard Gesell heard the trial and the pleas relating to the break-in into the office of Daniel Ellsberg's psychiatrist; Charles Richey handled a number of civil suits, including the one brought by the Democratic National Committee against the Watergate burglars. Judges William Bryant,

---

53. "Watergate," as the term is used here, encompasses all criminal and civil proceedings connected with the burglary of the Democratic National Committee offices in the Watergate complex and the efforts to cover up the connection between the burglary, the Committee to Re-Elect the President, and the White House. It also includes all those criminal and civil proceedings involving members or former members of the Nixon administration and the campaign committee that resulted from revelations produced by efforts of the Watergate Special Prosecution force, the Senate Watergate Committee, the House Judiciary Committee, and the press that were brought before the resignation of President Nixon on August 8, 1974.

In addition to other sources cited in the bibliography, much of the material in this section derives from Judge Sirica's memoir *To Set the Record Straight* (1979) and from discussions the author had with Sirica and with most of the judge's colleagues of the time who were still living in 1990–91. Judge Gesell also wrote for this author a three-page memorandum entitled "Sirica-Watergate."

John L. Smith, John Pratt, Joseph Waddy and Barrington Parker also handled some Watergate matters.

Like Nixon, Sirica was a self-made conservative Republican. Born in Waterbury, Connecticut, in 1904, the son of a barber and a grocer, Sirica came of age in Washington, where his family moved when he was fourteen. Never an intellectual, young Sirica was not academically motivated and as a young man worked as an automobile mechanic, a lifeguard, and a prize fighter. Three times he began law school and twice he dropped out before finally graduating from Georgetown in 1926. Sirica spent much of his early professional life as a "Fifth Street lawyer," in solo practice trying criminal cases in the local courts. In 1949 he joined Hogan & Hartson as a litigator, filling the slot opened by the departure of Edward Bennett Williams. His involvement in Republican politics paid off in 1957, when President Eisenhower appointed him to the District Court. Sixty-eight years old in 1972, now Chief Judge of the District Court and comfortable in his social associations, which were more country club than courthouse, Sirica seemed finally to have succeeded in a life-long search for professional and social recognition.

However, Sirica's fifteen years on the bench had not been particularly distinguished, and at the time his self-assignment of the Watergate burglary case did not seem particularly wise. Conservative and mercurial, neither scholarly nor intellectually agile, Sirica had been one of the trial judges most often reversed by the Court of Appeals. He was not a first-rate case manager nor a particularly self-confident judge. Now he would be responsible for a case with the highest profile imaginable, where any misstep might prove disastrous, both legally and politically.

The pressures on Sirica grew as the national impact of what was happening in his courtroom became greater and greater. He did not sleep well and paced up and down the courthouse corridors in the early mornings. Sirica turned over to George Hart, an excellent administrator, the day-to-day running of the District Court. Among his colleagues on the bench, he sought advice most often from Matthew McGuire and Gerhard Gesell, but as Gesell would later relate, Sirica "could ignore advice as readily as he would accept it and always did what he thought best."

Burglary, Cover-Up, and Presidential Privilege

At two in the morning of June 17, 1972, seven men were apprehended in the act of burglarizing the headquarters of the Democratic National Committee in the Watergate complex. A cover-up of the ties between the burglars, the President's campaign committee and the White House began almost at once. Documents were destroyed, safes emptied, the FBI pressured, hush money raised, perjury suborned. The burglars were immediately arraigned in the Court of General Sessions, but they would not be indicted in District Court until September 15. Almost immediately, however, a civil suit was brought by the Democratic Party Chairman, Larry O'Brien, against the burglars and the Committee to Re-Elect the President.[54] The case was randomly assigned to Judge Charles Richey, where it did not move rapidly.

Sirica assigned the criminal case to himself and set the trial for November, but later postponed it until January because of medical problems.[55] He also took two actions that limited the impact of the scandal on the 1972 election campaign: he imposed a gag order on lawyers, witnesses and defendants, thereby hobbling a potential congressional investigation, and requested Richey to put off the trial of the civil suit so that the criminal trial would not be prejudiced. Prior to the trial nothing solid was established linking the burglary to the White House or the reelection committee, and Sirica's prodding of the U.S. Attorney for the District of Columbia to broaden the investigation was ineffective.

Sirica's stubborn desire to get to the bottom of the case became evident when the seven burglars came to trial in January 1973. He refused at first to take the guilty plea of E. Howard Hunt, the first of the defendants to plead, because, as he said, "The Court sees as an element of its discretion and as part of its duty proper representation of the public interest in justice." He ultimately did take Hunt's plea and that of four other defendants, which dramatically reduced the scope of the trial. During the trial of James McCord and G. Gordon Liddy, Sirica showed obvious dissatisfaction with the prosecution's questioning, prodded defense lawyers, and questioned witnesses at length himself. He was, he told Liddy's lawyers, exercising his "judgment as a federal judge and chief judge of this court [to] examine witnesses when [he] thought all the facts were not brought out by counsel on either side."

In the sentencing phase, too, Sirica repeated over and over again his desire that the full truth be disclosed, employing a carrot-and-stick approach that implied leniency for cooperation and heavy sentences for defiance. On March 20, three days before sentencing was scheduled, James McCord showed up unexpectedly in Sirica's chambers and handed him a letter,

---

54. *O'Brien v. Finance Comm. to Re-elect the President*, Civ. No. 1233-72.

55. While generally assignments of cases were made randomly in the District Court, the Chief Judge had the authority to assign to any judge a potentially protracted case. The prosecution urged that this be done with the case of the Watergate burglaries.

which the judge read in open court three days later. In it, McCord stated that "[t]here was political pressure applied to the defendants to plead guilty and remain silent."[56] McCord's sentencing was delayed, and he began talking with the U.S. Attorney.

The sentences for the other burglars were harsh, ranging up to forty years. Sirica was sharply criticized for the sentences, but he considered them "tentative" and intended to take cooperation into consideration when he imposed final sentences. The sentences were later reduced; even Liddy, who never cooperated, was given only five years.

Shortly after McCord began cooperating, the cover-up cracked wide open. Mid-level White House officials connected with the cover-up began to deal with the prosecutors. That, in turn, led to the resignations of the President's Chief of Staff, H. R. Haldeman, and his chief domestic advisor, John Ehrlichman, as well as the acting Attorney General and the acting head of the FBI. On May 17, hearings of the select Senate Committee investigating the Watergate scandal commenced. The next day Archibald Cox, a Harvard Law School professor and former Solicitor General, was named Special Prosecutor by the President. On June 12, Sirica denied Cox's request to bar radio and television coverage of the hearings because they might prejudice later criminal trials. There were not, Sirica said, any defendants to protect—nobody had yet been charged.

In mid-July the Senate hearings revealed, almost by accident, that the President had an extensive tape-recording system operating in his offices in the White House. After Nixon refused to surrender the tapes to either the Special Prosecutor or the Senate committee, Sirica signed, at Cox's request, a subpoena for the tapes and other White House records. In a letter dated July 25, the President responded:

> With the utmost respect for the court of which you are Chief Judge, and for the branch of government of which it is part, I must decline to obey the subpoena. In doing so, I follow the example of a long line of my predecessors as President of the United States who have consistently adhered to the position that the President is not subject to compulsory process from the courts.

Nixon said that he would, like his predecessors, always make relevant material available to the Court "except in those rare instances when to do so would be inconsistent with the public interest."

---

56. McCord later called Sirica "the lone man I felt I could depend on in this case.... The man is honest and genuine."

Cox presented Sirica with an order to be served on the President to show cause why the documents should not be produced. At this dramatic moment, Sirica called the two grand juries into open court to ascertain that they wished him to sign the order to show cause. As their names were called in turn, each juror rose. Sirica asked each of them if he or she had an objection to the show cause order. None did. Sirica signed the order on the bench. Thus began one of the great constitutional battles in American history.

Two of the nation's great legal scholars—Cox and Charles Alan Wright of the University of Texas Law School, then the President's attorney—argued the case before Sirica. The issue was momentous, if not complex, but there were almost no direct precedents. Presidents had asserted executive privilege since George Washington, but only once, in the treason trial of Aaron Burr in 1807, had the privilege been asserted by the President in response to a subpoena in a criminal case. Then, Thomas Jefferson was President and John Marshall was the trial judge. At best it was an ambiguous precedent. Jefferson had not acknowledged the constitutional validity of the subpoena, but he had made most of the subpoenaed documents available for the trial through the U.S. District Attorney.

Now, President Nixon was arguing that the institution of the presidency would be irreparably injured if he had to turn over the tapes. Cox argued that the President himself was hardly in a position to judge the public interest in keeping the tapes secret since "the evidence on the tapes also may be material to public accusations against the respondent himself…a question to which he can hardly be indifferent." Indeed, Sirica would relate in his memoir that "[a]long with the press and the public, I was becoming increasingly suspicious that Nixon was more interested in protecting himself than in advancing the constitutional principles his counsel was arguing." There were ominous leaks from the White House that the President might consider nothing less than a definitive order of the Supreme Court to be binding on him.

Sirica read his decision in open court on August 29th. He ordered the President to turn over the tapes for *in camera* examination. He held that the Court had the authority to order a President to obey the command of a grand jury subpoena, reaffirming the generally accepted premise that the grand jury has a right to every man's evidence. The history of the Constitution and the Constitution itself, Sirica said, "revealed a general disfavor of government privileges, or at least uncontrolled privileges." The validity and scope of executive privilege was to be determined, not by the executive, but by the courts.

Sirica further held that courts generally, and the U.S. District Court for the District of Columbia in particular, "have not hesitated to rule on nondiscretionary acts [of coordinate branches] when necessary." For that principle, he cited to four cases, three of which had arisen in the D.C. Circuit: the Steel Seizure case of 1952, *Powell v. McCormack*, and *D.C. Federation of Civic Associations v. Volpe,* part of the Three Sisters Bridge litigation (see chapters five and seven). He added, "The Court cannot say that the Executive's persistence in withholding the tape recordings would 'tarnish its reputation,' but must admit that it would tarnish the Court's reputation to fail to do what it could in pursuit of justice."[57]

Neither the White House nor the Special Prosecutor's office was pleased by the decision. The latter had hoped that Sirica would order that the tapes be turned over directly to the grand jury, but Sirica had held that he would examine each tape to decide if it was privileged. The President, as expected, filed an appeal. The case was heard *en banc*, as all major Watergate matters would be.

The Court of Appeals approached the tapes case like a skittish horse. Two days after oral argument, the Court issued a memorandum without a dissent, urging Nixon and Cox to try to reach an out-of-court compromise which would embrace examination of the tapes by Nixon (or his delegate), Wright, and Cox.[58] The Court expressed its hope that the President and the Special Prosecutor could "agree as to the material needed for the grand jury's functioning." That way the national interest would be served, with neither the President nor the Special Prosecutor having surrendered or subverted the principle for which they had contended. A week later Wright informed the Court of Appeals that efforts to that end had not been fruitful.

When the Court of Appeals finally decided the case, on October 12, it divided 5–2. The opinion for the majority (Bazelon, Wright, McGowan, Leventhal, and Robinson) was *per curiam*. MacKinnon and Wilkey dissented. Tamm and Robb had disqualified themselves.[59] While stressing the "unique circumstances of the case," the majority denied that the President was absolutely immune from the judicial process: "Though the President is elected by nationwide ballot, and is often said to represent all the people, he does not embody the nation's sovereignty. He is not above the law's commands."

---

57. *In re Subpoena to Nixon*, 360 F. Supp. 1 (1973). The fourth case Sirica cited was *United States v. U.S. District Court*, 407 U.S. 297 (1972), in which the Supreme Court rejected the executive's contention of inherent power to wiretap domestic organizations.

58. The memorandum is set out in *Nixon v. Sirica*, 487 F.2d 700, Appendix 1.

59. *Nixon v. Sirica*, 487 F.2d 700 (1973). It is surmised that Robb recused himself because he had been a law partner of Kenneth Parkinson, who had been implicated in the case, and that Tamm did so because of his previous affiliation with the FBI.

The court rejected the President's claim that, at least with respect to conversations with his advisers, the privilege is absolute and up to him to assert. It stood on its own language in the *Seaborg* case: "Any claim to executive absolutism cannot override the duty of the court to assure that an official has not exceeded his charter or flouted the legislative will."[60] If mere invocation of executive privilege by the President could deprive the courts, grand juries, or citizens access to all documents, the "Freedom of Information Act could become nothing more than a legislative statement of unenforceable rights. Support for this kind of mischief," the Court added, "simply cannot be spun from incantation of the doctrine of separation of powers."

Judge MacKinnon's thirty-four-page dissent laid out the case for recognition of an absolute privilege for confidential presidential communications. "To recognize only a qualified privilege," he wrote, "is to invite every litigant, both civil and criminal, to demonstrate his or her own particularized need for evidence contained in presidential deliberations."

In a thoughtful thirty-seven-page dissent, Judge Wilkey distinguished between the "common-sense common law privilege of governmental confidentiality, codified in statute in the Freedom of Information Act," which, when asserted, the courts do weigh as to scope and applicability, and the "constitutional privilege" derived from the separation of powers, which was not subject to weighing and balancing by the courts. When the latter is asserted, as in this case, "the President has an *unqualified, constitutional* privilege to decide whether it is in the public interest to disclose records in his possession to a co-equal Branch of Government," Wilkey wrote.

Nixon chose not to appeal the Court's decision. Instead, he tried to force Cox to accept transcripts of the tape recordings, verified by Senator John Stennis of Mississippi. Cox refused. On October 20, three days before the deadline for turning the tapes over to Judge Sirica, Nixon ordered Cox fired. Attorney General Elliot Richardson refused to carry out the order and resigned. So did the Deputy Attorney General, William D. Ruckelshaus. The new acting Attorney General, Robert Bork, fired Cox.

This action, which became known as the "Saturday Night Massacre," shocked the nation. In its uncertain aftermath, Sirica tried to alleviate some of the anxieties of the grand jurors. Calling both grand juries to his packed courtroom on the morning of the 23rd, he told them that "the grand juries

---

60. *Nixon v. Sirica,* at 714, quoting from *Committee For Nuclear Responsibility v. Seaborg,* 463 F.2d 788, at 793.

on which you serve remain operative and intact [and] will continue to function and pursue their work. You are not dismissed and will not be dismissed
except by this court as provided by law." He also called members of the Special Prosecutor's office to his chambers and urged them to proceed with
their work while he considered what more he could do.

The tapes were supposed to be turned over to the Court that afternoon.
No one expected them to be, though, and Sirica was ready to deal with the
consequences of the President's refusal. He drafted an order calling upon the
President to appear in court the following day to show cause why he should
not be held in contempt. Sirica was ready to use fines to enforce his order,
the way Judge Goldsborough had handled John L. Lewis and the United Mine
Workers in 1946 (see chapter five). Like everyone else, he was amazed when
Charles Alan Wright announced that the President "would comply in all respects" with the District Court's order as modified by the Court of Appeals.

Two weeks after Cox's firing, Judge Gesell held that Cox had been illegally removed. Ralph Nader and members of Congress, including Sen.
Frank Moss of Utah and Rep. Bella Abzug of New York City, had sought an
injunction to reinstate Cox and halt the Watergate investigation until he
had resumed control. Gesell denied that motion from the bench because
Cox had not entered into that particular litigation and Leon Jaworski had
already been sworn in to succeed him. However, the plaintiffs also pressed
for a declaratory judgment as to the legality of the discharge and of the temporary abolition of the Office of Watergate Special Prosecutor.

Gesell held that Nader lacked standing, but granted it to the congressional plaintiffs because bills attempting to insulate the Watergate inquiries
from executive interference were pending in the Congress, as were resolutions seeking the impeachment of the President. Gesell also held that the
matter was not moot, because the new Special Prosecutor derived his authority and independence from a Department of Justice regulation almost
identical to the one Cox had operated under and because of the "insistent
demand for some degree of certainty with regard to these distressing events
which have engendered considerable distrust of government." The danger
that the President's "challenged conduct" might be repeated with regard to
the new Watergate Special Prosecutor "forces decision."

Once he reached the merits, Gesell did not find them difficult. The Justice Department regulation setting forth the duties of the Watergate Special Prosecutor provided that he would not be removed "except for extraordinary improprieties on his part." Cox had not been discharged for such
improprieties, and the regulation had been rescinded retroactively after his
dismissal. Gesell held that the agency regulation had the force and effect of

law at the time Cox was fired and, following *Vitarelli v. Seaton*, that an executive department may not discharge one of its officers in a manner inconsistent with its own regulations. The abolition of the Office of Watergate Special Prosecutor was similarly illegal. The revocation of the regulation "was simply a ruse to permit the discharge of Mr. Cox," which was arbitrary and unreasonable.[61]

The grand jury returned indictments on March 1, 1974, against seven former members of the White House staff and staff of the Committee to Re-Elect the President, including Haldeman, Ehrlichman, and former Attorney General John Mitchell. With the indictments, it gave Sirica a sealed report listing the major facts linking the President to the cover-up and an overstuffed briefcase containing evidence. The request was opposed, not by the President's lawyers, but by counsel for those under indictment. On March 18, Sirica ruled that the evidence could go to the Judiciary Committee.[62]

In April, the second litigation over the White House tapes began. The new Special Prosecutor, Leon Jaworski, subpoenaed sixty-four tape recordings, and Sirica approved the request in a short opinion. When the White House moved to quash the subpoena, Jaworski revealed, in an *in camera* reply brief, that the grand jury had named the President an unindicted coconspirator. Sirica enforced the subpoena.

The Supreme Court granted Jaworski's request to bypass the Court of Appeals and grant certiorari. Oral argument took place on July 8. As the nation waited for the decision of the Supreme Court, it watched on television the final deliberations of the House Judiciary Committee considering articles of impeachment against the President. On July 24, a unanimous Supreme Court affirmed Sirica. While the Court took a generous view of the scope of executive privilege, the essence of its decision was that "[t]he generalized assertion of privilege must yield to the demonstrated specific need for evidence in a pending criminal trial."[63]

Two days later, James St. Clair, the President's lawyer, appeared in Sirica's courtroom for a hearing on delivery of the tapes. Sirica required St. Clair

---

61. *Nader v. Bork*, 366 F. Supp. 104 (1973). Gesell refused to appointed a special prosecutor on his own authority, as Sirica and Richey had at other times: *O'Brien v. Finance Comm. to Re-Elect the President*, Civ. No. 1233-72; *United States v. Liddy*, Crim. No. 1827-72 (1972). The judges of the District Court also discouraged passage of legislation authorizing that court or the Court of Appeals to appoint a Special Prosecutor.

62. *In re Report and Recommendation of June 5, 1972, Grand Jury Concerning Transmission of Evidence to the House of Representatives*, 370 F. Supp. 1219 (1974).

63. *United States v. Nixon*, 418 U.S. 683 (1974).

to take personal charge of their copying and indexing. In preparing to turn
the tapes over, the President's attorneys listened to the tape of June 23, 1972,
for the first time. That tape provided the "smoking gun," the direct evidence
of Nixon's involvement in the cover-up, which would have assured his impeachment and conviction. President Nixon resigned on August 8, 1974.
One month later, President Ford gave him a full pardon.[64]

The sixty-one day trial of the cover-up defendants began on October 1.
It would be marked by considerable tension between Sirica and Haldeman's
counsel, 73-year-old John J. Wilson, who had been involved in the Steel
Seizure case and who had been a friend of Sirica's for forty years. Twenty
hours of White House tapes were played at the trial and "the profanity, the
scheming, the plotting, the development of false stories," as Judge Sirica
later characterized it, could be heard by all.

The jury began deliberating on December 30 and reached its verdicts on
New Year's Day. Haldeman and Mitchell were found guilty on five counts,
Ehrlichman on four; their convictions were upheld on appeal. All three
went to prison, and were released in the fall of 1977. Robert Mardian, the
former Assistant Attorney General in charge of the Internal Security Division, was convicted on one count; the conviction was reversed on appeal
and he was not retried. Kenneth Parkinson, a "small fry," was found not
guilty. A total of thirty Nixon administration officials, presidential campaign officials and financial contributors would plead guilty or be found
guilty of Watergate-related offenses. Twenty-five of them went to jail. Sirica believed that Nixon, too, should have gone to jail.

Judge Gesell tried the prosecution of Ehrlichman, Liddy, Charles Colson
and others for the burglary of the office of Daniel Ellsberg's psychiatrist.
Ehrlichman was given twenty months to five years; Colson and Liddy, one

----

64. In 1973 the Court of Appeals had decided what would become the leading case
on the pardon power. It involved Maurice Schick, court martialed for the premeditated
murder of an eight-year-old girl in 1954 and sentenced to death. Schick had had his sentence commuted by President Eisenhower to imprisonment for life, upon the express
condition that he should not have any rights or claims arising under the law of parole.
When Schick applied for parole in the 1970s, there was no death penalty and there was
also a statutory provision that a prisoner given a life sentence would be eligible for parole after serving fifteen years. Both Judge Hart and the Court of Appeals ruled against
Schick, although not on constitutional grounds. Less than three months after Ford's pardon of Nixon, the Supreme Court held (Chief Justice Burger writing) that the pardon
power flows from the Constitution alone, not from any legislative enactments and therefore cannot be modified, abridged, or diminished by Congress. *Schick v. Reed,* 483 F.2d
1266 (1973) (*RRobb*-WMil/*Wri*), aff'd, 419 U.S. 263 (1974).

to three years. Gesell suspended the sentences of two others, whose convictions were then reversed on appeal for serious errors in applying the "following orders" defense,[65] which became critical during the Iran-Contra trials fifteen years later. Judge Hart handled the trial of former Secretary of the Treasury John Connally, who, represented by Edward Bennett Williams, was acquitted of taking a $10,000 bribe to lobby Nixon to raise milk price supports. Hart also took the plea of former Attorney-General Richard Kleindienst for refusing to answer the questions of a congressional committee. Kleindienst was sentenced to a month in prison and a fine of $100.

Aftermath

Two kinds of cases related to the Watergate scandals would occupy the Circuit for years: the battle over control of Richard Nixon's papers and tape recordings of White House conversations, and civil suits against Nixon and members of his administration for alleged violations of constitutional or statutory rights. The litigation over the Nixon tapes and presidential papers, which stretched into the 1990s, turned on issues of separation of powers, privacy, and executive privilege. The ex-President repeatedly challenged government policies and acts of Congress that would open the documents to scrutiny and prevent their destruction. In these cases, the District Court once again played the central role.

On September 8, 1974, the day he granted Nixon a full pardon, President Ford announced an agreement between Nixon and the Administrator of the General Services Administration, Arthur F. Sampson, similar to those made by other recent presidents. The agreement, which covered some forty-two million pages of documents and 4,000 hours of tape recordings, gave the GSA temporary custody of the material, but Nixon would control access to it and essentially had the right to destroy any tapes and documents he chose. Almost immediately, the Special Prosecutor sought documents from the Nixon papers and Nixon brought suit to prevent their release by the GSA. In order to permit the production of materials pursuant to court order, Judge Richey enjoined the government from effectuating the Nixon-Sampson agreement and disposing of the tapes.[66]

Concerned about the effect of the Nixon-Sampson agreement upon ongoing prosecutions, Congress rapidly passed the Presidential Recordings

---

65. *United States v. Barker*, 546 F.2d 940 (1976) (*per curiam Wilk*(c)-*Merhige*(D. Va.)(c)/*Lev*).

66. *Nixon v. Sampson*, 389 F. Supp. 107 (1974), order stayed, 513 F.2d 427 (1975) (*per curiam* Rob-Wilk).

and Materials Preservation Act, giving the federal government control of the Nixon papers and tapes.[67] The Act, like some others of the period, contained a section, 105(a), which provided for expeditious judicial review. The District Court of the District of Columbia was given exclusive jurisdiction to hear challenges to the law and was mandated to give such cases "immediate consideration and resolution." Because litigation over the tapes was already pending before Judge Richey—litigation which might serve as the vehicle to speedily resolve challenges to the new law—Congress eliminated a provision requiring a three-judge district court.

The day after the law went into effect, the ex-President brought suit to enjoin its enforcement, asking for the convening of a three-judge district court to determine the constitutionality of the statute. That suit was consolidated with three others pending before Judge Richey. Less than six weeks later—impatient for once with delay in litigation involving his tapes—Nixon asked the Court of Appeals to mandamus Judge Richey to order an immediate decision on the convening of the three-judge court.

A contretemps developed. On January 31, 1975, a motions panel of the Court of Appeals (Spottswood Robinson and Malcolm Wilkey) refused to issue the writ of mandamus but held that Richey should give Nixon's application priority over the consolidated cases and decide his case right away.[68] On the same day, Richey, emphatically denying that he was acting in response to the Court of Appeals, issued a decision in the consolidated cases rejecting most of Nixon's claims.[69] Although his decision was not released until ninety minutes after the Court of Appeals had ruled, Richey insisted that he had signed his order at two that morning. The Court of Appeals, acting *per curiam* (Robinson, Wilkey, and Bastian), made it clear that it did not accept Richey's explanation. Concerned that the decision in the consolidated cases might "unilaterally narrow the ambit of a three judge tribunal," it stayed the effectuation of Richey's decision until the three-judge court could adjudicate the issue of the priority of cases.[70]

Almost a year later, on January 7, 1976, the three-judge District Court, composed of Appeals Court Judges Tamm and McGowan and District Judge Aubrey Robinson, upheld the Presidential Recordings and Materials Act on its face. In a forty-five-page opinion written by McGowan, the court rejected

---

67. 88 Stat. 1695 (1974).
68. *Nixon v. Richey*, 513 F.2d 427 (1975) (*per curiam* Rob-Wilk).
69. *Nixon v. Sampson*, 389 F. Supp. 107 (1975).
70. *Nixon v. Richey*, 513 F.2d 430 (1975).

Nixon's separation-of-powers contentions, that Congress was unable to take an action which impinged on another branch of government and that presidential control over the disposition of presidential papers was an essential part of executive power. Rejecting a "stiffly formal and mechanistic view of government" requiring three airtight departments, the judges embraced "a more pragmatic, flexible, functional approach." Such an approach meant considering "whether the impact of an Act on one branch of government is justified by the need to pursue objectives whose promotion is assigned by the Constitution to a different branch," and in this case it was.[71]

The court thought that the established process for screening presidential documents would not be likely to "stifle free and open communications in the future" and that Congress had a legitimate reason for concern that this particular President, because of the circumstances under which he departed from office, might destroy documents which cast him in an unfavorable light. While the Court also rejected Nixon's claim that his right to privacy extended to forty-two million pages of documents, it was more sympathetic to the less extensive privacy claims for the tapes, which contained some conversations the President had had with members of his family. The opinion warned that while the law was constitutional on its face, "sensitivity to constitutional protections cannot end with the act itself."

The decision was upheld by a fractured Supreme Court. The plurality opinion took the lower court's pragmatic, flexible approach to the separation-of-powers issues. It upheld screening of the documents by archivists against the claim of executive privilege and rejected the argument that the Act was tantamount to a general warrant authorizing the search and seizure of all presidential papers and effects. Nevertheless, not only the dissents of Chief Justice Burger and Justice William Rehnquist but the four concurring opinions demonstrated that the members of the Court were troubled by the implications of the decision.[72]

Litigation over the Nixon tapes continued for over a decade. Meanwhile, a series of suits was brought by individuals against Nixon and members of the Nixon administration for violation of their civil rights. The leading case in this group was *Halperin v. Kissinger.* Morton Halperin had had his phone tapped for twenty-one months during and after the time he was an assistant to Henry Kissinger in the White House. The eavesdropping was motivated by leaks to the press of foreign policy documents and classified in-

---

71. *Nixon v. Administrator of Gen. Servs.*, 408 F. Supp. 321 (1976) (*McGowan*-Tamm-A. Robinson).

72. *Nixon v. Administrator of Gen. Servs.*, 433 U.S. 425 (1977).

formation, including the secret bombing raids on Cambodia. These wire-taps (and many others undertaken by the Nixon administration) were made without a warrant and were justified on the basis of the inherent power of the President.

Judge John Lewis Smith Jr. held that Nixon, John Mitchell, and H. R. Haldeman were jointly liable; he awarded summary judgment for the re-maining defendants and awarded only nominal damages. The Court of Ap-peals (Judge Wright writing) affirmed as to the liability of Nixon, Mitchell, and Haldeman, and rejected claims that the President was entitled to ab-solute immunity. Wright wrote that a "proper regard for separation of pow-ers does not require that the courts meekly avert their eyes from presiden-tial excesses while invoking a sterile view of three branches of government entirely insulated from such power." However, the Court reversed Smith on the proper measure of damages and held that his grant of summary judg-ment to Kissinger was in error. By an equally divided vote, the Supreme Court affirmed.[73]

As a result, however, of the High Court's intervening decision in the *Fitzgerald* case, Judge Smith on remand granted summary judgment in favor of all the defendants in the *Halperin* case.[74] The Court of Appeals then held that "if the facts establish that the purported national security moti-vation would have been reasonable," the immunity defense would prevail. However, the defendants were not shielded by qualified immunity from the Fourth Amendment reasonableness claims.[75] The case was remanded to de-termine whether the putative national security purpose of the wiretap was objectively reasonable. Finally, in 1989, Judge John Pratt awarded summary judgment to Kissinger and Haldeman, the only remaining defendants.[76]

Judging Sirica

How does one assess Sirica's performance at the storm center of the Wa-tergate cases? By the standards of most protracted or complex litigation, Watergate was fairly simple. If the constitutional issues were very great, they were not an enormously hard study. Even as a political trial it was com-

---

73. *Halperin v. Kissinger*, 424 F. Supp. 838 (1976); 434 F. Supp. 1193 (1977), rev'd, 606 F.2d 1191 (1979)(*Wri*-Rob-*Gesell*(c)), aff'd, 452 U.S. 713 (1981).

74. *Halperin v. Kissinger*, 578 F. Supp. 231 (1984).

75. *Halperin v. Kissinger*, 807 F.2d 180 (1986) (*Sca-Mik*(c)-Rob). On the latter point, Scalia disagreed with the concurring judges, Mikva and Robinson.

76. 723 F. Supp. 1535 (1989).

paratively tame; Sirica was spared the problems with unruly defendants or insolent lawyers in the courtroom that Eicher had in the Great Sedition case, or that some of the D.C. District Court judges had in cases involving Vietnam War demonstrators. Nor did Sirica have to decide major constitutional issues under the extreme pressure of time, as Pine had in the Steel Seizure case and Gurfein and Gesell had in the Pentagon Papers litigation. Those qualifiers granted, it is equally true that probably no judge in American history had for so long responsibility for litigation which repeatedly posed issues of the gravest political and constitutional significance, or so often had to confront occasions on which a misstep could have brought grief. In contrast to his prior judicial career, Sirica was never guilty of a short temper or careless legal errors. The worst criticism that honorably might have been attached to Sirica's performance was that he had unnecessarily disrupted the McCord-Liddy trial with his questions and that his "tentative" sentences in that case were draconian.

Sirica kept cheap politics from his courtroom. He devised and unleashed the process that got at the truth. He "handled the press like a pro," according to Gerhard Gesell—no small matter in this case. If in private Sirica could be nervous and excitable, in the courtroom he was dignified, nonpartisan and, almost always, strong. He worked well with the Special Prosecutors and the grand juries, while giving the President and the cover-up defendants no legitimate cause for complaint. The law he made in the tapes cases was solid and shrewd, giving the White House no reason, other than self-preservation, to refuse to cooperate. Apparently realizing the President's complicity earlier than virtually any other major actor in the drama outside the White House, Sirica never pulled back. He did not flinch from enforcing the subpoenas and would not have flinched from holding the President in contempt. He stayed the course and at its end, in his sentencing, fairly apportioned what was fitting and proper for the meek and for the powerful.

Sirica would not seem to have been well cast for his role in Watergate. He was not a man with great legal learning, and his judicial career did not produce many examples of brilliantly wrought law. He was not the wisest, the most astute, the quickest witted, the most balanced of trial judges. Yet to him came the greatest test ever demanded of an American trial judge. That test he met with courage, humility, and wisdom.

Chapter 9

"Active Partner in a Whirlwind Era"

Overseer of the Administrative Agencies in the 1970s

By the middle of the 1970s, Washington had emerged as a world-class city, rivaling Paris for beauty and, within the United States, a bona fide contender for second place to New York for richness of culture. While the "other Washington"—that city of poverty, crime and drugs—continued to exist, progress towards representative government and home rule quickened. In 1971, the residents of the District elected a delegate (non-voting) to the Congress for the first time. The District of Columbia Self-Government Act, passed by Congress in 1973, led to a home-rule charter and the popular election of a Mayor and a thirteen-member City Council.[1] But it was home rule with a shrinking population and tax base, without real representation in Congress, a veto on congressional legislation for the District, or control of the local budget.

As we saw in the previous chapter, in the 1970s the U.S. District Court for the District of Columbia emerged as a national court, intimately engaged in checks and balances at the national level. In the same period, the U.S. Court of Appeals emerged as the national court of administrative law, becoming, in the words of Judge Patricia Wald, "an active partner in a whirlwind era of expanded federal regulation."

In this decade federal courts throughout the country were generally not embarrassed to employ judicial power, and the judges of the D.C. Circuit were no exception. The factors affecting judicial activism elsewhere—Warren Court precedents, including liberalized rules of jurisdiction and standing, an invigorated public interest bar, ambiguous laws of Congress, and

---

1. 87 Stat. 784.

concern about the excesses of executive power—also affected the Circuit. But there were also factors unique to the D.C. Circuit: exclusive jurisdiction in crucial areas; a national outlook; a lack of illusion about presidential, legislative and bureaucratic power (which may have come from first-hand exposure to it); and the Circuit's heritage of activism. In any event, during a time in which there was a loss of faith in government, judges throughout the country were willing to reach out and confront hard problems that others in government were ducking. In this, the courts of the D.C. Circuit were at the forefront.

The U.S. Court of Appeals

The nine regular judges who sat together during the seventies were a talented group.[2] After President Nixon made his three appointments to the Court of Appeals, in 1969 and 1970, the regular membership of the Court remained intact until the death of Harold Leventhal in 1979. There were four "liberal" members, appointed by presidents Truman, Kennedy and Johnson—Judges Bazelon (who continued as Chief Judge until 1978), Wright, Leventhal and Robinson—and four conservative judges: Tamm (a Johnson appointee) and the three Nixon appointees, Roger Robb, George MacKinnon and Malcolm Wilkey. Carl McGowan, a Kennedy appointee, who was at the center of the discordant court of the 1960s, can be classified as a "moderate liberal" during this period. Six senior judges—Edgerton, Prettyman, Miller, Washington, Danaher and Bastian—sat on very few cases and wrote virtually no opinions. Charles Fahy, close to eighty at the beginning of the decade, does not appear to have been anything like the influence he had been in the fifties and sixties.

Although David Bazelon had made a large part of his reputation in the fields of criminal and mental health law, he now, seemingly without missing a beat, established himself as a force in administrative law through his creative approaches to the problems raised by the new administrative agencies. J. Skelly Wright continued to be, with Bazelon, the least constrained by traditional canons of judicial restraint. Although here and there jurisprudential differences arose between them, the two were ordinarily on the same wavelength. They were joined there by Spottswood Robinson, a

---

2. Some insights into relations on the Court during this period were provided in interviews with the author by Judge George MacKinnon, December 6, 1990, and Justice Ruth Bader Ginsburg, February 8, 1995.

peacemaker beloved by those around him, a careful craftsman but a very slow worker. Harold Leventhal was a liberal of a different school than Bazelon and Wright, far more traditional in his judicial craft, more tough-minded and pragmatic. While in many matters he joined with Bazelon, Wright, and Robinson, he parted from them on some important issues, such as the way the Court should oversee administrative agencies and the regulation of indecent speech. He was among the most brilliant and eloquent American judges of his time, and his premature death in 1979 at the age of sixty-four was a grievous blow to the Court.

In the 1970s Carl McGowan came into his own as a judge. McGowan played no small role in the transformation of the Court of Appeals into the premier national administrative tribunal. In those administrative cases where there were liberal/conservative divisions, McGowan would vote with the liberals. He was also clearly a judicial liberal where poverty law was concerned, but in major criminal cases heard *en banc* he joined Leventhal in the middle of the Court, refusing to accept the "advanced" approaches of Bazelon and Wright and preferring a remand to a clear-cut Court of Appeals decision.

Although Edward Tamm's background was in law enforcement and he was distinctly unsympathetic in criminal cases to the approaches of Bazelon and Wright, in administrative law his outlook was closer to the liberal wing of the Court than that of the Court's three newest members. He emerged during the 1970s as an independent and strong voice in administrative law, an advocate of expansion of intervention in administrative proceedings and the Court's strongest supporter of the Fairness Doctrine.

President Nixon's three appointees to the Court of Appeals had qualities in common. All had prosecutorial experience, for instance, and each was a staunch conservative voice. But the three men differed considerably from each other in style and, in certain respects, in outlook.

Roger Robb was appointed on May 6, 1969, at the age of sixty-two. He was the son of Judge Charles H. Robb, who had served on the Court of Appeals from 1906 to 1937. The younger Robb had had a distinguished career at the bar, where his clients included Earl Browder, Barry Goldwater, Fulton Lewis Jr., and the Personnel Security Board of the Atomic Energy Commission, which took away the security clearance of J. Robert Oppenheimer. Robb had also been retained by the judges of the U.S. Court of Customs and Patent Appeals to argue before the Supreme Court that they were Article III judges. Senate Judiciary Committee Chairman James Eastland was a strong supporter of Robb's appointment.

Affable and able, Robb was slow to anger in print. In the limelight less than any of his colleagues save Robinson, Robb nevertheless would have the best "batting average" with the Supreme Court of any of the judges. Although he was generally in accord with the views of MacKinnon and Wilkey, Robb nevertheless differed from them in such significant cases as the Pentagon Papers. In a court which came to be known for the length of its opinions, Robb would not join in any opinion over fifty pages, concurring only in the judgment in such cases.

Although technically George E. MacKinnon was named to fill the vacancy left by Judge Danaher's taking senior status, in effect he replaced Warren Burger. Taking his seat on the bench only a few days before Burger left, MacKinnon was the same age as Burger and was, like Burger, a Minnesotan who had been active in Republican politics as a supporter of Harold Stassen. MacKinnon's experience in the Minnesota legislature and as a member of Congress (1947–49) proved useful on the Court of Appeals.

Not only was MacKinnon similar to Burger in judicial philosophy, of the Nixon appointees he was most akin to Burger temperamentally. He saw himself as an intellectual counterweight and counterpuncher to the liberals, often responding indignantly in dissent point by point to a Bazelon or Wright opinion. In an obituary broadcast on May 5, 1995, NPR's legal affairs correspondent Nina Totenberg characterized MacKinnon as "gruff, direct, in your face…an incredibly hard worker who called the shots as he saw them." In twenty-five of the twenty-nine cases in which cases with MacKinnon opinions reached the Supreme Court, the High Court agreed with him. Although miles apart from the Court's liberal majority, MacKinnon would turn out to be a very different kind of "judicial conservative" than the appointees of Ronald Reagan in the 1980s.

The most junior member of the Court of Appeals during this decade was Malcolm Richard Wilkey, appointed in February 1970 at the age of fifty-two, twelve years younger than MacKinnon. Wilkey came to the Court after a career which included service as general counsel of Kennecott Copper, U.S. Attorney for the Southern District of Texas, and Assistant Attorney General for both the Criminal Division and the Office of Legal Counsel. Wilkey had a strong, analytical mind and wrote with considerable legal grace.

The strongest of the more conservative judges on the Court of Appeals during the 1970s, Wilkey was thoughtful, scholarly, and thorough. Although he dissented in both the Pentagon Papers case and the Nixon tapes case, it was already clear that he would not be a reflexive conservative, as he soon demonstrated in cases involving the duties of landlords, military surveillance of civilian political activity, and racially restrictive covenants.[3] On the other hand, as a powerful opponent of the Exclusionary Rule, Wilkey differed strongly from the Bazelon wing of the Court in the area of criminal law. In an important dissent in *United States v. Bailey*, Wilkey stressed individual accountability in rejecting duress and related defenses by prisoners who claimed they had escaped from prison to avoid inhumane conditions.[4]

Wilkey's career in private law practice and government service had encompassed a great deal of experience in international law,[5] and he added particular strength to the Court of Appeals in this field. If the D.C. Circuit had had few important cases involving principles of international law and U.S. foreign relations law in its first 175 years, by the end of Wilkey's tenure it was confronting them with some frequency. Among the holdings in Wilkey's opinions in these areas were that the International Organizations Immunity Act made the World Bank immune from suit under American law for sexual harassment and discrimination; that a default judgment entered in an Israeli court could be enforced in U.S. courts; and that the Base Labor Agreement, which governed the employment of Filipino civilians on U.S. military bases in the Philippines, was not a "treaty" that superseded U.S. employment discrimination laws.[6]

In other important decisions in this field, Wilkey considered conflicts of antitrust jurisdiction, the extraterritorial application of U.S. environmental laws, and the subpoena service provision of the Federal Trade Commission. Wilkey's opinion in *Laker Airways v. Sabena* upheld an injunction re-

---

3. *Kline v. 1500 Massachusetts Ave. Apartment Corp.*, 439 F.2d 477 (1970) (*Wilk-Tamm/MacK*); *Tatum v. Laird*, 444 F.2d 947 (1971) (*Wilk-Tamm/MacK*(c/d)), rev'd, 408 U.S. 1 (1972).

4. 585 F.2d 1087 (1978) (*Wri-McG/Wilk*), rev'd, 444 U.S. 394 (1980).

5. Wilkey practiced international law as General Counsel of Kennecott Copper, served as U.S. delegate to the International Conference on Judicial Remedies against Abuse of Administrative Authority (1959), and was Reporter to the Commission on International Rules and Judicial Procedure. He was an editor of *The International Lawyer* and was the only sitting judge on the board of advisors of the Restatement of the Foreign Relations Law of the United States. In April 1981, President Reagan appointed Wilkey as one of three arbitrators on the U.S.-Iran Claims Tribunal, but Wilkey withdrew from the appointment after evaluating the effect his absence would have on the work of the Court of Appeals.

6. *Mendaro v. The World Bank*, 717 F.2d 610 (1983) (*Wilk-Rob-Markey*(Fed. Cir.)); *Attorney General v. The Irish People, Inc.*, 684 F.2d 928 (1982) (*per curiam* Wilk-*Wald*(c)-*Baz*(c)); *Tahan v. Hodgson*, 662 F.2d 862 (1981) (*Wilk-McG-Wald*); *Rossi v. Brown*, 642 F.2d 553 (1980) (*Wilk-McG-Davies*(Sr. D.J. N.D.)), rev'd sub nom. *Weinberger v. Rossi*, 456 U.S. 25 (1982).

straining the Belgian national airline from participating in a foreign action designed to prevent the District Court from hearing antitrust claims against it. In *Natural Resources Defense Council v. Nuclear Regulatory Commission,* Wilkey (with Spottswood Robinson concurring) upheld the NRC decision to license the export of a nuclear reactor without evaluating the health, safety, and environmental impact within the recipient nation. And in *FTC v. Compagnie de Saint-Gobain,* Wilkey concluded that established and fundamental principles of international law disfavor methods of extraterritorial subpoena service and oppose judicial enforcement of investigatory subpoenas abroad.[7]

In 1985, after fifteen years on the Court, Malcolm Wilkey retired, quite possibly because it had become evident that Spottswood Robinson would not leave the Chief Judgeship in time for Wilkey to assume that position.

This, then, was the Court of Appeals of the seventies, nine judges who would deserve the label increasingly applied to their court, "the nation's second most important court." During this period, the gap between the Court of Appeals and the District Court lessened somewhat as the Nixon appointees and Tamm lunched regularly with the trial judges. And tensions within the Court of Appeals diminished marginally, perhaps, with the elevation of Burger and the arrival of Nixon's appointees.

Jurisprudence

One effect of the Court Reform Act of 1970 (see chapter seven) was a considerable increase in the workload of the Court of Appeals. Although there was a short-term decline in filings (from 1973 to 1975 the number of criminal and private civil cases were halved), at the same time the number of agency cases and civil actions involving the United States more than doubled. By 1978, cases involving the review of agencies or oversight of federal officials — either direct review of the agencies or review of District Court decisions in these matters — accounted for almost three-quarters of the Court of Appeals' caseload. These cases, which concerned communications, power, the environment, health, and safety, and dealt with challenges to the

---

7. *Laker Airways v. Sabena,* 731 F.2d 909 (1984) (*Wilk-MacK/Sta*); *Natural Resources Defense Council v. Nuclear Regulatory Commission,* 647 F.2d 1345 (1981) (*Wilk-Rob*(c)-RGin); *FTC v. Compagnie de Saint-Gobain,* 636 F.2d 1300 (1980) (*Wilk-McG/Gesell*(D.D.C.)).

validity of the acts of federal agencies and officials, were also the most time-consuming. In the year ending June 30, 1981, the Court of Appeals ranked tenth among the eleven circuits in the number of opinions per judgship and ninth in the median time from filing to termination.[8]

Not coincidentally, the reduction in the local workload of the federal courts of the Circuit—also a result of the court reorganization—led to employment of the Circuit as the exclusive forum for litigation arising out of the new regulatory statutes passed in the early and mid-1970s, a development Chief Judge Bazelon had anticipated in his testimony on the court reform. The courts of the Circuit were given exclusive jurisdiction over certain suits arising out of the Clean Air Act Amendments of 1970, the Occupational Safety and Health Act of 1970, the Federal Water Pollution Control Act Amendments of 1972, the Federal Election Campaign Act Amendments of 1974, the Presidential Recordings and Materials Preservation Act of 1974, the Safe Drinking Water Act of 1974, and the Foreign Sovereign Immunities Act of 1976.[9]

A variety of measures served to deal with the added work. Two new judges were added in 1978. There was also a circuit executive, a central legal staff, a Civil Appeals Management Plan for large multi-party cases and to assist in preparing the Court's calendar, and the judges of the District Court sat with the Court of Appeals on a rotating basis. However, the workload of both federal courts of the District of Columbia Circuit must be viewed in the context of the surge of cases in the federal courts generally. After 1960, the creation of many rights by Congress, judicial interpretations of the Constitution, and a variety of procedural developments, such as expanded use of class actions, led to increased caseloads for all the federal courts. These factors also led to broadened popular recognition and acceptance of the federal courts as the forum for vindication of the personal rights of the citizen. The result of this would be more judgeships, more judicial adjuncts and surrogates, and a greater emphasis on case management.

---

8. Although a high percentage of opinions went unpublished, the Court of Appeals was rendering longer and longer opinions. The Court had the highest percentage of any of the circuits of opinions over 5,000 words—16.7 percent in 1978–79.

9. Clean Air Act Amendments, 84 Stat. 1676 (1970); Occupational Safety and Health Act, 84 Stat. 1590 (1970); Federal Water Pollution Control Act Amendments, 86 Stat. 816 (1972); Federal Election Campaign Act Amendments, 88 Stat. 1263 (1974); Presidential Recordings and Materials Preservation Act, 88 Stat. 1695 (1974); Safe Drinking Water Act, 88 Stat. 1660 (1974); Foreign Sovereign Immunities Act of 1976, 28 U.S.C. 1391 (4)(4) (1982).

While administrative law commanded more and more of the Court of
Appeals' attention during this period, the federal courts of the District of
Columbia Circuit continued to hear cases in their other traditional areas of
jurisdiction, both federal and local. Several important separation-of-powers issues came before them, including constitutional challenges to the executive's treaty-making power and to the campaign reform law of 1974.
While the Circuit's courts had been formally divested of their local jurisdiction by the court reorganization, they still decided a great many cases of
local importance — especially in the early years of the decade — thanks to
the vast extension of jurisdiction of the federal courts nationally. The
courts' work in this decade in the areas of poverty and mental-health law
has already been considered (see chapter seven); another important area of
jurisprudence in this period was civil rights. Because of its location at the
hub of government, and jurisdiction over certain cases exclusive to it, the
D.C. Circuit in the 1970s began to encounter cases involving national civil
rights policy. Two important lines of affirmative action cases developed in
the Circuit, one dealing with national issues of equal opportunity, the other
with racial discrimination in local institutions.

Affirmative Action

During the 1970s the Court of Appeals was often asked to consider the extent to which the Federal Communications Commission was required to
investigate broadcasters' equal-opportunity performance before it renewed
a broadcast license.[10] Because of the gross under-representation of minority owners of broadcast media, in 1973 the Court of Appeals required the
FCC to provide a comparative preference for racial minorities in the interest of program diversity. In an opinion written by Judge Charles Fahy, the
Court held that there was a connection between the FCC's public-interest
goal of providing the diversity of ideas and expression required by the First
Amendment and the longstanding FCC policy of promoting diversity of
ownership.[11]

The most important case of the late 1970s involving this issue was *Bilin-
gual Bicultural Coalition on Mass Media v. FCC*, in which the Court of Ap-

---

10. In addition to the cases discussed below, see *Stone v. FCC*, 466 F.2d 316 (1972)
(*Wilk*-Baz-Matthews(D.D.C.)); *Garrett v. FCC*, 513 F.2d 1056 (1979) (*Rob*-McG-
Weigel(Sr. D.J. No. Cal.)); *National Organization for Women v. FCC*, 555 F.2d 1002 (1977)
(*Wilk*-Lev-Rob); *Alianza Federal de Mercedes v. FCC*, 539 F.2d 732 (1976) (*Lev*-RRobb-
Solomon(Sr. D.J. Ore.)).

11. *TV 9 v. FCC*, 495 F.2d 929 (1973) (*Fahy*-Baz-Rob).

peals, sitting *en banc*, attempted to definitively state its position on the Commission's obligation to investigate equal-opportunity performance before it renewed broadcast licenses. Although it acknowledged that the FCC "is not the Equal Opportunity Commission," the Court of Appeals nevertheless held that where responsible and well-pleaded claims of discrimination were made, the FCC might be required to hold a hearing to resolve the charges before granting the renewal of a license.[12] The Carter administration's active support of race- and gender-conscious initiatives in broadcasting would continue to keep the courts of the Circuit busy in the 1980s.

The D.C. Circuit also confronted difficult affirmative action problems involving the local institutions of the District of Columbia. African-Americans had long been discriminated against by the D.C. Metropolitan Police Department in hiring and promotion. Naturally, this had taken a toll in police-community relations. In the early 1970s, a written examination testing verbal ability, which was used in the selection of recruits for the police academy, was challenged on the ground that it had a disproportionate impact on black applicants and had not been demonstrated to be related to job performance. From 1968 to 1971, fifty-seven percent of black officers taking the test had failed it, compared to only thirteen percent of the white officers.

The test was upheld by Judge Gesell, who ruled that it had a direct and reasonable relationship to the requirements of the police training program. A divided Court of Appeals (Judges Robinson and McGowan in the majority, Judge Robb dissenting) reversed. The Court held that, as there was evidence in the record that the test had a racially disproportionate impact, the government had not met its heavy burden of showing that the exam was related to job performance. Dissenting, Judge Robb believed that modern law enforcement demanded more than "issuing a badge and a gun to a semi-literate." The Supreme Court agreed with the dissenter, holding that the written objective test did not in itself constitute purposeful discrimination. To prevail, the High Court ruled, those challenging the test would have to establish some proof of a racially discriminatory purpose in the administration of the test.[13]

In the civil rights arena, the courts of the Circuit also issued several important decisions concerning school segregation. In one ruling, a three-judge District Court made up of Harold Leventhal, Joseph S. Waddy and

---

12. 595 F.2d 621 (1978) (*Wilk-Wri*(c)-Tamm-Lev-MacK-RRobb-*Baz*(c)/*Rob*(d. in part)).

13. *Davis v. [Walter E.] Washington*, 348 F. Supp. 15 (1972), rev'd, 512 F.2d 956 (1975) (*Rob*-McG/*RRobb*), rev'd, 426 U.S. 229 (1976).

John H. Pratt enjoined the Secretary of the Treasury from granting tax exemptions to private, white-only schools set up in southern states in response to court-ordered integration of public schools.[14] Later, Judge Pratt affirmed and enforced the obligation of the Department of Health, Education and Welfare to withhold federal funds from segregated schools pursuant to Title VI of the 1964 Civil Rights Act.[15]

Separation of Powers

The courts of the D.C. Circuit heard a great many cases with separation-of-powers implications during the 1970s. Attempts by members of Congress and others to use the courts to restrain alleged abuses of power by the executive included not only Watergate-related matters (see chapter eight) but two important cases that challenged the executive's power to make and break treaties. Some litigation was literally "brought" by statute—Congress providing for test cases in the D.C. Circuit of new legislation of which members of Congress themselves had constitutional doubts. Much of the litigation pivoted on threshold questions of standing, ripeness and justiciability; it is possible that a majority of the judicial time spent on separation-of-powers cases was spent dealing with such threshold issues.

If the work of an intermediate appellate court in dealing with major constitutional litigation often seems futile, there may be some consolation that deliberations above may be assisted by thorough analysis below. Perhaps no such case has ever demanded so much of an intermediate appellate court as *Buckley v. Valeo*, a case testing the constitutionality of the comprehensive campaign reform statute.

---

14. *Green v. Kennedy*, 309 F. Supp. 1127 (1970) (*per curiam* Leventhal-Waddy-Pratt). A later opinion by Judge Leventhal placed the burden on Mississippi schools to demonstrate that they did not discriminate, indicated doubt that educational organizations that practiced racial discrimination could qualify as charitable trusts under general trust law, and prodded the IRS to make its rules consistent nationally. *Green v. Connally*, 330 F. Supp. 1150 (1971) (Leventhal-Waddy-Pratt), aff'd sub nom. *Coit v. Green*, 404 U.S. 997 (1971). The litigation resumed in 1976, yielding an important Supreme Court decision on standing, *Allen v. Wright*, 468 U.S. 737 (1984).

15. *Adams v. Richardson*, 356 F. Supp. 92 (1973), modified, 480 F.2d 1159 (1973). The Court of Appeals' opinion was *per curiam*; Judge MacKinnon did not participate. Following this case, the District Court continued to oversee HEW's Office of Civil Rights, not only with regard to racial claims but for those brought for Mexican-Americans, women, and the blind. A second prong of this litigation involved forcing HEW to withhold funds from higher education systems that discriminated on the basis of race. *Adams v. Bell*, 711 F.2d 161 (1983) (*Wilk*-MacK-Tamm-Edw-RGin-Sca/*Wri*-Rob-Mik-Wald).

The litigation that immediately flowed from the passage of the Federal Election Campaign Act Amendments of 1974[16] raised both separation-of-powers and First Amendment issues. Passed in the wake of Watergate, the law placed limitations on campaign contributions and expenditures, required disclosure of them, and provided for public financing of qualified candidates and political parties in the presidential campaign. A new agency, the Federal Election Commission, was established to administer the Act. It was given rule-making, subpoena, investigative, and other powers, including the power to impose a temporary disqualification on a candidate who failed to file a report.

Section 437(h) of the statute provided for judicial review in a unique way. Any voter could institute an action for a declaratory judgment as to the Act's constitutionality. In that event, the District Court was to immediately certify all constitutional questions to the Court of Appeals, which was to sit *en banc* to resolve them. The decision of the Court of Appeals was reviewable by appeal directly to the Supreme Court. Such a suit was brought in the District Court of the District of Columbia on the first business day after the Act went into effect, January 2, 1975. The plaintiffs included Senator James L. Buckley of New York (later a judge of the Court of Appeals), former Senator Eugene McCarthy, the Conservative Party of New York State, and the New York Civil Liberties Union.

On May 19 Judge Howard Corcoran certified twenty-eight constitutional questions or subquestions to the Court of Appeals. The case was argued on June 13 simultaneously before the *en banc* Court of Appeals and a three-judge District Court made up of Corcoran, Spottswood Robinson and Chief Judge Bazelon. The cases were decided on August 15. The eight-judge Court of Appeals (Robb did not sit) upheld virtually every part of the statute, although it declined to rule on certain provisions, believing the issues were not ripe.[17] The three-judge District Court, which dealt with issues relating to the public financing of presidential campaigns, adopted the Court of Appeals' opinion as to those matters and simply entered an order.

The Court of Appeals upheld the Act's disclosure provisions, its limitations on contributions from individuals and political committees, and the ceiling on candidates' personal campaign expenditures. Judges Tamm (writing) and Wilkey dissented as to the expenditure limits, believing that the First Amendment prohibits any restriction of access "to the political dialog

---

16. 88 Stat. 1263, amending the 1971 Federal Election Campaign Act.

17. *Buckley v. Valeo*, 519 F.2d 821 (1975) (*per curiam* Wri-McG-Lev-Rob-Baz(c/d)-MacK(c/d)/*Tamm*-Wilk).

and electoral process, whether the individual's major resource is time or money." Tamm and Wilkey, joined by Chief Judge Bazelon, also dissented as to the disclosure requirements.

The method by which the Federal Election Commission was constituted posed separation-of-powers problems. Two members were to be appointed by the House, two by the Senate, and two by the President, with the Senate's Secretary and the House's Clerk serving *ex officio*. The Court of Appeals' *per curiam* decision held the method of appointment constitutional for the performance of "legislative functions." However, the question as to whether the Commission as constituted could perform quasi-judicial or quasi-executive functions was left for another day when they might be better decided "in the context of a particular factual controversy." (Judges Tamm, Wilkey, and MacKinnon thought this part of the Act unconstitutional.)

Buckley v. Valeo was argued before the Supreme Court on November 10, 1975, and decided *per curiam* on January 30, 1976. Five of the nine justices dissented in part. The High Court dealt with Congress's handiwork much less charitably than the Court of Appeals had, reversing it in a number of respects. It upheld the law's disclosure provisions, its provisions for public funding of elections, and its limitations on contributions when public funding is accepted; however, the Court struck down the ceilings on expenditures, including the limitation on candidates' expenditures of personal or family resources. Finally, finding the issue of the Commission's powers ripe for review, the High Court held their exercise unconstitutional in almost every respect on separation-of-powers grounds, because Congress cannot reserve for itself the power to appoint members to a body exercising executive powers. The decision, marked by internal inconsistencies and different standards of review, made a hash of campaign finance laws.[18]

As already has been seen, during the 1970s the Congress became more active in litigation. One of the most interesting developments of the early 1970s was judicial recognition of the standing of members of Congress to attack executive actions which arguably diluted their constitutional powers, so long as the injury was concrete enough.[19] However, during the latter part of the seventies, the courts were on the whole wary of suits brought by members of Congress, and used standing, ripeness, or political-question doctrines to dismiss such cases.

---

18. *Buckley v. Valeo*, 424 U.S. 1 (1976).

19. For example, *Kennedy v. Sampson*, 511 F.2d 430 (1974), holding that a senator could challenge the President's exercise of the pocket veto (see chapter eight).

Nonetheless, in two important congressional challenges to the power of the executive branch, both of which involved the making and breaking of treaties, members of Congress were able to convince the courts of the Circuit to reach the merits. *Edwards v. Carter* and *Goldwater v. Carter* each dealt with a foreign policy issue of great moment: in one case, the return of the Panama Canal to Panama; in the other, relations with China. Both raised fundamental constitutional questions.

At issue in *Edwards* were two treaties with Panama, signed by President Carter in September 1977, under which Panama was to assume territorial sovereignty over all real property in the Canal Zone. The treaties also provided that the United States would continue to operate the Canal until the year 2000. While the treaties were awaiting ratification in the Senate, Representative Mickey Edwards of Oklahoma and fifty-nine other members of the House of Representatives sued in their official capacities to vindicate their rights under Article IV Section 3, Clause 2 of the Constitution, which provides that "Congress shall have Power to dispose of... the Territory or other Property belonging to the United States."

The representatives sought from the District Court a declaratory judgment that the President's action in submitting these treaties only to the Senate deprived the United States of property without the prior concurrence of the full Congress, thus thwarting the members of the House in the performance of their constitutional duties. On February 20, 1978, Judge Barrington Parker held that the members of Congress lacked standing because there was no "particular concrete injury" and because there were possible legislative alternatives available to the plaintiffs.

The Senate consented to one of the treaties on March 14, 1978. The appeal in *Edwards* was heard on an expedited basis and decided on April 6. Over Judge MacKinnon's sharp dissent, a panel of the Court of Appeals affirmed on the merits, siding with the executive. The *per curiam* opinion saw the transfer of property as "part of a broader effort in the conduct of our foreign affairs to strengthen relations with another country." The Property Clause, the Court declared, had not been intended to restrict the treaty-making clause, nor had the Framers of the Constitution intended to preclude the use of self-executing treaties as a means of disposing of U.S. property. On May 15 the Supreme Court denied certiorari. The transfer of sovereignty went forward.[20]

---

20. *Edwards v. Carter*, 445 F. Supp. 1279 (1978), aff'd, 580 F.2d 1055 (1978) (*per curiam* Fahy-McG/MacK*), cert denied, 436 U.S. 907 (1978).

In December 1978 President Carter gave the Republic of China (Taiwan) notice that the United States would unilaterally terminate the 1954 Mutual Defense Treaty between the two countries on January 1, 1980. That treaty provided for termination by either party on one years's notice. Nine days after Taiwan was notified of the treaty termination, the United States recognized the People's Republic of China (Beijing) as the sole legal government of China.

Eight members of the Senate, including Barry Goldwater, and sixteen members of the House sought a declaratory judgment from the District Court that termination could not occur without either the advice and consent of the United States Senate or the approval of both houses of Congress. Judge Oliver Gasch dismissed the complaint on June 6, 1979, because there was a substantial likelihood of resolving the treaty termination issue in the Congress. Within hours of the Court's initial ruling, the Senate passed a sense-of-the-Senate resolution that its approval was required to terminate any mutual defense treaty, but took no further action.

On October 17, Judge Gasch agreed to consider the substance of the lawsuit. He held that the plaintiffs had standing because they were suffering an injury in fact to their legislative right to be consulted and that the issue was justiciable because the Court was confronted with a clash of authority between two political branches in a posture suitable for judicial resolution.

The issue before Gasch on the merits was an important one of first impression: did the President have the authority to terminate a valid, binding treaty without formally consulting the Congress? Gasch said that the President did not have the authority. "Taken as a whole," Gasch wrote, "the historical precedents support rather than detract from the position that the power to terminate treaties is a power shared by the political branches of this government." The conduct of foreign relations was not, after all, "a plenary executive power." Gasch issued a declaratory judgment and enjoined the Secretary of State from taking any action to implement the President's notice of termination until that notice was approved by the Congress.[21]

The appeal from Gasch's ruling was heard *en banc* on November 13, 1979, and decided *per curiam* seventeen days later. Five members of the seven-person court were willing to reach the merits; the same majority held that there was standing, and saw "no reason... to refrain from judgment" because of the justiciability issue. On the merits, a 4–3 majority of the Court of Appeals held that the determination of the conduct of the United

---

21. *Goldwater v. Carter*, 481 F. Supp. 949 (1979).

States with regard to treaties comes under the "foreign affairs power of the President," who was therefore empowered to terminate the treaty in accordance with its terms. To hold otherwise would lock the United States into all of its obligations, giving one-third of the members of the Senate plus one a veto. Judge MacKinnon again strongly dissented, arguing that historical practice bore out Gasch's conclusion that congressional participation in treaty termination had been the prevailing practice.

It would turn out that the Court of Appeals had treated the justiciability problem too cavalierly. When the Supreme Court dealt with the matter (without hearing oral argument), it vacated that decision and remanded the case to the District Court for dismissal of the complaint.[22]

Administrative Law

By the late 1970s questions of administrative law dominated the docket of the Court of Appeals. The burst of new regulation that had begun in the mid-sixties with the Great Society social-welfare legislation gained momentum. In the seventies Congress passed twenty-nine major regulatory laws and created seven new regulatory agencies dealing with energy, consumer protection, workplace safety and the environment. This period of explosive growth and rapid change in government regulation—occurring in the context of high inflation, energy shortages, a weakened presidency and a more assertive Congress, and the emergence of public-interest citizen groups and law firms—brought new and difficult problems for reviewing courts.

The two most prominent of the new agencies were the Environmental Protection Agency (EPA) and the Occupational Safety and Health Administration (OSHA). These operated not under the broad public-interest standards of the independent regulatory commissions, but under detailed congressional guidelines, and had to cope with extremely complex scientific and technological problems.

The most important judicial oversight of the new agencies occurred in the D.C. Circuit, and during this period the Court of Appeals emerged as a national court of administrative appeals. Because of the location of the agencies and the new public interest organizations in Washington and be-

---

22. *Goldwater v. Carter*, 617 F.2d 697 (1979) (*per curiam* McG-Rob-Wilk-Wald-Wri(c)-Tamm/*MacK*(c/d), vacated, remanded, 444 U.S. 996 (1979).

cause of respect for the capacity of its judges, Congress entrusted the Court with more exclusive jurisdiction. Unsurprisingly, the judges reached out to confront hard problems that others in government were avoiding—sometimes as active partner with the agencies, sometimes as gadfly, sometimes as kibitzer.

Over and over again, the Court of Appeals had to consider just how much regulation Americans had asked for, how well that regulation was working, and, from time to time, how much regulation the American economy could take. These questions were met by a group of unusually able judges who made little effort to paper over their differences. If not all of their work survived Supreme Court review, much did—broader public participation in the administrative process, higher conflict of interest standards, the scope of environmental impact statements.

Although the courts of the Circuit continued to hear important cases involving the older regulatory agencies, especially the FCC, perhaps their most significant contributions to administrative law during the 1970s were made in cases in which they considered the proper role of the reviewing court, especially where the newer agencies were concerned, and in which they supported greater openness and public access. Much of this support was given in cases involving rules for standing and intervention and conflict-of-interest issues. This was also true of cases involving the Freedom of Information Act, in which the District of Columbia Circuit was the principal forum for litigation.

Standing, Intervention, and Conflicts of Interest

One of the most significant developments in administrative law during the 1970s was the flourishing of public interest groups. As the D.C. Circuit continued to broaden the category of those who had access to the courts to challenge agency actions (while the Supreme Court was playing catch-up), such groups benefitted greatly. In the past, standing had been limited to those who had established legal rights. The new rule for standing was that the plaintiff had to show an injury in fact, that the injury was traceable to the action complained of and that the plaintiff was within the congressional zone of interest. Under such liberalized rules, as Chief Judge Patricia M. Wald pointed out some years later, "consumers, users of the wilderness, competitors, air breathers and water drinkers [could] sue to enforce regulatory statutes passed for their benefit."

Perhaps the most important standing case was *Students Challenging Regulatory Agency Procedures (SCRAP) v. United States*, in which a public-interest group challenged Interstate Commerce Commission rules which, it contended, would discourage the use of recyclable materials. SCRAP claimed standing because its members used the forests, streams, and mountains in the Washington area for camping and hiking, and charged that this use would be disturbed by the environmental impact of nonrecyclable materials. A three-judge District Court, Judge Wright writing, agreed that there was standing, then enjoined the Commission's action because it had not supplied an environmental impact statement. The *SCRAP* litigation would reach the Supreme Court twice. In the first of these cases, the High Court agreed with the D.C. Circuit as to standing, but ultimately disagreed with it on the merits, holding that the environmental impact statement was sufficient.[23]

Later in the decade, the Supreme Court tightened the rules for standing, requiring a particular injury and one redressable by the Court's remedial power. Determining standing thus became a fact-specific issue; as Chief Judge Wald later noted, "Uninvolved 'do-gooders' were out." Nonetheless, when standing again became a hotly contested issue in the D.C. Circuit in the 1980s, much of the ground won early in the seventies would be held.

The D.C. Circuit was also, on the whole, hospitable to the right to intervene in agency proceedings in this period. While that right, unlike standing, is rarely dealt with by statute, it is similar to standing in that the decisions involve a determination as to what interests are deserving of legal protection. In *National Welfare Rights Organization v. Finch*, the Court of Appeals, building upon the foundation of the *United Church of Christ* case (see chapter seven), held that an organization of welfare recipients was entitled to intervene in proceedings before the Secretary of Health, Education and Welfare.[24] After this and similar decisions, the right to intervene in trial-type proceedings before agencies was seldom denied.

The Court of Appeals wrestled repeatedly with conflict-of-interest problems in the administrative agencies, which frequently arose from commissioners' sometimes overly cozy relationships with representatives of the industries they were charged with regulating. In *Moss v. CAB*, for example, thirty-two members of Congress argued that the Civil Aeronautics Board had been "captured" by the industry. They contended that the Board had excluded the public from *ex parte* meetings with representatives of the airline industry and then, *after* approving a six percent rise in domestic air fares, had held a perfunctory hearing. Writing for himself and Judges McGowan

23. *SCRAP v. United States,* 346 F. Supp. 189 (1972) (*Wright-Richey-Flannery*(c)), 412 U.S. 669 (1972); *SCRAP v. Aberdeen and Rockfish Railroad Co.,* 371 F. Supp. 1291 (1974) (*Wright*-Richey/*Flannery*), rev'd, 422 U.S. 289 (1975).

24. 429 F.2d 725 (1970) (*Wri*-Baz-McG).

and Robinson, Judge Wright reminded the CAB that Congress had required "public participation in making rates because it is the public who pays for them. . . . No requirement of Board operation on policy of the Act seems to support the Board's blatant attempt to subvert the statute's scheme."[25]

Two 1977 FCC cases involved extensive *ex parte* contacts, first by the whole Federal Communications Commission in a rule-making proceeding for cable television (the list of contacts ran to sixty pages), then by its chairman, who had worked out a closed-door agreement with the television industry postponing regulation of advertising on children's television to allow time to assess the effectiveness of self-regulation. In the first case, the Court of Appeals remanded for an evidentiary hearing on the nature and scope of the contacts.[26] In the second, a District Court panel held that *ex parte* contacts were void only when an agency was attempting to resolve conflicting claims to a valuable privilege, and not, as in this case, during informal rulemaking.[27] It would not be until 1981, in its wide-ranging opinion in *Sierra Club v. Costle*, that the Court of Appeals would settle on final rules authorizing more extensive *ex parte* contacts in administrative rulemaking than would be permissible in judicial proceedings.[28]

The Freedom of Information Act

The major thrust of the work of the courts of the District in reviewing cases involving the Freedom of Information Act (FOIA) was to facilitate the purpose of the statute — greater openness in government.[29] Under the law, any person, for whatever reason, may file for an agency record. The record must be turned over unless it falls within one of a number of exemptions, most of them protecting classified records, internal procedures, and personal or commercial privacy. If the agency refuses to disclose the document, judicial review is provided on a priority basis; the case is to be decided without deference to the agency.

FOIA was enacted on July 4, 1966, but little use was made of the law in its early years.[30] Amendments added in 1974, overruling the effects of sev-

---

25. *Moss v. CAB*, 430 F.2d 891 (1970) (*Wri*-McG-Rob).

26. *Home Box Office, Inc. v. FCC*, 567 F.2d 9 (1977) (*per curiam* Wri-*Weigel*(c)-*MacK*(c)).

27. *Action for Children's Television v. FCC*, 564 F.2d 458 (1977) (*Tamm*-MacK-Wilk).

28. 657 F.2d 298 (1981) (*Wald*-RGin-*RRobb*(c)).

29. 80 Stat. 250 (1966).

30. Between 1967 and 1972 only about 200 cases were filed in court to overturn agency decisions not to turn over information.

eral D.C. Circuit and Supreme Court decisions, provided for agency and judicial oversight procedures intended to achieve openness, uniformity, and speed in the bureaucratic processing of FOIA requests. The number of such requests and the amount of litigation challenging agency denials of requests increased dramatically. And one unexpected use of the law developed: businesses invoked it, not to achieve greater oversight of government agencies but to seek information about competitors.

Hospitable for the most part to the Act in the 1970s — Chief Judge Bazelon had written in *Soucie v. David*, "The policy of the Act requires that the disclosure requirements be construed broadly, the exemptions narrowly"[31] — the D.C. Circuit became the forum of choice for litigants seeking to overturn agency refusals. A remarkably wide diversity of cases invoking FOIA were decided by the courts of the Circuit, which rendered important decisions interpreting each of the seven major exemptions.[32]

One of the early contributions of the Circuit to FOIA law was the so-called Vaughn Index. In *Vaughn v. Rosen*, a law professor attempted to get documents from the Civil Service Commission, purportedly evaluations of personnel management programs of governmental agencies. Concerned that an agency might "sweep a document under a general allegation of exemption" and that existing procedures fostered inefficiency and unfairly burdened "a court system never designed to act in an adversary capacity," the Court (Judge Wilkey writing) held that the government was responsible for itemizing and indexing documents so as to specify in detail which portions of the documents were disclosable and which exempt.[33] This came to be known as a Vaughn Index, a device which helped the federal courts survive the substantial increase in FOIA litigation. In a later opinion, Judge

---

31. *Soucie v. David*, 448 F.2d 1067, 1080 (1971).

32. Among the most important of these cases were *National Park and Conservation Association v. Morton*, 498 F.2d 765 (1974) (*Tamm*-Wri-Baz) and *National Parks & Conservation Ass'n v. Kleppe*, 547 F.2d 673 (1976) (*Tamm*-MacK-Kaufman(D. Md.)), both concerning Exemption 4's protection of commercial privacy; *Cuneo v. Schlesinger*, 484 F.2d 1086 (1973) (*Wilk*-Rob-*Baz*(c)), which involved a manual of the Defense Contract Audit Agency and arguably fell into the exception for internal agency practices and rules (Exemption 2); and *Getman v. NLRB*, 450 F.2d 670 (1971) (*Wri*-RRobb-*MacK*(c)), involving personal privacy (Exemption 6). In *Weisberg v. U.S. Department of Justice*, 489 F.2d 1195 (1973) (*Dan*-Tamm-MacK-RRobb-Wilk-McG-Rob-Lev-Wri/*Baz*), the *en banc* Court of Appeals, Judge Danaher writing, vacated a panel decision and affirmed Judge Sirica, holding that FBI materials relating to the Kennedy assassination were exempt (the spectrographic analyses of the bullets had been sought).

33. *Vaughn v. Rosen*, 484 F.2d 820 (1973) (*Wilk*-Rob-Kaufman).

Wilkey provided a workable framework for courts considering requests for expedited treatment.[34]

The "Hard Look" Doctrine

One of the characteristic features of the work of the Court of Appeals during the 1970s was an ongoing debate over the proper role of the courts in overseeing administrative agencies when dealing with highly technical matters and when the agency was engaged in informal rulemaking. This dialogue was carried on especially in the environmental cases. While it was less bitter than the exchanges in the 1960s over the proper approach to the criminal law, it was a vigorous debate which spilled over into lecture halls and law reviews.

The debate was less over *how much* judicial review was called for—a clear majority of the Court supported a more demanding and skeptical mode of review than had previously been applied—than over *what kind* was most appropriate. While every member of the Court contributed to the dialogue, the differences between Chief Judge Bazelon and Judge Leventhal, two of the most influential participants, best illustrate the aspects of the debate that gained the widest attention. Whereas Bazelon's approach focused on administrative process, Leventhal's "hard look" doctrine required appraisal of the *substance* of agency decision making. It would be the Leventhal approach that would prevail.

In Bazelon's view, the Court's focus should be on assuring fairness, regularity and reasonableness in agency rule-making through quasi-procedural scrutiny of that process. Courts, Bazelon believed, should require administrative agencies to articulate the standards and principles that govern their discretional decisions in as much detail as possible. "Therefore," he declared, "even society's most technical decisions must be ventilated in a public forum with public input and participation." His approach entailed focusing on the way an agency went about its decision, rather than engaging in battles with agency experts over statistics and technology. Sometimes, especially for Judges Bazelon and Wright, this meant engrafting new procedures for the agency on top of those required by the governing statute or the Administrative Procedure Act to compel agencies to disclose data, detail reasoning, and respond to comments from aggrieved parties. In environmental law, where administrative action "touches on fundamental per-

---

34. *Open American v. Watergate Special Prosecution Force*, 547 F.2d 605 (1976) (*Wilk-*MacK-*Lev*(c)).

sonal interests in life, health and liberty," this also implied a standard of strict judicial scrutiny.[35]

Leventhal first articulated what became known as the "hard look doctrine" in an FCC case in which the Commission had terminated the license for Boston television station WHDH. The reasons for termination included excessive media concentration and improper approaches to the Commission. Leventhal argued,

> Its supervisory function calls on the court to intervene not merely in cases of procedural inadequacies or bypassing of the mandate in the legislative charter, but more broadly if the court becomes aware, especially from a combination of danger signals, that the agency has not really taken a "hard look" at the salient problems and has not genuinely engaged in reasoned decision-making.[36]

"[T]here is a will in the courts," Leventhal wrote a year and a half later, in a case which had come from the EPA, "to study and understand what the agency puts before it. And there is a will to respect the agency's choices if its has taken a hard look at its hard problems."[37]

Environmental Law

Some of the most important work of the Court of Appeals in the seventies occurred in the rapidly developing field of environmental law. The Environmental Protection Agency was brought into existence by Richard Nixon on December 2, 1970, through a reorganization that consolidated several existing agencies. New environmental and health and safety laws passed in 1974 and 1976, with virtually no presidential initiative, gave the EPA the authority to protect the air and water and to control solid waste, toxic substances and hazardous waste. The statutes included standards, deadlines and procedures that were fairly specific and not always practical.

During the 1970s the Court of Appeals dealt with many, perhaps a majority, of the important environmental cases decided in the federal courts. For example, the Court held up construction of the 789-mile Alaska

---

35. *Environmental Defense Fund v. Ruckelshaus*, 439 F.2d 584, 586 (1971) (*Baz*-Rob-RRobb). See also, e.g., *Friends of the Earth v. United States Atomic Energy Commission*, 485 F.2d 1031 (1973) (*per curiam Baz*(c)-*Lev*(c)); *International Harvester Co. v. Ruckelshaus*, 478 F.2d 615 (1973) (*Lev*-Tamm-*Baz*(c)).

36. *Greater Boston Television Corp. v. FCC*, 444 F.2d 841, 851 (1970) (*Lev*-Tamm-MacK).

37. *Environmental Defense Fund v. EPA*, 465 F.2d 528, 591 (1972) (*Lev*-Fahy-Rob).

Pipeline, ruling that the Secretary of the Interior lacked the authority to grant the necessary rights-of-way and special land use permits.[38] It also upheld decisions by the EPA administrator to prohibit the manufacture and sale of pesticides shown to be harmful to human health.[39] Judge Charles Richey's decision in *Committee for Humane Legislation v. Richardson* in 1976 belatedly put into effect strong regulations under the Marine Mammal Act of 1972 to prevent the mass killing of porpoises through "purse seines" tuna fishing.[40]

There was a particularly large number of important decisions under the Clean Air Act, not only in the Court of Appeals but also in the District Court, which played a major role in environmental litigation. Judge Thomas A. Flannery modified and approved a settlement in litigation over the Clean Air Act, mandating the EPA to promulgate regulations to control sixty-five toxic pollutants, which set in motion sweeping changes in U.S. water policy.[41] Another case involving the Clean Air Act — *Alabama Power v. Castle*, concerning sulfur dioxide reduction standards in coal burning utility plants and decided by the Court of Appeals — illustrates how extraordinarily unwieldy the new litigation could be. There were eighty parties in the case, seventeen categories of issues, a record of several thousand pages, twelve volumes of appendices, eight hundred pages of briefs, a preliminary opinion, and a final opinion with a part written by each member of the panel.[42]

38. *Wilderness Society v. Morton*, 495 F.2d 1026 (1973) (*Wri*-Baz-Rob-Lev/*MacK*(c/d)-*RRobb*(c/d)-*Wilk*(c/d)), rev'd sub nom. *Alyeska Pipeline Service Co. v. Wilderness Society,* 421 U.S. 40 (1975).

39. The Court of Appeals pressed the EPA administrator to ban the use of pesticides containing DDT and later upheld his decision to do so. See *Environmental Defense Fund v. Hardin*, 325 F. Supp. 1401 (1971); *Environmental Defense Fund v. Ruckelshaus*, 439 F.2d 584 (1971) (*Baz*-Rob-RRobb); *Environmental Defense Fund v. EPA*, 489 F.2d 1247 (1973) (Wilk-Tamm-Rob). In *Environmental Defense Fund v. EPA*, 548 F.2d 998 (1976) (*Lev*-Rob-Wilk), the Court upheld the EPA administrator's decision to suspend registrations and prohibit the manufacture and sale of the pesticides Aldrin and dieldrin.

40. 414 F. Supp. 297 (1976), aff'd, 540 F.2d 1141 (1976) (*per curiam* Wri-Rob-Wilk).

41. Important decisions under the Clean Air Act included *Kennecott Copper Corp. v. EPA*, 462 F.2d 846 (1972) (*Lev*-Wri-Tamm), in which the Court dealt with national secondary ambient air quality standards for sulfur oxide, and *Essex Chemical Corp. v. Ruckelshaus*, 486 F.2d 427 (1973) (*Tamm*-Wri-Davies(Sr. D.J. N.D.)), concerning source performance standards for sulfuric acid plants and coal-fired steam generators. See also *Natural Resources Defense Council v. Train*, 519 F.2d 287 (1975) (*RRobb*-Lev/*Nichols*(Ct.Cl.)); *Natural Resources Defense Council v. Castle*, 561 F.2d 904 (1977) (*Wilk*-RRobb-MacK); *Environmental Defense Fund v. Castle*, 636 F.2d 1229 (1980) (*Wri*-Rob-Swygert(7th Cir.)).

42. 606 F.2d 1068 (1979) (*per curiam* Lev-Rob-Wilk).

On the whole, the era of environmental regulation was welcomed warmly by the D.C. Circuit. As Judge J. Skelly Wright saw it, the Court's role was "to see that important legislative purposes, heralded in the halls of Congress, are not lost or misdirected in the vast hallways of the federal bureaucracy." This opinion came down in *Calvert Cliffs Coordinating Committee v. U.S. Atomic Energy Commission,* a pivotal case concerning the environmental impact of atomic energy. Although in the early 1970s atomic power was increasingly looked to as an important energy source and as an alternative to the pollution emitted by conventional generating plants, a majority of the members of the Court of Appeals were skeptical about the claims made for nuclear power and its regulation. In *Calvert Cliffs* the Court issued one of its farthest-reaching decisions in this field. But later in the decade it overreached and received one of the sharpest rebukes it had ever been given by the Supreme Court.

Although the National Environmental Policy Act required that federal agencies weigh the environmental impact of their activities and take corrective measures when necessary, the Atomic Energy Commission was concerned that an expansive interpretation of such authority would cause long delays in licensing new plants. Accordingly, it was cautious and restrictive in applying the new law, reluctant to involve itself with environmental hazards other than radiation. The AEC was also unwilling to make independent appraisals of anticipated environmental effects, relying instead on evaluations and standards of other federal and state authorities.

The AEC's approach was challenged by a local protest group (joined by the Sierra Club and the National Wildlife Federation) in a case involving an application the Commission had approved for the construction of a nuclear plant at Calvert Cliffs on the Chesapeake Bay, forty-six miles from Washington on the rural Western Shore of Maryland. Judge Wright's opinion for the Court of Appeals, delivered on July 23, 1971, was the first major appellate interpretation of the National Environmental Policy Act of 1969 (NEPA)[43] and a milestone in environmental law. Its influence would go well beyond the field of nuclear power.

NEPA, Judge Wright stated, "makes environmental protection a part of the mandate of every federal agency and department... as much a part of their responsibility as is protection and promotion of the industries they regulate.... We believe that the Commission's crabbed interpretation of NEPA makes a mockery of the Act." The Court ordered the AEC to provide for independent review of an environmental impact statement prepared by

---

43. 83 Stat. 852 (1970).

the AEC staff. It required new environmental impact statements for projects licensed after January 1970 and evaluation of the environmental impact of projects which had received construction permits before NEPA was in effect.[44]

The AEC did not appeal the decision, but rewrote regulations, reviewed applications, conducted hearings and trained staff members. Furthermore, thanks in large part to the *Calvert Cliffs* decision, other federal agencies assumed the same obligations in applying NEPA. Although later decisions modified or bypassed *Calvert Cliffs*, it remained a landmark ruling that established the broad-ranging effects of NEPA and the responsibilities of the federal government to carry out its purposes.

Later in the decade, however, in another case involving nuclear power, the Supreme Court administered to the Court of Appeals one of the harshest tongue lashings in its history. The chastisement specifically admonished the Bazelon-Wright wing of the Court for its procedural innovations in overseeing the administrative agencies.

Vermont Yankee Nuclear Power Corp. v. Natural Resources Defense Council brought together two cases from the Court of Appeals. *Aeschliman v. United States Nuclear Regulatory Commission* challenged AEC orders granting construction permits for two pressurized water nuclear reactors in Midland, Michigan. A local environmental group unsuccessfully argued that the Environmental Impact Statement for the project was fatally defective because it failed to examine energy conservation as an alternative to a plant of this particular size. The NRC, however, held that before licensing boards had to explore energy conservation alternatives, intervenors had to overcome a threshold test, which had not in this case been met. The Court of Appeals, Bazelon writing, reversed, holding that the Commission should not have refused to consider energy conservation alternatives.[45]

Chief Judge Bazelon also wrote the opinion in *Natural Resources Defense Council v. United States Nuclear Regulatory Commission*, decided by the Court of Appeals on the same day as *Aeschliman*, July 21, 1976.[46] The NRDC had objected to the granting of a license to the Vermont Yankee Nuclear Power Corporation to build a plant near Vernon, Vermont. In the hearing on the application, the issue of the environmental effects of operations to reprocess fuel or dispose of wastes resulting from the reprocessing operations was excluded, even though the plant was expected to pro-

---

44. *Calvert Cliffs Coordinating Committee v. AEC*, 449 F.2d 1109 (1971) (*Wri*-Rob-Tamm).

45. 547 F.2d 622 (1976) (*Baz*-Fahy-Tamm).

46. 547 F.2d 633 (1976) (*Baz*(&c)-Edw-*Tamm*(c)).

duce 160 pounds of plutonium wastes each year. The AEC had, however, instituted a rule-making proceeding on the general question of environmental effects associated with the uranium fuel cycle in the individual cost-benefit analyses for light-water-cooled nuclear power reactors.

The Court of Appeals held that, absent effective generic proceedings, the issue of reprocessing and waste disposal should be dealt with in individual licensing proceedings: "Once a series of reactors is operating it is too late to consider whether the wastes they generate should have been produced." The court then held the agency's rule-making proceeding inadequate, even though the agency employed all the procedures required by the statute and more. The notice and comment proceedings were not, the Court held, "sufficient to ventilate the issues," but were summary and conclusory. It was the role of the reviewing court, Bazelon stated, to "scrutinize the record as a whole to insure that genuine opportunities to participate in a meaningful way were provided, and that the agency has taken a good, hard look at the major questions before it." The court held that there was an insufficient record to sustain a rule so limiting consideration of the environmental effects of nuclear waste disposal.

Judge Tamm, concurring, agreed that the inadequacy of the record demanded a remand in order to ensure that the Commission had taken a hard look at the waste disposal problem, but expressed his concern that "the majority's insistence upon increased adversariness and procedural rigidity, uneasily combined with its non-direction toward any specific procedures, continues a distressing trend toward over-formalization of the administrative decision-making process which ultimately will impair its utility," Bazelon, writing an opinion concurring with his own opinion for the Court (something Leventhal also did from time to time), attempted to answer Tamm by stating that he did not believe that the need for reliable fact-finding necessarily implies transplanting trial type procedures.

In a scorching opinion—no mere rap on the knuckles, but a piling on— the Supreme Court, Justice William Rehnquist writing (two justices not sitting), unanimously reversed. The High Court said that the review by the Court of Appeals "fundamentally misconceives the nature of the standard for judicial review of an agency rule." The Supreme Court accused the Court of Appeals of misreading or misapplying the law, of engrafting its own notion of proper procedures upon the agencies, of "judicial intervention run riot," even of being "Kafkaesque."[47]

47. *Vermont Yankee Nuclear Power Corp. v. Natural Resources Defense Council*, 435 U.S. 519 (1978).

Vermont Yankee put a stop to judicial innovation in the procedural arena of administrative law, warning the courts against fashioning procedural requirements beyond those contained in the Administrative Procedure Act and administered by the agency involved. The Supreme Court essentially said that Congress had made a choice to at least try nuclear energy and had established a review process in which courts were to play only a limited role. Absent constitutional constraints or extremely compelling circumstances, the Court said, the administrative agencies should be free to fashion their own rules of procedure and to pursue methods of inquiry that would permit them to discharge their multitudinous duties. This ruled out the Bazelon approach to review of administrative action, but, as time would demonstrate, it did not make the Leventhal "hard look" impossible. Ironically, there would be a profound change in public opinion about nuclear power the following year, as a result of the accident at Three Mile Island on March 28, 1979, and the ten million dollar jury verdict in litigation brought by the estate of Karen Silkwood relating to the escape of plutonium from an Oklahoma nuclear plant.

Review of the Older Agencies

While the largest number of significant agency cases came from the Federal Communications Commission, major issues came before the courts of the District from the Securities and Exchange Commission, the Federal Trade Commission, the Civil Aeronautics Board and the various commissions regulating energy. In some of these cases the judges engaged questions that went to the heart of the regulatory agencies' charters: issues of competition and the public interest, agency rule-making powers and policies, and corporate accountability, among others.

A case from the SEC, heard by the Court of Appeals at the beginning of the decade, provided an important example of the Court's assertiveness in overseeing the agencies and its willingness to use judicial power to oversee corporate power and promote corporate democracy. The case involved an anti-war group with a few shares of the stock of Dow Chemical. The company had refused the group's request to include a resolution in its proxy statement requiring the company to stop making napalm, the critical ingredient in fire bombs used in Vietnam. After seeking relief from the SEC, which declined to take any action, the Committee sought judicial review of what the SEC argued was an unreviewable order committed to its discretion.

The opinion in *Medical Committee for Human Rights v. SEC* was written by Edward Tamm, generally no strong supporter of judicial activism. The court held that "[t]here is a substantial public interest in having important questions of corporate democracy raised before the Commission and the courts by interested responsible parties." Tamm further noted that "'discretion' can be merely another manifestation of the venerable bureaucratic technique of exclusion by attrition, of disposing of controversies through calculated non-decisions that will eventually cause eager supplicants to give up in frustration and stop 'bothering' the agency." He saw a "clear and compelling distinction" between management's legitimate exercise of discretion in day-to-day operations and its "patently illegitimate claim of power to treat modern corporations as personal satrapies implementing personal political or moral predilections."[48]

The Federal Trade Commission came to life during the Nixon administration under the chairmanships of Caspar Weinberger and Miles Kirkpatrick,[49] and during the 1970s the Court of Appeals backed the newly assertive FTC in several major cases. *National Petroleum Refiners Assn. v. FTC*, decided by the Court of Appeals in 1973, became the leading case on an agency's power to promulgate legislative rules. The case concerned a trade regulation rule adopted by the FTC which provided that failure to put octane numbers on gasoline constituted an unfair or deceptive practice. Although Judge Aubrey Robinson of the District Court held that the Commission lacked the authority to promulgate trade regulation rules that had

---

48. *Medical Committee for Human Rights v. SEC*, 432 F.2d 659 (1970) (*Tamm*-McG-Rob), vacated as moot, 404 U.S. 403 (1972). Certiorari was granted, but the case became moot when Dow included the Committee's proposal in a later proxy statement. Less than three percent of the shares voting supported the proposal. See also *Environmental Defense Fund v. Ruckelshaus*, 439 F.2d 584 (1971).

While the D.C. Circuit was not the major forum for review of the SEC, some other cases coming before it dealt with important issues. For example, *SEC v. National Student Marketing Corp.*, 457 F. Supp. 682 (1978) (Parker) considered the obligations of lawyers in securities transactions. In *National Assn. of Securities Dealers v. SEC*, 420 F.2d 83 (1969) (*per curiam* Baz(c)-Bur(c)-WMil), the Court of Appeals upheld government approval of First National City Bank's plan to operate a collective investment fund (a new form of banking activity similar to an open-end mutual fund) against opposition from the National Association of Securities Dealers, but was reversed by the Supreme Court, *Investment Co. Inst. v. Camp*, 401 U.S. 617 (1971). And in *SEC v. Dresser Industries*, 628 F.2d 1368 (1980), the Court of Appeals unanimously approved parallel investigations by the SEC and the Justice Department into the secret use of corporate funds to bribe foreign government officials.

49. Under Carter appointee Michael Pertschuk, however, the FTC became too vigorous for its own good. It became a symbol of government overregulation and in the early eighties was almost eviscerated by the Congress.

the effect of substantive law, the Court of Appeals reversed, stressing the need to "interpret liberally broad grants of rulemaking authority." As Judge Wright observed, "Increasingly, courts are recognizing that use of rule-making to make innovations in agency policy may actually be fairer to regulated parties than total reliance on case-by-case adjudication."[50]

In the 1970s the courts of the District acted to enhance competition and the public interest in the domestic airline industry. Following the Court of Appeals decision in *Moss v. CAB* (see above), which struck down the Civil Aeronautics Board's procedures for approving increases in domestic air fares, the agency instituted a series of rule-making proceedings that would allow for wider public comment and stricter judicial review. The Court of Appeals began to expound an explicitly procompetitive position in 1975, when the Court set aside a CAB order overruling an administrative-law judge who had recommended certification of competitive nonstop activity between San Diego and Denver. Writing for the Court, Judge Leventhal made it clear that "Section 102 of the Federal Aviation Act requires the Board to foster competition as a means of enhancing the development and improvement of air transportation service on routes generating sufficient traffic to support competing carriers."[51]

In an energy-conscious decade, the Federal Power Commission and its successor, the Federal Energy Regulatory Commission, repeatedly took steps to meet the energy shortages of the mid-1970s. Some of these efforts were upheld when reviewed by the Court of Appeals, some were not. The Court, for example, approved the replacement of area price ceilings for natural gas with a single nationwide ceiling, and held that the FPC's duties under the Natural Gas Act trumped its obligation to issue an environmental impact statement when establishing a temporary curtailment plan based upon end use.[52] But the Court was willing to go only so far; it rejected several of the

---

50. 340 F. Supp. 1343 (1972), rev'd, 482 F.2d 672 (1973) (*Wri*-Baz-Rob). The Court of Appeals also upheld the FTC's power to go beyond a traditional cease-and-desist order and require a company to inform consumers of inaccuracies in past advertising, even though it had not asserted that power for half a century. *Warner-Lambert v. FTC*, 562 F.2d 749 (1977) (*Wri*-Baz/*RRobb*). Although the Magnuson-Moss Act of 1974 authorized industry-wide rule-making authority for the FTC, congressional resentment of the FTC's vigorous assertion of those powers for consumer protection led in 1980 to enactment of a legislative veto over all such FTC rules.

51. *Continental Airlines v. CAB.* 519 F.2d 944 (1975) (*Lev*-Wri-Weigel).

52. *American Public Gas Ass'n v. FPC*, 567 F.2d 1016 (1977) (*Lev*-Gesell(D.D.C.)-*Fahy*(c/d)); *American Smelting & Refining Co. v. FPC*, 494 F.2d 925 (1974) (*Tamm*-

Commission's attempts to create production incentives and to relax price restrictions and certification standards.[53]

The Federal Communications Commission

Regulation of the broadcast industry during the 1970s was a vastly more complex process than it had previously been. To the perennial players—the FCC, the broadcast companies, the Washington communications bar, Congress, and the Court of Appeals—were added the White House, citizens' groups with much more muscle than before, congressional staff and, intermittently, the Supreme Court. If the industry and the Commission were as regulation-shy as before, the Court of Appeals, in a kind of *de facto* partnership with citizens' groups, and with a wary eye on the White House, demonstrated its dissatisfaction with the Commission again and again. For its part, the FCC reacted at times with undisguised rebellion.

Court and Commission disagreed on almost every important issue to come before them during the decade: license renewals, format changes, duopoly, indecent language and obscenity, affirmative action, and the future of cable.[54] Tensions between regulatory prerogatives and First Amendment

---

Fahy(c)-MacK). In the latter case, the FPC was required to make express findings demonstrating a "statutory" conflict prohibiting compliance with NEPA.

53. For example, in the Texas Gulf Coast Area gas rate cases, the Court did not approve incentives for production of oil from the Texas Gulf Coast dedicated to the interstate market in the form of higher rates, among other factors approved by the FPC, because of the absence of an adequate justification between the price adjustments and the supply problem. *Public Service Comm. for the State of New York v. FPC*, 487 F.2d 1043 (1973) (*Lev-Baz*(c/d)-*Richey*(D.D.C.)(c/d)), vacated and remanded, 417 U.S. 964 (1974). In *Consumer Federation of America v. FPC*, 515 F.2d 347 (1975) (*Lev*-Wilk-Dan), the Court set aside an FPC order allowing pipelines to make "emergency" purchases of gas on a short-term basis at rates higher than area rates, on the ground that it was not supported by statute and the Commission was neglecting its rate-control responsibilities under the Natural Gas Act. Optional certification procedures had been upheld in *Moss v. FPC*, 502 F.2d 461 (1974) (*RRobb*-Tamm-MacK), but in *Public Service Commission v. FERC*, 589 F.2d 542 (1978) (*Lev-Baz/RRobb*), the Court rejected an optional certification standard under which the Commission had permitted producers to recoup research and development costs, accusing the Commission of lapsing into "'kid glove' acquiescence to the desires of material producers."

54. Only in the area of children's programming did the Court of Appeals support the Commission in a decision not to regulate. In the controversial "kidvid" case, the Court upheld the FCC's decision to postpone action and rely on the industry's codes rather than impose rules governing programming for children on television, including

rights arose repeatedly, primarily but not exclusively in cases involving the application of the Fairness Doctrine to both commercial and noncommercial speech. Although the Court of Appeals frequently reversed or remanded to the Commission, its influence was blunted by Supreme Court intervention and other factors.

License Renewal

The widespread controversy over its decision not to renew the license of television station WHDH led the FCC, on January 15, 1970, to adopt a policy statement on renewal challenges. The policy, intended to achieve predictability and stability in the broadcast industry, provided for a two-stage process. The past performance of the applicant for renewal would first be examined, and only if its service was found to be substandard or "otherwise characterized by seriously deficiencies" would the incumbent be directly compared with the challenger, with no preference going to incumbency.[55] The Commission sought to avoid judicial review of the policy statement by arguing that it was not a formal rule, but rather a general guideline which the Commission might or might not choose to follow in particular cases.

The Court of Appeals would have none of that. In 1971 the statement was struck down as a violation of the FCC Act. Writing for the Court, Judge Wright pointed out that a pro-incumbent bias suffocated new voices. In a footnote which foreshadowed much litigation over the next two decades, he wrote, "As new interest groups and hitherto silent minorities emerge in our society, they should be given some stake in and chance to broadcast on our radio and television frequencies." According to the Court, the FCC had not achieved industry stability, but rather had "produced rigor mortis"—not a single renewal challenge had been filed in the year since the policy statement had been issued. The Court saw its decision as restoring healthy competition.[56]

The decision was condemned by the industry. *Broadcasting* magazine considered it "a new prescription for anarchy in broadcast regulation...a formula for dismemberment." The Commission's response, however, was to deal with comparative renewals on a case-by-case basis, consistently favoring incumbents. Ultimately, after several judicial remands, the FCC ar-

---

the elimination of commercials. *Action for Children's Television v. FCC*, 564 F.2d 458 (1977) (*Tamm*-MacK-Wilk).

55. "Policy Statement Concerning Comparative Hearings Involving Regular Renewal Applicants," 22 F.C.C. 2d 424 (1970).

56. *Citizens Communications Center v. FCC*, 447 F.2d 1201 (1971) (*Wri*-Wilk-MacK(c)).

ticulated a standard that related an incumbent broadcaster's level of past performance to the degree of preference it would receive in a comparative renewal hearing, but with no rebuttable presumption of renewal.[57] This standard was upheld by the Court of Appeals in 1982.[58] In the end, the broadcasters secured license stability, but at a price — the need to bargain with citizens' groups on an *ad hoc* basis over matters such as hiring and program format.

The Fairness Doctrine

A series of cases in the early 1970s involving the Fairness Doctrine inspired some of the most distinguished work of the D.C. Circuit in this period. The courts balanced the doctrine against the demands of the First Amendment and, in most cases, found them compatible, though some of these decisions provoked dissents from the Court of Appeals' most liberal judges. FCC rulings were reversed in several cases involving the airing of public issues, and upheld in at least one controversial license-renewal case. Laying the groundwork in the 1960s had been the *Red Lion* case, in which the D.C. Court of Appeals and then the Supreme Court had upheld the Fairness Doctrine against a First Amendment challenge (see chapter seven), and *Banzhaf v. FCC,* in which the Court of Appeals had approved an FCC order to a television station that it must run free public-service advertisements about the dangers of cigarette smoking.[59]

In 1971, a three-judge District Court upheld a law passed by Congress in 1969 that completely prohibited cigarette advertising in the broadcast media. Judges Oliver Gasch and June Green held that the law had no substantial effect on the exercise of the broadcasters' First Amendment rights. They "have lost no right to speak," Judge Gasch wrote, "they have only lost an ability to collect revenue from others for broadcasting their commercial messages." J. Skelly Wright dissented. Since the *Banzhaf* decision had been predicated upon the judgment that cigarette smoking and its dangers were important and controversial matters of public interest, Wright argued, Congress could hardly suppress the ventilation of information about it. "No amount of attempted balancing of alleged compelling state interests against

---

57. "Formulation of Policies Relating to the Broadcast Renewal Applicant, Stemming from the Comparative Hearing Process," 66 F.C.C. 2d 419 (1977).

58. *Central Florida Enterprises v. FCC,* 683 F.2d 503 (1982) (*Wilk*-Rob-Flannery(D.D.C.)).

59. *Red Lion Broadcasting Co. v. FCC,* 381 F.2d 908 (1967), aff'd, 395 U.S. 367 (1969); *Banzhaf v. FCC,* 405 F.2d 1082 (1968) (*Baz*-Wri/*WMil*(in part)).

freedom of the press can save this Act from constitutional condemnation under the First Amendment," he wrote. "The heavy hand of government has destroyed the scales."[60]

The Court of Appeals overruled the FCC in two important cases testing the right of broadcasters to refuse advertisements on controversial issues. In *Friends of the Earth v. FCC*, a New York station that had been running commercials for automobiles and gasoline was challenged for its refusal to accept paid advertisements presenting the case against auto pollution. The Commission upheld the station, but Judge McGowan—writing for himself and Judge Robb (Judge Miller dissented without opinion)—saw no significant difference between automotive advertisements and those for cigarettes: "Commercials which continue to insinuate that the human personality finds greater fulfillment in the large car with the quick getaway do, it seems to us, ventilate a point of view which not only has become controversial but involves an issue of public information."[61]

But another case decided the same month—August 1971—led to a Supreme Court decision that placed advertising on public policy issues in the same realm as broadcast journalism, where freedom of the press outweighs strict issues of fairness. In *Business Executives Move for Vietnam Peace v. FCC*, an antiwar organization had sought unsuccessfully to buy time on a District of Columbia radio station. A Court of Appeals panel (Judge McGowan dissenting) rejected the Commission's position that a flat ban on all editorial advertising was permissible. Judge Wright, joined by Judge Robinson, viewed broadcast licensees as the "proxies" of the people, administrators "of a highly valuable communications resource." Once broadcasters had opened their forum to commercial speech, they could not close it to political speech.[62] A divided Supreme Court, consolidating the D.C. case with another one challenging CBS over the same issue, reversed. In the leading opinion of five written by the justices, Chief Justice Burger held that the "unmistakable Congressional purpose" was to "maintain—no matter how difficult the task—essentially private broadcasting journalism held only broadly accountable to public interest standards." But if the First Amendment "could not command FCC mandates of political advertising," Burger reminded the media that fairness was relevant to license renewal.[63]

---

60. *Capitol Broadcasting Co. v. Mitchell*, 333 F. Supp. 582 (1971), aff'd, 405 U.S. 1000 (1972).
61. 449 F.2d 1164 (1971).
62. 450 F.2d 642 (1971) (Wri-Rob/McG).
63. *CBS v. Democratic National Committee*, 412 U.S. 94 (1973).

In a case recalling the *Red Lion* and *WLBT* cases of the 1960s (see chapter seven), the Court of Appeals upheld the FCC's refusal to renew the license of a right-wing radio station. But the decision prompted a notable dissent from Judge Bazelon on First Amendment grounds. WXUR of Media, Pennsylvania, just outside of Philadelphia, broadcast religious programming flavored with anti-Semitism and attacks on the Supreme Court and the United Nations. The FCC had received numerous protests and the Pennsylvania House of Representatives had called for an FCC investigation. Overruling its hearing examiner, the Commission rejected the license-renewal application because the station had failed to provide reasonable opportunities for contrasting views and had deceived the FCC by misrepresenting its program plans. On September 25, 1972, a panel of Tamm (writing), Wright and Bazelon unanimously upheld the FCC.[64]

Bazelon, however, had second thoughts. On November 4 he delivered a remarkable dissent that reexamined the value, purposes and effects of the Fairness Doctrine. He urged the FCC to

> draw back and consider whether time and technology have so eroded the necessity for governmental imposition of fairness obligations that the doctrine has come to defeat its purposes in a variety of circumstances: that we ask whether an alternative does not suggest itself— whether, as with printed press, more freedom for the individual broadcaster would enhance, rather than retard, the public's right to a marketplace of ideas.[65]

The line between free-speech rights and fairness obligations was perhaps drawn most sharply in a case arising from the FCC's first application of the Fairness Doctrine to a television documentary. The NBC film *Pensions: The Broken Promise*, an attack on abuses in private pension plans, had won the Peabody Award; but according to a conservative public-interest group, Accuracy in Media, the documentary presented a "grotesquely distorted picture of the private pension system of the United States." The Commission ordered NBC to submit a statement indicating how it intended to fulfill its fairness obligations. NBC petitioned for review.

Arrayed against NBC in the Court of Appeals were the FCC and both conservative and liberal public-interest groups. A panel of the Court of Appeals set the Commission's decision aside as a misapplication of the Fairness Doctrine. Application of the doctrine, Judge Leventhal held (Fahy concur-

---

64. *Brandywine-Main Line Radio v. FCC,* 473 F.2d 16 (1972) (*Tamm-Wri(c)/Baz*).
65. Ibid., 79.

ring), "must still recognize the enduring values of wide latitude of journalistic discretion in the licensee." Judge Tamm, concerned about the tremen-
dous power of the broadcast industry and the capacity of makers of docu-
mentaries to manipulate their presentations, dissented.[66] The FCC did not
appeal. However, after granting a request to rehear the case *en banc*, the
Court, over the vigorous dissent of Chief Judge Bazelon, remanded to the
panel on the issue of possible mootness. The panel, again divided, remanded
the issue to the FCC, which had sought permission to vacate its order.

Another arena where the Court of Appeals and the FCC wrestled over the
tension between free speech and regulation was that involving changes in
radio stations' format. During the 1970s, the Court of Appeals consistently
overturned FCC decisions (or, to be more exact, non-decisions) allowing
changes in programming format. Where the FCC preferred to let market
forces shape programming choices, the Court sought to preserve diversity
and minority listening interests within broadcast markets. As Judge Mc-
Gowan wrote for the Court in the first of these rulings, in 1970, "[I]t is surely
in the public interest for all major aspects of contemporary culture to be ac-
commodated by the commonly-owned public resources whenever that is
technically or economically feasible."[67] The Court of Appeals overruled the
Commission in three more such cases during the decade, two of them involving the loss of classical-music programming to popular-music formats.
Then, in 1980, the Supreme Court finally intervened on the side of the Commission, upholding the FCC's preference for the workings of the market over
judicial oversight of format changes on behalf of disaffected listeners.[68]

Indecent Speech

In an era when both the broadcasting industry and the Commission were
coming under considerable pressure to do something about sex and violence on television and suggestive song lyrics on the radio, the Court of Appeals supported several FCC moves to draw boundaries around such con-

---

66. *NBC v. FCC*, 516 F.2d 1101 (1974) (*Lev-Fahy*(c)/*Tamm*).

67. *Citizens Committee to Preserve WGKA v. FCC*, 436 F.2d 263 (1970) (*McG*-Tamm-
RRobb).

68. *WNCN Listeners Guild v. FCC*, 610 F.2d 838 (1979) (*McG*-Wri-Rob-RRobb-
Wilk-*Lev*(c)-*Baz*(c)/*Tamm*-MacK), rev'd, 450 U.S. 582 (1981). The other three cases in
which the Court overruled the FCC on this issue were *Citizens Committee to Preserve
WGKA v. FCC*, 436 F.2d 263 (1970) (*McG*-Tamm-RRobb); *Citizens Committee to Keep
Progressive Rock v. FCC*, 478 F.2d 926 (1973) (*Tamm*-McG—Jameson(Sr. D.J. Mont.);
Citizens Committee to Save WEFM v. FCC, 506 F.2d 246 (1974) (*McG*-Fahy-Wri-Lev-
Tamm-Rob-Wilk-*Baz*(c)/*RRobb*-MacK).

tent, and was reversed by the Supreme Court in one important instance when it did not.

In April 1971 the FCC issued a "Memorandum and Order on Drug Oriented Songs."[69] The statement was a classic example of "regulation by raised eyebrow"—a way of indicating without a rulemaking proceeding that allowing certain kinds of material on the air might subject renewal applications to particular scrutiny. Several weeks later the Commission's staff handed out a list of twenty-two songs identified as having "so-called drug-oriented lyrics." A panel of the Court of Appeals (Wilkey writing, Danaher and Robinson) upheld the rule against facial attack, expressing astonishment that a licensee would argue that it should not be required to have any knowledge of material it put out over the air waves.[70] Chief Judge Bazelon would have reheard the case *en banc.*

Two months later, a day after the FCC announced an inquiry into the broadcasting of obscene, indecent or profane material, FCC Chairman Dean Burch urged self-restraint on the industry in a speech to the National Association of Broadcasters. Two weeks after that, the Commission issued a notice of apparent liability to an Illinois station proposing forfeiture of $2,000 for the broadcast of a radio call-in program on a sex-related topic. Saying that it could not afford litigation, the station paid the fine. However, a citizens' group and the American Civil Liberties Union sought to apply to the FCC for remission of the forfeiture. The Commission allowed them to apply, but refused to grant remission. A unanimous panel of the Court of Appeals, Judge Leventhal writing, upheld the Commission, holding that the FCC could constitutionally determine that "explicit discussions of ultimate sexual acts in a titillating context" during a daytime broadcast were obscene. Chief Judge Bazelon, however, saying that the episode illustrated a whole range of "raised eyebrow tactics," and seeing the decision as a general attack on all sex-oriented talk shows, unsuccessfully sought rehearing *en banc.*[71]

In 1975 the television networks, under pressure from FCC Chairman Richard Wiley, established a so-called "family hour" during the first hour of evening prime time broadcasting. The same year, the Commission and the Court confronted the "seven filthy words" case. The case involved an afternoon broadcast by New York radio station WBAI of a monologue by comedian George Carlin. Mocking the restrictions on radio and television

69. 31 F.C.C. 2d 377 (1971).

70. *Yale Broadcasting v. FCC,* 478 F.2d 594 (1971).

71. *Illinois Citizens Committee for Broadcasting v. FCC,* 515 F.2d 397 (1974) (*Lev-Fahy-Rob*).

broadcasters, Carlin laced his monologue with seven "filthy" words which were not allowed to be heard on radio and television. Responding to a complaint, the FCC held that it had the power to regulate indecent language describing sexual or excretory acts, even where the language itself did not fit the legal test for obscenity, at times of the day when children might be in the listening audience. However, the only sanction it imposed on WBAI was an entry into a file.

A divided panel of the Court of Appeals reversed the Commission. Judge Tamm, joined by Chief Judge Bazelon, overturned the order as going outside the Commission's statutory power because it was overbroad and vague. Tamm did not reach the constitutional issue, but he did state that "the order is censorship, regardless of what the Commission chooses to call it" and pointed out that the FCC order would prohibit the broadcast of Shakespeare's *The Tempest* and *The Two Gentlemen of Verona*. In his concurring opinion, Chief Judge Bazelon, not surprisingly, did reach the constitutional issue, holding that the Constitution limited the government's power to select programming for children. Judge Leventhal dissented, seeing broadcast exposure to children as a "special enclave in the law of freedom of publication" and the FCC decision as reflecting a broad societal consensus that families would consider the language dangerous to their children. Divided 5–4 and without complete agreement on a majority opinion, the Supreme Court sided with the Commission and Judge Leventhal. The High Court held that because of the "uniquely pervasive presence of the broadcast media" the FCC could use a looser test for obscenity than what would apply to the print media.[72]

At the end of the 1970s, after an extraordinary decade in which it became the nation's prime overseer of administrative regulation, the Court of Ap-

---

72. *Pacifica Foundation v. FCC*, 556 F.2d 9 (1977) (*Tamm-Baz*(c)/*Lev*), rev'd, 438 U.S. 726 (1978).

Regulation of "indecent" programming continued to be a problem through the 1980s. In 1988 the Court of Appeals upheld FCC rules permitting the telecasting of "indecent" programming (material that falls short of being obscene or pornographic, but is considered contrary to contemporary standards for the broadcast medium) between the hours of midnight and 6 a.m., but remanded as to the time period and age group. *Action for Children's Television v. FCC*, 852 F.2d 1332 (1988) (*RGin*-Rob-Sen). Congress then imposed a blanket ban, which the Court of Appeals invalidated on constitutional grounds. Next, Congress required the FCC to prohibit the broadcasting of indecent programs between 6 a.m. and midnight. The Court of Appeals stayed the new rule and ordered the FCC to follow an interim "safe harbor" rule. *Action for Children's Television v. FCC*, 932 F.2d 1504 (1991) (*Mik*-Edw-Tho).

peals was only just beginning to deal with its obverse: deregulation. The movement toward increasing deregulation would be spurred by the incoming Reagan administration, which would also significantly reshape the Court of Appeals. A court once bitterly divided over loyalty-security and criminal cases, as well as matters of administrative law, would now divide over issues of standing, statutory interpretation, and constitutional law in cases involving the dismantling of major portions of the regulatory agencies' dominions.

Chapter 10

Changing Course
The "Reagan Court" of the 1980s

During most of the 1980s, the executive branch of the U.S. government was in the hands of the most conservative administration since that of Herbert Hoover. Ronald Reagan's administration paid conscientious attention to its appointments to the federal judiciary, achieving unusual success in choosing judges who shared its conservative philosophy: judges who would curb the power of the Congress and federal bureaucracy, who would be tougher on crime and more sympathetic to property rights, who would limit themselves to deciding narrowly defined cases and controversies.

During this decade, the most important cases coming before the courts of the District of Columbia Circuit represented a tapestry of the jurisprudential staples of the Circuit's long history. Separation-of-powers questions arose in challenges to Congress's "legislative veto" of administrative actions, the Gramm-Rudman-Hollings deficit-reduction act, and the Independent Counsel law. Civil rights issues were at the heart of cases involving affirmative action policies affecting broadcast media and municipal police and fire departments. First Amendment freedoms were tested in lawsuits seeking the right to demonstrate at symbolic sites in the capital and in libel actions for defamation in newspaper articles. The District Court was once again the seat of high-profile criminal trials, arising from the attempted assassination of the President and from the Iran-Contra scandal. And in an era of accelerating deregulation, the Court of Appeals confirmed its position as the leading forum for oversight of the nation's regulatory agencies.

As members of the Court of Appeals appointed by presidents Kennedy, Johnson and Nixon passed from the scene and were replaced by very able Carter and Reagan appointees, the old differences and personal feistiness seemed to be inherited by the new judges. The widespread acceptance of the importance of the Court and of the caliber of its judges was reinforced by the nominations of three of its members to the Supreme Court (although only one was appointed); two more would be elevated in the 1990s. In short, in a decade when an activist administration began to devolve power from the federal government to the states, the federal courts of the D.C. Circuit, both trial and appellate, continued to be extraordinarily influential.

Although monumental Washington grew ever grander during the decade, in some respects the city had still not recovered from the riots of the 1960s. In the face of declining schools and other city services and increased drug-related violent crime, the middle-class exodus from the city continued, with the black middle class constituting a large proportion of those fleeing to the suburbs. By 1990 the city's population was nearly two-thirds black and less than one-third white. Washington was split into two cities, one privileged, white, and safe, the other poor, black, and dangerous.

Such home rule as Congress permitted Washington was not a success. Homegrown politics had been stunted by a century of congressional domination, disenfranchisement and racism. During Marion Barry's tenure as mayor from 1978 to 1990, the District's government was reduced to one-party, one-man rule characterized by cronyism and corruption. The city entered the 1990s with a government much too large for its tax base, crippled by the tax-free 57 percent of the District's property and by Congress's refusal to allow a commuter tax.

Changes on the Bench

Between 1979 and 1987 the membership of the Court of Appeals turned over almost completely, as almost every judge took senior status and then retired completely or died. Counting those appointed to fill the three new judgeships Congress created in 1978 and 1982, twelve new judges took their seats in eight years, four appointed by Jimmy Carter and eight by Ronald Reagan. Among the Reagan appointees the jurisprudential affinities were such that after they constituted a majority, in 1986, it is appropriate to speak of a "Reagan Court."

The first change in the Court of the 1970s occurred in 1978 with the death of Harold Leventhal. David L. Bazelon retired as Chief Judge that same year, took senior status in 1979 and retired from the bench in 1985. J. Skelly Wright served as Chief Judge until 1981, took senior status in 1986 and died in August 1988. Carl McGowan served briefly as Chief Judge in 1981, took senior status the same year and died in December 1987. Edward Tamm died in September 1985 and Roger Robb in December 1985, at the age of seventy-eight; Malcolm Wilkey left the Court the same year. George MacKinnon took senior status in 1983, remaining active until his death in 1995. Of the nine judges in regular, active status between 1970 and 1978, only one remained at the end of the Reagan administration: Spottswood W. Robinson III, who took senior status in 1989, the year Reagan left office.

Carter's Appointments

Four of President Carter's five appointments to the District Court for the District of Columbia had served almost a decade on the Superior Court. In these appointments he recognized prior judicial experience while also reaching out to African-Americans (John Garrett Penn, appointed in 1979, and Norma Holloway Johnson, appointed in 1980) and women (Johnson and Joyce Hens Green, appointed in 1979). Harold Greene, appointed in 1978, had been Chief Judge of the Superior Court; the most visible of the Carter appointees, he will be discussed at greater length later in this chapter. Carter's first appointment to the District Court, Louis F. Oberdorfer, named in 1977, had been Assistant Attorney General in charge of the Tax Division under Robert Kennedy and had been chairman of the Lawyers Committee on Civil Rights under Law.

Jimmy Carter made four appointments to the Court of Appeals—two in 1979 to fill the new seats created by Congress, and two in 1980 to fill the vacancies caused by Harold Leventhal's death and David Bazelon's decision to take senior status. As it did in other federal jurisdictions, the Carter administration reached out to groups who traditionally have been underrepresented on the federal bench.

Carter's first nominee, Patricia M. Wald, was the first woman appointed to the Court of Appeals. She had been a frequent civil liberties advocate before the D.C. Circuit and a witness at congressional hearings dealing with legislation affecting the District of Columbia Circuit. Wald had served with the National Conference on Law and Poverty, the President's Commission on Law Enforcement and Administration of Justice, and the President's Commission on Crime in the District of Columbia; she had also been Assistant Attorney General for Legislative Affairs in the Carter administration. A group of conservative senators mustered 21 votes against her confirmation.

Carter appointed Abner Mikva to the second of the newly created seats. He had served five terms in the U.S. Congress, where he was among its most liberal members. His confirmation was bitterly fought by the gun lobby, which marshaled 31 votes against him.[1]

---

1. After Mikva's confirmation, Idaho Sen. James A. McClure brought suit in the D.C. District Court to have the appointment overturned on the grounds that it violated the Ineligibility Clause of Article I, section 6 of the Constitution (Congress had raised fed-

Harry T. Edwards was appointed in 1980 to fill the Bazelon seat. The second African-American to serve on the Court of Appeals, Edwards is a noted authority on labor law and on arbitration. He graduated from the University of Michigan Law School and taught law there and at the Harvard Law School.

To the vacancy left by the death of Harold Leventhal, Carter appointed Ruth Bader Ginsburg. She had taught law at Rutgers and Columbia, and had been the architect of the gender equality campaign mounted by the Women's Rights Project of the American Civil Liberties Union.[2] Ginsburg served on the Court of Appeals from 1980 until her appointment to the Supreme Court of the United States in June 1993. Her tenure on the D.C. Circuit was characterized by collegiality, moderation, and a keen appreciation for the metes and bounds of the law. Although she voted more often with Republican than with Democratic appointees (especially in criminal matters), Ginsburg was sympathetic to standing claims and generally voted to uphold affirmative action programs.

Reagan's Appointments

Few administrations in the twentieth century have come to power headed by men as concerned with changing the direction of the federal courts, and as interested in altering so many specific jurisprudential areas, as Ronald Reagan's. Reagan himself was not knowledgeable in the law, but two of his closest advisors, attorneys general William French Smith and Edwin Meese, were.

Reagan made six appointments to the District Court for the District of Columbia. The first, Thomas Penfield Jackson, appointed in 1982, had practiced law in the District with Jackson, Campbell & Parkinson. Thomas F. Hogan, appointed the same year, had clerked for William B. Jones and served as counsel to the National Commission for the Reform of Federal

---

eral judges' salaries during Mikva's tenure in the House). McClure, however, was denied standing because his claim to it was based on a law he himself had authored for the purpose of bringing this suit. *McClure v. Carter*, 513 F. Supp. 265 (D. Idaho, 1981), aff'd sub. nom. *McClure v. Reagan*, 454 U.S. 1025 (1981).

2. Ginsburg served as counsel in several cases brought by the project which came before the Supreme Court in the 1970s. See, e.g., *Frontiero v. Richardson*, 411 U.S. 677 (1973); *Weinberger v. Wiesenfeld*, 420 U.S. 636 (1975). In that decade she also authored several law journal articles on women's rights under the law: "Gender and the Constitution," *University of Cincinnati Law Review* 44 (1975): 1–42; "The Progression of Women in the Law," 1971, reprinted in *Valparaiso University Law Review* 28 (1994): 1161–82; "Sex and Unequal Protection: Men and Women as Victims," *Journal of Family Law* 11 (1971): 347–62.

Criminal Laws. Stanley S. Harris, appointed in 1983, was the son of the legendary "Bucky" Harris, manager of the Washington Senators. Harris had served on the D.C. Superior Court and the D.C. Court of Appeals, and had been U.S. Attorney for the District of Columbia. George H. Revercomb, the son of a Republican senator from West Virginia, had also served on the D.C. Superior Court before his appointment to the District Court in 1985. He died of cancer after eight years' service.

The most visible of the Reagan appointees to the District Court was Stanley Sporkin, appointed in 1985. He had made his career as an attorney for the SEC, rising to direct the Division of Enforcement when William T. Casey chaired the Commission. In 1981, when Casey was named head of the CIA, he appointed Sporkin General Counsel. Some conservative and business groups attempted unsuccessfully to block Sporkin's nomination to the District Court because they regarded his enforcement efforts at the SEC as anti-business. Reagan's final appointment to the District Court, Royce C. Lamberth, had been chief of the Civil Division of the U.S. Attorney's office in the District prior to his nomination.

In many of its appointments to the federal appellate courts, the Reagan administration looked for smart, strong and relatively young men who would come to the bench with their judicial philosophy well formulated. Through these appointments, the administration sought to lessen the power of the federal government in domestic affairs and to curb the power of Congress, the federal bureaucracy and the federal courts. They wanted judges who would limit themselves to deciding narrowly defined cases and controversies. They wanted the courts to be tougher on crime and more sympathetic to property rights; to achieve more accommodation and less separation between church and state; to greatly limit, if not eliminate, affirmative action programs, and to overturn *Roe v. Wade*. The administration sought "strict constructionists" who would confine interpretation of the Constitution to the perceived intent of the Framers, especially regarding restraints on the powers of the federal government; who would limit the use of legislative history in the interpretation of statutes; and who would be less likely to defer to recent precedents with which they disagreed.

President Reagan made nine appointments to the Court of Appeals for the D.C. Circuit, more than any other President. One, Judith Richards Hope, was not confirmed; the Senate declined to act on her appointment. Three—Kenneth Starr, James Buckley, and Stephen Williams—had been intended for appointment to other circuits (the Fourth, Second, and Tenth respectively), but because of the opposition of Republican senators they ended up in the D.C. Circuit. Both of Reagan's first two appointees were nominated for seats on the Supreme Court shortly after their arrival on the Court of Appeals.

The first of these was the preeminent conservative legal intellectual, Robert Bork, fifty-five years old and a professor of law at Yale. It was Bork who, as Solicitor General in the second Nixon administration, wrote the brief which may have persuaded Vice President Spiro Agnew to resign. He also carried out the removal of Special Prosecutor Archibald Cox in the "Saturday Night massacre" during the Watergate affair. In articles and lectures before, during, and after his tenure on the Court of Appeals, Bork laid out a philosophy of fidelity to the original text of the Constitution. "What does it mean," he wrote in 1990, "that a judge is bound by law? It means that he is bound by the only thing that can be called law, the principles of the text, whether Constitution or statute, as generally understood at the enactment."

Bork had been sent a clear signal when the Reagan administration took office, that he would have to serve on the Court of Appeals if he wanted the Supreme Court. Some of the intellectual baggage Bork carried into his Supreme Court confirmation hearings derived from opinions he had written on the Court of Appeals. From the beginning of his service on the Court of Appeals, Bork articulated positions that distinguished him sharply from the Carter appointees and the older liberals on the Court. Never comfortable with the primarily administrative law docket of the Court of Appeals, Bork had been considering leaving the Court at the time he was nominated for the Supreme Court. On January 7, 1988, just a few months after the failure of his bid for the High Court, Bork resigned from the Court of Appeals.

Reagan's second appointee to the Court of Appeals — and four years later, his second appointee to the Supreme Court — was Antonin Scalia. The great strength in administrative law Scalia brought to the D.C. Circuit included experience as General Counsel of the White House Office of Telecommunications Policy (1971–72), where he played a leading role in tinkering the compromise that led to the growth of cable television. He served as chairman of the Administrative Conference of the United States (1972–74) and as Assistant Attorney General in charge of the Office of Legal Counsel (1974–77). Scalia taught at the University of Virginia Law School in the late sixties and from 1977–82 at the University of Chicago Law School, where he had been one of the strongest critics of the prevailing administrative jurisprudence of the D.C. Circuit. Scalia served on the Court of Appeals from 1982 until his unanimous confirmation as Associate Justice of the Supreme Court on September 17, 1986.

On the Court of Appeals, Scalia was a leading exponent of restricting standing to sue and argued forcefully that the only legitimate interpretive guide is the text of the statute or related provisions of enacted law. He tended to vote against plaintiffs in race and gender discrimination cases, was unsympathetic to First Amendment claims, and was generally deferential to executive power. Gregarious and combative, Scalia has on both courts been known for his wit and lively participation in oral argument, as well as for his distinctive, passionate prose.

Like Bork and Scalia, Kenneth Starr, Reagan's third appointee to the Court of Appeals, did not have a long tenure there. Thirty-seven at the time of his appointment, Starr had clerked for Chief Justice Warren Burger (1975–77) and had practiced law in Los Angeles and Washington. As Attorney General William French Smith's chief of staff, Starr played an important role in the appointments of Robert Bork to the D.C. Circuit and Sandra Day O'Connor to the Supreme Court and was a major contributor to the legal ferment in the Justice Department during the early Reagan years. Starr served from October 1983 to May 1989, leaving the Court to be Solicitor General in the Bush administration. Although often voting with the conservative wing of the Court of Appeals, Starr was more moderate on First Amendment issues than most of the other Reagan appointees. He was respected by all for his affability and honesty. In August 1994 Starr was appointed Independent Counsel to investigate the Whitewater affair.

Laurence H. Silberman was fifty-five at the time of his appointment to the Court of Appeals in 1985. He has been considered for appointment to the Supreme Court several times, coming particularly close for the vacancy which went to Judge David H. Souter in 1990. He was a mentor to and strong supporter of Clarence Thomas during the battle over his confirmation to the Supreme Court. An independent conservative, Silberman has had a strong intellectual impact on the Court of Appeals, but his powerful and sometimes abrasive personality has contributed to its internal tensions.

James L. Buckley, Reagan's fifth Court of Appeals appointee, began his judicial service in 1986. The brother of the noted conservative commentator William F. Buckley, James Buckley was elected to the United States Senate from New York in 1970, serving one term. When the Republicans regained the White House in 1981, Buckley served as Undersecretary of State for Security Assistance. Although Buckley appeared to be headed to the U.S. Court of Appeals for the Second Circuit, opposition from the New York City Bar Association and Senator Lowell Weicker of Connecticut diverted him to the D.C. Circuit, which had been his first preference, when a vacancy was created by the death of Edward Tamm. Thoughtful, philosophical and polite to counsel, Buckley tended in his rulings to be pro-business and pro-government when they were not mutually exclusive.

The appointment of Stephen F. Williams to the Court of Appeals, in 1986, came just before his fiftieth birthday. From 1969 until his appointment to the bench, Williams was a professor of law, primarily at the University of Colorado Law School. Williams has written extensively on energy law and policy and on property rights, and has brought to the Court of Appeals considerable strength in these important areas of the Court's work.

Douglas Ginsburg was appointed to the Court of Appeals in October 1986 at the age of forty. He had clerked for Carl McGowan and Justice Thurgood Marshall. As a professor at the Harvard Law School (1975–83), Ginsburg had specialized in administrative law and antitrust, and was the author of *Regulation of Broadcasting: Law and Policy towards Radio, Television and Cable Communications* (1979). A market-oriented conservative, Ginsburg had worked in the Reagan Justice Department and the Office of Management and Budget as a specialist in regulatory affairs; in 1985–86 he served as Assistant Attorney General in charge of the Antitrust Division.

When Robert Bork was denied confirmation to the Supreme Court, conservatives at the Justice Department outmaneuvered more moderate and cautious aides to the President and secured the nomination of Ginsburg. However, Ginsburg lost the support of conservatives in the Congress over accusations of conflicts of interest while in the Justice Department and for overstating his trial experience and admitting to having smoked marijuana in the 1970s. His nomination was withdrawn.

David B. Sentelle was appointed to the Court of Appeals in October 1987. Sentelle had judicial experience, having served as a district judge of the North Carolina General Courts of Justice (1970–74) and as U.S. District Judge for the Western District of North Carolina (1985–87). He also had been visiting professor at the University of North Carolina's Charlotte and Chapel Hill campuses. His appointment to the District of Columbia Circuit was controversial because of his close association with Senator Jesse Helms and his membership in an all-male, all-white club.

During the Reagan years the Court of Appeals was such an intellectually high-powered court that it was known jocularly as "the Court of Appeals for the Academic Circuit." In 1988, for example, the Court had six members who had been full-time law professors and three others who had clerked for noted judges. In the 1980s, opinions of the Court of Appeals grew still longer and more heavily footnoted (although Judge Mikva abandoned footnoting entirely) and separate statements of opinion proliferated.

The Court of Appeals also continued to be a place of considerable discord. Some of this was undoubtedly the result of the unprecedented turnover between 1978 and 1986. Although well over 90 percent of the total number of cases were decided without dissent, differences between the Kennedy-Johnson-Carter appointees and the Reagan appointees were pronounced in important cases involving standing, attorneys' fees, deference to administrative agencies, the Freedom of Information Act and the First Amendment. As Judge Mikva wrote in 1989, "Pick a controversial subject in our democracy, and you can find at least two points of view expressed by judges of the D.C. Circuit."[3]

Once President Reagan's appointees constituted a majority, in 1986, Judge Bork led them in employing rehearings *en banc* to overturn panel decisions with which they disagreed—a tactic that led to ill feelings on the part of the other judges. Even though the number of *en bancs* was not that much higher than it had been during the 1970s, the cases were significant—over half involved constitutional questions, administrative law, or energy regulation. Friction was also caused by elaborate dissents in panel cases, which often were ill-disguised invitations to the Supreme Court to reverse the Court of Appeals—invitations the High Court accepted far more often than in cases coming from other circuits. As Patricia Wald wrote in 1993, in this court, more than in most circuits, could be found "the parade of horribles, the slippery slope, the barbed jibe, the ad hominem jab, the bitter accusation, the catastrophic prediction."

Judicial Administration

The District Court

Rising caseloads made effective judicial administration vitally important to federal courts throughout the nation in the 1980s. Although the overall number of cases filed in the U.S. District Court for the District of Columbia did not increase much during the 1980s, an increase in the number of cases brought against the United States added considerable complexity to the docket. Two developments in particular contributed to an overflowing docket in the District Court: new federal sentencing guidelines and the war on drugs.

In the mid-1980s, Congress created a Sentencing Commission, on which Judge George E. MacKinnon served, charged with establishing sentence ranges for every federal crime. The sentencing guidelines created by the Commission assigned every crime a level of heinousness and every crimi-

---

3. Judge MacKinnon and Judge Wilkey, both Nixon appointees, began to find their newest colleagues too ideological for them, according to interviews the author had with them in December 1990 and February 1995, respectively.

nal a degree of nefariousness. Elaborate grids representing these variables measured each convict's offense and criminal history and mandated sentences accordingly, although federal judges could depart from the guidelines if certain mitigating or aggravating circumstances were found. As mandatory minimum sentences decreased defendants' incentive to plea bargain, the number of jury trials increased substantially.

One of the strategies in the war against drugs was to bring relatively trivial prosecutions in federal rather than state courts because federal courts were more likely to impose long sentences. Between 1984 and 1990 the percentage of drug defendants as a proportion of all defendants in criminal cases in federal courts rose from 32.6 percent to 68.1 percent. By the late eighties drug offenders were overcrowding federal prisons and drug cases clogged the dockets and caused security problems within the courthouse (leading drug dealers were tried in bulletproof courtrooms). These developments, intersecting with the impact of sentencing reform, created a crisis of morale among U.S. district judges throughout the country.

Where drug offenses were concerned, the length of an offender's sentence was determined primarily by the weight of the drugs involved in the offense. Mandatory minimum sentences had to be imposed for crimes involving certain quantities of drugs, regardless of whether the defendant was a high-level operator or merely a "mule" carrying drugs. By the end of the 1980s, forty-two percent of the male population of Washington, D.C. between the ages of eighteen and thirty-five were in prison or under some form of court supervision, such as probation or parole. Federal judges in the District of Columbia, like those throughout the country, grew increasingly disturbed over the harshness of the sentences they had to impose.[4]

At a time when judicial administration mattered, the District Court for the District of Columbia was fortunate to have a decisive, independent, nononsense judge with considerable "people skills." The formal powers held by chief judges of federal courts—the power to empanel grand juries, receive indictments from the grand juries, and dispose of matters requiring immediate action in cases already assigned to any judge—are ordinarily not very significant, and give a chief judge little leverage over his life-

---

4. Responding to years of criticism of the policy as capricious, fundamentally unfair and choking dockets with low level drug cases, in 1993 interim U.S. Attorney J. Ramsey Johnson announced that the office would emphasize the prosecution of mid-level drug organizations which controlled street corners and neighborhoods, with lower level figures prosecuted in Superior Court. Only if a defendant was caught with more than 50 grams of crack cocaine would the case be brought in federal court.

tenured colleagues (although they undoubtedly contributed to Chief Judge
John Sirica's remarkable Watergate performance). To a much greater extent,
the influence chief judges can wield derives from the impact of their personalities. The intangible qualities necessary to be an effective judicial administrator were embodied in Aubrey E. Robinson Jr., who was Chief Judge
for almost a decade, from September 1982 to March 1, 1992.

Robinson, born in 1922 to an middle-class African-American family in
Madison, New Jersey, was a graduate of Cornell University Law School. He
came to Washington to work for the civil rights attorney-activist Belford V.
Lawson, at whose home he lived while studying for the bar. In 1953 Robinson opened his own law firm with Charles R. Duncan, who later would become D.C. Corporation Counsel. Although historically African-American
attorneys in the District had survived primarily by handling criminal cases,
Robinson's firm focused on domestic and landlord-tenant matters, as well
as estate law. While he was in practice, Robinson was involved with a number of social-welfare organizations and was particularly concerned with the
young. He was, therefore, a particularly apt choice to succeed Marjorie
McKenzie Lawson as judge of the Juvenile Court in 1965. One year later,
Lyndon Johnson appointed him to the District Court.

Combining considerable warmth with a very thick hide, Robinson was
a strong, but not a domineering chief judge. Coming to the Chief Judgeship at a relatively young age, Robinson was flexible and able to think ahead.
He worked well with the chief judges of the Court of Appeals and won the
cooperation and good will of his court's officers and administrative employees. Aware, as he put it, that "judges only speak to themselves and God,"
he never tried to force change on his colleagues. The success of the experiment in Alternative Dispute Resolution was one example of his method.
Rather than simply impose this system of mediation and case evaluation
on his fellow judges, Robinson made it a voluntary option for those who
wanted to try it, and it soon caught on.[5] On some matters, though, he was

---

5. In 1989, the District Court began to experiment with Alternate Dispute Resolution (ADR) with two programs—mediation and early neutral evaluation (ENE), a
process in which parties obtain from an experienced neutral party a non-binding, reasoned, oral evaluation of their case on its merits. The program was voluntary for the
parties as well as the judges. Three types of cases were chosen: contract, auto personal
injury, and other personal injury. In the first two and one-half years, about 700 cases
were diverted to the program. 55 percent of the mediated cases and 49 percent of those
given Early Neutral Evaluation were settled. By 1991, seventeen district judges were involved in the program. By 1993, over a thousand cases had gone through the District

tough. Believing that most elderly judges were hostile to change, Robinson would not let senior judges vote on policy matters.

Robinson was responsible for a distinct improvement in the treatment of jurors, the principal point of contact between the Court and the public. Believing that pleasant physical surroundings affect people's attitudes and help them work and produce well, Robinson worked for the creation of a new juror lounge, a bigger and brighter space that opened in 1992. His Chief Judgeship was also marked by improvements in physical security, a reduction in the number of grand juries and the beginning of the reorganization of the Clerk's Office.

During this period, some progress was made in the provision of legal services for the poor. Resolutions adopted by the Circuit Judicial Conference, followed up by bench-bar committees spurred by Judges Oberdorfer and Gesell, led to the establishment of a volunteer panel of attorneys, law firms, and law school clinics to represent indigent litigants in the District Court, where as many as 25 percent of the civil cases are filed *pro se*. Over the first three years of the program, counsel were appointed in 200 cases, primarily in prisoner litigation, job discrimination, and Freedom of Information Act cases. A Civil Litigation Fund was also established to compensate attorneys for expenses incurred in representing indigent clients. In addition, the Federal Defender's Office was established in 1990 to provide representation to indigent defendants charged with federal criminal offenses.

The Court of Appeals

During the 1980s, the Court of Appeals' caseload grew in both quantity and complexity. By fiscal year 1982 almost two-thirds of the Court's work consisted of agency cases, which were considerably more complex, on average, than the local cases that had been the Court's staple until the 1970s. Although enlarged by the addition of two regular judgeships in 1978 and another one in 1982, the Court of Appeals still required the assistance of senior, visiting and district judges. Like most of the regional courts of appeals, the U.S. Court of Appeals for the District of Columbia Circuit resolved many cases summarily—by boilerplate order or short opinion *per curiam*. While many of the 300 signed opinions it issued each year were much longer and

---

Court ADR programs, including a major class action suit involving more than 25,000 class members and a $38 million settlement. What had begun as a modest experiment in 1989 had within a very few years become an established and accepted case-management tool.

more heavily footnoted than the Court's opinions a generation before, these signed opinions represented only a minority of the cases it heard.

Patricia Wald, the best administrator of the Court of Appeals in generations, became Chief Judge in 1986 and served until 1991.[6] Her tenure saw considerable reform in the ways the Court coped with its caseload. In addition to computerization of several systems within the courthouse,[7] a new case-management process was introduced, alternative dispute resolution programs were begun, and greater reliance was placed upon the Office of Staff Counsel.

The Court of Appeals began implementing the new case-management process in 1986. By encouraging dispositive motions to dismiss or by summary affirmance or reversal, the Court was able to dispose of more cases more quickly. A three-track system was created for cases: those that could be disposed of by special panels without oral argument; those to be given regular treatment; and those cases (perhaps a dozen each year) of such length and complexity that specially designated panels would manage them from beginning to end.

An appellate mediation program began in 1987 with eleven volunteer mediators. Its creation was stimulated by the Circuit Executive, Linda Finkelstein (now Ferren), who had created the Multi-Door Dispute Resolution Program of the Superior Court. By 1991, the mediation program was settling one-third of its cases, with government cases settling at a higher rate than private cases.[8]

The Office of Staff Counsel had been established in the late 1970s to administer the Civil Appeals Management Plan for large, multi-party cases

---

6. After Bazelon's fifteen-year tenure, the office of Chief Judge of the Court of Appeals was held by J. Skelly Wright (March 1978–January 1981), Carl McGowan (January–May 1981), and Spottswood Robinson (May 1981–July 1986), before Wald took that office.

7. Automation came to the courts of the Circuit in the 1980s, when all chambers were equipped with personal computers with direct access to legal research services. In 1989 the Court of Appeals adopted a new system for printing slip opinions. They were prepared in chambers on computer, transmitted electronically to the printer using a modem and telephone lines, typeset by the printer on an automatic system, and returned via fax to chambers. In 1992 the Court of Appeals began using a new electronic docketing system, called NewAIMS, and the Judges' Library began to develop a CD-ROM reference collection.

8. The program was reorganized in 1989, when cases began to be screened for mediation by the Chief Staff Counsel's Office. Nancy Stanley, an attorney and an experienced mediator, joined the staff of the Circuit Executive's Office in 1989 as coordinator of the program.

and to assist in preparing the Court's calendar. In the 1980s the office became the Court's central legal staff, drafting orders for contested motions and emergency matters and screening every appeal in order to recommend which cases could be disposed of without oral argument and which might be included in the appellate mediation program.

Separation of Powers

While the courts of the Circuit reached the merits in several major separation-of-powers cases in the 1980s, a great many more were decided on threshold issues. Perhaps the major battlefield for these cases in the D.C. Circuit of the 1980s was the issue of standing. Throughout the early years of the decade, members of Congress often pursued political goals through the courts. Most of these challenges were dismissed for lack of standing on various grounds, from "prudential concerns" to "equitable discretion" to "ripeness" to "political question." On the whole, the Reagan appointees on the Court of Appeals were especially hostile to congressional standing, writing several dissents from decisions dismissing on prudential grounds, a route often taken by the Nixon appointees.[9]

Early in the decade, when affirming the dismissal of a suit brought by Senator Donald W. Riegle challenging certain procedures under the Federal Reserve Act, Judge Robb employed a doctrine of circumscribed discretion to reflect separation-of-powers concerns: "Where a Congressional plaintiff could obtain substantial relief from his fellow legislators through the enactment, repeal, or amendment of a statute, this court should exercise its equitable discretion to dismiss the legislator's action."[10] Judge June Green invoked the doctrine of equitable discretion to dismiss a suit brought by members of Congress against the President and Secretary of State challenging the constitutionality of the military action in Grenada.[11]

That case was one of a series in which members of Congress unsuccessfully appealed to the courts of the Circuit to prevent unilateral resort to the

---

9. See Judge Scalia's concurring opinion in *Moore v. United States*, 733 F.2d 946 (1984) (*Wilk*-Gasch(D.D.C.)-*Sca(c)*), and Judge Bork's opinions in *Vander Jagt v. O'Neill*, 699 F.2d 1166 (1982) (*Gordon*-RRobb-*Bork(c)*) and *Barnes v. Kline*, 759 F.2d 21 (1984) (*McG*-Rob/*Bork*).

10. *Riegle v. Federal Open Market Committee*, 656 F.2d 873, 881 (1981) (*RRobb*-Edw-Penn(D.D.C.)).

11. *Conyers v. Reagan*, 578 F. Supp. 324 (1984), appeal dismissed, 765 F.2d 1124 (1985) (*Tamm*-Wald-Bork).

war powers by the executive. In a suit involving military aid to El Salvador, brought by members of Congress under the War Powers Act, Judge Joyce Green declined to exercise equitable discretion to settle what she saw as a dispute between partisan legislators. In another, Judge Howard Corcoran dismissed a challenge to the administration's support of the Nicaraguan Contras because it presented a non-judicial political question. And later in the decade Judge Revercomb, on prudential and political-question grounds, declined jurisdiction of a suit contesting the President's actions in the Persian Gulf.[12]

In what probably were the three most important separation-of-powers cases in the Circuit during this period, the judges wrestled with the constitutionality of the legislative veto, the budgetary process Congress established in the 1985 Gramm-Rudman-Hollings Act, and the Independent Counsel mechanism. All three were held unconstitutional by courts of the circuit. The Supreme Court agreed about the first two, but not about the third.

The Legislative Veto

The "legislative veto" was created by the Congress in the 1930s as a way to retain some control over the President's power to reorganize executive branch agencies. Through it, Congress broadly delegated power to the executive branch but reserved the authority to review and veto executive action taken pursuant to the grant. During the 1970s Congress created scores of legislative vetoes—some of which were single-house vetoes—to control executive and bureaucratic excess. In the post-Watergate era, the legislative veto became a thorn in the side of presidents in battles over the war powers, impoundments, and arms sales. Presidents Carter and Reagan both opposed it, although the latter appreciated its value in limiting government regulation.

In the early 1980s a D.C. Circuit case seemed poised to be the vehicle by which the constitutionality of the legislative veto would finally be confronted by the Supreme Court, which had previously considered the issue

---

12. *Crockett v. Reagan*, 558 F. Supp. 893 (1982), aff'd, 720 F.2d 1355 (1983) (*per curiam* Edw-Lumbard(2d Cir.)-*Bork*(c)); *Sanchez-Espinoza v. Reagan*, 568 F. Supp. 596 (1983), aff'd, 770 F.2d 202 (1985) (*Sca*-Tamm-*RGin*(c)); *Lowry v. Reagan*, 676 F. Supp. 333 (1987).

In the run-up to the 1991 Gulf War, when 54 members of Congress filed suit to prevent the United States from going to war with Iraq without a congressional declaration, Judge Harold Greene rejected the sweeping executive claim that the determination as to whether certain types of military actions require a declaration of war was never one for the courts. Nevertheless, he found the action unripe. *Dellums v. Bush*, 752 F. Supp. 1141 (1990). Compare *Ange v. Bush*, 752 F. Supp. 509 (1990) (Lamberth).

unripe.[13] In the end, it was addressed in the Ninth Circuit's *Chadha* case, involving a legislative veto to oppose Immigration and Naturalization Service exemptions to deportation orders. But Malcolm Wilkey's comprehensive and impressively reasoned opinion in the D.C. case would be closely tracked in the Supreme Court's *Chadha* opinions, both the Chief Justice's opinion for the Court and Justice Powell's important concurring opinion.[14]

Consumer Energy Council v. Federal Energy Regulatory Commission involved an incremental pricing program administered by the FERC which shifted part of the price increase caused by the deregulation of new natural gas from residential to industrial users. The House of Representatives had vetoed one of the regulations imposed under the program. On June 29, 1982, the Court of Appeals held that the legislative veto "contravenes the constitutional procedures for making law." In his opinion, Malcolm Wilkey discussed the effect of the veto on the President's ability to protect his authority from encroachment and on his capacity to check unwise legislation. The exercise of the legislative veto may, Wilkey argued, "enable one house of Congress effectively to dictate that a specific type of rule be promulgated" and therefore allows Congress "to expand its role from one of oversight, with an eye to legislative revision, to one of shared administration" — a contravention of "the fundamental purpose of the separation of powers doctrine."[15]

---

13. In *Buckley v. Valeo* (see chapter 9), the Supreme Court ruled that Congress could not reserve for itself the power to appoint members to a body exercising executive powers, but held that it would *not* decide the legislative veto issue at that time. 424 U.S. 1, 140 n.176 (1976). The issue returned to the courts of the D.C. Circuit in 1977 in *Clark v. Valeo*, another case involving the Federal Election Campaign Act Amendments of 1974. In *Clark*, regulations of the newly constituted Federal Election Commission subject to legislative veto were challenged. Only two members of the Court believed the central issues ripe for review — Spottswood Robinson, who wanted to hear further argument on the merits, and George MacKinnon, who thought the legislative veto unconstitutional. "The point," Judge MacKinnon argued in one of his finest opinions, "is that the Congressional veto scheme, whether exercised or not, makes Congress a working party in the executive functioning of the agency" and greatly increases the authority of a small minority of the entire Congress to achieve a legislative result. 559 F.2d 642 (1977) (*per curiam* McG-Wilk-*Tamm*(c)-Baz-Wri-*Lev*(c)/*Rob-MacK*).

14. *INS v. Chadha*, 462 U.S. 919, 959 (1983).

15. *Consumer Energy Council of America v. Federal Energy Regulatory Commission*, 673 F.2d 425 (1982) (*Wilk*-Baz-Edw), aff'd, 463 U.S. 1216 (1983). Aware that the case was likely to reach the High Court, Wilkey had announced himself "determined to cover every blooming point that could be raised about the veto, in part for my own personal satisfaction, but also to do a job for the Supreme Court."

Following this decision, the Court of Appeals acted in other cases involving the legislative veto with unusual agreement, brevity, and dispatch. Unanimously, and in two pages, the Court held a statutory provision which permitted a veto of FTC regulations unconstitutional, and soon afterward struck down a scheme which permitted a veto of HUD reorganizations by a congressional committee.[16] When it decided *Chadha*, the Supreme Court vigorously reasserted formal separation-of-powers principles and rejected congressional encroachment on executive powers. One week later, without opinion, the High Court upheld the Court of Appeals in the FERC and FTC cases.

The Gramm-Rudman-Hollings Act

The Balanced Budget and Emergency Deficit Control Act of 1985, better known as the Gramm-Rudman-Hollings Act, became law on December 12, 1985.[17] The law set maximum federal deficits for fiscal years 1986–91 and required automatic reductions in federal spending programs should the federal deficit exceed the maximum deficit amount in any given year. In such an event, the Comptroller General (an officer appointed by the President but removable only by Congress) was to specify the budget reductions needed to ensure compliance and report his conclusions to the President, who was then required to issue a sequestration order mandating the budget reduction.

Within hours of the bill becoming law, Representative Mike Synar of Oklahoma filed a complaint seeking declaratory relief. Shortly afterward, an identical suit was filed by the National Treasury Employees Union. The two actions were consolidated and heard before a special three-judge District Court provided for under the Act.[18]

The three-judge court, made up of Judges Antonin Scalia, Norma Holloway Johnson, and Oliver Gasch, held that there was standing. It also held that Congress had the authority to delegate its budgetary powers as part of an "intricate administrative mechanism" to address the goal of a balanced

---

16. *Consumers Union v. Federal Trade Commission*, 691 F.2d 575 (1982), aff'd sub nom. *United States House of Representatives v. FTC*, 463 U.S. 1216 (1983); *American Federation of Government Employees, AFL-CIO v. Pierce*, 697 F.2d 303 (1982). Three judges—Wald, Mikva, and Wright—would have granted a rehearing of the latter case *en banc*.

17. 99 Stat. 1038.

18. The history of the litigation is given in Judge Gasch's opinion in *Synar v. United States*, 670 F. Supp. 410 (1987).

budget by fiscal year 1991. However, the Court ruled that the delegation of powers to the Comptroller General was unconstitutional, since those powers were executive powers, which could not constitutionally be exercised by an officer removable by Congress. As a result, the automatic reduction process to which those powers were central could not be implemented.[19] That this mechanistic view of legislative and executive powers also had serious implications for the independent regulatory commissions, whose functions were both executive and legislative and which often were exceedingly responsive to the Congress, was suggested by the dictum of the District Court, which was widely quoted: "It is not as obvious today as it seemed in the 1930s that there can be such things as genuinely 'independent' regulatory agencies, bodies of impartial experts whose independence from the President does not entail correspondingly greater dependence upon the committees of Congress to which they are then immediately accountable."

In Warren Burger's last opinion as Chief Justice, the Supreme Court affirmed by 7–2, on grounds similar to those given by the District Court.[20] In dissent, Justice White argued that as a practical matter the Comptroller General was not unduly dependent upon Congress, but was one of the most independent officers in the entire federal establishment.

The Independent Counsel

The Supreme Court's decisions in the *Chadha* and Gramm-Rudman-Hollings Act cases raised serious doubts about the constitutionality of the statutory mechanism for appointment of Independent Counsel. In the Ethics in Government Act of 1978,[21] one of the series of oversight laws passed in the wake of Watergate, Congress had established a permanent mechanism for such appointments. Attempting to strike a balance between executive responsibility for enforcement of the laws and the need to effectively oversee the executive, Congress divided responsibility for the appointment and oversight of Independent Counsel between the Attorney General and the judiciary.

The law provided for the establishment of a special division of the Court of Appeals for the District of Columbia Circuit—a three-judge panel to be constituted by the Chief Justice of the United States from senior or retired circuit judges from anywhere in the nation, the presiding judge to come from the D.C. Circuit. Since it was instituted, the Special Division has been headed by Roger Robb, George MacKinnon, and David Sentelle. Under the

19. *Synar v. United States*, 626 F. Supp. 1374, 1391 (1986).
20. *Bowsher v. Synar*, 478 U.S. 714 (1986).
21. 92 Stat. 1824.

statutory scheme, the Attorney General was charged with conducting a preliminary investigation of alleged violations of federal criminal laws by high-ranking officials of the executive branch, the results of which were to be filed with the Special Division and were not reviewable. If the Attorney General recommended further investigation, the Special Division was to select a special prosecutor.

The Special Division remains an unusual court. It does not convene in public and rarely has had an adversarial proceeding before it, other than disputes over payment of legal fees. Its discretionary decisions are not reviewable. Its role is to compile a list of possible special prosecutors, select one when requested by the Attorney General, and define his or her investigative and procedural jurisdiction. The Special Division has the power to expand the jurisdiction of the Independent Counsel beyond that requested by the Attorney General, retains supervisory power, and receives and reviews the prosecutor's report.[22]

The Carter administration had lived grudgingly with the special prosecutor law and the Reagan administration was actively hostile to it. By 1987, the Reagan administration had more than separation-of-powers reasons for hostility to the Act: Independent Counsels had been or were investigating several of the President's closest personal and political friends, including former presidential aides Michael Deaver and Franklyn C. Nofziger for offenses related to lobbying activities after they left the White House. Furthermore, Lawrence Walsh had been appointed Special Prosecutor to investigate the Iran-Contra affair. In these circumstances, Reagan had little option but to sign the Independent Counsel Reauthorization Act of 1987, reauthorizing the Independent Counsel mechanism with new reporting requirements limiting some of the Attorney General's discretion.[23]

---

22. One of the unusual features of the D.C. Circuit is the presence of several specialized tribunals, which are either housed in the U.S. Courthouse or whose members, chosen by the Chief Justice, ordinarily include judges from the Circuit. for example, the Foreign Intelligence Surveillance Court, created in 1978, has authority to grant orders approving electronic surveillance of foreign governments and their representatives anywhere in the United States, as well as groups suspected of involvement in international terrorism. The first Chief Judge of the Foreign Intelligence Surveillance Court was George L. Hart Jr. John Lewis Smith was Chief Judge from 1982 to 1988 and Joyce Hens Green, appointed to the Court in 1988, became Chief Judge in 1990. There is also a three-judge Foreign Intelligence Surveillance Court of Review, which reviews denials of any applications for a surveillance order, of which George MacKinnon was chief judge for several years.

23. 101 Stat. 1293.

Serious constitutional challenges to the revised law were soon posed in litigation in the D.C. Circuit. Michael Deaver and National Security Council operative Oliver North, a target of the Iran-Contra investigation, sued in the District Court to have the investigations against them enjoined and the law declared unconstitutional. Both suits were rebuffed, Deaver's by Thomas Penfield Jackson, who ruled that Deaver had a remedy which would be available to him after indictment, North's by Barrington Parker, who held the action not ripe for judicial review.[24] Both judges at least implied that they believed the law would not be held unconstitutional.

Deaver was tried before Judge Jackson and convicted of three counts of perjury. Nofziger, prosecuted by Independent Counsel James McKay before Thomas Flannery, was convicted, but a divided panel of the Court of Appeals overturned the conviction by narrowly construing the Ethics in Government Act.[25] Responding to the Nofziger decision and to Independent Counsel Whitney North Seymour's argument that the Ethics in Government Act of 1978 was virtually unenforceable and offered little real protection to the Congress created a sweeping ban on lobbying by former senior government officials.

The constitutional issue reached the U.S. Supreme Court in a case fraught with partisanship. The case, involving Theodore Olson, Assistant Attorney General for the Office of Legal Counsel, had begun as a dispute between Congress, the Environmental Protection Agency, the Justice Department, and the President over the release of documents relevant to the toxic waste disposal program. It was alleged that Olson had lied to a congressional subcommittee about advice regarding executive privilege given to the President by the Justice Department.

Two years after Olson appeared before the subcommittee, the Democratic majority of the House Judiciary Committee asked the Attorney General to appoint an Independent Counsel. Meese referred the allegations to the Special Division, which appointed Alexia Morrison as Independent Counsel.[26] After the Special Division somewhat expanded Morrison's jurisdiction at her request,[27] her authority was challenged on constitutional grounds in motions to quash her subpoenas. That challenge was backed by the Depart-

---

24. *Deaver v. Seymour*, 656 F. Supp. 900 (1987); *North v. Walsh*, 656 F. Supp. 414 (1987).

25. *United States v. Nofziger*, 878 F.2d 442 (1989) (*Buc*-Will/*Edw*).

26. James C. McKay was first appointed Independent Counsel in this case, but resigned because of a conflict of interest.

27. *In re Olson*, 818 F.2d 34 (1987).

ment of Justice. Chief Judge Aubrey Robinson upheld the statute as a "measured response to the recurrent question of how to enforce the laws of the United States when they are violated by high government officials."[28]

In January 1988 a divided panel of the Court of Appeals struck down the Independent Counsel provisions of the Act.[29] In a lengthy opinion, Judge Silberman held that the statute violated the Appointments Clause of Article II of the Constitution, the Article III limitations on the doctrine of separation of powers and the clause which requires the President to faithfully execute the laws. "[T]he Act viewed as a whole," Silberman wrote, "taking into account its appointment, removal, and supervisory provisions, so deeply invades the President's executive prerogatives and responsibilities and so jeopardizes individual liberty as to be unconstitutional."

Ruth Bader Ginsburg dissented. She argued that the arrangement was not an undue intrusion into executive prerogatives and that the role of the Special Division, taken as a whole, was more administrative than advisory. She concluded that the Act, "a carefully considered congressional journey into the sometimes arcane realm of the separation of powers doctrine," was "designed to prevent Congress's own appropriation of the functions it insulates from executive supervision," and that it "implements a fundamental control essential to our Constitution's doctrine of separated powers: the control of mutual checks."

The Supreme Court immediately noted probable jurisdiction and added to the drama by establishing an expedited schedule for briefing and oral argument.[30] In view of the High Court's preference for a formalistic rather than flexible approach to separation of powers, as manifested in the *Chadha* and Gramm-Rudman-Hollings Act cases, there was considerable doubt that the law could withstand High Court review. Interest in argument was so high that Olson himself, a prominent member of the District of Columbia bar, was able to get into the hearing only by joining the public line at 5 a.m.

Deciding the case in the middle of the Iran-Contra scandal, the Supreme Court stepped back from "the slippery slope of formalism," upholding the Independent Counsel mechanism by a vote of 7–1.[31] Only Justice Scalia dissented. Writing for the Court, Chief Justice Rehnquist held that judicial appointment of Independent Counsel was a logical way for Congress to insure independent investigation; that the Appointments Clause did not

28. *In re Sealed Case*, 665 F. Supp. 56 (1987).
29. 838 F.2d 476 (1988) (*Sil-Will/RGin*).
30. 484 U.S. 1058 (1988).
31. *Morrison v. Olson*, 487 U.S. 654 (1988).

prohibit interbranch appointments; and that there was no threatening intrusion into executive functions.

After an investigation of close to three years, Morrison did not seek to indict Olson, whose lawyers' fees totaled over $1,250,000. After a troubled life, the statute authorizing the Independent Counsel was allowed to lapse on June 30, 1999.

Administrative Law

The Court of Appeals entered the 1980s somewhat chastened by the Supreme Court's 1976 *Vermont Yankee* decision (see chapter 9) and would be further constrained by reversals in two other important cases, *Chevron U.S.A. v. Natural Resources Defense Council* and *Heckler v. Chaney*. Further, divisions between the Court's Carter and Reagan appointees on issues of standing and statutory interpretation pervaded agency cases.[32] Nevertheless, much of Judge Leventhal's "hard look" approach survived and the Court of Appeals made important contributions to administrative law, particularly in the environmental and communications fields. During this period, the Court of Appeals was hearing about one-fifth of agency cases (exclusive of the NLRB) appealed to all the circuits, and was generally supportive of the agencies.

Throughout the 1980s there was considerable dialogue between members of the Court of Appeals—in opinions and law review articles—on statutory interpretation. Underlying the debate were disagreements over the amount of leeway the judiciary has to enforce congressional preferences upon the executive. In her 1982 commencement address at Catholic University's Columbus School of Law, Chief Judge Wald neatly described the difficulties of interpreting congressional statutes: "The syntax is convoluted; surplusage and redundancy abound; participles dangle; phrases twist aimlessly in the wind" and legislative history is apt to be a jumble of different

---

32. On the whole, the Carter appointees to the Court of Appeals afforded litigants and organizations more access to the courts to contest agency policies than did the Reagan (and later, Bush) appointees. See, e.g., *American Hospital Ass'n v. Bowen*, 834 F.2d 1037 (1987) (*Wald-Sil/Mik(c/d)*); *Action Alliance of Senior Citizens v. Bowen*, 846 F.2d 1449 (1988) (*Will-Sta/Wald*); *Center for Auto Safety v. Thomas*, 806 F.2d 1071 (1986) (*Wald-RGin(c)-Bork(c)*), 847 F.2d 843 (1988) (*per curiam Wald-Rob-Mik-Edw-RGin/Buc-Sta-DGin-Will-Sil*), vacated, 856 F.2d 1557 (1988) (*per curiam*); *Hazardous Waste Treatment Council v. Thomas*, 885 F.2d 918 (1989) (*DGin-Sil/Wald*).

voices and themes. Furthermore, in the modern-day legislative process, it is not unknown for interest groups, staffers and members of Congress to "insert" into the legislative history of a statute statements favorable to their positions in the hope that a court will be persuaded to construe the statutory language in light of those statements.[33]

During the 1980s, the more liberal wing of the Court of Appeals, tilting to the legislative branch, was willing to draw upon a variety of different sources—text, statutory context, other relevant statutes, and legislative history—to extrapolate meaning from language. Other judges, most notably Scalia and Starr, more conservative and tilting toward the executive, refused to resort to legislative history in the construction of statutes, in effect challenging Congress to express its intent clearly in the text. The consistent use of text-only techniques, which had the effect of giving narrow applications to statutory enactments, was challenged by Patricia Wald, who argued in a 1990 law review article that "to disregard committee reports as indicators of Congressional understanding because we are suspicious that nefarious staffers have planted certain information for some undisclosed reason, is to second-guess Congress' chosen form of organization and delegation of authority and to doubt its ability to oversee its own constitutional functions effectively."

Many agency cases involved the application of the most important administrative case of the 1980s, *Chevron U.S.A. v. National Resources Defense Council*, in which the Supreme Court restricted the role of the federal judiciary in interpreting statutes. Applying a term in the Clean Air Act which Congress had not specifically defined, the Court of Appeals panel had interpreted the statute based on its view of the legislative purpose. In reversing, the Supreme Court stated that the Court of Appeals had "misconceived the nature of its role in reviewing the regulations at issue" and held that when the intent of Congress is not clear, the court must ask whether the agency's answer is based on a permissible construction of the statute.[34]

Chevron thus appeared to leave most statutory ambiguities to be resolved by the executive branch, for, as Judge Silberman pointed out, it demanded respect for legislative compromises, administrative expertise and political accountability. After *Chevron*, judicial affirmances of agency decisions in-

---

33. See *Nat. Small Shipments Traffic Conf. v. CAB*, 618 F.2d 819 (1980) (*Wri-Baz-RRobb*).

34. *Natural Resources Defense Council v. Gorsuch*, 685 F.2d 718 (1982) (*RGin-Mik-Jameson*(Sr. D.J. Mont.), rev'd sub nom. *Chevron U.S.A. v. Natural Resources Defense Council*, 467 U.S. 837 (1984).

creased by fifteen percent. Nevertheless, *Chevron* did not dictate deference in all cases; judges were still able to determine what the issue was in a particular case, whether Congress had addressed the issue, whether Congress had intended to delegate interpretation to the agency or the courts, and whether the agency's interpretation was "reasonable." The judges could even disagree over which materials should be used to infer congressional intent.

The other major D.C. Circuit case that led to a Supreme Court decision limiting judicial discretion in agency affairs was *Heckler v. Chaney*.[35] There, the Commissioner of the Food and Drug Administration had refused the petition of prison inmates to ban the use of lethal injections as a means of execution, deeming it not to be the best use of his discretionary enforcement authority. The Court of Appeals held that the FDA had erred. The Supreme Court reversed, largely on the basis of Judge Scalia's dissent in the Court of Appeals. It held that the Administrative Procedure Act precluded review of agency action committed by law to agency discretion. The decision amounted to a court-announced presumption of the unreviewability of agency inaction.

Deregulation

The "public interest" era had run its course by the time the Reagan administration came into office. Deregulation was already occurring in the airline, railroad, trucking, and broadcasting industries. Following through on his promise to reduce "inefficient and burdensome regulations," President Reagan ordered a review of federal regulations by the Office of Management and Budget and required that all existing and proposed regulations be subject to cost-benefit and/or cost-effectiveness analysis. The administration also cut agency budgets, reduced staffs, and appointed reluctant regulators such as John S. R. Shad to chair the SEC and Mark Fowler to head the FCC.

In 1978 Harold Leventhal had established the Court's attitude toward deregulation in a case involving the Interstate Commerce Commission's application of the Railroad Revitalization and Regulatory Act of 1976.[36] The Act removed the ICC's jurisdiction to regulate railroad rates, except where a railroad possessed "market dominance." An ICC order setting out four

---

35. 718 F.2d 1174 (1983) (*Wri*-Weigel(Sr. D.J. No. Cal.)/*Sca*), rev'd, 470 U.S. 821 (1985).

36. 90 Stat. 31.

fact situations which would trigger a rebuttable presumption of market dominance was challenged by the Atchison, Topeka and Santa Fe Railway Company in a suit in which numerous other interested parties, including the Justice Department and the Federal Trade Commission, intervened. In his opinion largely upholding the ICC's approach, Judge Leventhal saw the Court's role as "one of deference and deferral." The agency's presumptions were to be tested according to whether a rational connection existed between the facts giving rise to the presumption and the fact presumed. Such presumptive regulation was, the Court thought, entitled to deference, especially where the regulations at issue represented the Commission's initial attempt at interpreting and implementing a new regulatory concept.[37]

During the 1980s, the Federal Communications Commission accomplished a deregulation revolution without running afoul of the courts or seeking new authority from the Congress. Even before the Reagan administration came into office, the FCC's deregulation efforts had affected the telephone, broadcast, satellite and cable industries. Indeed, just one week before President Reagan was sworn in, the FCC, by a vote of six to one, deregulated major portions of the radio broadcasting industry. Basing its policy on the assumption that the market would self-regulate, the Commission eliminated restrictions on commercials, specific time requirements for public affairs programming and rules requiring stations to log their programming and survey the needs of the community. Most of this policy was upheld by the Court of Appeals, which accepted a requirement that stations merely make a short boilerplate statement indicating that they understood and intended to comply with their public service obligations.[38] In 1986 the Court itself ordered a further deregulatory step, invalidating the FCC's "must carry" rule requiring cable television stations to carry local programming.[39]

During the 1970s the necessity, utility, and constitutionality of the Fairness Doctrine had increasingly been questioned, and during the 1980s the Court of Appeals had been nudging the FCC to abolish the Fairness Doctrine on its own, rather than waiting for Congress to do it. The Court held

---

37. *Atchison, Topeka & Santa Fe Ry. Co. v. ICC [Market Dominance]*, 580 F.2d 623 (1978) (*Lev*-MacK-RRobb).

38. *Office of Communication of United Church of Christ v. FCC*, 707 F.2d 1413 (1983) (*Wri*-Jameson-*Bork*(c)).

39. *Quincy Cable TV v. FCC*, 768 F.2d 1434 (1985) (*Wri*-RGin-Bork). The ruling was based on the First Amendment and on the fact that there no longer was a scarcity of television outlets.

in 1986 that, absent congressional action, the doctrine lacked statutory support; the 1959 Congressional Amendment to the Fairness Doctrine had not statutorily mandated it but had merely ratified the Commission's longstanding position that the doctrine had been authorized by the public-interest standard.[40] The following year Congress attempted to codify the doctrine, but President Reagan vetoed the bill as unconstitutional. On August 4, 1987, the FCC, pointing out that the number of television stations had grown several fold since 1969 (although station ownership was in fewer hands), unanimously abolished the doctrine on the ground that it violated the First Amendment. Finally, in 1989, nearly two decades after Bazelon had first raised the issue, the Court of Appeals upheld the repeal of the Fairness Doctrine.[41]

Deregulation of the airline industry during the 1970s had resulted from widespread opposition, coming from government, the industry, and consumer groups to Civil Aeronautics Board policies. Extensive congressional hearings in 1974 were followed by the appointment of a new CAB chairman more sympathetic to deregulation. As early as 1975, the CAB took a much more liberal view of market entry and supported expansion of low-fare service by existing carriers and in 1978 advanced several deregulatory initiatives. Finally, the CAB unanimously endorsed regulatory reform. The result, the Airline Deregulation Act of 1978,[42] was an attempt to deregulate the entire industry. It provided for an end to the CAB's authority over domestic routes by the end of 1981 and domestic fares by the end of 1982, and for abolition of the CAB itself by the end of 1984.

But deregulation, which was intended to increase efficiency and low-cost service in the airline industry, also spawned bitter labor-management disputes. The battle between Eastern Airlines and unions representing its employees repeatedly found its way into the courts of the Circuit, exposing sharp differences between the District Court and the Court of Appeals. District Court decisions enjoining attempted structural and staffing changes by the airline, which was in fiscal crisis, were reversed on three occasions by the Court of Appeals. In one instance, the District Court had found that Eastern's unilateral furlough of thousands of employees was the result of a conscious effort to transfer assets and corporate activities to a less-union-

---

40. *Telecommunications Research & Action Center v. FCC*, 801 F.2d 501 (1986) (*Bork-Sca/MacK*(c/d)).

41. *Syracuse Peace Council v. FCC*, 867 F.2d 654 (1989) (*Will-Sta/Wald*(c/d)).

42. 92 Stat. 1705.

ized subsidiary; the Court of Appeals, however, concluded that the staff reductions were motivated by economic pressures, not anti-union animus.[43]

The Breakup of AT&T

By pushing the FCC toward a real marketplace in telecommunications, the
courts of the District of Columbia Circuit played an important role in the
breakup of AT&T's monopoly in long-distance telephone service.[44] The antitrust prosecution of AT&T, which would affect everyone in the nation who
had a telephone, was in the District Court for ten full years. The suit had
been filed in 1974 and assigned to Judge Joseph Waddy. When Waddy died
in 1978, Judge Harold Greene drew the case, on his first day at work.

Fifty-eight years old in 1981, Greene had been appointed to the District
Court by Jimmy Carter in 1978. He had come to the United States in his
youth as a refugee from Germany, and after law school had clerked for Bennett Champ Clark of the Court of Appeals (1953–54). He then made a distinguished career as a public lawyer, as an Assistant U.S. Attorney for the
District of Columbia, in the Office of Legal Counsel of the Department of
Justice, and then in the Civil Rights Division of the Justice Department,
where he headed its Appeals Section. Greene was appointed to the Court
of General Sessions by Lyndon Johnson in 1965 (becoming Chief Judge in
1966), and when the Superior Court succeeded that court as the trial court
of general jurisdiction of the District of Columbia in 1971, Greene was its
first Chief Judge. He rapidly became respected as an able administrator.

---

43. *Air Line Pilots Ass'n Int'l v. Eastern Airlines*, 703 F. Supp. 962 (1988) (Parker),
rev'd, 863 F.2d 891 (1988) (*Will-Buc-Sen*). The other two cases were *Int'l Assn. of Ma-
chinists & Aerospace Workers v. Eastern Airlines*, No. 87-1720 (1987) (Pratt), rev'd, 849
F.2d 1481 (1988) (*Edw-Will-Oberdorfer(D.D.C.)*); and *Air Line Pilots Ass'n Int'l v. Eastern Airlines*, 683 F. Supp. 845 (1988) (Parker), rev'd, 869 F.2d 1518 (1989) (*Edw-Rob-
Sen*).

44. In the 1970s the Court of Appeals had also contributed to the deregulation of
the telecommunications field in the litigation over MCI's attempts to introduce its Execunet telecommunications services. The Execunet cases tested the FCC's policy of approving new carriers' entry into the specialized communications field except when the
"public interest would be served by creating an AT&T monopoly." In two suits over
AT&T's refusal to provide the local physical connections necessary for the MCI services — and the FCC's inaction over those refusals — the Court of Appeals ordered compliance. *MCI Telecommunications Corp. v. FCC*, 561 F.2d 365 (1977) (*Wri-Tamm-Wilk*);
MCI Telecommunications Corp. v. FCC, 580 F.2d 590 (1978) (*Wri-Tamm-Wilk*). The consequences of the Execunet decisions were profound. Microwave private lines, computer-
based terminal equipment, and domestic satellite delivery now offered the opportunity
to create new services and new ways of delivering older services.

Despite the weakened antitrust environment of the early 1980s, and in the face of strong support within the Reagan administration for dropping the AT&T prosecution, Greene refused to be cowed. Having previously reaffirmed Waddy's opinion that the Court need not defer to the FCC,[45] he refused to dismiss the suit, saying the evidence demonstrated that the company had repeatedly violated the antitrust laws. The first of one hundred government witnesses testified on March 4, 1981. The government rested after four months, with 4,627 exhibits having been placed into evidence by the two sides. On September 11, in a seventy-four page decision, Greene again threw out AT&T's motion to dismiss, stating that the documentary evidence adduced by the government demonstrated that the Bell system had violated the antitrust laws in a number of ways over a lengthy period of time.[46]

When the two sides reached a settlement in January 1982, Greene once again refused to dismiss the suit, allowing competitors and consumer groups an opportunity to present their objections to the settlement and invoking his authority under the Tunney Act, which provided judicial review of antitrust settlements under certain conditions to protect the public interest. By the time he signed the consent decree in August 1982, it had been so modified that the "Baby Bells," the seven regional holding companies carved out of the AT&T monopoly, had been given the lucrative Yellow Pages service and the right to reenter the telephone equipment sales market. AT&T was given eighteen months to divest itself of twenty-two local phone companies.[47] The divestiture took place on January 1, 1984.[48]

---

45. *United States v. AT&T*, 427 F. Supp. 57 (1976) (Waddy); *United States v. AT&T,* 461 F. Supp. 1314 (1978) (Greene).

46. *United States v. AT&T*, 524 F. Supp. 1336 (1981).

47. *United States v. American Telephone & Telegraph Co.*, 552 F. Supp. 131 (1982), aff'd sub nom. *Maryland v. United States,* 460 U.S. 1001 (1983).

48. The Baby Bells were not permitted to provide long distance service, offer electronic information services, or manufacture telecommunications equipment. In 1987 Judge Greene denied requests to lift these exclusions, although he did eliminate some restrictions on the Baby Bells, including the requirement that their outside holdings be limited to ten percent of their revenues. In 1988 Greene ruled that local telephone companies could offer information transmission services, such as voice messaging and electronic mail, but would not be permitted to offer content-based information services. Prodded by the Court of Appeals in 1991, Greene reluctantly agreed to allow the Baby Bells to offer electronic information services over phone lines, but with palpable reservations. *United States v. W. Electric Co.,* 673 F. Supp. 525 (1987); 714 F. Supp. 1 (1988); 767 F. Supp. 308 (1991).

Greene won wide praise for his handling of the AT&T divestiture. It was described as the "most significant act of judicial statesmanship since desegregation" and Greene was a runner-up for *Time* magazine's 1984 Man of the Year. But he also endured some strong criticism. One of his harshest critics was Rep. John Dingell of the House Committee on Energy and Commerce, who, in the *Wall Street Journal* of September 11, 1987, accused the judge of "arrogating power to determine whether and when the American people will be allowed to receive advanced new services."

Affirmative Action

Under Ronald Reagan's presidency, race- and gender-conscious initiatives launched in the 1970s were subjected to the hostility of his administration and the skepticism of his judicial appointees. Opposition within the Court of Appeals to affirmative action programs grew with each new Reagan appointee. The courts of the Circuit were the scenes of bitter clashes over affirmative action between the liberal and conservative wings of the Court, notably in several cases testing policies established by the Federal Communications Commission and by municipal departments in the District.

Minorities and Women in Broadcasting

During the Carter administration, the FCC had adopted a policy that gave tax breaks to broadcasters who sold their stations to minority owners and had approved a "distress sale" exception permitting licensees subject to revocation or renewal hearings to transfer their licenses to minority applicants at lower-than-normal prices. In 1984, in *West Michigan Broadcasting v. FCC*, the Court of Appeals, with a strong opinion by Judge Wright, upheld the FCC policy of considering minority ownership as a plus factor in a multi-factor selection system "as a way of increasing the overall diversity of perspectives represented in the broadcast mass media."[49]

However, the following year Judge Scalia joined Judge Tamm in invalidating an FCC policy that considered female ownership as a plus factor in a comparative licensing procedure, on the ground that it exceeded the FCC's statutory authority.[50] While the decision was not reached on constitutional grounds, the Court indicated that the assumptions and premises

---

49. 735 F.2d 601 (1984) (*Wri-RGin-McG*).
50. *Steele v. FCC*, 770 F.2d 1192 (1985).

underpinning minority preferences ran counter to fundamental constitutional principles. The majority thought such preferences "questionable as a matter of fact" and "offensive as a matter of principle." In dissent, Judge Wald argued that "women having ownership interests and policymaking roles in the media are likely to enhance the probability that the varying perspectives and viewpoints of women will be fairly represented in the broadcast media."

The full court vacated the panel decision and set the case for rehearing. However, at the Commission's request, the case was remanded to the FCC, which instituted a proceeding to reconsider the basis for the preferences and determine whether there was evidence that its minority and general-preference policies were likely to lead to enhanced diversity. In response, an outraged Congress attached a rider to an appropriations bill, prohibiting the repeal, retroactive revision, or further reexamination of the FCC's policy in this area.[51] That brought the FCC inquiry to a halt and forced the D.C. Circuit to come to terms with the issue of constitutionality.

In 1989, in *Winter Park Communications v. FCC*, relying upon its own 1984 *West Michigan* decision, a panel of the Court of Appeals (Judge Edwards writing) upheld the constitutionality of FCC consideration of minority ownership as a qualitative enhancement factor in comparative licensing proceedings for broadcast stations.[52] Dissenting, Judge Williams contended that *West Michigan* had been largely undermined by intervening Supreme Court decisions—in one of which, *City of Richmond v. J.R. Croson Co.*, a widely divided Court had set aside an affirmative action program as not justified by a compelling governmental interest and not narrowly tailored to accomplish a remedial purpose.[53] Williams further argued that the stated goal of the Commission was undefined and seemingly not definable except in racial terms. He found the program diversity theory unconstitutional because it was based on impermissible racial stereotypes and lacked in remedial justification.

A month earlier, in *Shurberg Broadcasting v. FCC*, another divided panel of the Court of Appeals had held the FCC's distress-sale policy unconstitutional because it had not been tailored narrowly enough to remedy past

---

51. 101 Stat. 1329–31 (1987).

52. 873 F.2d 347 (1989) (*Edw*-Friedman(Fed. Cir.)/*Will*(c/d)).

53. 488 U.S. 469 (1989). The other decision was *Wygant v. Jackson Board of Education*, 476 U.S. 267 (1986), in which a similarly divided Court held that a school board's policy of protecting certain employees against layoffs because of their race violated the Fourteenth Amendment.

discrimination or lack of programming diversity, because it unduly burdened competitors, and because it was not reasonably related to the interests it sought to vindicate.[54] The decision produced three important opinions that attempted to decipher the Supreme Court's affirmative action opinion in the *Croson* case.

Judges Silberman and MacKinnon constituted the majority, but differed in their analyses. Judge Silberman was troubled by the fact that the FCC rules in no way required the preference to be tied to the extent of disadvantage suffered by the minority enterprise. "There must be some opportunity to exclude those individuals for whom affirmative action is merely another business opportunity," he maintained. MacKinnon argued that the policy presented "opportunities for minorities to be insulated from all competition and to receive very substantial subsidies that are not in any way related to past discrimination." Chief Judge Wald dissented: "In casting off a thoughtfully conceived and monitored program aimed at attaining a legitimate congressionally mandated end, the majority has too rigidly applied Supreme Court affirmative action guidelines designed for other types of programs, ignored firm precedents in this circuit, and failed to credit the explicit intent of Congress."

The Supreme Court granted certiorari in *Shurberg* and consolidated it with *Winter Park* (sub nom. *Metro Broadcasting, Inc. v. FCC*). By a vote of 5–4, the High Court upheld both the enhancement in comparative licensing proceedings and the FCC's distress-sale policies.[55] In one of his final opinions, Justice William Brennan, employing intermediate level constitutional scrutiny, held that the program was substantially related to the achievement of important governmental objectives within the power of Congress. Of particular importance was the fact that Congress had found that there had been "past inequities stemming from racial and ethnic discrimination" and had acted to remedy them.

Municipal Services

In the mid-1980s voluntary affirmative action plans entered into by the District's police and fire departments were tested in the courts of the Circuit, engendering profound controversy. Both departments had had long histories of segregation. The Fire Department, for example, had separate white and black companies until 1962, and racial segregation was the norm within

---

54. 876 F.2d 902 (1989) (*Sil-MacK/Wald*).
55. 497 U.S. 547 (1990).

the firehouses until 1971, at which time the force was about 25 percent black. In 1985, when Judge Charles Richey ruled on a new affirmative action plan for hiring and promotion, nearly two-thirds of the District's firefighters were white males (who also predominated among the officers), and one-tenth of one percent were women.

The affirmative action plan, which had been adopted voluntarily after a consent decree had been entered in a suit against the Fire Department, set an interim rate for selection of candidates of sixty percent black and five percent female. In *Hammon v.* [Mayor Marion S.] *Barry*, against challenges under Title VII of the 1964 Civil Rights Act and the Constitution, Judge Richey upheld the hiring aspects of the plan as narrowly tailored, although he admitted that he was "not comfortable with racially based distinctions." He held most the plan's provisions for promotion invalid under Title VII.[56]

A divided Court of Appeals reversed Richey on the hiring plan.[57] Writing for the panel, Judge Starr (joined by Judge Silberman) made clear that he saw the case as one in which a black political majority was disadvantaging a white minority. Interpreting recent Supreme Court decisions on affirmative action, the Court held that "the absolutely indispensable element of the legality of remedies which differentiate human beings on the basis of race" was remediation of present discrimination, not restitution for past injustices. The court saw "no present day impediments to black hiring" and found the hiring scheme not only not narrowly tailored but "not tailored at all." In dissent, Judge Mikva considered the plan within the "history of discrimination against blacks by the Fire Department," a history which had had "severe and lasting effects on the firefighting force."

Rehearing the case six months later, the same panel held that its earlier opinion had not been undermined by an intervening Supreme Court decision, *Johnson v. [Santa Clara] Transportation Agency*, which upheld an affirmative action plan favoring minorities and women.[58] In his concurring opinion, Judge Silberman argued that under the Constitution the District of Columbia may not "insist on proportional representation of blacks in government employment." In a provocative statement, Silberman added, "It is manifestly inappropriate for us to take judicial notice of the unlikely proposition that all ethnic or racial groups in our society have the same

---

56. 606 F. Supp. 1082 (1985).
57. *Hammon v. Barry*, 813 F.2d 412 (1987).
58. 480 U.S. 616 (1987).

relative interests or capability for performing the various jobs in our economy." Judge Mikva again dissented fiercely, writing, "The majority pretends
that there have been happy times in the District's Fire Department since
the time of the Korean conflict," adding that blacks "weren't happy with
the plantation... no matter how comfortable the separate but equal sleeping facilities."[59]

Between the two decisions in *Hammon v. Barry*, a different Court of Appeals panel upheld the voluntary affirmative action plan of the D.C. Metropolitan Police Department.[60] The majority, Judges Edwards and Wald,
held that there had been manifest imbalance before the plan, that there was
a valid remedial purpose, and that the legitimate interests of non-minority
or male employees were not trampled upon. However, the Court remanded
for the Department to demonstrate that it had a strong basis for believing
that affirmative action was necessary to remedy the present effects of past
discrimination.

Rehearing *en banc* was granted for both the police and firefighters cases,
but was then vacated by a vote of 6–5. The court vacated its earlier opinions and judgment in the Police Department case, which was then settled.[61]
The panel decision in the firefighters case stood, as the Court (the six Reagan appointees voting together) revoked its decision to rehear *Hammon* en
banc.[62] In 1990 Judge Richey approved a settlement for the firefighters that
provided for 180 immediate promotions, a new platoon of firefighters with
a new corps of officers, payment of $3.5 million to the *Hammon* plaintiffs,
and the development of fair promotional tests.[63]

First Amendment Cases

The members of the Court of Appeals differed often and vigorously in the
1980s over First Amendment cases, which comprised an unusually high
portion of the docket. Although the Vietnam War belonged to the past,
demonstrations of various kinds still took place, involving some of the most
symbolic sites in the capital. Two libel cases in the Circuit attracted wide

---

59. *Hammon v. Barry*, 826 F.2d 73 (1987).
60. *Ledoux v. District of Columbia*, 820 F.2d 1293 (1987) (*Edw*-Wald/*Revercomb*((D.D.C.)(c/d)).
61. 833 F.2d 367 (1987), vacated, 841 F.2d 426 (1987).
62. 841 F.2d 426 (1988).
63. *Hammon v. Barry*, 752 F. Supp. 1087 (1990).

attention, partially because of the divisions on the Court of Appeals, which were revealed in these cases in divergent views on the limits of freedom of the press.

Demonstrations

From the beginning, the nation's capital has been the nation's soapbox, the national stage on which groups of citizens representing the full spectrum of opinion have gathered to demand "redress of grievances." Among the most significant free-speech cases the courts of the District heard in this decade were two challenging no-protest zones around buildings in the capital and one testing a novel form of symbolic speech.

The original first named defendant in *Grace v. Burger* was Chief Justice Warren E. Burger; the case involved the sidewalk in front of the Supreme Court. The named plaintiff, Mary Terese Grace, had been prevented by a court police officer from displaying a sign on which was reproduced the text of the First Amendment. The other plaintiff, Thaddeus Zywicki, had been attempting to distribute leaflets and pamphlets at that location and had been threatened with arrest under a statute which made it "unlawful to parade, stand or move in processions or assemblages in the Supreme Court Building or grounds, or to display therein any flag, banner, or device designed or adapted to bring into public notice any party, organization, or movement."[64]

Judge Louis Oberdorfer dismissed the suit because the plaintiffs had failed to exhaust their administrative remedies.[65] On appeal, Harry T. Edwards, joined by Ruth Bader Ginsburg, held the statute void on its face because of its absolute prohibition of expression on the Court grounds.[66] "[W]e believe that it would be tragic if the grounds of the Supreme Court, unquestionably the greatest protector of First Amendment rights, stood as an island of silence in which those rights could never be exercised in any form," Edwards wrote. Although it clearly was an "interested" party, the Supreme Court heard the case and agreed with the Court of Appeals, holding unconstitutional that part of the statute pertaining to the public sidewalks forming the perimeter of the Supreme Court because they are "public forums."[67]

---

64. 63 Stat. 617 (1949).
65. *Grace v. Burger*, 524 F. Supp. 815 (1980).
66. *Grace v. Burger*, 665 F.2d 1193 (1981) (*Edw*-RGin/*MacK*(c/d/).
67. *United States v. Grace*, 461 U.S. 171 (1983).

Boos v. Barry involved a provision of the District of Columbia Code which regulated demonstrations in front of embassies. The law made it unlawful to demonstrate within five hundred feet of a foreign embassy with placards or other signs designed to criticize, intimidate, or bring a foreign government, its policies, or its actions "into public odium [or] public disrepute" without a police permit.[68]

The Act was challenged by conservative groups wanting to carry placards opposing the Soviet and Nicaraguan governments. Judge Oliver Gasch upheld the law, and the Court of Appeals affirmed.[69] Writing for the Court, Robert Bork emphasized the unusually strong case for judicial deference to the political branches, not only in the area of foreign relations but in dealing with a statute which both Congress and the President had declared necessary to comply with treaty obligations and international law. The statute, Bork wrote, "does not eliminate any point of view from our political discourse, but sets aside the space immediately surrounding foreign embassies as an area free from hostile protest."

Judge Wald dissented, arguing that the majority, "by blindly deferring to the political branches and unquestioningly accepting their assertion of an ill-defined interest in protecting [foreign governments] from annoyance and insult," had effectively erased "an enormously important category of political speech from First Amendment protection." By a vote of 5–3, the Supreme Court reversed as to the clause prohibiting the display of placards, finding it a content-based restriction that did not survive the most exacting scrutiny.[70]

One of the most intriguing First Amendment cases in this period involved a demonstration designed to draw attention to the widespread problem of homelessness in the capital and the nation. The Community for Creative Non-Violence, an unincorporated religious association, applied to the National Park Service for a permit to conduct round-the-clock demonstrations on the Mall and in Lafayette Park.[71] The permit granted by the Park Service allowed construction of a symbolic campsite, but made clear that sleeping at the campsite would violate anti-camping regulations. That

---

68. D.C. Code Ann. §22-1115 (1981).

69. *Finzer v. Barry*, 798 F.2d 1450 (1986) (*Bork*-Davis(Fed. Cir.)/*Wald*).

70. *Boos v. Barry*, 485 U.S. 312 (1988).

71. Previously, the CCNV had, through litigation, established that demonstrators had the right to place tents in Lafayette Park for a week and sleep in them, even though the park was not a designated camping area. *Community for Creative Non-Violence v. Watt*, 670 F.2d 1213 (1982) (*per curiam* Rob-Wald-Edw).

restriction was challenged on First Amendment grounds. The *en banc* Court of Appeals, dividing 6–5, struck the regulations down. The vote reflected what had essentially become the lineup of the Court of Appeals in the 1980s in "hot-button" cases, but the search for a rationale fragmented the Court further. In addition to the announcement of the judgment *per curiam,* six judges wrote opinions.[72]

Judge Mikva (joined by Judge Wald) saw the proposed demonstration, including the sleeping, as carefully designed to express the message that homeless people have nowhere else to go. In this context, he thought, sleeping was sufficiently expressive to implicate First Amendment scrutiny. Judge Ruth Bader Ginsburg, the apparent swing vote, concurred, but found the case "close and difficult" and hesitated to treat this demonstration as indistinguishable from soapbox speech or leaflet distribution.

In the principal dissenting opinion, Judge Wilkey wrote that the First Amendment does not guarantee a right to deliver a message in the most effective manner possible: "Not a whit more justification is needed to ban spitting in the street by a parade of tobacco farmers protesting a new tax on chewing tobacco than is needed to prevent such activity by the public at large." In an opinion in which Judges Bork and MacKinnon joined, Judge Scalia took the position that a law proscribing conduct for a reason having nothing to do with its communicative character need only meet minimal requirements of the Equal Protection Clause. the First Amendment fully protects only spoken and written thought, he argued, and flatly denied "that sleeping is or can ever be speech for First Amendment purposes." Judge Ginsburg responded that "it would be surprising if those who poured tea into the sea and who refused to buy stamps did not recognize that ideas [can be] communicated, disagreements expressed, protests made other than by word of mouth or pen."[73]

The Supreme Court agreed with the dissenters, holding, through Justice White, that the judiciary did not have "the authority to replace the Park Service as the manager of the Nation's parks."[74]

Litigation by the Community for Creative Non-Violence would enliven the dockets of the Circuit's courts throughout the 1980s. The group sought to place a modern depiction of homeless people over a steam grate in close

---

72. *Community for Creative Non-Violence v. Watt,* 703 F.2d 586 (1983) (per curiam *Mik*-Wald-*Wri*(c)-Rob-*Edw*(c)-*RGin*(c)/*Wilk*-Tamm-*Sca*-MacK-Bork).

73. She was quoting from Louis Henkin, "The Supreme Court, 1967 Term — Foreword: On Drawing Lines," *Harvard Law Review* 82 (1968): 79.

74. *Clark v. Community for Creative Non-Violence,* 468 U.S. 288 (1984).

proximity to a traditional Christmas display; challenged the regulation of speech on Washington's public transit system; and, under the Constitution's religion clauses, challenged the practice of having spectators rise for the judge in Superior Court.[75]

In 1990, sixty-five years after its notorious march down Pennsylvania Avenue, the Ku Klux Klan sought to march from the Washington Monument to the Capitol via Constitution Avenue. The proposed march would have taken the participants by the U.S. Courthouse. A previous march weeks earlier had ended in violence when a hostile mob attacked police lines. Rejecting the so-called "heckler's veto," Judge Louis Oberdorfer ordered that a permit issue for the full march. Noting that "the full route from the Washington Monument to the Capitol is the premier public forum in the nation," Oberdorfer, in his final opinion of this series, found that there had been no showing of a credible threat that the violence would be beyond reasonable control.[76]

Libel

Two media-related libel cases that came before the Court of Appeals in the early 1980s exposed the fissures in the Court as much as any litigation in this period.

In a nationally syndicated column published on May 4, 1978, Rowland Evans and Robert Novak sharply criticized Professor Bertell Ollman, who was under consideration to chair the Department of Political Science at the University of Maryland. They questioned Ollman's scholarly reputation and suggested that, as a Marxist and political activist, Ollman desired to use the classroom as an instrument to prepare for revolution. Ollman brought an action for defamation against the columnists. The trial judge, Aubrey Robinson, held that, although Evans and Novak might have written a biased column, such opinion was afforded the same constitutional protection as writing thought of as "balanced." The column, Robinson held, contained

---

75. *Community for Creative Non-Violence v. Hodel*, 623 F. Supp. 528 (1985) (Oberdorfer); *Community for Creative Non-Violence v. Turner*, 714 F. Supp. 29 (1989) (Sporkin), 729 F. Supp. 868 (1989) (Sporkin), clarified by, amended by, substituted opinion at *Community for Creative Non-Violence v. Turner*, 893 F.2d 1387 (1990) (*Mik*-Edw-Will(c)); *Community for Creative Non-Violence v. Hess*, 745 F.2d 697 (1984) (*Rob*-Wald-Palmieri(Sr. D.J. S.D.N.Y.)).

76. *Christian Knights of the Ku Klux Klan Invisible Empire v. District of Columbia*, 751 F. Supp. 212 (1990), vacated, 919 F.2d 148 (1990) (*per curiam Edw*(c)-*Ran*(c)/Wald), opinion remand, 751 F. Supp. 218 (1990), aff'd, 972 F.2d 365 (1992) (Ran-Buc-Hen).

"merely the opinions of two people," rather than "false and defamatory statements of fact."[77]

A panel of the Court of Appeals reversed and remanded,[78] but the decision was vacated and the case reheard by the Court *en banc*. The full court, by a vote of seven to five, also upheld the District Court, but fractured in an unusual way. Four groups of judges combined in ad hoc alliances, issuing a total of seven opinions. Starr, writing for the Court, was joined by Tamm and Mikva; Bork, MacKinnon, Wilkey, and Ginsburg concurred, but on different grounds; Robinson dissented, joined by Wright, and Wald, Scalia, and Edwards dissented on different grounds.[79] Judge Starr's opinion expressed the fear that "the contraction of liberty's breathing space can only mean inhibition of the scope of public discussion on matters of general interest and concern." Judge Bork, concerned about the effect of excessive damage awards on freedom of the press, wrote, "The American press is extraordinarily free and vigorous, as it should be, not because it is free of inaccuracy, oversimplification and bias, but because the alternative to that freedom is worse than those failings."[80]

In a front-page article published November 30, 1979, the *Washington Post*, citing the fact that the son of William Tavoulareas, president of Mobil Oil, had an interest in the Atlas Maritime Company, implied that extensive business transactions between Mobil and Atlas were the result of nepotism. The elder Tavoulareas brought a lawsuit against the *Post* and the jury awarded him $250,000 compensatory damages and $1.8 million punitive damages (the amount of his legal bill) — a verdict that one observer called "a citizen vote on the merits of a story." Notwithstanding the verdict, Judge Gasch awarded judgment for the *Post*.[81]

A panel of the Court of Appeals, with Judges MacKinnon (writing) and Scalia in the majority and Judge Wright dissenting in part, reversed Gasch, concluding that the evidence adduced had been sufficient to establish actual malice.[82] After consideration of the editorial decisions of the *Post* in

---

77. *Ollman v. Evans*, 479 F. Supp. 292 (1979).

78. *Ollman v. Evans*, 713 F.2d 838 (1983) (*per curiam Rob*(c)-*Wald*(c)-*MacK*(c)).

79. *Ollman v. Evans*, 750 F.2d 970 (1984) (*Sta*-Tamm-Mik/*Bork*(c)-Wilk-RGin-*MacK*/*Rob*(d)-Wri/*Wald*(d)-*Sca*-*Edw*(c/d)).

80. In words that eerily presaged his personal trials three years later, Judge Bork added, "Those who step into areas of public dispute, who choose the pleasures and distractions of controversy, must be willing to bear criticism, disparagement, and even wounding assessments."

81. *Tavoulareas v. Washington Post Co.*, 567 F. Supp. 651 (1983).

82. *Tavoulareas v. Piro*, 759 F.2d 90 (1985) (*MacK*-Sca/*Wri*(c/d).

printing the article, MacKinnon wrote that "the falsehoods contained in the article were published not merely through negligence or inadvertence, but with reckless disregard of whether they were false or not." According to the panel majority, the reporter had been out to get Tavoulareas and had deliberately slanted the article, rejecting evidence contrary to the central premise of the story. Dissenting, Judge Wright believed the effect on freedom of expression would be incalculable if an excessive jury verdict on the particular "mundane, flimsy facts" of the case was upheld.

The Court of Appeals voted to rehear the case *en banc*. Although the case was argued on October 3, 1985, the decision did not come down until March 13, 1987. By then Judge Scalia had been elevated to the Supreme Court and the Court of Appeals had three new appointees—Buckley, Williams, and Douglas Ginsburg—who did not participate in the decision. Two others, Bork and Silberman, recused themselves. The *en banc* court reversed the panel by a vote of 7–1.[83] The majority opinion, written jointly by Wright and Starr (the one Reagan appointee who sat), emphasized that an adversarial stance in a newspaper article "is certainly not indicative of actual malice" under circumstances where "the reporter conducted a detailed investigation and wrote a story that is substantially true." The Supreme Court denied certiorari.

Criminal Cases

During the 1980s, the District Court was the scene of several extremely high-profile criminal cases. As noted above, the Independent Counsel brought prosecutions against friends and associates of President Reagan for violations of the Ethics in Government Act. Two of the seven trials resulting from the "Abscam" investigation into political corruption by members of Congress and other politicians were held in the District of Columbia Circuit.[84] Most significant of all were the trial of John Hinckley for attempted assassination of the President and the prosecutions growing out of the Reagan administration's abuses of power in the Iran-Contra scandal.

83. *Tavoulareas v. Piro*, 817 F.2d 762 (1987) (*Sta-Wri*(c)-Rob-Mik-Edw-Wald(c)-*RGin*(c)/*MacK*).

84. *United States v. [Rep. John W.] Jenrette*, 594 F. Supp. 769 (1983) (Penn), aff'd, 744 F.2d 817 (1984) (*Tamm*-Wri-Sta); *United States v. [Rep. Richard] Kelly*, 539 F. Supp. 363 (1982) (Bryant), rev'd, remanded, 707 F.2d 1460 (1983) (*per curiam* Rob-*MacK*(c)-*RGin*(c)), aff'd, 748 F.2d 691 (1984) (*Gesell*(D.D.C.)-Bork-Sca).

The Hinckley Prosecution

On March 30, 1981, as Ronald Reagan was walking out of the Washington Hilton Hotel after a speech, twenty-six-year-old John Hinckley fired six bullets, the last of which hit the President. Press Secretary Jim Brady was struck in the head and permanently paralyzed. A District policeman and a Secret Service agent were also wounded.

Almost exactly a century after the trial of Charles Guiteau for the assassination of James A. Garfield, the federal courts of the District of Columbia Circuit once again struggled with the insanity defense raised by a man who had attempted to take the life of the President of the United States. The trial of John Hinckley was the fifth time the fate of a presidential assassin was determined in the D.C. Circuit.

The trial began on May 4, 1982, and lasted seven weeks. The trial judge was Barrington Parker, who handled more than his share of high-profile cases in sixteen years as a District Court judge.[85] Like his father, George, with whom he had practiced law, Parker was a liberal Republican and a staunch advocate of racial civil rights. His last years on the bench were difficult ones. Crippled in an automobile accident, he was cantankerous and feisty, irascible and impatient, a difficult colleague and a martinet in the courtroom. But at the time of the Hinckley trial Parker was still capable of doing first-class work. He would try Hinckley with skill and compassion.

There was only one issue at the trial—whether Hinckley was not guilty by reason of insanity. Since *United States v. Brawner* in 1972 (see chapter seven), the District of Columbia had followed the Model Penal Code's test for insanity, which held that a person suffering from a "mental disease or defect" is not held responsible for criminal conduct if he or she cannot tell right from wrong or refrain from wrongful behavior.

The definition of "mental disease" in the D.C. Circuit in effect at the time of the Hinckley trial was that of *McDonald v. United States*: "any abnormal

---

85. Among these was the month-long trial in 1979 of three men for the car-bomb assassination of the Chilean ambassador, Orlando Letelier, in Washington's Sheridan Circle. Parker was reversed on appeal, although the number and complexity of issues led the judges of the Court of Appeals to share the writing of the opinion. *United States v. Sampol*, 636 F.2d 621 (1979) (*per curiam* MacK-RRobb-Corcoran(D.D.C.)). Parker also tried Fawaz Younis, a Lebanese Shi'ite Muslim charged with hijacking a Royal Jordanian airliner in 1985. In that case, Parker ruled that the manner of Younis's arrest by the FBI—he had been subjected to a "relentless interrogation" for four days on a Navy ship—had deprived him of his rights.

condition of the mind which substantially affects mental or emotional processes and substantially impairs behavior controls."[86] The 1970 court reform act had shifted the burden of proof of insanity to the defense, and had directed that it was to apply in federal as well as local trials; however, the practice still prevailing among federal judges, including Parker in the Hinckley case, was to place the burden on the government.

The trial was primarily a battle of experts. Hinckley's experts agreed that he was psychotic at the time of the offense, having progressively withdrawn into an inner world as his anchor to reality slipped away, but they disagreed as to a precise diagnosis. The government experts agreed that Hinckley had a "schizoid personality disorder," but believed he had functioned within normal limits and had been in touch with social reality during the months he had stalked the President. He was, to be sure, narcissistic and emotionally cold, with a grandiose sense of self-importance and marked feelings of inferiority and shame. Some reporters ironically dubbed his traits "dementia suburbia."

The jury deliberated for three days before returning with a verdict of not guilty on all counts by reason of insanity. The government considered an extraordinary appeal on the burden-of-proof issue, but decided against it. The verdict was unpopular. The "cascade of public outrage" reported by the *New York Times* found sustenance in the Congress, already under pressure to deal with violent crime. Soon after the trial twenty-six bills were introduced to limit the insanity defense, even though insanity acquittals in the federal system were rare and even more rarely contested.[87]

The reconsideration of the insanity defense stimulated by the Hinckley trial took it back to the pre-*Durham* era. Within three years Congress and half the states enacted limitations on the insanity defense. The new federal law restricted the Model Penal Code approach of *Brawner* and revived *M'-Naghten*. Acquittal by reason of insanity required a "severe mental disease" and the volitional part of the defense was eliminated. The defendant was to have the burden of proving the defense of insanity by clear and convincing evidence.

Hinckley was committed to St. Elizabeths Hospital under orders that he not be released except by order of the Court upon a showing that he was no longer mentally ill or dangerous to himself or others. For years after-

---

86. 312 F.2d 847, 851 (1962).

87. Only four defendants using the insanity defense were acquitted throughout the federal system in 1981; there were twenty-six insanity acquittals in the District of Columbia between 1979 and 1983, twenty-four of which were uncontested.

ward, Judge Parker monitored Hinckley's confinement, ruling on a series of furlough requests and complaints about confinement.[88]

The Iran-Contra Affair

The 1980s, which had begun with the final dispositions of the series of trials growing out of abuses of power by the Nixon administration, ended with several major prosecutions arising from the biggest scandal of the Reagan era. The Iran-Contra affair seriously weakened the Reagan administration during its final years, and was the occasion of another major state trial in the D.C. Circuit—part of a line dating back to Bollmann and Swartwout.

At its core Iran-Contra was far less complex than Watergate. In defiance of the policy of the U.S. government, and belying its own rhetoric, the Reagan administration had sold arms to the Iranian government in the hope that it would win release of American hostages held in the Middle East. Most of the money made from overcharging the Iranians in those transactions was secretly funneled, in apparent violation of U.S. law, to the Contra rebels attempting to overthrow the leftist government of Nicaragua.

After the scandal broke, there was an unsatisfactory preliminary investigation handled personally by Attorney General Ed Meese. Meese then asked for the appointment of an Independent Counsel. The Special Division named Lawrence Walsh, a seventy-five-year-old former federal judge and Deputy Attorney General. Walsh's investigation, impeded by the Justice Department, the White House, congressional committees, and intelligence agencies, lasted seven years and cost more than $35 million dollars. Walsh concluded in his final report that "the President's most senior advisers and the Cabinet members on the National Security Council" had acted to make "scapegoats" of NSC staff members Bud McFarlane, John Poindexter, and Oliver North.

Eleven of the fourteen people against whom criminal charges were brought either pleaded guilty or were convicted after trial. The convictions of the two most important officials tried, North and Poindexter, were upset on appeal and the highest official charged, Defense Secretary Caspar W. Weinberger, was pardoned before trial. Four others, including McFarlane, were pardoned by George Bush after conviction. Higher-ups in the administration, implicated in Walsh's report, escaped prosecution.

---

88. In 1987 Parker ruled, in an action having nothing directly to do with Hinckley, that all mental patients who had been held at St. Elizabeths under voluntary civil commitments—some 600—were entitled to hearings to determine if they were being held unconstitutionally.

The prosecution of Oliver North, the official most actively involved in the Iran-Contra plot, proved the final great case in Gerhard Gesell's career. North was accused of obstructing congressional investigations, making false statements to a congressional committee and the Attorney General, wire fraud, shredding and altering official documents, theft of government property, and acceptance of an illegal gratuity. His defense was primarily that administration officials, including the President, had been aware and approved of his activities—something Reagan denied in written answers to interrogatories.

The North case was extraordinarily complex. Over 100 motions were filed before the trial began. By the day of the verdict, Gesell had issued 193 separate written opinions. His first important decision, made in March 1988, was to sever North's case from the prosecutions of three other defendants on the ground that the others' intentions to use the immunized testimony of their co-defendants in their own defenses prevented a joint trial. This decision greatly slowed the work of the Independent Counsel.

Defense demands for discovery of hundreds of thousands of classified documents raised complex problems. Applying the Classified Information Procedure Act (CIPA), Gesell ordered the construction of a secure facility to house the classified documents; a large downtown office was remodeled to serve that purpose. The Independent Counsel would ultimately produce more than 100,000 pages of classified documents and 200,000 pages of unclassified documents. Nevertheless, at Walsh's request, Gesell dismissed the two broad conspiracy counts against North—counts which described the Iran-Contra conspiracy in detail—because the administration refused to make available classified documents for North's defense. This meant that North would be tried on what were essentially minor charges.[89]

Perhaps the most difficult problem faced by the prosecution resulted from the congressional hearings on the scandal. North had been granted

---

89. Noting that "it probably was never contemplated that classified information problems of this magnitude would be presented to a trial judge in a single case," Gesell took a flexible approach to the application of CIPA procedures because "strict application of the statute to this proceeding would not only be difficult, but impossible to accomplish consistent with a fair and expeditious resolution." *United States v. Poindexter*, 698 F. Supp. 316, 319–20 (1988). On the day before opening statements were to be made in the North case, Attorney General Richard Thornburgh tried to intervene, seeking complete adherence to CIPA procedures. Gesell and the Court of Appeals denied the motions on standing grounds. Ultimately, on appeal, the Court of Appeals would find that Gesell had erred in not adhering to the CIPA procedures, but held that it had not been reversible error.

use immunity to testify before Congress. As a result, under *Kastigar v. United States*,[90] the prosecution could not use any evidence that came to it by way of those hearings. Walsh and his staff were prohibited from reading congressional reports and were sealed off from exposure to the immunized testimony; newspaper clippings and transcripts of testimony were redacted by nonprosecuting personnel. Ruling on a petition for mandamus during the pretrial, the Court of Appeals held that Judge Gesell had "a considerable degree of discretion to fashion the procedure most conducive to resolving fully and fairly all issues regarding the use of immunized testimony at trial."[91] However, in the end the problem of immunized evidence led to the reversal of North's conviction.

The trial took place between January 31 and May 4, 1989. Gesell insisted that North was entitled to a fully open, public trial. The judge refused to monitor the opening or closing statements in advance or to subject witness's testimony to advance scrutiny.[92] The lawyer-journalist Jeffrey Toobin, who covered the trial, said Gesell looked "as jolly as a Franz Hals peasant— red-faced, white-haired, and ready for action," sometimes presenting a smile "that every reporter covering the trial compared...to Santa Claus," and sometimes showing "an epochal scowl."

North did not deny that he had performed the acts he was charged with, but argued that his motives had not been criminal. He insisted that his actions had been approved by his superiors, that they were justified in light of the need for covert action in a dangerous world, and that he never believed any of his actions were unlawful. Forty-nine witnesses were heard. Many of the government's, including McFarlane, Meese, and North's secretary, Fawn Hall, were hostile to the prosecution. To mount his higher-authorization defense, North sought to subpoena ex-President Reagan and President Bush. Gesell quashed the Bush subpoena for lack of a showing that the President had material information, and insisted that a sufficient showing be made that Reagan's testimony was essential to assure a fair trial.[93] He placed Reagan on call to testify, but ultimately quashed the subpoena. Reagan, though, had cooperated much more with the Independent Counsel than President Nixon had during Watergate, answering interrogatories and making available his personal diary.

---

90. 406 U.S. 441 (1972).
91. *United States v. Poindexter*, 859 F.2d 216 (1988) (*per curiam* Buc-DGin-Sen).
92. *United States v. North*, 708 F. Supp. 389 (1988).
93. *United States v. North*, 713 F. Supp. 1448 (1989).

The jury deliberated for twelve days before pronouncing North not guilty on nine counts and guilty on three: aiding and abetting an obstruction of congressional inquiries, destroying and falsifying official NSC documents, and receiving an illegal gratuity. Under the sentencing guidelines, North could have received up to 57 months in prison, but Gesell, noting that North was "really a low-ranking subordinate working to carry out initiatives of a few cynical superiors," sentenced him to two years' probation, $50,000 in fines, and 1,200 hours of community service.

The conviction on the most important counts was reversed on appeal by a divided panel, on July 20, 1990. The Court of Appeals ruled that Gesell had failed to keep the trial free of taint from North's immunized congressional testimony and remanded for a witness-by-witness and, if necessary, line-by-line and item-by-item inquiry into content and sources. A petition for rehearing was granted in part and denied in part. The panel released a long opinion that did not modify its judgment. A suggestion for rehearing *en banc* was denied, with dissents by Judges Wald and Ginsburg. On May 28, 1991, the Supreme Court denied the petition for certiorari.[94] After two days of remand hearings before Judge Gesell, the Independent Counsel consented to dismissal of the remaining counts.

John Poindexter was tried for obstructing official inquiries and proceedings and making false statements to Congress in the wake of the exposure of the Iran-Contra connection. He, too, mounted a higher-authorization defense, claiming that he had deliberately withheld information from Reagan in order to give the President "deniability." He sought to subpoena Reagan's notes and diaries, as well as the testimony of the former President himself. Harold Greene, who tried the case, upheld the subpoenas.[95] President Reagan gave a seven-hour videotaped deposition on February 17, 1990. He did not claim executive privilege, but repeatedly claimed memory lapses. Though he exhibited virtually no detailed knowledge of the Iran-Contra matter, he made it clear that the actions had had his imprimatur.

The one-month trial ended on April 7, 1990, with Poindexter's conviction on five counts. Judge Greene sentenced him to six months' imprisonment. On November 15, 1991, a divided panel of the Court of Appeals reversed Poindexter's convictions, largely on the same ground it had

---

94. 910 F.2d 843 (*per curiam* Sen-*Sil*(c/d)-*Wald*(c/d)), op. withdrawn and superseded in part on reh'g, 920 F.2d 940 (1990), cert. denied, 500 U.S. 941 (1991).

95. *United States v. Poindexter*, 732 F. Supp. 135 (1990); 732 F. Supp. 142 (1990).

overturned North's: that the trial had been impermissibly tainted by Poindexter's immunized congressional testimony. Judge Mikva dissented. The Supreme Court denied certiorari.[96]

96. *United States v. Poindexter*, 951 F.2d 369 (1991) (*DGin*-Sen/*Mik*), cert. denied, 506 U.S. 1021 (1992).

Epilogue

The D.C. Circuit in the Nineties

Through the 1990s and into the turn of the new century, the courts of the District of Columbia Circuit have been among the nation's most influential, each the primary seat for important classes of litigation. By the close of the 1980s the District Court had become the major forum for lawsuits embodying differences between the executive and legislative branches. It also continued to be the nation's principal venue for oversight of the executive branch of the federal government and for the trial of attempted crimes against the President. Almost two decades after the District of Columbia Court Reorganization Act, the problems of the city of Washington continued to be raised in cases, both civil and criminal, before the District Court.

The Court of Appeals has become the nation's undisputed chief tribunal for administrative law. It confronts a steady stream of complex issues involving science, health, the environment, and technology, and is constantly wrestling with difficult questions of deference to the administrative agencies, statutory interpretation, and constitutional law. If, as a result of the Reorganization Act, the docket of the Court of Appeals is less varied than it once had been, it still hears appeals on a wide range of social cases coming from the District Court.

As this volume goes to press, the courts of the D.C. Circuit are celebrating their bicentennial and embarking upon their third century of service to the nation. From their modest beginnings in the embryonic federal city, they have steadily grown in stature to meet the diverse and exacting needs of the District and of the federal government, both of which have expanded far beyond the visions of the founding fathers to become the political capital of the world.

The judges of the Court of Appeals today are Harry T. Edwards, C.J., Stephen F. Williams, Douglas H. Ginsburg, David Bryan Sentelle, Karen LeCraft Henderson, A. Raymond Randolph, Judith W. Rogers, David S. Tatel, and Merrick B. Garland; Laurence H. Silberman and James J. Buckley are senior Circuit judges. They are an able, diverse and hard-working collegial group. Six former judges of the Court of Appeals have served on the Supreme Court: Chief Justices Frederick M. Vinson and Warren Burger and Justices Wiley Rutledge, Antonin Scalia, Clarence Thomas, and Ruth Bader Ginsburg. A former Chief Judge of the court, Patricia Wald, is a member of the International Criminal Tribunal for the Former Yugoslavia, which sits at the Hague.

On the District Court are Chief Judge Norma Holloway Johnson and Judges Thomas Penfield Jackson, Thomas F. Hogan, Royce C. Lamberth,, Paul L. Friedman, Gladys Kessler, Ricardo M. Urbina, Emmet G. Sullivan, James Robertson, Colleen Kollar-Kotelly, Henry H. Kennedy Jr., Richard W. Roberts, Ellen Segal Huvelle, and senior Judges William B. Bryant, June L. Green, Thomas A. Flannery, Louis F. Oberdorfer, John Garrett Penn, Joyce Hens Green, and Stanley S. Harris. Senior judges over the years have made a most important contribution to work of both courts, particularly the District Court, on which six to eight senior judges have regularly carried a heavy load of cases.

President John Adams and Judge William Cranch would certainly take great satisfaction in the court system they set in motion two centuries ago.

Appendix A

Judges of the Courts of the District of Columbia Circuit

Circuit Court of the District of Columbia, 1801–63[1]

Chief Judges Asst. Judges	Served
Thomas Johnson[2]	(1801)
William Kilty	1801–06
William Cranch	1801–55
James Marshall	1801–03
Nicholas Fitzhugh	1801–15
William Cranch	1806–55
Allen B. Duckett	1806–09
Buckner Thruston	1809–45
James S. Morsell	1815–63
James Dunlop	1845–63
James Dunlop	1855–63
William Merrick	1855–63

---

1. Created by the Act of February 27, 1801, 2 Stat. 103.
2. Johnson was appointed and confirmed, but declined the appointment and never served.

Supreme Court of the District of Columbia, 1863–1936

District Court of the United States for the District of Columbia, 1936–48

U.S. District Court for the District of Columbia, 1948–2000[3]

Chief Justices Assoc. Justices	Served
David K. Cartter	1863–1887
George P. Fisher	1863–70
Abram B. Olin	1863–79
Andrew Wylie	1863–85
David C. Humphreys	1870–79
Arthur MacArthur	1870–87
Alexander B. Hagner	1879–1903
Walter S. Cox	1879–99
Charles P. James	1879–92
William M. Merrick	1885–89
Edward F. Bingham	1887–1903
Martin V. Montgomery	1887–92
Andrew C. Bradley	1889–1902
Louis E. McComas	1892–99
Charles C. Cole	1893–1901
Harry M. Clabaugh	1899–1914
Job Barnard	1899–1914
Thomas H. Anderson	1901–16
Ashley M. Gould	1902–21
Harry M. Clabaugh	1903–14
Jeter C. Pritchard	1903–04
Daniel T. Wright	1903–14
Wendell P. Stafford	1904–31

---

3. Supreme Court of the District of Columbia, created by the Act of March 3, 1863, 12 Stat. 762-65; designated as the District Court of the United States for the District of Columbia, Act of June 25, 1936, 49 Stat. 1921; and as the United States District Court for the District of Columbia, Act of June 25, 1948, 62 Stat. 991. By the 1948 Act (62 Stat. 991), members of the District Court, hitherto called "justices," were denominated "judges."

Chief Justices/Judges Assoc. Justices/Judges	Served (S.J. = Senior Justice/Judge)
J. Harry Covington	1914–18
Walter T. McCoy	1914–29
Frederick L. Siddons	1915–31
William Hitz	1916–31
Thomas J. Bailey	1918–50 (S.J. 1950–63)
Walter T. McCoy	1918–29
Adolph A. Hoehling Jr.	1921–27
Peyton Gordon	1928–41 (S.J. 1941–46)
Alfred A. Wheat	1929–41 (S.J. 1941–43)
Alfred A. Wheat	1930–41
Jesse C. Adkins	1930–46 (S.J. 1946–55)
Oscar R. Luhring	1930–44
Joseph W. Cox	1930–39
James M. Proctor	1931–48
F. Dickinson Letts	1931–61 (S.J. 1961–65)
Daniel W. O'Donoghue	1931–46 (S.J. 1946–48)
Bolitha J. Laws	1938–58
T. Alan Goldsborough	1939–51
James W. Morris	1939–60
David A. Pine	1940–65 (S.J. 1965–70)
Matthew F. McGuire	1941–66 (S.J. 1966–86)
Edward C. Eicher	1942–44
Bolitha J. Laws	1945–58
Henry A. Schweinhaut	1944–56 (S.J. 1956–70)
Alexander Holtzoff	1945–67 (S.J. 1967–69)
Edward M. Curran	1946–71 (S.J. 1971–88)
Richmond B. Keech	1947–66 (S.J. 1966–86)
Edward Allen Tamm	1948–65
Charles F. McLaughlin	1949–64 (S.J. 1964–76)
James R. Kirkland	1949–58
Burnita Shelton Matthews	1949–68 (S.J. 1968–88)
Walter M. Bastian	1950–54
Luther W. Youngdahl	1951–66 (S.J. 1966–78)
Joseph C. McGarraghy	1954–67 (S.J. 1967–75)
John J. Sirica	1957–77 (S.J. 1977–92)
F. Dickinson Letts	1958–59
George L. Hart Jr.	1958–79 (S.J. 1979–84)
Leonard P. Walsh	1959–71 (S.J. 1971–80)

Chief Judges Assoc. Judges	Served (S.J. = Senior Judge)
David A. Pine	1959–61
Matthew F. McGuire	1961–66
William B. Jones	1962–77 (S.J. 1977–79)
Spottswood W. Robinson III	1964–66
Howard F. Corcoran	1965–77 (S.J. 1977–89)
Oliver Gasch	1965–81 (S.J. 1981–99)
William B. Bryant	1965–82 (S.J. 1982–)
Richmond B. Keech	1966
Edward M. Curran	1966–71
John Lewis Smith Jr.	1966–83 (S.J. 1983–92)
Aubrey E. Robinson Jr.	1966–92 (S.J. 1992–2000)
Joseph C. Waddy	1967–78
Gerhard A. Gesell	1967–93
John H. Pratt	1968–89 (S.J. 1989–95)
June L. Green	1968–84 (S.J. 1984–)
Barrington D. Parker Sr.	1969–85 (S.J. 1985–93)
Charles R. Richey	1971–97
Thomas A. Flannery	1971–85 (S.J. 1985–)
John J. Sirica	1971–74
George L. Hart, Jr.	1974–75
William B. Jones	1975–77
Louis F. Oberdorfer	1977–92 (S.J. 1992–)
William B. Bryant	1977–81
Harold H. Greene	1978–95 (S.J. 1995–2000)
John Garrett Penn	1979–98 (S.J. 1998–)
Joyce H. Green	1979–95 (S.J. 1995–)
Norma Holloway Johnson	1980–
Thomas Penfield Jackson	1982–
Thomas F. Hogan	1982–
John Lewis Smith Jr.	1981–82
Aubrey E. Robinson Jr.	1982–92
Stanley S. Harris	1983–96 (S.J. 1996–)
George H. Revercomb	1985–93
Stanley Sporkin	1985–1999 (S.J. 1999–2000)
Royce C. Lamberth	1987–
Michael Boudin	1990–92

Chief Judges Assoc. Judges	Served (S.J. = Senior Judge)
John Garrett Penn	1992–97
Gladys Kessler	1994–
Paul L. Friedman	1994–
Ricardo M. Urbina	1994–
Emmet G. Sullivan	1994–
James Robertson	1994–
Norma Holloway Johnson	1997–
Collen Kollar-Kotelly	1997–
Henry H. Kennedy Jr.	1997–
Richard W. Roberts	1998–
Ellen Segal Huvelle	1999–

Court of Appeals of the District of Columbia, 1893–1934

United States Court of Appeals for the District of Columbia, 1934–42

United States Court of Appeals for the District of Columbia Circuit, 1942–2000[4]

Chief Justices Assoc. Justices/Judges	Served (S.J. = Senior Justice/Judge)
Richard H. Alvey	1893–1905
Martin F. Morris	1893–1905
Seth Shepard	1893–1917
Seth Shepard	1905–17
Charles Holland Duell	1905–06
Louis Emory McComas	1905–07
Charles H. Robb	1906–37 (S.J. 1937–39)
Josiah A. Van Orsdel	1907–37
Constantine J. Smyth	1917–24
George Ewing Martin	1924–37 (S.J. 1937–48)
William Hitz	1931–35
Duncan Lawrence Groner	1931–48 (S.J. 1948–57)
Harold M. Stephens	1935–55
Duncan Lawrence Groner	1938–48
R. Justin Miller	1937–45
Henry W. Edgerton	1937–63 (S.J. 1963–70)
Fred Vinson	1937–43
Wiley Rutledge	1939–43
Thurman Arnold	1943–45
E. Barrett Prettyman	1945–62 (S.J. 1962–71)
Wilbur K. Miller	1945–64 (S.J. 1964–76)
Bennett Champ Clark	1945–54

4. The Court of Appeals of the District of Columbia, created by the Act of February 9, 1893, 27 Stat. 434; redesignated as the United States Court of Appeals for the District of Columbia, Act of June 7, 1934, 48 Stat. 926; and as the United States Court of Appeals for the District of Columbia Circuit by the Act of December 29, 1942, 56 Stat. 1094.

Until 1948, judges of the Court of Appeals were called "justices"; by the Act of June 25, 1948, 62 Stat. 991, they were denominated "judges."

Chief Judges Assoc. Judges	Served (S.J. = Senior Judge)
Harold M. Stephens	1948–55
James M. Proctor	1948–53
David L. Bazelon	1949–79 (S.J. 1979–93)
Charles Fahy	1949–67 (S.J. 1967–79)
George T. Washington	1949–65 (S.J. 1965–71)
John A. Danaher	1953–69 (S.J. 1969–90)
Walter M. Bastian	1954–65 (S.J. 1965–75)
Henry W. Edgerton[5]	1955–58
Warren E. Burger	1956–70
E. Barrett Prettyman	1958–60
Wilbur K. Miller	1960–62
David L. Bazelon	1962–79
J. Skelly Wright	1962–86 (S.J. 1986–88)
Carl McGowan	1963–81 (S.J. 1981–87)
Edward Allen Tamm	1965–85
Harold Leventhal	1965–79
Spottswood W. Robinson III	1966–89 (S.J. 1989–98)
George E. MacKinnon	1969–83 (S.J. 1983–95)
Roger Robb	1969–82 (S.J. 1982–85)
Malcolm Richard Wilkey	1970–84 (S.J. 1984–85)
J. Skelly Wright	1978–81
Carl McGowan	1981
Spottswood W. Robinson III	1981–86
Patricia M. Wald	1979–1999
Abner J. Mikva	1979–94
Harry T. Edwards	1980–
Ruth Bader Ginsburg	1980–93
Robert H. Bork	1982–88
Antonin Scalia	1982–86
Kenneth W. Starr	1983–89
Laurence H. Silberman	1985–2000 (S.J. 2000–)
James L. Buckley	1985–96 (S.J. 1996–2000)
Stephen F. Williams	1986–

5. Under the Act of June 25, 1948, 62 Stat. 87, the Chief Judge cannot be over 70 years of age, and the Chief Judgeship, previously a presidential appointment, passes automatically to the most senior associate judge under 70.

Chief Judges Assoc. Judges	Served (S.J. = Senior Judge)
Patricia M. Wald	1986–91
Douglas H. Ginsburg	1986–
David B. Sentelle	1987–
Clarence Thomas	1990–91
Karen LeCraft Henderson	1990–
A. Raymond Randolph	1990–
Abner J. Mikva	1991–94
Judith W. Rogers	1994–
Harry T. Edwards	1994–2001
David S. Tatel	1994–
Merrick B. Garland	1997–

Appendix B

Abbreviations of Judges' Names in Case Citations

When reported, the record of votes in a decision is given parenthetically at the end of the footnoted case citation, if not specified in the text. In citations of cases in the Court of Appeals (and its nineteenth-century forebears), the names of the participating judges are abbreviated according to the following chart. Names are abbreviated to the first three letters, except in the case of four-letter names, which are fully spelled out, and when an additional letter is necessary to avoid confusion between two names. (The names of District Court judges and visiting judges from other circuits are spelled out.) The majority and minority are separated by a solidus (slash) and judges issuing written opinions are italicized. (c) indicates a concurring opinion, (c/d) means concurring in part and dissenting in part.

Abbreviations	Judges cited in footnoted decisions
Alv	Alvey, Richard H.
Arn	Arnold, Thurman
Bas	Bastian, Walter M.
Baz	Bazelon, David L.
Bin	Bingham, Edward F.
Bork	Bork, Robert H.
Buc	Buckley, Edward F.
Bur	Burger, Warren E.
Cla	Clark, Bennett Champ
Dan	Danaher, John A.
Edg	Edgerton, Henry W.
Edw	Edwards, Harry T.
Fahy	Fahy, Charles
RGin	Ginsburg, Ruth Bader

DGin	Ginsburg, Douglas
Gro	Groner, Duncan Lawrence
Hag	Hagner, Alexander B.
Hen	Henderson, Karen LeCraft
Hitz	Hitz, William
Jam	James, Charles P.
Lev	Leventhal, Harold
MacA	MacArthur, Arthur
MacK	MacKinnon, George E.
Mar	Martin, George Ewing
McG	McGowan, Carl
Mer	Merrick, William
Mik	Mikva, Abner J.
JMil	Miller, R. Justin
WMil	Miller, Wilbur K.
Mor	Morris, James W.
Pre	Prettyman, E. Barrett
Pro	Proctor, James M.
Ran	Randolph, A. Raymond
CRobb	Robb, Charles H.
RRobb	Robb, Roger
Rob	Robinson, Spottswood W., III
Rut	Rutledge, Wiley
Sca	Scalia, Antonin
Sen	Sentelle, David B.
She	Shepard, Seth
Sil	Silberman, Laurence H.
Smy	Smyth, Constantine J.
Sta	Starr, Kenneth W.
Ste	Stephens, Harold M.
Tamm	Tamm, Edward Allen
Tho	Thomas, Clarence
Van	Van Orsdel, Josiah A.
Vin	Vinson, Fred
Wald	Wald, Patricia M.
Was	Washington, George T.
Wilk	Wilkey, Malcolm Richard
Will	Williams, Stephen F.
Wri	Wright, J. Skelly

Sources

General Sources

Judicial History and Biography[1]

Almanac of the Federal Judiciary. Edited by Barnabas D. Johnson and others. Chicago: LawLetters, 1984–89; Englewood Cliffs, N.J.: Prentice Hall Law and Business, 1989–94; New York: Aspen Law & Business, 1994–date.

The American Bench: Judges of the Nation. 9 eds., 1977–97. Minneapolis: Reginald Bishop Forster & Assocs.; Sacramento: Forster-Long.

Banks, Christopher P. *Judicial Politics in the D.C Circuit Court.* Baltimore: Johns Hopkins University Press, 1999.

Cannon, Mark W., and David M. O'Brien, eds. *Views from the Bench: The Judiciary and Constitutional Politics.* Chatham, N.J.: Chatham House, 1985.

Chase, Harold, Samuel Krislov, Keith O. Boyum, and Jerry N. Clark, comps. *Biographical Dictionary of the Federal Judiciary.* Detroit: Gale Research Co., 1976.

Edwards, Harry T. "The Judicial Function and the Elusive Goal of Principled Decisionmaking," *Wisconsin Law Review* (1991): 837–65.

———. "Public Misperceptions Concerning the 'Politics' of Judging: Dispelling Some Myths about the D.C. Circuit." *University of Colorado Law Review* 56 (1985): 619–46.

Emerson, Thomas I., David Haber, and Norman Dorsen. *Political and Civil Rights in the United States: A Collection of Legal and Related Materials.* 3d ed. 2 vols. Boston: Little, Brown, 1967.

Fish, Peter Graham. *The Politics of Federal Judicial Administration.* Princeton: Princeton University Press, 1973.

Ginsburg, Ruth Bader. "Speaking in a Judicial Voice." *New York University Law Review* 67 (1992): 1185–1209

———. "Styles of Collegial Judging: One Judge's Perspective." *Federal Bar News,* March–April 1992, 199–201.

Goulden, Joseph C. *The Benchwarmers: The Private World of the Powerful Federal Judges.* New York: Weybright & Talley, 1974.

---

1. See **Other Sources** by chapter, below, for sources on individual judges.

A History of the District of Columbia Circuit Judicial Conference, 1940–1989. Written by the Office of the Circuit Executive for the District of Columbia Circuit Judicial Conference. Washington, D.C., 1989.

Johnson, John W., ed. *Historic U.S. Court Cases 1690–1990: An Encyclopedia.* New York: Garland, 1992.

Judicial Conference of the United States, Bicentennial Committee, Subcommittee on Biographical Directory. *Judges of the United States.* Washington, D.C.: Judicial Conference of the United States, Bicentennial Committee, 1978 [1980].

McGuire, Matthew F. *An Anecdotal History of the United States District Court for the District of Columbia, 1801–1976.* Washington, D.C.: The Court, 1977.

Miller, Loren. *The Petitioners: The Story of the Supreme Court of the United States and the Negro.* New York: Pantheon Books, 1966.

Morris, Jeffrey B. "The Second Most Important Court: The United States Court of Appeals for the District of Columbia Circuit." Ph.D. diss., Columbia University, 1972.

Noel, F. Regis. *The Court-house of the District of Columbia.* Washington, D.C.: Law Reporter Printing Co., 1939.

United States Court of Appeals (District of Columbia Circuit). *History of the United States Court of Appeals for the District of Columbia Circuit in the Country's Bicentennial Year.* Washington, D.C.: The Court, 1977.

U.S. Senate Committee on the Judiciary. *Legislative History of the United States Circuit Courts of Appeals and the Judges Who Served During the Period 1801 through March 1958.* 85th Cong., 2d Sess., 1958. Committee Print.

Wald, Patricia M. "Ghosts of Judges Past." *George Washington Law Review* 62 (1994) 675–82.

———. "Making 'Informed Decisions' on the District of Columbia Circuit." *George Washington Law Review* 60 (1982) 135–54.

———. "The Problem with the Courts: Black-Robed Bureaucracy, or Collegiality under Challenge?" *Maryland Law Review* 42 (1983): 766–86.

Who Was Who in America, vols. 1–8 (1897–1985). Chicago: Marquis, 1942–85.

Who Was Who in America, Historical Volume, 1607–1896. Chicago: Marquis, 1963.

Williams, E. Melvin, and Frederick L. Siddons. "The Circuit Court of the District of Columbia, 1801–63," "The Supreme Court of the District of Columbia, 1863–1928," "The Court of Appeals of the District of Columbia, 1893–1928." Chapters 21–23 of *Washington, Past and Present: A History,* edited by John Clagett Proctor. New York: Lewis Historical Publishing Co., 1930.

History of the District of Columbia

Bryan, Wilhelmus Bogart. *A History of the National Capital, from Its Foundation through the Period of the Adoption of the Organic Act.* 2 vols. New York: Macmillan, 1914–16.

Evelyn, Douglas E., and Paul A. Dickson. *On This Spot: Pinpointing the Past in Washington, D.C.* Washington, D.C.: Farragut Publishing Co., 1992.

Fitzpatrick, Sandra, and Maria R. Goodwin. *A Guide to Black Washington: Places and Events of Historical and Cultural Significance in the Nation's Capital.* New York: Hippocrene Books, 1990.

Gillette, Howard, Jr. *Between Justice and Beauty: Race, Planning, and the Failure of Urban Policy in Washington, D.C.* Baltimore: Johns Hopkins University Press, 1995.

Green, Constance McLaughlin. *The Secret City: A History of Race Relations in the Nation's Capital.* Princeton: Princeton University Press, 1967.

————. *Washington.* Vol. 1, *Village and Capital, 1800–1878;* vol. 2, *Capital City, 1879–1950.* Princeton: Princeton University Press, 1962–63.

Gutheim, Frederick. *The Potomac.* New York: Holt, Rinehart & Winston, 1974.

Gutheim, Frederick, and Wilcomb E. Washburn. *The Federal City, Plans and Realities: The History.* 2d ed. Washington, D.C.: Smithsonian Institution Press, with the National Capital Planning Commission, 1981.

Jaffe, Harry S., and Tom Sherwood. *Dream City: Race, Power, and the Decline of Washington, D.C.* New York: Simon & Schuster, 1994.

Junior League of the City of Washington. *The City of Washington: An Illustrated History,* edited by Thomas Froncek. New York: Knopf, 1977.

Melder, Keith, ed. and comp. *City of Magnificent Intentions.* Developed by the D.C. Curriculum Project, a project of Associates for Renewal in Education. Washington, D.C.: Intac, 1983.

Proctor, John Clagett, ed. *Washington, Past and Present: A History.* 4 vols. New York: Lewis Historical Publishing Co., 1930.

Administrative Law and Regulatory Agencies

Breyer, Stephen G., and Richard B. Stewart. *Administrative Law and Regulatory Policy: Problems, Text, and Cases.* 3d ed. Boston: Little, Brown, 1992.

Friendly, Fred W. *The Good Guys, the Bad Guys, and the First Amendment: Free Speech vs. Fairness in Broadcasting.* New York: Random House, c.1976.

Gardner, Warner W., and I. Michael Greenberger. "Judicial Review of Administrative Action and Responsible Government." *Georgetown Law Journal* 63 (1974): 7–38.

Gellhorn, Walter, Clark Byse, and Peter L. Strauss. *Administrative Law: Cases and Comments.* 7th ed. Mineola, N.Y.: Foundation Press, 1979.

Heffron, Florence, with Neil McFeeley. *The Administrative Regulatory Process.* New York: Longman, 1983.

Kahn, Frank J., ed. *Documents of American Broadcasting.* 4th ed. Englewood Cliffs, N.J.: Prentice-Hall, 1984.

Kohlmeier, Louis M., Jr. *The Regulators: Watchdog Agencies and the Public Interest.* New York: Harper & Row, 1969.

Krasnow, Erwin G., Lawrence D. Longley, and Herbert A. Terry. *The Politics of Broadcast Regulation.* 3d ed. New York: St. Martin's Press, 1982.

Krislov, Samuel, and Lloyd D. Musolf, eds. *The Politics of Regulation: A Reader.* Boston: Houghton Mifflin, 1964.

Michael, James R., with Ruth C. Fort, eds. *Working on the System: A Comprehensive Manual for Citizen Access to Federal Agencies.* New York: Basic Books, 1974.

Prettyman, E. Barrett. *Trial by Agency.* The Henry L. Doherty Lectures, 1958. Charlottesville: Virginia Law Review Association, 1959.

Wald, Patricia M. "Comments: The 'New Administrative Law' — with the Same Old Judges in It?" *Duke Law Journal* (1991): 647–70.

———. "The Contribution of the D.C. Circuit to Administrative Law." *Administrative Law Review* 40 (1988): 507–59.

Wilson, James Q., ed. *The Politics of Regulation.* New York: Basic Books, 1980.

Woll, Peter. *American Bureaucracy,* chap. 3, "Administrative Law and the Courts." 2d edition. New York: Norton, 1977.

Other Sources

Chapter 1

Adams, John Quincy. *Memoirs,* edited by Charles Francis Adams, vol. 8. Philadelphia: Lippincott, 1876.

Ames, William E. *A History of the National Intelligencer.* Chapel Hill: University of North Carolina Press, 1972.

Arnebeck, Bob. *Through a Fiery Trial: Building Washington, 1790–1800.* Lanham: Madison Books, 1991.

Beveridge, Albert J. *The Life of John Marshall,* vol. 3. Boston: Houghton Mifflin, 1919.

Burr, Aaron. *Political Correspondence and Public Papers of Aaron Burr: Selections,* edited by Mary-Jo Kline. 2 vols. Princeton: Princeton University Press, 1983.

Clark, Allen C. *Greenleaf and Law in the Federal City.* Washington, D.C.: W. F. Roberts, 1901.

Cox, Walter S. "Efforts to Obtain a Code of Laws for the District of Columbia." *Records — Columbia Historical Society of Washington, D.C.* 3 (1898): 115–35.

———. "Reminiscences of the Courts of the District." *Washington Law Reporter* 23, no. 32 (August 8, 1895): 498–502.

Delaplaine, Edward S. *The Life of Thomas Johnson.* New York: F. H. Hitchcock, 1927.

Dewey, Donald O. *Marshall versus Jefferson: The Political Background of Marbury vs. Madison.* New York: Knopf, 1970.

DiGiacomantonio, William C. "All the President's Men: George Washington's Federal City Commissioners." *Washington History* 3 no. 1 (1991): 52–75.

Hagner, Alexander B. "William Cranch." In *Great American Lawyers,* edited by William Draper Lewis, vol. 3. Philadelphia: John C. Winston Company, 1907–09.

Haskins, George Lee, and Herbert A. Johnson. *Foundations of Power: John Marshall, 1801–15.* History of the Supreme Court of the United States, vol 2. New York: Macmillan, 1981.

Newman, Helen. "William Cranch: Judge, Law School Professor, Reporter." *Law Library Journal* 26 (October 1933): 74–91.

Porter, John Addison. *The City of Washington: Its Origin and Administration.* Johns Hopkins University Studies in Historical and Political Science, 3d series, 11–12. Baltimore: N. Murray, for Johns Hopkins University, 1885.

U.S. House of Representatives. *Case of Judge Thruston.* Hearings. 24th Cong., 2d Sess., H.R. Rept. 327, 1837.

Warren, Charles. *The Supreme Court in United States History,* vol. 1, 1789–1835. Rev. ed. Boston: Little, Brown, 1928.

White, G. Edward, with Gerald Gunther. *The Marshall Court and Cultural Change, 1815–35.* History of the Supreme Court of the United States, vols. 3–4. New York: Macmillan, 1988.

White, Leonard Dupee. *The Jeffersonians: A Study in Administrative History, 1801–1829.* New York: Macmillan, 1951.

Chapter 2

Barnard, Job. "The Early Days of the Supreme Court of the District of Columbia." *Washington Law Reporter* 36, no. 3 (January 17, 1907): 30–40.

Bullard, F. Louristan. "Lincoln and the Courts of the District of Columbia." *American Bar Association Journal* 24 (1938): 117–20.

Busch, Francis X. "The Trial of Mary Eugenia Surratt and Others for the Murder of President Abraham Lincoln (May–June 1865)." In *Enemies of the State.* Notable American Trials series. Indianapolis: Bobbs-Merrill, 1954.

"The Case of Brig. Gen. Graham." *Washington Evening Star,* October 10, 1861, 3.

Fairman, Charles. *Reconstruction and Reunion, 1864–88.* 2 vols. History of the Supreme Court of the United States, vols. 6–7. New York: Macmillan, 1971–87.

Indritz, Phineas. "Post-Civil War Ordinances Prohibiting Racial Discrimination in the District of Columbia." *Georgetown Law Journal* 42 (1954): 179–209.

Kunhardt, Dorothy Meserve, and Philip B. Kunhardt Jr. *Twenty Days: A Narrative in Text and Pictures of the Assassination of Abraham Lincoln and the Twenty Days and Nights that Followed.* New York: Harper & Row, 1965.

Leech, Margaret. *Reveille in Washington, 1860–1865.* New York and London: Harper & Brothers, 1941.

Leland, Earl J. *The Post Office and Politics, 1876–1884: The Star Route Frauds.* Ph.D. diss., University of Chicago, 1964.

"Mr. Justice Walter Smith Cox: Meeting of the Bar of the District to Take Action Relative to His Retirement." *Washington Law Reporter* 27, no. 45 (November 9, 1899): 717–24.

Supreme Court of the District of Columbia. *Proceedings in the Trial of the Case of the United States vs. John W. Dorsey, John R. Miner, John M. Peck, Stephen W. Dorsey, Harvey M. Vaile, Montfort C. Rerdell, Thomas J. Brady, and William H. Turner, for Conspiracy.* 3 vols. Washington, D.C.: U.S. Government Printing Office, 1882; microfiche reprint, Englewood, Colo.: Microcard Editions, 1975 (Historical Trials Relevant to Today's Issues, 4).

―――. *Proceedings in the Second Trial of the Case of the United States vs. John W. Dorsey [et al.], for Conspiracy.* 4 vols. Washington, D.C.: U.S. Government Printing Office, 1883.

Maury, William M. *Alexander "Boss" Shepherd and the Board of Public Works.* George Washington Studies, no. 3. Washington, D.C.: George Washington University, 1975.

―――. "Alexander R. Shepherd and the Board of Public Works." *Records — Columbia Historical Society of Washington, D.C.* (1971–72): 394–410.

Rosenberg, Charles E. *The Trial of the Assassin Guiteau: Psychiatry and Law in the Gilded Age.* Chicago: University of Chicago Press, 1968.

Saint Elizabeths Hospital Centennial Committee, eds. *Centennial Papers: Saint Elizabeths Hospital, 1855–1955.* Washington, D.C.: Saint Elizabeths Hospital Centennial Commission, 1956. (See especially Winfred Overholser, "An Historical Sketch of Saint Elizabeths Hospital," and Nolan D. C. Lewis, "Review of the Scientific Contributions of Saint Elizabeths Hospital, 1855–1955.")

U.S. House of Representatives. *Confiscation Law in the District of Columbia.* 37th Cong., 3d sess., Ex. Doc. 32, 1863.

The War of the Rebellion: A Compilation of the Official Records of the Union and Confederate Armies, series 2, vol. 2. Washington, D.C.: U.S. Government Printing Office: 1891.

White, Leonard Dupee, with Jean Schneider. *The Republican Era, 1869–1901: A Study in Administrative History.* New York: Macmillan, 1958.

Whyte, James H. "Divided Loyalties in the Civil War." *Records — Columbia Historical Society of Washington, D.C.* 62 (1960): 103–22.

Chapter 3

Allen, Frederick Lewis. *Only Yesterday: An Informal History of the Nineteen-Twenties.* 2d ed. New York and London: Harper & Brothers, 1931.

Baker, Leonard. *Brandeis and Frankfurter: A Dual Biography.* New York: Harper & Row, 1984.

Bernstein, Irving. *The Lean Years: A History of the American Worker, 1920–1933.* Boston: Houghton Mifflin, 1960.

Busch, Francis X. "The Trial of Albert B. Fall and Others for Bribery and Conspiracy to Defraud the United States of the Teapot Dome and Elk Hils Oil Reserves." In *Enemies of the State.* Notable American Trials series. Indianapolis: Bobbs-Merrill, 1954.

Clark, Blue. *Lone Wolf v. Hitchcock: Treaty Rights and Indian Law at the End of the Nineteenth Century.* Lincoln: University of Nebraska Press, 1994.

Cohen, Lester. *Frank Hogan Remembered: Reminiscences.* Washington, D.C.: Hogan & Hartson, 1985.

Hill, Walter Bernard. "The Federal Judicial System." *American Bar Association Report* 12 (August 28, 1889): 289–326.

"In Memoriam: Proceedings in Memory of Honorable Charles H. Robb and Honorable Josiah A. Van Orsdel, Associate Justices of the United States Court of Appeals for the District of Columbia." 71 App. D.C. v (May 20, 1940).

McDonald, Kevin. "Antitrust and Baseball: Stealing Holmes." *Journal of Supreme Court History* 2 (1998): 88–128.

McMurry, Donald L. *Coxey's Army: A Study of the Industrial Army Movement of 1894.* Boston: Little, Brown, 1929.

"Memorial to the Late Mr. Chief Justice Smyth." 54 App. D.C. vii (May 28, 1924).

"Mr. Justice Walter Smith Cox: Meeting of the Bar of the District to Take Action Relative to His Retirement." *Washington Law Reporter* 27, no. 45 (November 9, 1899): 717–24.

Perrett, Geoffrey. *America in the Twenties: A History.* New York: Simon & Schuster, 1982.

"Retirement of Associate Justice Morris." 26 App. D.C. xxi (December 22, 1905).

"Retirement of Chief Justice Alvey." 24 App. D.C. xvii (December 30, 1904).

"Retirement of Chief Justice Shepard." 46 App. D.C. xxiii (April 28, 1917).

Ryan, Bernard, Jr. "The Teapot Dome Trials, 1926–30." In *Great American Trials,* edited by Edward W. Knappman. Detroit: Visible Ink Press, 1994.

Whipple, Leon. "The Woman's Suffrage Movement." In *The Story of Civil Liberty in the United States.* New York: Vanguard Press, American Civil Liberties Union, 1927.

Chapter 4

Burns, James MacGregor. *Roosevelt: The Lion and the Fox.* New York: Harcourt, Brace, 1956.

———. *Roosevelt: The Soldier of Freedom.* New York: Harcourt Brace Jovanovich, 1970.

"D. Lawrence Groner—Chief Judge, U.S. Court of Appeals, District of Columbia." Third in a series on the Senior Judges of the U.S. Circuit Courts of Appeals. *American Bar Association Journal* 33 (January 1947): 36–39.

Edgerton, Henry W. *Freedom in the Balance: Opinions of Judge Henry W. Edgerton Relating to Civil Liberties,* edited by Eleanor Bontecou. Cornell Studies in Civil Liberty. Ithaca: Cornell University Press, 1960.

———. "A Liberal Judge: Cuthbert W. Pound." *Cornell Law Quarterly* 21 (1935): 7–45.

Pacifico, Michele. "'Don't Buy Where You Can't Work': The New Negro Alliance of Washington." *Washington History* 6, no. 1 (Spring-Summer 1994): 66–88.

Pollak, Louis H. "Wiley Blount Rutledge: Profile of a Judge." In *Six Justices on Civil Rights,* edited by Ronald D. Rotunda. David C. Baum Memorial Lectures. London and New York: Oceana Publications, 1983.

Ribuffo, Leo P. "*United States v. McWilliams*: The Roosevelt Administration and the Far Right." In *American Political Trials*, edited by Michal R. Belknap. Contributions in American History, no. 94. Westport, Conn.: Greenwood Press, 1981.

Stevens, John Paul. "Mr. Justice Rutledge." In *Mr. Justice*, edited by Allison Dunham and Philip B. Kurland. Rev. ed. Chicago: University of Chicago Press, 1964.

Torrey, E. Fuller. *The Roots of Treason: Ezra Pound and the Secret of St. Elizabeths.* New York: McGraw-Hill, 1984.

Vose, Clement E. *Caucasians Only: The Supreme Court, the NAACP, and the Restrictive Covenant Cases.* Berkeley: University of California Press, 1959.

Wald, Patricia M. Remarks, Thurman Arnold Centennial Celebration, Washington, D.C., October 30, 1991, unpublished.

Chapter 5

Arnold, Thurman. *Selections from the Letters and Legal Papers of Thurman Arnold.* [Washington, D.C.?], 1961.

Clark, Tom C. "E. Barrett Prettyman." *Georgetown Law Journal* 53 (1964): 1–4.

———. Papers. Attorney General Files, 1945–49. Truman Library, Independence, Mo.

Donovan, Robert J. *Conflict and Crisis: The Presidency of Harry S. Truman, 1945–1948.* New York: Norton, 1977.

Ginsburg, Ruth Bader. "Tribute in Memory of the Honorable Burnita Shelton Matthews, 1894–1988." In *Tributes*, pamphlet distributed at District of Columbia Circuit Judicial Conference, Williamsburg, Va., May 22–24, 1988.

Goulden, Joseph C. *The Best Years: 1945–1950*, chap. 6, "We Want More!" New York: Atheneum, 1976.

Indritz, Phineas. "Racial Ramparts in the Nation's Capital." *Georgetown Law Journal* 41 (1953): 297–329.

Konvitz, Milton R. *Expanding Liberties: Freedom's Gains in Postwar America.* New York: Viking Press, 1966.

Marcus, Maeva. *Truman and the Steel Seizure Case.* New York: Columbia University Press, 1977.

Matthews, Burnita Shelton. "Leader of Women's Rights Movement Recalls Suffrage Fight and Appointment to Bench" (excerpts from an interview with Judge Matthews). *Third Branch* 17 no. 3 (March 1985): 1, 6–9.

McCoy, Donald R. *The Presidency of Harry S. Truman.* American Presidency Series. Lawrence: University Press of Kansas, 1984.

McCullough, David G. *Truman.* New York: Simon & Schuster, 1992.

Miller, Merle. *Plain Speaking: An Oral Biography of Harry S. Truman.* New York: Berkley, 1974.

Truman, Harry S. Papers. Official Files, 41-G (U.S. District Court for the District of Columbia) and 41-H (U.S. Court of Appeals for the District of Columbia Circuit). Truman Library, Independence, Mo.

Westin, Alan F. *The Anatomy of a Constitutional Law Case: Youngstown Sheet and Tube Co. v. Sawyer: The Steel Seizure Decision.* New York: Macmillan, 1958.

Chapter 6

Brownell, Herbert. Interview, by Jeffrey B. Morris and Seth Muraskin. 9 March 1995.

Burger, Warren E., David J. McCarthy, and Milton Eisenberg. "In Memoriam: John A. Danaher." Tributes. *George Washington Law Review* 59 (1991): 1001–07.

Burns, James MacGregor. *The Crosswinds of Freedom.* The American Experiment, vol. 3. New York: Alfred A. Knopf, 1989.

Danaher, John A. Interview by John T. Mason Jr. 15 February 1968. Oral History Research Office, Columbia University, New York.

Gasch, Oliver. "Recollections." *Washington Lawyer* 7, no. 2 (November/December 1992): 22–29.

Kutler, Stanley I. *The American Inquisition: Justice and Injustice in the Cold War.* New York: Hill & Wang, 1982.

"Memorial Service for the Honorable Wilbur K. Miller and the Honorable Walter M. Bastian." 220 U.S. App. D.C. xxi (May 11, 1976).

Packer, Herbert L. "Two Models of the Criminal Process." *University of Pennsylvania Law Review* 113 (1964): 1–68.

Prettyman, E. Barrett. "Three Modern Problems in Criminal Law." *Washington and Lee Law Review* 18, no. 2 (Fall 1961): 187–241.

Rosenblum, Victor G. "How to Get into TV: The Federal Communications Commission and Miami's Channel 10." In *The Uses of Power: Seven Cases in American Politics,* edited by Alan F. Westin. New York: Harcourt, Brace & World, 1962.

Wechsler, Herbert. "The Criteria of Criminal Responsibility." *University of Chicago Law Review* 22 (1955): 367–76.

Chapter 7

Advisory Panel Against Armed Violence. Report, prepared for Senate Committee on the District of Columbia. 91st Cong., 1st session, 1969. Committee Print. Washington, D.C.: U.S. Government Printing Office, 1969.

Arens, Richard. *Make Mad the Guilty: The Insanity Defense in the District of Columbia.* Springfield, Ill.: C. C. Thomas, 1969.

Attorney General's Committee on Poverty and the Administration of Federal Criminal Justice, U.S. Department of Justice. *Report: Poverty and the Administration of Federal Criminal Justice.* Washington, D.C., 1963.

Baker, Liva. *Miranda: Crime, Law, and Politics.* New York: Atheneum, 1983.

Bass, Jack. *Unlikely Heroes: The Dramatic Story of the Southern Judges of the Fifth Circuit Who Translated the Supreme Court's Brown Decision into a Revolution for Equality.* New York: Simon & Schuster, 1981.

Bazelon, David L. "The Defective Assistance of Counsel." *University of Cincinnati Law Review* 42 (1973): 1–75.

———. "Implementing the Right to Treatment." *University of Chicago Law Review* 36 (1969): 749–54.

———. "Psychiatrists and the Adversary Process." *Scientific American,* June 1974, 18–23.

Burger, Warren E. "Tribute to Judge Edward Allen Tamm." *Georgetown Law Journal* 74 (1986): 1571–72.

Clayton, James C. "Six Years after Durham." *Judicature* 44 (June 1960): 18–21.

Cortner, Richard C. "Case Study: Broadcasting and the Bureaucracy: The FCC and the Red Lion Case." In *The Bureaucracy in Court: Commentaries and Case Studies in Administrative Law.* Port Washington, N.Y.: Kennikat Press, 1982.

Frankfurter, Felix. Papers, box 73 (correspondence, 1962). Library of Congress.

"In Memoriam: Judge J. Skelly Wright." Memorial tributes by John R. Brown, Louis Claiborne, Susan Estrich, Gerhard A. Gesell, Ruth Bader Ginsburg, Louis F. Oberdorfer, Barrington D. Parker, Spottswood W. Robinson III, Abraham D. Sofaer, and John Minor Wisdom. *George Washington Law Review* 57 (1989): 1029–59.

Judicial Conference of the United States. *Report of the Proceedings of the Judicial Conference of the United States [and] Annual Report of the Director of the Administrative Office of the United States Courts.* Washington, D.C.: U.S. Government Printing Office, 1964.

Judicial Council of the District of Columbia Circuit, Committee on the Administration of Justice. *Court Management Study,* for Senate Committee on the District of Columbia. 91st Cong., 2d Sess., 1970. Committee Print. Washington, D.C.: U.S. Government Printing Office, 1970.

Kluger, Richard. *Simple Justice: The History of Brown v. Board of Education and Black America's Struggle for Equality.* New York: Knopf, 1976.

Landis, James M. *Report on Regulatory Agencies to the President-elect.* Washington, D.C.: U.S. Government Printing Office, 1960.

"The Legacy of Judge David L. Bazelon." Tributes by Abner J. Mikva ("The Real Judge Bazelon"), Martha Minow ("Questioning Our Policies: Judge David L. Bazelon's Legacy for Mental Health Law"), and Patricia M. Wald ("Tribute to Judge Bazelon"). *Georgetown Law Journal* 82 (1993): 1–26.

Leventhal, Harold. "The Role of Price Lawyers." Part 2 of *Problems in Price Control: Legal Phases,* by Leventhal and Nathaniel L. Nathanson. Historical Reports on War Administration, 11. Washington, D.C.: Office of Price Administration, 1947.

Miller, Arthur Selwyn. *A "Capacity for Outrage": The Judicial Odyssey of J. Skelly Wright.* Westport, Conn.: Greenwood Press, 1984.

Molleur, Richard R., director, and the staff of the D.C. Bail Project. *Bail Reform in the Nation's Capital: Final Report.* Washington, D.C.: Georgetown University Law Center, 1966.

Morris, Jeffrey B. "The American Jewish Judge: An Appraisal on the Occasion of the Bicentennial." *Jewish Social Studies* 38 (Summer–Fall 1976): 195–223.

Moscovitz, Myron. "Rent Withholding and the Implied Warranty of Habitability—Some New Breakthroughs." *Clearinghouse Review* 4, no. 2 (June 1970): 49, 62–67.

Pike, David F. "The D.C. Supercircuit." *National Law Journal,* March 30, 1981, 1.

"Portrait Presentation Ceremony, J. Skelly Wright," 784 F.2d lxxix (October 25, 1985).

"Portrait Presentation Ceremony of Spottswood W. Robinson, III," 920 F.2d lxxxiii (June 9, 1989).

"Presentation of the Edward J. Devitt Distinguished Service to Justice Award to Honorable Edward A. Tamm," 800 F.2d ciii (April 8, 1986).

President's Commission on Crime in the District of Columbia. *Report of the President's Commission on Crime in the District of Columbia on the Metropolitan Police Department.* Washington, D.C.: U.S. Government Printing Office, 1966.

"Recent Cases: Insane Persons...*Rouse v. Cameron....*" *Harvard Law Review* 80 (1967): 898–903.

Robinson, Spottswood W., III. "The D.C. Circuit: An Era of Change." *George Washington Law Review* 55 (1987): 715–17.

Subin, Harry I. *Criminal Justice in a Metropolitan Court: The Processing of Serious Criminal Cases in the District of Columbia Court of General Sessions.* New York: Da Capo Press, 1973.

Tamm, Edward A. "Oral History: Judge Edward Tamm." Interview by Alice O'Donnell, November 12 and 29, 1983. Transcript in Federal Judicial Center, Washington, D.C.

Task Force on Assessment of Crime. *Task Force Report: Crime and Its Impact—An Assessment.* Washington, D.C.: President's Commission on Law Enforcement and Administration of Justice, U.S. Government Printing Office, 1967.

U.S. Senate, Committee on the District of Columbia and Subcommittee on Improvements in Judicial Machinery, Committee on the Judiciary. *Crime in the National Capital: Reorganization of District of Columbia Courts.* Hearings, May–August 1969. 91st Cong., 1st session, part 3. Washington, D.C.: U.S. Government Printing Office, 1969.

Wald, Patricia M. *Law and Poverty: 1965.* Prepared as a working paper for the National Conference on Law and Property, 1965. Washington D.C.: U.S. Government Printing Office, 1965.

Wilson, Jerry V. *The War on Crime in the District of Columbia, 1955–75.* Washington, D.C.: Dept. of Justice, Law Enforcement Assistance Administration, National Institute of Law Enforcement and Criminal Justice, 1978.

Wright, J. Skelly. "A Colleague's Tribute to Judge David L. Bazelon, on the Twenty-fifth Anniversary of His Appointment." *University of Pennsylvania Law Review* 123 (1974): 250–53.

———. "The Courts Have Failed the Poor." *New York Times Magazine,* March 9, 1969.

———. "Public School Desegregation: Legal Remedies for De Facto Segregation." *New York University Law Review* 40 (1965): 285–309.

Chapter 8

Dionisopoulos, P. A. *Rebellion, Racism, and Representation: The Adam Clayton Powell Case and Its Antecedents.* DeKalb: Northern Illinois University Press, 1970.

Doyle, James. *Not above the Law: The Battles of Watergate Prosecutors Cox and Jaworski: A Behind-the-Scenes Account.* New York: Morrow, 1977.

Fisher, Louis. *Constitutional Dialogues: Interpretation as Political Process.* Princeton: Princeton University Press, 1988.

Jacobs, Andy. *The Powell Affair: Freedom Minus One.* Indianapolis: Bobbs-Merrill, 1973.

Kleindienst, Richard G. *Justice: The Memoirs of Attorney General Richard Kleindienst.* Ottawa, Ill.: Jameson Books, 1985.

Knappman, Edward W., and others, eds. *Watergate and the White House.* 2 vols. New York: Facts on File, 1974.

Pyle, Christopher H. "CONUS Intelligence: The Army Watches Civilian Politics." *Washington Monthly,* January 1970, 4–16.

"Separation of Powers and Executive Privilege: The Watergate Briefs." *Political Science Quarterly* 88 (1973): 582–654.

Seymour, Whitney North, Jr. *United States Attorney: An Inside View of "Justice" in America under the Nixon Administration,* chap. 10, "Pentagon Papers Revisited." New York: Morrow, 1975.

Shapiro, Martin, ed. *The Pentagon Papers and the Courts: A Study in Foreign Policy-Making and Freedom of the Press.* San Francisco: Chandler, 1972.

Sirica, John J. *To Set the Record Straight: The Break-In, the Tapes, the Conspirators, the Pardon.* New York: Norton, 1979.

Ungar, Sanford J. *The Papers and the Papers: An Account of the Legal and Political Battle over the Pentagon Papers.* New York: Dutton, 1972.

U.S. Senate Committee on the Judiciary, Subcommittee on Constitutional Rights. *Military Surveillance of Civilian Politics: A Report.* 93d Cong., 1st session, 1973. Committee Print. Washington, D.C.: U.S. Government Printing Office, 1973.

Chapter 9

Archibald, Sam. "The Early Years of the Freedom of Information Act—1965 to 1974." *PS: Political Science and Politics,* December 1993, 726–31.

Ayer, Donald B., "Judge Wilkey's Contributions to Criminal Law"; Harold Hongju Koh, "Judge Wilkey's Contributions to International Law and the Foreign Relations Law of the United States"; Stephen S. Rosenthal, "Judge Wilkey's Contributions to Administrative Law on the Separation of Powers." *Brigham Young University Law Review* (1985): 613–56.

Bazelon, David L. "The Impact of the Courts on Public Administration." *Indiana Law Review* 52 (1976): 101–110.

Bermant, Gordon, Patricia A. Lombard, and Carroll Seron. *The Cases of the United States Court of Appeals for the District of Columbia Circuit* [in fiscal 1980]. Washington, D.C.: Federal Judicial Center, 1982.

Bouchard, Robert F., and Justin D. Franklin, eds. *Guidebook to the Freedom of Information and Privacy Acts.* New York: C. Boardman Co., 1980. Supplement, edited by Bouchard. New York: Boardman, 1985.

Breyer, Stephen G., and Paul W. MacAvoy. *Energy Regulation by the Federal Power Commission.* Washington, D.C.: Brookings Institution, 1974.

Butzel, Albert K. "Intervention and Class Actions before the Agencies and the Courts." *Administrative Law Review* 25 (1973): 135–46.

Cortner, Richard C. "Case Study: Banzhaf's Bandits Strike Again: Standing in the SCRAP Case." In *The Bureaucracy in Court: Commentaries and Case Studies in Administrative Law,* 18–42. Port Washington, N.Y.: Kennikat Press, 1982.

Derthick, Martha, and Paul J. Quirk. *The Politics of Deregulation.* Washington, D.C.: Brookings Institution, 1985.

Dyk, Timothy B., and Sarah L. Wanner, "The F.C.C.'s Indecency Proposals under Fire." *Legal Times,* May 17, 1993, 25.

Federal Judicial Center, Research Division. *Appellate Court Caseweights Project.* FJC staff paper. [Washington, D.C.]: Federal Judicial Center, 1977.

Judicial Conference of the United States, Federal Courts Study Committee. *Report of the Federal Courts Study Committee.* [Philadelphia:] 1990.

McGowan, Carl. "Symposium: A Reply to Judicialization." *Duke Law Journal* (1986): 217–37.

Melnick, R. Shep. "Judicial Capacity and Environmental Litigation: The Case of the Clean Air Act." Paper presented at the meeting of the American Political Science Association, 1980.

Reynolds, William L., and William M. Richman. "An Evaluation of Limited Publication in the United States Court of Appeals: The Price of Reform." *University of Chicago Law Review* 48 (1981): 573–631.

Wald, Patricia M. "The D.C. Circuit: Here and Now." *George Washington Law Review* 55 (1987): 718–28.

———. "The Freedom of Information Act: A Short Case Study in the Perils and Payback of Legislating Democratic Values." *Emory Law Journal* 33 (1984): 649–83.

Chapter 10

"Affirmative Action: From *Bakke* to *Croson*—The Affirmative Action Quagmire and the D.C. Circuit's Approach to FCC Minority Preference Policies," by Jennifer M. Bott; "Ethics in Government Act: Statutory Interpretation of Ambiguous Criminal Statutes—An Analysis of Title 18, Section 207(c) of the United States Code," by Beth Frensilli; "Federal Communications Commission: Laying the Fairness Doctrine to Rest—Was the Doctrine's Elimination Really Fair?" by Linda Harowitz. The D.C. Circuit Review, September 1988–August 1989. *George Washington Law Review* 58 (1990): 845–76, 972–1018.

Baer, Donald. "Court in Transition: Reagan Reshapes D.C. Circuit." *Legal Times,* July 28, 1986, 6.

Bendavid, Naftali. "Who's Minding the Sentencing Store?" *Legal Times,* April 4, 1994, 1.

Brill, Steven. "Inside the Jury Room at the *Washington Post* Libel Trial." In *Trial by Jury*, by Steven Brill and the editors and reporters of *American Lawyer*. New York: Simon & Schuster, 1989.

Brisbin, Richard A., Jr. *Justice Antonin Scalia and the Conservative Revival*, chaps. 1–3. Baltimore: Johns Hopkins University Press, 1997.

Brown, Anthony E. *The Politics of Airline Deregulation*. Knoxville: University of Tennessee Press, 1987.

Caplan, Lincoln. *The Insanity Defense and the Trial of John W. Hinckley, Jr.* Boston: D. R. Godine, 1984.

Coll, Steve. *The Deal of the Century: The Breakup of AT&T*. New York: Atheneum, 1986.

Coyle, Marcia. "Starr Potential." *National Law Journal*, September 25, 1989, 1.

Craig, Barbara Hinkson. *Chadha: The Story of an Epic Constitutional Struggle*. New York: Oxford University Press, 1988.

Edwards, Harry T. "A Judge's View on Justice, Bureaucracy, and Legal Method." *Michigan Law Review* 80 (1981): 259–69.

Evans, Colin. "Abscam Trials: 1980 and 1981." In *Great American Trials*, edited by Edward W. Knappmann, 699–703. Detroit: Visible Ink Press, 1994.

"Federal Court Centralizes Pro Se System." *Washington Lawyer*, March–April 1991, 22–29.

Finkelstein, Linda, and Nancy Stanley. "ADR at the U.S. District Court." *Washington Lawyer*, May–June 1992, 32–35, 53.

Gasch, Oliver. "Recollections." *Washington Lawyer*, November–December 1992, 22, 29.

Ginsburg, Douglas H., and Donald Falk. "The D.C. Circuit Review: The Court En Banc, 1981–1990." *George Washington Law Review* 59 (1991): 1008–37.

Greene, Robert W. *The Sting Man: Inside Abscam*. New York: Dutton, 1981.

Harriger, Katy Jean. "Symbol of Justice: The Federal Special Prosecutor in American Politics." Ph.D. diss., University of Connecticut, 1986.

Hickey, Mary C. "The Decade of ADR." *Washington Lawyer*, May–June 1992, 26–29, 50.

Hirrel, Michael J. "The F.C.C.'s Fairness Doctrine Revisited." *Legal Times*, May 17, 1993, 25.

Horwitz, Robert Britt. *The Irony of Regulatory Reform: The Deregulation of American Telecommunications*. New York: Oxford University Press, 1989.

"Investiture Ceremony of the Honorable Kenneth W. Starr." 734 F.2d xcvii (October 25, 1983).

Karpay, Kenneth. "En Banc Furor, Liberal Fury." *American Lawyer*, June 1988, 10

Kifner, John. "Washington Buckling under Home Rule." *New York Times*, February 12, 1995, A1

Low, Peter W., John Calvin Jeffries Jr., and Richard J. Bonnie. *The Trial of John W. Hinckley, Jr.: A Case Study in the Insanity Defense*. Mineola, N.Y.: Foundation Press, 1986.

McGowan, Carl. "Symposium: A Reply to Judicialization." *Duke Law Journal* (1986): 217–37.

Mikva, Abner J. "Sturm und Drang at the D.C. Circuit." *George Washington Law Review* 57 (1989): 1063–68.

"New Juror Lounge Opens at Federal Courthouse." *Washington Lawyer,* January–February 1992, 20.

Rodriguez, Eva M. "Prosecutor Shift on Low-Level Drug Cases." *Legal Times,* July 12, 1993, 15.

Savage, David G. *Turning Right: The Making of the Rehnquist Supreme Court,* chap. 4, "Robert Bork and the Intellectual Feast." New York: Wiley, 1992.

Schultz, Mark F. "Attorneys' Fees under the Independent Counsel Act: How the Grinch Stole Lyn Nofziger's Wallet." *George Washington Law Review* 60 (1992): 1311–56.

Silberman, Laurence H. "Chevron: The Intersection of Law and Policy." *George Washington Law Review* 58 (1988): 821–28.

Smith, Christopher George. "The United States Court of Appeals for the District of Columbia and the First Amendment since the Appointment of Chief Judge Patricia Wald." Honors thesis, University of Pennsylvania, 1987.

Starr, Kenneth W. "Of Forests and Trees: Structuralism in the Interpretation of Statutes." *George Washington Law Review* 56 (1988): 703–10.

Stone, Alan. *Wrong Number: The Breakup of AT&T.* New York: Basic Books, 1989.

Temin, Peter, with Louis Galambos. *The Fall of the Bell System: A Study in Prices and Politics.* Cambridge and New York: Cambridge University Press, 1987.

Toobin, Jeffrey. *Opening Arguments: A Young Lawyer's First Case, United States v. Oliver North.* New York: Viking, 1991.

Wald, Patricia M. "Changing Course: The Use of Precedent in the District of Columbia Circuit." *Cleveland State Law Review* 34 (1985–86): 477–518.

———. "Collegiality on a Court: Its Practices, Problems, and Pitfalls." *Federal Bar News & Journal* 40 (1993): 521–28.

———. "Commencement Address, 1982." *Catholic University Law Review* 32 (1982): 1–12.

———. "…Doctor, Lawyer, Merchant, Chief." *George Washington Law Review* 60 (1992): 1127–50.

———. "Life on the District of Columbia Circuit: Literally and Figuratively Halfway between the Capitol and the White House." *Minnesota Law Review* 72 (1987): 1–22.

———. "The Sizzling Sleeper: The Use of Legislative History in Construing Statutes in the 1988–89 Term of the United States Supreme Court." *American University Law Review* 39 (1990): 277–310.

———. "Some Observations on the Use of Legislative History in the 1981 Supreme Court Term." *Iowa Law Review* 68 (1983): 195–216.

Walsh, Lawrence E. *Iran Contra: The Final Report.* New York: Times Books, 1994.

Table of Cases

Index